ROYAL HISTORICAL SOCIETY

STUDIES IN HISTORY

New Series

THE SCOTTISH MIDDLE MARCH, 1573–1625
POWER, KINSHIP, ALLEGIANCE

Studies in History New Series
Editorial Board

Professor John Morrill (*Convenor*)
Professor Barry Doyle (*Economic History Society*)
Professor Nigel Goose (*Economic History Society*)
Dr Emma Griffin (*Literary Director*)
Dr Rachel Hammersley
Professor Michael Hughes (*Honorary Treasurer*)
Professor Colin Kidd
Professor Daniel Power
Dr Bernhard Rieger
Professor Alec Ryrie
Dr Selina Todd (*Past and Present Society*)

This series is supported by annual subventions from the
Economic History Society and from the Past and Present Society

PAST & PRESENT
a journal of historical studies

THE SCOTTISH MIDDLE MARCH, 1573–1625

POWER, KINSHIP, ALLEGIANCE

Anna Groundwater

THE ROYAL HISTORICAL SOCIETY
THE BOYDELL PRESS

© Anna Groundwater 2010

All Rights Reserved. Except as permitted under current legislation no part of this work may be photocopied, stored in a retrieval system, published, performed in public, adapted, broadcast, transmitted, recorded or reproduced in any form or by any means, without the prior permission of the copyright owner

The right of Anna Groundwater to be identified as the author of this work has been asserted in accordance with sections 77 and 78 of the Copyright, Designs and Patents Act 1988

First published 2010
The Royal Historical Society, London
in association with
The Boydell Press, Woodbridge
Paperback edition 2013
The Boydell Press, Woodbridge

ISBN 978 0 86193 307 5 hardback
ISBN 978 1 84383 838 8 paperback

Transferred to digital printing

The Boydell Press is an imprint of Boydell & Brewer Ltd
PO Box 9, Woodbridge, Suffolk IP12 3DF, UK
and of Boydell & Brewer Inc,
668 Mt Hope Avenue, Rochester, NY 14620–2731, USA
website: www.boydellandbrewer.com

A CIP catalogue record for this book is available
from the British Library

The publisher has no responsibility for the continued existence or accuracy of URLs for external or third-party internet websites referred to in this book, and does not guarantee that any content on such websites is, or will remain, accurate or appropriate.

This publication is printed on acid-free paper

Contents

List of maps	vi
Acknowledgements	vii
Abbreviations and conventions	ix
Family tree	xi
Prologue	1
Introduction	5
1 A frontier society?	23
2 The socio-political structure of the Middle March	47
3 The administrative structure of the Middle March	73
4 Middle March men in central government	104
5 Crime, feud and violence	128
6 The road to pacification, 1573–1597	154
7 Pacification, 1597–1625	181
Conclusion	205
Bibliography	215
Index	225

List of Maps

1. The Borders in the sixteenth century   6
2. Roxburghshire, Selkirkshire and Peeblesshire in the Middle March   24
3. Landholdings of the major surnames on the Middle March   48

Acknowledgements

Hard as it is for me to believe, but nine years have passed since I took my first tentative steps back into the world of academia and started this project now coming to fruition. It has been a long and occasionally painful process but one that has also been invigorating, enlightening and hilarious at times. What started under the towering walls of the Hermitage castle, its blank stone windows looking out over the bleak moors of Liddesdale, has taken me on a journey through the fortified towers of Branxholme, Smailholm and Newark, to the wynds of Edinburgh and the panelled chambers of Holyrood, and finally to the palace of Whitehall. Gradually these places have been peopled by the vibrant figures that leap from the crackling parchment over which countless happy hours have been spent here in Edinburgh at the National Library and National Archives.

Massive thanks are due to many for their encouragement, advice and time along the way, helping me to produce a coherent (I hope) something out of the original nebulous musings. In particular I would like to thank those who got the whole process going: primary amongst these are Professor Michael Lynch and Dr Julian Goodare. Michael's breadth of vision opened my eyes to exciting new ways of seeing things, Julian's own works introduced to me new concepts of government that I would have never formulated on my own, and both of them spent painstaking days reading and advising on my first stumbling drafts. Julian's clarity and precision has inculcated much-needed discipline in my thought and writing, whilst Michael's encouragement kept me going when problems seemed insurmountable. So heartfelt thanks to them both.

But perhaps I need to go back even further than this to my early days at Cambridge, so very long ago, and a young and enthusiastic tutor who inspired academic excitement and then put up with my subsequent distraction. Despite my appalling academic record, Professor John Morrill, as he is now, was kind enough to set me on my way to Edinburgh, and since then has steered my work through its transformation into a more readable, and a better thought-out book. One of the joys of this whole project has been re-finding John, and, I hope, making up for my previous performance. Very many thanks are due to him.

There are others too, to whom I would like to show my appreciation: my examiners Professor Mike Braddick and Dr Steve Boardman for a stimulating and kindly-managed *viva*, and to Steve for his entertaining paleography classes; to the Scottish history department at Edinburgh for the sense of community, the opportunity to teach and for some very late evenings; to Dr Tom Webster for kick-starting my teaching in British history, which has done so much to widen my perspectives; and to all for repeatedly providing references, often at short notice. Needless to say, any errors that remain, after so much help, are mine.

On a more practical level, thanks are due also to the patient staff at the NLS, NAS and the Borders Archives at Selkirk and Hawick, to Walter Elliot for guiding me through the Walter Mason papers, and to Ray Harris, the last non-computerised cartographer at the University of Edinburgh for his excellent maps. Thanks too to Christine Linehan for her exacting editing that did much to pull this book into shape. And finally many thanks also to the dukes of Roxburgh and Buccleuch, the marquess of Lothian, the Pringles of Torwoodlee and the Murrays of Elibank for access to their papers in the NAS. On a personal level, I would like to thank my parents for the huge part that they have played in encouraging my love of history throughout my life, to Bob Younger for living with the Middle March for so many years, and to my children for providing the necessary displacement activity. But finally, my thanks are to the wonderfully strident men and women of the Middle March in the late sixteenth and early seventeenth centuries who have kept me amused and gripped for so long. I salute them!

Anna Groundwater,
February 2010

Abbreviations and Conventions

During the period covered by this book the designation of two of the main families changed. These were the Scotts of Branxholme, referred to increasingly frequently as Buccleuch by the 1590s, and the Kers of Cessford who became Roxburgh on the ennoblement of Robert Ker in 1600. They are referred to by the designation by which they were known at the time referred to.

Adv. MS	Advocates' MS
BA	Borders Archives, Hawick
BUK	*Booke of the universall Kirk of Scotland*, ed. A. Peterkin, Edinburgh 1839
CBP	*The Border papers: calendar of letters and papers relating to the affairs of the Borders of England and Scotland*, ed. J. Bain, Edinburgh 1894–6
CSP Dom.	*Calendar of state papers, domestic series, 1603–1704*, ed. M. A. Green and others, London 1856–1947
CSP Scot.	*Calendar of the state papers relating to Scotland*, ed. J. Bain, G. G. Simpson and J. D. Galbraith, Edinburgh 1881–8
CSP Venetian	*Calendar of state papers …Venice, 1603–75*, ed. R. Brown, G. Cavendish Bentinck, H. F. Brown and A. B. Hinds, London 1864–1947
EHR	*English Historical Review*
ER	*The exchequer rolls of Scotland*, ed. J. Stuart and others, Edinburgh 1878–1908
HJ	*Historical Journal*
HMC	Historic Manuscripts Commission
NAS	National Archives of Scotland
NH	*Northern History*
NLS	National Library of Scotland
NRAS	National Register of Archives of Scotland
RMS	*The register of the great seal of Scotland*, ed. J. M. Thomson, P. J. Balfour, J. H. Stevenson and W. K. Dickson, Edinburgh 1882–1914
RPC	*The register of the privy council of Scotland, 1545–1625*, ed. J. Buron and D. Masson, Edinburgh 1877–98
RPS	*The records of the parliaments of Scotland to 1707*, ed. K. M. Brown, G. H. MacIntosh, A. J. Mann, P. E. Ritchie and R. J. Tanner, St Andrews 2007–9; www.rps.ac.uk

RSS	*The register of the privy seal of Scotland*, ed. M. Livingstone, Edinburgh 1908
SHR	*Scottish Historical Review*
SHS	Scottish History Society
SRS	Scottish Record Society
STS	Scottish Text Society
TA	*Abstracts of the treasurer's accounts* (Bannatyne Club, 1867)

Marriage links between the Scotts, the Murrays and the Kers of the Middle March, 1573 to 1625

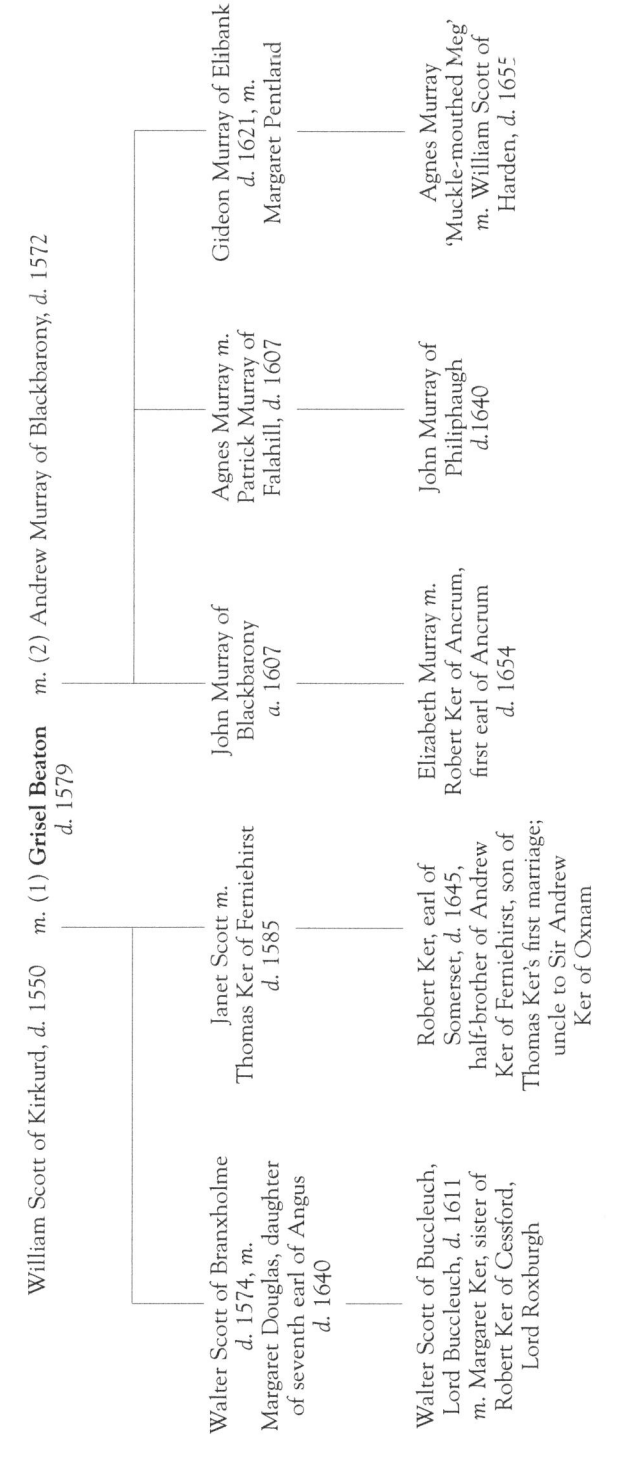

William Scott of Kirkurd, *d.* 1550   m. (1) **Grisel Beaton**   m. (2) Andrew Murray of Blackbarony, *d.* 1572
                                              d. 1579

- Walter Scott of Branxholme
  d. 1574, m.
  Margaret Douglas, daughter
  of seventh earl of Angus
  d. 1640

  - Walter Scott of Buccleuch,
    Lord Buccleuch, *d.* 1611
    m. Margaret Ker, sister of
    Robert Ker of Cessford,
    Lord Roxburgh

- Janet Scott m.
  Thomas Ker of Ferniehirst
  d. 1585

  - Robert Ker, earl of
    Somerset, *d.* 1645,
    half-brother of Andrew
    Ker of Ferniehirst, son of
    Thomas Ker's first marriage;
    uncle to Sir Andrew
    Ker of Oxnam

- John Murray of
  Blackbarony
  a. 1607

  - Elizabeth Murray m.
    Robert Ker of Ancrum,
    first earl of Ancrum
    d. 1654

- Agnes Murray m.
  Patrick Murray of
  Falahill, *d.* 1607

  - John Murray of
    Philiphaugh
    d. 1640

- Gideon Murray of Elibank
  d. 1621, m.
  Margaret Pentland

  - Agnes Murray
    'Muckle-mouthed Meg'
    m. William Scott of
    Harden, *d.* 1655

Prologue

'Now I was to begin in a new world; for by the King's coming to the crown, I was to lose the best part of my living. For my office of Wardenry ceased … And hereupon I bethought myself with what grace and favour I was ever received by the Kings of Scots.'[1]

On 26 March 1603 Robert Carey staggered into James VI's bedchamber at Holyrood to announce his succession to the English throne. For James, it was the defining moment in his life, the glittering prize that for so long he had striven. For Carey, exhausted after his three-day ride from London, it was his opportunity to secure a heady future at the English court. No longer would he be confined to the turbulent wastelands of his wardenry in the Middle March of the English Borderlands.[2] For his Scottish counterpart too, the recently ennobled Robert Ker, Lord Roxburgh, it marked the beginning of a new life: the rough comfort of Cessford castle's thick walls was replaced by the court at Whitehall and the dark rooms of the privy council in Edinburgh. The significance of the Anglo-Scottish border, as a barrier between two, often hostile, kingdoms lapsed, as did Roxburgh's and Carey's offices as warden.

Whilst James's succession undoubtedly transformed these men's lives, they were also affected by a variety of longer-term processes in which the Scottish crown had begun to harness judicial authority, and the use of violence, to settle disputes throughout Scotland. The increasing intrusion of crown authority into the localities that resulted might have been expected to alienate prominent local officials, such as Roxburgh. What was notable, however, was the way in which the landed elite had co-operated with James, rewarded by new office and confirmation of their landholdings. By carefully including Roxburgh within an evolving framework of government, James retained the authority that this borderer exerted in the Scottish Middle March, as its warden, and through his leadership of the great Ker kindred. Whilst Roxburgh's experience was determined largely by border-specific circumstances, he was also the creature of James's policies affecting much of Scotland. So, similarly, was the experience of the Middle March that he had governed. Furthermore, in the prospering of Roxburgh's career can be found an illustration of broader concepts such as the interplay of kinship, alliance and patronage within the governance of a Scotland that, after 1603, was now

---

[1] *Memoirs of Robert Carey*, ed. J. H. Mares, Oxford 1972, 58, 65.
[2] Carey was appointed a gentleman of the Bedchamber but lost his place in James's purge of Englishmen from his household in London.

part of James's new 'Great Britain'. But whilst the processes of government in the Middle March were affected by the proximity of the border, they were also, collectively, an example of what was happening elsewhere in Scotland.

The period from 1573 to 1625 spanned a watershed in the history of the Borders. In the late sixteenth century the region was defined by its position on the border with England. It was inevitable that any change in Anglo-Scottish relations would have an immediate effect in the region. James's succession marked the official ending of the separate entities of the Scottish and English marches. They were subsumed into a wider cross-border region christened, too hopefully, 'the Middle Shires', at the supposed heart of the new Great Britain. Government in the former Scottish marches, however, remained inextricably linked with what had gone before: it involved the same people, similar mechanisms and nearly identical administrative regions. Local kindreds and alliances continued to provide much of the structure of society and power in each of the three marches. But all of these were affected by both diplomatic changes and the growing power of the state, and it is impossible to understand what was happening in the Borders without placing them within the wider context of national political and diplomatic circumstances.

The aim, in concentrating on the Middle March alone, is to provide a socio-political framework for an administrative region defined as such by contemporary government and given physical form by its topographical boundaries. The region has been notorious for its reported levels of crime, and whilst crime there will be assessed, this is not primarily a study of crime in the region. Instead it is about the response of the crown to the reports of crime. Government periodically prioritised the suppression of crime in the region, but at other times it appeared reluctant to deal with it. The crown's fluctuating approach to this area will be placed within changes in the diplomatic and political spheres, and within an increasing intensification of government in all the Scottish regions. Conversely, the involvement of borderers in government in Edinburgh is also assessed. Whilst such inclusion could be interpreted as a deliberate crown policy to bring people from an area of concern into line, it could equally show the active participation of such people within national governmental processes and the political structure of the kingdom. Previous analysis of the region has tended to emphasise its location on the margins of the kingdom and the isolating effect this had on its inhabitants.[3] In contrast, it can be shown that these people were not alienated from their country's highest levels of power: they were part of it. Some of the conclusions of this study may be applicable to the other marches but, it will be suggested, some were also applicable to other regions of Scot-

---

[3] 'The administrative problem in the borders arose from the isolation of the region and the turbulent character of its inhabitants': T. I. Rae, *The administration of the Scottish frontier, 1513–1603*, Edinburgh 1966, 1.

land, including the Lowlands: the Middle March did not exist in a separate, peripheral bubble.

The first chapter of this book provides a brief description of social, economic and ecclesiastical conditions in the Middle March, placing them within the context of the kingdom as a whole, and questioning the degree to which it could be termed a 'frontier society'. Chapter 2 outlines the sociopolitical framework of the Middle March upon which local authority was based. The fundamental importance of kinship and alliance in the march's society is demonstrated, though parallels here will be drawn with the way in which kinship retained its significance throughout Scotland. Kinship and alliance determined the ties of obligation, service and responsibility and the chapter shows how central government was able to utilise these links in implementing policy in the region. Chapter 3 looks at local office-holding, including the layer of border-specific office, and the continuity of the same families in office. It considers how the government in Edinburgh was able to affect local government: this amounted to an increasing intrusion of crown authority under James VI, which, though the crown had additional concerns peculiar to the Borders, had similarities to that underway in the Lowlands too. The fourth chapter illustrates the inclusion of prominent Middle March figures within central government, showing their involvement in national political life, in particular on the privy council and within the royal households, and how this survived the translation of James's court to London. Chapter 5 assesses the reporting of crime, feud and violence in the Middle March, analysing central government's changing response to such activities. Government policy in the march is placed within the context of the crown's increasing control of the kingdom's judicial system, including the suppression of feud and the gradual replacing of private with public justice, and fluctuating Anglo-Scottish relations. Throughout, the themes of continuity, inclusion, co-operation, obligation, kinship, allegiance and reward will be explored alongside those of governmental innovation, social, political and diplomatic change, border-specificity, enmity and the exclusion of those who did not co-operate.

The sixth and seventh chapters set a narrative history of the region against a shifting political background in Scotland and fluctuating Anglo-Scottish relations. They illustrate the change in government policy in the region arising from concern over James's impending succession to the English throne, but they also set this changing policy within processes at work elsewhere in the kingdom. It is suggested that mechanisms for effective government were already in place for James to implement his new policies. Chapter six details the last few years of the old way of life in the Middle March, the changes to which were increasingly evident from the late 1580s, whilst the final chapter provides an account of moves towards a pacification of crime in the region between 1597 and 1605 and the pacification itself between 1605 and 1625. Two strands can be identified here: the suppression of feud, which was a nationwide project, and the suppression of cross-border raiding which was specific to the region. Whilst the latter was perhaps more speedily achieved than the former, the chapter also considers what the experience of the Middle March after Union demonstrated of the problems that James was to encounter in his pursuit of full political union. It is within the bigger picture of politics and diplomacy, government and society that this survey of the Middle March is intended.

Any balanced assessment of the Middle March has to consider the pervasive influence, over several hundred years, of the stereotypical images of a borderer and the Borders on the histories of the region. The effect of this characterisation on subsequent histories is evident in the largely damning historiography of the Borders. The legend needs to be stripped away, and replaced by concentration, instead, on the contemporary records of government and events. Then, with the Middle March placed within the broader processes at work in Scotland, it will be possible to draw a more representative portrait of the region, at a definitive moment in its history, and not just another caricature. At the same time it is hoped to suggest how the experience of the Middle March, as one region in Scotland, can inform a more general history of governance in Scotland as it underwent crucial and long-term change.

Introduction

I

In administrative terms, in the reign of James VI, the Borders were divided into three sections. These included the area stretching back some miles from the frontier line itself, which formed the administrative regions of the East, Middle and West Marches. There was a similar framework to the south of the border which formed the English East, Middle and West Marches, though their boundaries did not meet their Scottish counterparts at the same points on the frontier. The national frontier of the the Scottish Middle March coincided with half of that of the English East March and all of the English Middle March, with its last eight miles adjoining the English West March. Thus the Scottish Middle March's stretch of frontier was the longest and involved its officials in interaction with their counterparts in all three English Marches.

The physical geography of the region and its medieval administrative areas, the sheriffdoms, determined the internal divisions between each Scottish march. The Middle March comprised the shires of Roxburgh, Peebles and Selkirk and included the lordship of Liddesdale, which fronted onto the border. The Moorfoot Hills marked its northern edge, whilst the hills of the Southern Uplands formed a barrier to the West March. The outer edge of the Merse, to the east, sloped down into the East March.[1] The topographical layout of the land, particularly the moor-covered uplands of the western half of the march, lent itself to an image of remote wasteland. However, it was not inaccessible, the rivers cutting through it providing corridors of communication: the valleys of upper Tweeddale and Teviotdale and the rivers Jed, Ettrick and Yarrow facilitated communications within the region, whilst those of the Leader and Gala rivers gave access northwards to Edinburgh through the passes of Soutra and Fala respectively. Its principal towns were Jedburgh, Selkirk and Peebles, the administrative centres of its sheriffdoms, and Kelso, Melrose and Hawick.

The day-to-day administration in the marches, as elsewhere in Scotland, was led by its resident sheriffs; in the Middle March these were the sheriffs of the shires of Roxburgh, Selkirk and Peebles. The march, however, had an extra layer of officialdom, which was peculiar to the Borders, the warden whose primary duty was concerned with the regulation of cross-border affairs.

---

[1] *RPC* iii, 344. *See* map 1.

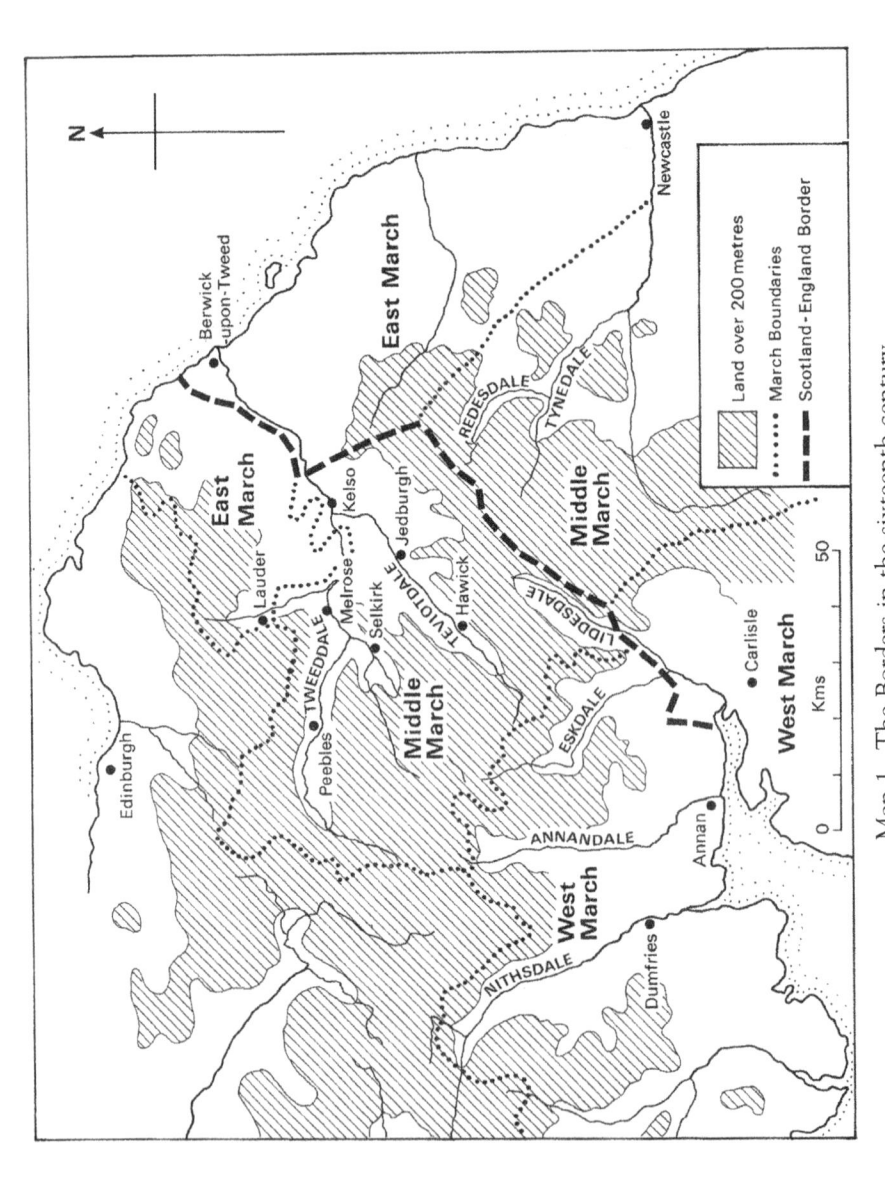

Map 1. The Borders in the sixteenth century

There was also a keeper appointed to the lordship of Liddesdale, who held separate jurisdiction and was accountable directly to the king.[2] The exercise of authority in the region was delineated by the administrative districts of the shires and the march, but it was built largely on the socio-political framework provided by local kindreds. Again this is not unlike elsewhere in Scotland, where kinship remained of fundamental importance in determining allegiance, identity and enmity, though it was, perhaps, beginning slowly to decline in significance by the end of the sixteenth century.[3] So whilst the Middle March was in itself a coherent entity, there was inevitably interaction with the other marches and within kindreds, which, combined with overlapping private jurisdictions, to some extent blurred the margins between the marches.

In 1573, the beginning point of this study, the Middle March was recovering from the Marian civil wars, which had exacerbated the divisions between some of its inhabitants. In 1570 the house and lands of Walter Scott of Buccleuch at Branxholme and the town of Hawick were burned in a raid by the English earl of Sussex, which suspiciously bypassed the lands of Buccleuch's enemy, William Ker of Cessford, the Middle March warden. Cessford's support for the king's party was directly in opposition to the devotion of his cousin (but enemy), Ker of Ferniehirst to Mary. The ending of the siege of Edinburgh castle, following English intervention in 1573, and the death of Kirkcaldy of Grange, Ferniehirst's father-in-law, forced Ferniehirst into exile for the next few years. Instead, the affiliates of the new regent James Douglas, earl of Morton, were to prosper from his ascendancy through to 1578. Over the next few years, his attempts to solidify amicable relations with England led to a number of judicial raids to the Borders. This severity was not to outlast his regency. In 1584 Ferniehirst became warden under the earl of Arran's regime but was ousted at his fall in 1585. He was replaced by the Kers of Cessford (later Roxburgh), in whose hands the wardenry remained until 1603.

The distinct entities of the three marches came to an end with the regnal union of 1603. James abolished the term 'the Borders' and replaced it with that of 'the Middle Shires', which included the counties and sheriffdoms of both sides of the frontier. Subsequently, the separate marches were not used as official designations of administrative areas in the former Borders region. Instead, proclamations referred either to the Middle Shires, or the 'late borderis', or to the individual sheriffdoms of Berwick, Roxburgh, Selkirk, Peebles and Dumfries and the stewartries of Kirkcudbright and Annan – and in England the counties of Northumberland, Durham, Westmorland and Cumberland. As the framework of the marches faded, an attempt was made by James's government to treat the entire region, both north and south of the

---

[2] Rae, *Administration*, 35–6.
[3] J. Wormald, *Court, kirk and community: Scotland, 1470–1625*, Edinburgh 1981, 29–30, 40.

border, as one entity – or at least one entity with two subdivisions, Scottish and English. In 1603 the office of march warden ceased and, in 1605, was replaced by a body of border commissioners whose jurisdiction extended to the whole of their side of the border.

Within the former march, however, the administrative districts continued to be much as before, based on the ancient sheriffdoms. Where additional appointments were made, they were fitted within the existing outline of local administration; the area of jurisdiction of the first Justices of the Peace introduced in 1610 was identical to that of the sheriffdoms. Thus though the administrative entity of the Middle March may have disappeared, its former outline remained in that of the shires of Roxburgh, Selkirk and Peebles. Often contemporarily referred to in one breath, their grouping continued to be relevant as a basis for this study throughout the years of the pacification of the former Borders. James's death in 1625 marked the end of significant crown interest in the region and the scope of this study.

II

There are a small number of histories of the Borders in the sixteenth century. Ian Rae's definitive book covering the whole Scottish Borders, *The administration of the Scottish frontier, 1513–1603*, would be difficult to surpass in its analysis of the framework of administration and crown interest in the region, but of necessity could not deal with the intricacies of one march alone. Similarly circumscribed is D. L. W. Tough's *The last years of a frontier: a history of the Borders during the reign of Elizabeth I* which covers the entire Borders region on both sides of the frontier, focusing on cross-border relations and March law.[4] But since both these studies were published some time ago, in 1966 and 1928 respectively, they do not encompass more recent re-evaluation of Scottish government. Works by Julian Goodare, Jenny Wormald and Keith Brown have significant implications for the way in which government in the Borders should be viewed.[5]

Their conclusions have informed Maureen Meikle's study of an area she designates the Eastern Borders, from 1540 to 1603. She provides a comprehensive socio-economic historical analysis of the lairds and gentry of this region, in which she also included the English East March and the eastern

---

[4] Rae, *Administration*; D. L. W. Tough, *The last years of a frontier: a history of the Borders during the reign of Elizabeth I*, London 1928.

[5] J. Goodare, *State and society in early modern Scotland*, Oxford 1999, and *The government of Scotland*, Oxford 2004; Wormald, *Court, kirk and community*; *Lords and men in Scotland: bonds of manrent, 1442–1603*, Edinburgh 1985; 'Bloodfeud, kindred and government in early modern Scotland', *Past and Present* lxxxvii (1980), 54–97; and 'Taming the magnates', in K. J. Stringer (ed.), *Essays on the nobility of medieval Scotland*, Edinburgh 1985, 270–80; K. M. Brown, *Bloodfeud in Scotland, 1573–1625: violence, justice and politics in an early modern society*, Edinburgh 1986.

part of the Scottish Middle March.⁶ Her principal premise is that, given the degree of socio-economic connections and cultural similarity between the Eastern Borderers on either side of the frontier, any frontier line could almost be redrawn on a north-south axis, separating the more civilised Easterner from his reiving Western counterpart. She concludes that the reputation of the Easterner has been unfairly sullied by this proximity, anglo-centric prejudice colouring any attempt at a balanced evaluation of the Borders. However, in laying to rest the fallacy of the accepted orthodoxy of the barbarian borderer in the east, she risks creating another in her approach to the rest of the Borders.⁷

The image of the barbarian borderer was entrenched several centuries ago. Therefore this work's analysis of contemporary sources has the 'How representative were these records of the situation "on the ground"?' alarm ringing throughout. In the sixteenth century, report of the Borders was profoundly influenced by an increasing disdain for the 'wickit' borderers. Even worse, a shift has been identified in the government's perception of its Borders, in the act of 1587 'For the quieting and keping in obedience of the disorderit subjectis, inhabitantis of the bordouris, hieldandis, and ilis', which began to equate them with the troublesome and barbaric Highlands. And, as Julian Goodare and Michael Lynch note, 'perceptions – from the centre – were more significant than reality' in Scotland's borderlands.⁸ By the end of the sixteenth century the expression of government's contempt might be termed a 'language of opprobrium'. So borderers frequently appear in the privy council records as 'vagabundis', 'malefactouris', 'rebellis' and 'brokin men', and rarely of 'good rule'. Problematically, for the historian, most reports on the area were confined to those concerning disturbance, with little record of any outbreak of peace. Reports of events in one part of the Borders were not always applicable to another part, but they could affect the way in which government viewed and described the whole region. And the way in which a government referred to the Borders mattered: it affected the formulation of policy towards that area. When such weighted reports were received by a late sixteenth-century government, attempting to exert its authority in all its regions, they helped to create a perception of the stereotypical borderer and an 'out-countrey' in which the law held no remit. This perception has exercised an enduring influence on the way subsequent historians have viewed the region.

---

6   The lairds of Maureen Meikle's study lived in Berwickshire and the eastern parts of Roxburghshire and Selkirkshire: *A British frontier? Lairds and gentlemen in the eastern Borders, 1540–1603*, East Linton 2004.
7   Ibid. 1–2, 3, and 'A godly rogue; the career of Sir John Forster, an Elizabethan border warden', *NH* xxviii (1992), 126–63.
8   *RPS*, 1587/7/70, accessed 19 June 2009; J. Goodare and M. Lynch, 'The Scottish state and its Borderlands, 1567–1625', in J. Goodare and M. Lynch (eds), *Reign of James VI*, East Linton 1999, 186–207 at pp. 187–8, 197–8, 201–5, 207.

Contemporary histories were no less affected. Bishop Leslie's assertion that descriptions of 'Scottis to eit menis flesche ... can to na uther be attrubutet ... bot only to thame of Anandale', distancing their 'alde crueltie' from the behaviour of 'the hail Scottis natione' was not indicative of an unbiased approach. Borderers, he wrote, were 'persuadet that all the gudes of al men in tyme of necessitie, be the lawe of nature, ar commoune to thame and utheris'.[9] Contemporary diaries ring with disdain for the borderers. Robert Birrel, writing about the 'Tumult of Edinburgh' of December 1596, saw no need to explain further the terror caused by the 'grate rumour and word among the tounesmen, that the Kings Majestie sould send in Will Kinmond the comone thieff, and so many Southland men, as sould spulzie the toune of Edinburghe'. The fear inspired by mention of a borderer was implicit, the image of the violent and lawless borderer generally understood.[10]

This perception abounded in contemporary poetry. Sir Richard Maitland's complaint *Aganis the theivis of Liddisdaill* of the 1560s warned of the 'commoun thevis' of Liddesdale, guided by the 'mekle deill'. The thief in Sir David Lindsay's *Ane satyre of the thrie estaitis* in the 1550s rode with the notorious border surnames, Nicksons and Bells, Scotts of Ewesdale and Grahams. There 'was nocht ane in all Lidsdaill,/ That ky mair craftelie culd staill'. The easily identifiable caricature of the border bandit prevailed which, like most caricatures, was unrepresentative of all borderers.[11] Perhaps the border ballads have done the borderers no favours, peopled as they are by the violent (but patriotic) reiver.[12] Though the veracity of events described in the ballads is questionable, some are old enough to reflect how a borderer might have liked to portray himself during this period. Anthony Goodman notes of the ballads about the Battle of Otterburn (1388) that 'the social context in which the Otterburn ballads place the battle ... [was] probably based on contemporary local perceptions' and originated soon after the events.[13] But, unluckily for the Borders, the ballads have influenced much of

---

[9] *The historie of Scotland by John Leslie, bishop of Ross*, ed. E. G. Cody and W. Murison, trans. J. Dalrymple (1596) (STS, 1888–95), 10–11, 99–101; J. Lesley, *History of Scotland* (Bannatyne Club, 1830).
[10] R. Birrel, *Diary*, in J. G. Dalyell (ed.), *Fragments of Scottish history*, Edinburgh 1798, 1–64 at p. 41.
[11] *The Maitland folio manuscript*, ed. W. A. Craigie (STS, 1919), i. 301–3; *The works of Sir David Lindsay of the Mount, 1490–1555*, ed. D. Hamer (STS, 1931–6), ii. 359, 371.
[12] Collections of ballads include those by Sir Walter Scott and Francis Child: Sir Walter Scott, *Minstrelsy of the Scottish Border*, ed. T. F. Henderson, Edinburgh 1902; F. J. Child, *English and Scottish popular ballads*, Boston 1898.
[13] A. Goodman, 'Introduction', and A. Grant, 'The Otterburn War from the Scottish point of view', in A. Goodman and A. Tuck (eds), *War and border societies in the Middle Ages*, London 1992, 1–29 at pp. 7–8; 30–64 at pp. 32, 34, 53; E. J. Cowan, 'Introduction', and 'Sex and violence in the Scottish ballads', in E. J. Cowan (ed.), *The ballad in Scottish history*, East Linton 2000, 1–18, 95–115.

INTRODUCTION

the subsequent analysis of the region, whether it was the misleading romanticism of Sir Walter Scott or Tough's contempt for the barbaric borderer.[14]

There is much to illustrate the contemporary perception of the borderers in the principal records for the Borders, the *Calendar of Border papers*, from 1560 to 1603. This extensive collection of correspondence between mainly English wardens, agents in Scotland and Elizabeth I's government was inevitably concerned with reports of disturbances, especially those perpetrated by the Scots, and often included complaints about insufficient action by the Scottish wardens to control such activity. Since such a wealth of record has not survived from the Scottish side, the impression given by these English records is of a less civilised Scottish Borders, weakly governed and semi-anarchic. There is a greater amount of Scottish correspondence in the *State papers relating to Scotland*. However, again, this collection was created by the English government and cannot be taken accurately to represent the Scottish government's relations with its regions. Similarly English in origin are the papers for the years between 1603 to 1625, in the collections of Lord Salisbury and Lord Muncaster.[15] As a result, report on the Borders is dominated by that of English provenance. This is not necessarily to deny that the crimes described took place, but to question the representative nature of such material.

The letters and ordinances of the Scottish privy council provide a crucial counterbalance. Given the necessity for Borders's events to be evaluated within the context of broader developments in Scottish government, the *Records of the privy council of Scotland* is often as useful as the *Calendar of Border papers*. Whilst council papers also reflect concern over the Borders, rather than an appreciation of any stability or effective local government there, they do provide an indication of Scottish government policy in the Borders and its changing priorities. There are periods when border business disappears from view. This could have been a reflection of lessened tension in the area, decreased English complaints, real reduction in levels of crime there or government preoccupation with other affairs. Determining what government policy was during this period is complex: its inspiration and motives were not always obvious. However, crucial for this study is what the *RPC* reveals about the involvement of apparently 'civilised' Middle March inhabitants in central government. James's move to London in 1603 necessitated an increased correspondence between him and his agents in Scotland and a wealth of letters between James, his court and his Scottish councillors survive. These illuminate the way in which James's government operated, in his absence, demonstrating a network of authority and patronage that stretched from Whitehall to the Scottish regions, connecting the borderers

---

[14] Tough, *The last years*, 175.
[15] CBP; HMC, *The manuscripts of Lord Muncaster*, ed. H. Maxwell Lyte, London 1885, and *The manuscripts of the marquess of Salisbury*, ed. M. Guiseppie and O. Dyfnallt, London 1930–70.

to, and including them in, the highest levels of government. This correspondence allows the voices of Scotsmen to be heard unfiltered by English interpretation or prioritisation.[16]

But perhaps more insidious than the stereotyping, has been the subconscious perforation of a notion of English cultural and governmental superiority into the evaluation of government and society in Scotland. Most analysis of the Borders has, until quite recently, been dominated by that from an anglo-centric perspective. This lauded the development of the English state and government, whilst disdainfully pointing to the apparent lack of a similar development in Scotland. Contemporary English reports were similar, one in 1580 sneering that in 'making and abrogating laws, ... the Prince's authority is so limited that he has not so much as a negative, but must ratify that which is agreed on by suffrage of the greater part of the nobility and commons in their Parliaments'. The 'Prince has no universal authority' in justice thanks to the private and partisan jurisdictions of the feuding magnates and 'no absolute authority in league and war making'.[17] Thus, to subsequent historians, the benefits to Scotland, and especially to the Borders, of a seemingly inevitable union were deemed obvious.

Scholarly works on the whole Borders began to appear from the latter half of the eighteenth century. The first attempt to provide a history of the whole Borders region was by George Ridpath in 1776; however, his mostly balanced assessment was typically distorted by his unquestioning view of the Union: 'every unprejudiced mind must be sensible of the unspeakable advantages of this great event'. This limited much positive analysis of events before the Union.[18] Subsequently, Sir Walter Scott's enthusiasm for the Borders introduced a new appreciation of the borderer as a semi-independent patriot – but a patriot who simultaneously identified more closely with his English neighbour than his king and government in Edinburgh. This romanticism was equally as misleading as the English contempt. It spawned such accounts as Gordon MacDonald Fraser's entertaining *The steel bonnets* that build a sense of the alienation of the borderer, existing on a periphery, distanced from government. They do not allow for the implications of the evidence of borderers' involvement within that government.[19] In contrast, Tough's study of both sides of the border could not have been less romantic. His account came from a determinedly anglo-centric perspective, resonant in his comparison of English with Scottish border officials, which concluded that 'it is clear that we are dealing with two different stages of civilization'.[20]

---

[16] NLS, Denmilne MS, Adv. MS 33.1.1, vols 1–11; 33.3.12; 33.1.3; 33.1.7.
[17] *CSP Scot.* v, no. 638.
[18] G. Ridpath, *The Border history of England and Scotland*, London 1776, repr. Edinburgh 1979, 445–84, quotation at p. 484.
[19] G. MacDonald Fraser, *The steel bonnets: the story of the Anglo-Scottish border reivers*, London 1971.
[20] Tough, *The last years*, 175.

Such a view is still prevalent: a typical description of the Borders, by the English historian, Richard Spence, is of 'a near autonomous region' with 'endemic violence' perpetrated by 'numerous and unruly clans'.[21] This would have surprised the meticulous clerk of the weekly sheriff court at Jedburgh. However, recent re-evaluation, from a Scottish perspective, of Scottish monarchy and government is beginning to result in a more positive understanding of Scottish government in the late sixteenth century.

Such debate is particularly relevant to the marches since its effect has been to reassess how the crown was able to impose its will throughout Scotland. The traditional view, that weak kingship, exacerbated by frequent minorities, led to rampant magnates operating semi-autonomously within their own regions, has been systematically revised. The work in particular of Jenny Wormald and Michael Brown has shown that magnates generally found that it was in their own interest to co-operate with the crown, and that the crown was thus able to exercise some degree of authority in the regions.[22] More recently, for the eastern and central Highlands, Alison Cathcart has found evidence of similar co-operation in an area traditionally deemed beyond the crown's reach.[23] In a similar vein, Keith Brown's study of bloodfeud concludes that, far from resisting crown suppression of feud from the 1590s, the nobility found it to their advantage to work with James VI. Of specific relevance to the Middle March, Brown's analysis of the geographical spread of feud throughout Scotland found a more even distribution of it than the traditional notoriety ascribed to feud in the Borders suggested. Feuding 'was a Scottish experience, and not one which was a product of highland tribalism, or border lawlessness'. Tough, like many English border officials, ascribed much of the violence in the Borders to feuding. However, more recent studies of crime, such as that by Michael Wasser, have accepted that, whilst levels of violence are difficult to quantify, figures for the Borders are not hugely out of line with those for lowland Scotland. As a result, the traditional interpretation of the turbulent nature of late medieval Scottish border society, as a result of weak government, is open to reassessment.[24]

That this has not been fully appreciated before is due to too direct a comparison between English and Scottish forms of government. Scottish bureaucracy was certainly not nearly as developed as the English, but, as Alexander Grant warns, 'medieval governments should be judged by their

---

[21] R. T. Spence, 'The pacification of the Cumberland Borders, 1593–1628', *NH* xiii (1977), 59–160 at pp. 156–7.
[22] Wormald, 'Taming the magnates?'; *Court, kirk and community*, 3, 9–14, 16–17, 192; and *Lords and men*, 5; M. H. Brown, 'Scotland tamed? Kings and magnates in late medieval Scotland: a review of recent work', *Innes Review* xlv (1994), 120–46.
[23] A. Cathcart, *Kinship and clientage: highland clanship, 1451–1608*, Leiden 2006.
[24] Brown, *Bloodfeud*, 6–7, 241–3, 269, 277 appendix 1; M. Wasser, 'Violence and the central criminal courts in Scotland, 1603–1638', unpubl. PhD diss. Columbia 1995, 5–7, 13–14, 18, 38; Wormald, 'Bloodfeud'.

results, not by their machinery'. Power held by the magnates could be, in fact, a force for stability in their locality; magnates could provide good lordship, which included the settling of local disputes.[25] What this means for the Middle March is that though direct control by central government may have appeared less developed than the corresponding English system, this did not mean that the crown was not able to effect its will in the locality. It was generally in the interest of the greater lairds to co-operate with the crown: the reward for their service enhanced their ability to maintain their adherents, to exercise 'good lordship', thus securing (at least theoretically) the compliance of those dependants with crown policy.

This perhaps contrasts with the situation across the border. Mervyn James's work on the northern English nobility has identified the destabilising effect of the development of the Tudor state that was achieved at the expense of the 'overmighty subjects' in the north. This upset the 'local balance of interest and power, producing reactions of violence and revolt'. Problematically, an historical assumption of the similarity of the Scottish Borders and their English neighbours, has meant that the interpretation of the English Borders has influenced the way in which the Scottish have been evaluated.[26] But, in the sixteenth century, there was no equivalent to the Northern Rising, or the destruction of Lord Dacre, in the Scottish Borders. On a more positive note, James acknowledged the 'good qualities' of the 'old order', the good lordship and the 'protective and integrative influence of kinship', which were not recognised by a Tudor government intent on extending its own authority in the north.[27] Such recognition of the good things about kinship and strong local leaders needs to be applied to the north of the border, but care is also needed not to impose inappropriate English models onto different Scottish circumstances.

In the later fourteenth century a good relationship existed between the Scottish crown and some of its Borders magnates, and Alastair MacDonald has demonstrated that events in the Borders were more closely linked to government policy than has been appreciated. In the 1380s, the mutually-beneficial relationship between Robert II and James, earl of Douglas, saw Douglas well-rewarded for pursuing Robert's war against the English. The successful implementation of crown policy dovetailed with Douglas's own landed interests in the region. As Steve Boardman observes, royal grants to

---

[25] A. Grant, 'Crown and nobility in late medieval Britain', in R. A. Mason (ed.), *Scotland and England, 1286–1815*, Edinburgh 1987, 38–9, 49–50.

[26] Alastair MacDonald notes that as 'regards the late medieval Anglo-Scottish border there has been a relative abundance of recent work, although its focus has mainly been on northern England ... it has been assumed rather than demonstrated that the Scottish side of the border displayed similar characteristics': *Border bloodshed: Scotland and England at war, 1369–1403*, East Linton 2000, 200.

[27] M. E. James, *Society, politics and culture: studies in early modern England*, Cambridge 1986, 3.

INTRODUCTION

the Douglases in this period were 'something of a war subsidy'.[28] Michael Brown shows how this created a balance of power between the Douglases and the crown; it was only when the balance became upset by the increasing wealth and power of the Douglases in the 1450s that James II was forced to retaliate, killing the eighth earl and forfeiting the family. The affiliated kindreds, particularly in the Middle March, that had previously formed the local framework of Douglas power then filled the vacuum that the Douglas demise had left. They too found that it was beneficial to co-operate with the crown.[29] And this type of a relationship was to a great extent replicated in the sixteenth century in that between James VI, and the Kers of Cessford and Scotts of Buccleuch.

In contrast to the English experience in the sixteenth century, Macdonald notes the absence of the destabilising 'alienation' of Scottish borderers from their crown. He concludes for the late fourteenth century, as does this study for the sixteenth, that the assessment of political circumstances in the Scottish Borders, primarily from an English perspective, has resulted in the sweeping generalisation of a 'strongly entrenched orthodoxy'.[30] This has ignored real differences in political and social circumstances of English and Scottish borderers, to the underestimation of the efficacy of crown-locality relations and a misreading of crown policy in the region. It would have been interesting to see whether Ian Rae would have revised some of his conclusions in the light of these more recent works. Though he showed that central government was able to an extent to impose its will in the Borders, he concluded that the intrusion of other political and diplomatic factors, such as royal minorities or war with England, often limited the government's ability to use the existing machinery of local authority.[31] It is in his assessment of the weaknesses of central government and a crown beset by overpowerful magnates that he and the revisionists would diverge. His assessment remained influenced by a view of a Scottish government hampered by 'the nobility with their important semi-private jurisdictions and their tradition of independence and revolt'. As a result, Rae perhaps underestimated the effectiveness of the crown.[32]

One area, however, that might benefit from some consideration of more recent, non-border-specific research by English historians, is the consideration of what motivated the lower strata of society to comply with their superiors' orders. As yet the concepts of consensus and the negotiating power

---

[28] MacDonald, *Border bloodshed*, 62–3; S. Boardman, *The early Stewart kings: Robert II and Robert III, 1371–1406*, East Linton 1996, 117.
[29] M. H. Brown, *The Black Douglases: war and lordship in the late medieval Scotland, 1300–1455*, East Linton 1998, 1–6, 69–71, 283–6, 290–5, 308.
[30] MacDonald, *Border bloodshed*, 6–7, 241, quotation at p. 5.
[31] Rae, *Administration*, 12, 16–18, 28, 156–7, 177, 180–1, 215, 221–2.
[32] Ibid. 206.

of the subordinate have been little tested for Scotland.[33] In the Scottish Borders, whilst the tangible rewards of office, lands and jurisdiction, given to secure the co-operation of its kindred leaders with the crown, are detectable in the charters and commissions that recorded them, there is much less overt evidence of what was in it for their kinsmen and tenants. So far the Scottish historiography of this rests largely on a perception of the obligations and loyalty associated with kinship and the benefits of maintenance that good lordship could bring. The manifestation of the latter in the Borders can be seen in the tacks made to their adherents, in the intervention of leaders on behalf of their tenants in judicial processes, and in leaders standing surety for their dependants. If, as concluded in England, the absence of sufficiently developed institutions of government, and forms of coercion, meant that the elite had to negotiate the legitimacy and extent of their power with those below them, how much more so would this have been true of an even less developed system in Scotland?[34]

The dovetailing of interest between Scottish crown and regional elites was apparent in the co-operation of those elites, but the mutual interest in the perpetuation of a common ideology, identified by English historians as necessary to secure the co-operation of those of lower social status, has not been explored beyond the assumption of clan or kindred identity and loyalty. And that indeed may be where it should stay. Or rather, that the common interest may, perhaps, differ in England, from Scotland, where an emphasis on the significance of kinship, the replications of it in allegiance, and the use of its obligations by government, governors *and* governed, might go some way to explaining why people could be made to do things.[35] In both societies, however, kings, nobles and kindred leaders manipulated a 'discourse of rule', which sought to portray them as the defenders of the weak, in order to legitimise their authority.[36] Also, the significance of kinship in Scotland in determining relationships is thought to have been declining by the late sixteenth century. In the Borders, however, it may be that kinship continued to be of importance for longer, resounding, for instance, through the acts of caution that named several members of the same kin in dispute with similarly

---

[33] P. Griffiths, A. Fox and S. Hindle (eds), *The experience of authority in early modern England*, Basingstoke 1996; M. J. Braddick and J. Walter (eds), *Negotiating power in early modern society: order, hierarchy and subordination in Britain and Ireland*, Cambridge 2001.

[34] J. Walter, 'Public transcripts, popular agency and the politics of subsistence in early modern England', in Braddick and Walter, *Negotiating power*, 123–48 at pp. 123–5.

[35] Keith Wrightson notes the interdependence of all members of English households, loosely termed 'families', and similar 'areas of relative interdependence within the structure of society' that might correspond to aspects of the relationships within Scottish kindreds and alliances: 'The politics of the parish in early modern England', in Griffiths, Fox and Hindle, *Experience of authority*, 10–46 at pp. 13, 17, 32.

[36] John Walter identifies this discourse projecting 'a public policy acknowledging protection of the subject as its primary responsibility ... to secure consent to their right to rule': 'Public transcripts', 125–6, 128–9.

numerous members of another, with other relations standing surety, through their intermarriage, and in the continuation of members of the same kin acting as executors in their kinsmen's wills late into the seventeenth century. A qualitative assessment, of course, is all that is possible here but certainly the impression is that the obligations of kinship and alliance lingered on in the Borders.

The lack of records, commensurate with those available in England, means that it is very difficult to determine what the 'hidden transcript' behind the public discourse may have been. However, the voice of the 'ordinary' borderer can perhaps be heard in the ballads, and, occasionally, peeping through the 'public' transcript in kirk session and patchy judicial court records: for instance, William Tweedie in Peeblesshire in 1611 invited the Justices of the Peace to 'kiss his arse' since he 'wald nocht gif ane scab of his erse for thame!' The gesture that went with these words can be imagined. And the crown did not like such disrespect to its lawful officers, as a town official found out too late in Edinburgh, in 1601, when he was hanged for attempting to display the king's portrait hanging from the gibbet. Tweedie was prosecuted for 'unreverent and disdanefull speiches' by the High Court of Justiciary, but escaped lightly in contrast, being scourged through the streets of Edinburgh and subsequently banished.[37] A humourless crown was sensitive to any overt questioning of the legitimacy of its officers' authority that had the potential to hinder 'good rule'.[38]

Changes in the crown's approach to the Borders were influenced, not only by varying relations with England, but also by its wider development of government in Scotland in this period. James's attitude to his whole domain, and the participation of increasing numbers of his subjects within the expanding authority of the state, is the context to the intensification of the crown's power in the Borders, as elsewhere. The period between 1560 and 1625 saw a quadrupling of those holding local office in Scotland, and the Borders were no less affected.[39] But, additionally, the Borders, like the Highlands, were specifically targeted by government, and, as Goodare observes, whilst 'the Borders and Highlands were two distinct regions, it was very much the same general policy for them both'. The difference between

---

[37] J. C. Scott, *Domination and the arts of resistance: hidden transcripts*, New Haven–London 1990, pp. xii–xiii, 5–10, 19, 87; *Ancient criminal trials in Scotland*, ed. R. Pitcairn, (Bannatyne Club, 1839–45), ii/2, 349–51; iii/1, 220–1; M. J. Braddick, 'Introduction: the politics of gesture', and J. Walter, 'Gesturing at authority: deciphering the gestural code of early modern England', *Past and Present* cciii, suppl. 4 (2009), 9–35 at pp. 18, 24–6, 28; 96–127 at pp. 113–15, 126–7.

[38] As Michael Braddick notes, words could become 'magnified by the implications'. Credibility and effectiveness rested on a 'smooth representation of the collective authority of the magistracy', thus concern over any criticism: 'Administrative performance: the representation of authority in early modern England', in Braddick and Walter, *Negotiating power*, 166–87 at pp. 167, 171, 186–7.

[39] Goodare, *Government of Scotland*, 216–19.

them was that the Borders, unlike the Highlands, were subject to 'over-government': 'The lack of local nerve-ends of government in the Highlands meant that the crown was relatively insensitive to unauthorised violence. By contrast, it displayed a marked touchiness towards similar events in the Borders'. Thus Goodare concludes that the Borders were 'part of the structure of the state in a way that the Highlands hardly were'.[40] Government in the Borders was integrated into that of the kingdom and subject to processes underway throughout.

But border-specific circumstances continued to impact: James VI's succession to the throne of England in 1603 inevitably affected the Middle March as the international significance of the border disappeared. Where James had used instability in the borders to bargain with Elizabeth, he did not have to bargain with himself. A policy of 'pacification' was implemented consistently from 1605 in order to bring the Middle Shires into conformity with the rest of the united kingdoms. Two regional studies of the pacification in England, Sheldon and Susan Watts on Northumberland and Richard Spence on Cumberland, provide invaluable context for any evaluation of the northern side of the frontier. In particular the Watts's analysis of the effect of factionalism within Northumberland on the exaggerated or underplayed portrayal of disorder there, has direct relevance to the Scottish government's perception of its Borders. However, the situation in the English Borders cannot be directly equated with that in the Scottish, particularly in relation to Scottish borderer connections with their government.[41] James, however, after 1603, seems to have forgotten the differences in the Borders between his two kingdoms, creating the cross-border region of the Middle Shires. In his history of the pacification, from 1603 to 1625, Jared Sizer attempted to treat this entire Borders region, as 'one administrative entity', 'a single geographic, legal and religious entity'. He found that 'this was what they were not'. Both sides of the border continued to be administered under two separate commissions. This division resulted in the failure of James's vision of a united 'Middle Shires' and was symptomatic of his frustrated attempts to gain full Union.[42] However, Sizer's analysis of the Borders as 'separated' from the 'typical Lowland experience', and backward due to its isolation, is to superimpose perhaps his conclusions for the English Borders onto the Scottish situation.[43]

The problems James faced in the Borders, from 1603, explain much about the problems he faced in his pursuit of full Union – particularly in relation to the enduring distinct legal systems. As Brian Levack notes, 'what

---

[40] Idem, *State and society*, 255, 257–58.
[41] S. J. Watts and S. J. Watts, *From Border to Middle Shire: Northumberland, 1586–1625*, Leicester 1975; Spence, 'Pacification'.
[42] J. Sizer, 'Law and disorder in the "Middle Shires" of Great Britain, 1603–1625', unpubl. PhD diss. Cambridge 2001, 3, 5, 15, 284.
[43] Ibid. 20.

appeared necessary ... was the co-ordination, if not the union, of the judicial forces of the two states in this troubled area'. However 'Scotland in the seventeenth century was a free, independent kingdom, a sovereign state in its own right, possessing its own laws'. James's difficulties in standardising legal procedures in the whole Borders were seen in his frustrated attempts to enforce cross-border remanding; these should be set within Anglo-Scottish friction over legal integrity and broader fears of loss of sovereignty. Bruce Galloway observed that the parliamentary debate over hostile and border laws, from 1604 to 1607, took place 'against a background of mutual distrust'. Levack's description of the 'modified' version of the 1707 Union, in which legal systems remained independent, suggests an explanation for the failure to achieve uniformity of such systems in the Borders to 1625.[44]

Though his aspirations for Union dominated the early years of James's English rule, his policies in the Borders should be placed within the context of his kingship and government throughout Britain. As Galloway noted, border administration in 1605–6 was an area where 'it is difficult to separate action taken to advance the Union from the simple continuation of long-standing policy'; the pacification 'reflected James's emphasis on the extension of centralised authority throughout his dominions'.[45] Recent research has underlined how developments in the separate regions of the British archipelago have formed part of a wider 'British history'.[46] Steven Ellis's comparative study of the English northern border region and the English pale in Ulster under the Tudors usefully identifies the similarities between these two peripheral regions, which provides some context for the situation in the Scottish Borders. He shows how the 'marcher society' characteristics of 'clans and captaincies, joint responsibility and co-ownership of land' in both England and Ulster, increasingly conflicted with the demands of 'civil society' and Tudor government. Following the Reformation, Henry VIII was forced to pre-empt any rebellion by disaffected magnates such as Lord Dacre in the English north and the earl of Kildare in Ulster. For Ellis, the tensions he found in the development of Tudor government, using this 'collective

---

[44] B. P. Levack, *The formation of the British state: England, Scotland, and the Union, 1603–1707*, Oxford 1987, 6, 24, 62, 75, 86–7; B. Galloway, *The Union of Scotland and England, 1603 to 1608*, Cambridge 1986.
[45] Galloway, *Union of Scotland*, 65–8, 84–6, 120–7, quotation at p. 84.
[46] S. G. Ellis, 'Introduction: the concept of British history', and 'Tudor state formation and the shaping of the British Isles', in S. G. Ellis and S. Barber (eds), *Conquest and union: fashioning a British state, 1485–1726*, London–New York 1995, 1–7, 40–63; J. Morrill, 'The British problem, c.1534–1707', in B. Bradshaw and J. Morrill (eds), *The British problem, 1534–1707*, Basingstoke 1996, 1–38; M. J. Braddick, *State formation in early modern England* c. 1550–1700, Cambridge 2000; A. Macinnes and J. Ohlmeyer (eds), *The Stuart kingdoms in the seventeenth century: awkward neighbours*, Dublin 2002; G. Burgess (ed.), *The new British history: founding a modern state, 1603–1707*, London 1999; M. Greengrass (ed.), *Conquest and coalescence: the shaping of the state in early modern Europe*, London 1991. 'British history' is discussed further in the conclusion below.

approach' to history, help to explain the tensions apparent in the formation of the British state after unification.[47]

Whilst his analysis of the Tudor north conclusively shows the problems that Tudor governments had with England's peripheries, it should be emphasised that Ellis's concentration is on the English government: his works do not cover Scotland, though he draws conclusions from them for post-Union Scotland. As a result Ellis perhaps underestimates the significance of the very different circumstances north of the border, where those in the Middle March, at least, were not alienated from central government: increasingly they were involved within it. These differences continued after 1603 when the privy council in Edinburgh continued to govern on a day-to-day basis: policy was affected by English considerations but directed by a Scottish privy council exercising some discretion, through Scotsmen in the regions, within a Scottish governmental framework. Ellis's model for the English Borders should not be applied wholesale to those in Scotland: to do so would be to underestimate the effectiveness of royal authority in the Scottish Borders and links between centre and periphery, both before and after Union.

Awareness is needed, also, of one final consideration: the subconscious effect of the way in which the Borders and its inhabitants have been traditionally described by contemporary government and writers. By the end of the sixteenth century government's disdain might be termed a 'language of opprobrium'. When James's government, as it invariably did, used the terminology 'disorderit' to describe the borderers, it unwittingly formed the basis for future assumption that this was indeed the way most borderers were. When the term 'disorderit' was then linked with a description of the 'wicked' nature of the borderers, as in 'the wicked inclinatioun of the disorderit subjectis', it acquired a further level of meaning.[48] Disorder was equated with wickedness, thus any use of the term disorder inherently carried the meaning 'wicked'. Disorder to James represented a threat to the stability of his kingdom and an affront to his kingship. Given that James viewed his appointment as divine, such a personal challenge meant that it was ungodly, obviously 'wicked'. After 1603 he viewed any 'disorder' in the Borders as threatening to the establishment of full Union. Government's concern over 'disorder', however, only portrayed government's priorities at the time, and was not a methodical quantification of any such 'disorder', or, indeed, of those who were of 'good rule'.

The term 'disorder' throws up another problem: what exactly was this disorder and, intrinsic to an understanding of this, why was it occurring? At its most basic level, disorder in the Borders was described by government typically as 'reiff, thift or ressett of thift, depradationis opin and avowit, fyre

[47] S. G. Ellis, *Tudor frontiers and noble power: the making of the British state*, Oxford 1995, 253–4, 257–8, 263–4, 267.
[48] Preamble to act 'Anent the Highlands and Borders', *RPS*, 1587/7/70, accessed 19 June 2009.

raising upoun deidlie feidis'.[49] Such complaints abound from the English wardens, who equate the disorder with the inherently wicked borderers. But there is a problem with assuming that all these offences were motivated by the 'wicked' borderer: there is evidence that such 'disorder' was consciously condoned by the Scottish government. As late as 1597 the English ambassador Robert Bowes saw 'too little sinceritie' in James's public protestations of his intentions to impose 'order' in the Borders. This could be interpreted as diplomatic paranoia but, given the long-term favour shown by James in the 1590s to the very borderers that the English complained about, the English could be forgiven their scepticism. Governments may publicly declare one thing, whilst privately doing something completely different. Should disorder that was effectively state-sanctioned be viewed as disorder at all?[50]

III

The Middle March's experience from 1573 to 1625 was defined by its physical location on the border with England. This clearly affected central government's approach to the region and the evolution of some of the mechanisms within it. It is also important to understand that no matter how much this was the case, events in the Middle March were influenced by the evolving government of James VI and by a wider development in central government's policies towards its larger kingdom. From 1597, however, the increasing likelihood of James's succession to the throne of England prompted significant changes in his attitude to the Borders. No longer was disturbance there of use as leverage in negotiations with the English; instead it had come to be seen as a barrier. This inevitably affected the way in which the crown attempted to assert its authority in the region. From 1605 this took the form of a consistent and severely prosecuted pacification.

It is important, however, to separate the way in which borderers had been tacitly allowed to behave in the years before 1597 from the impression that their subsequent treatment has given. Similar caution should be applied to the terminology applied to the borderers throughout the sixteenth century, which suggested a tradition of violence in a region out of the control of central government. The image of the wicked borderers should not blind us to their participation in government both in the locality and at national level. To ignore this involvement would be to underestimate the mechanisms of government in place in the region. When government chose to exert its authority in the Borders, the mechanisms for it to do so were already there.

[49] Ibid.
[50] *CBP* ii, no. 603.

Sadly, for a balanced assessment of the Borders, the imagery associated with an anarchic region has coloured most histories of the region. Both the romanticism of Sir Walter Scott and the condemnation of anglo-centric historians have hindered a fuller understanding of the Borders in the late sixteenth century. It is intended here to challenge the stereotyping of the barbarous borderers of the Middle March. This case study will explore the ramifications of the findings of Jenny Wormald, Keith Brown and Michael Brown for the region and extend the socio-political parts of Maureen Meikle's work westwards. However, the significance of the Middle March's experience is not limited to discussion of government in Scotland. The conclusions that are drawn on the effectiveness of James's government, and the way in which it evolved in the Borders, will inform any wider debate on state formation within a nascent 'Great Britain'.

1

A Frontier Society?

'It is impossible that scottis men and inglis men can remane in concord undir ane monarche or ane prince because there naturis and conditions ar as indefferent as is the nature of scheip and wolvis ... [though] within ane ile and nythtbours, and of ane langage

for inglis men ar subtil and scottis men ar facile, inglis men ar ambitious in prosperite, and scottis men ar humane in prosperite, scottis men ar furious quhen thai ar violently subieckit, inglis men ar cruel quhen thai get victorie and scottis men ar merciful

[Yet] the familiarity that is betwix inglis men and scottis men in ane peace[ful] world at mercattis and conventions on the tua bordours is the cause of the treason that the scottis men committis contrar their natyfe country'[1]

It is a truism that the Middle March's geographical location on the frontier between two periodically hostile kingdoms affected its political, administrative, social, economical and cultural circumstances. The presence of that borderline inevitably meant that the Middle March developed border-specific characteristics that differentiated the region from Lowland Scotland. Additionally, the topographical nature of the land, moors, hills and 'wastelands', separated from the Lothians by the buttresses of the Moorfoot Hills and the Lammermuirs, contributes to an impression of an area 'apart' from its lowland neighbours: an 'out-countrey' divided from the 'incuntry'; the barbarian dales from the 'lawlands'; a region on the periphery of the kingdom, separated physically from its 'centre' in Edinburgh. Most recent work on frontier societies highlights these differences, pointing instead to the similarities, on some international borders, between the regions on either side: cross-border acculturation and/or assimilation, fraternisation and intermarriage, cultural and social similarities and militarisation which blurred the day-to-day significance of a political demarcation.[2] The result has been the identification of a frontier zone, stretching for some miles back either side

---

[1] *The complaynt of Scotland, c. 1550 by Robert Wedderburn*, ed. A. M. Stewart (STS, 1979), 83–4.
[2] G. Barrow, 'Frontier and settlement: which influence which? England and Scotland, 1100–1300', and A. Goodman, 'Religion and warfare in the Anglo-Scottish Marches', in R. Bartlett and A. MacKay (eds), *Medieval frontier societies*, Oxford 1992, 3–21, 245–66; Goodman, 'Introduction', to Goodman and Tuck, *War and border societies*, 1–3, and 'The Anglo-Scottish marches in the fifteenth century: a frontier society?', in Mason, *Scotland and England*, 18–33.

Map 2. Roxburghshire, Selkirkshire, and Peeblesshire in the Middle March

of the borderline. Thus for many historians, such as Patricia Bradley, the Anglo-Scottish border was not 'a line drawn on a map', but a 'distinct area' in which 'No distinction must or, indeed, can be made between the men who claimed allegiance to England and those who were Scottish subjects ... [T]hese men had far more in common with each other than with anyone else ... [sharing] a similar economy, a similar dialect, and similar dislike of outside authority.'[3]

What these studies obscure, however, are the differences between the two Borders regions and the effects of long-term hostility and administrative separation. As much as they might encourage intermixing, frontiers provided

---

[3] P. Bradley, 'Social banditry on the Anglo-Scottish Border during the late Middle Ages', *Scotia* xii (1988), 27–43 at pp. 29–31. Similar observations are made in Meikle, *A British frontier?*, 3; Sizer, 'Middle Shires', 14–15; Goodare, *State and society*, 218–19; and D. Newton, *North-east England, 1569–1625: governance, culture and identity*, Woodbridge 2006, 12–14, 83, 169.

points of intersection between two peoples that could trigger dispute or alienation, when confronted by the 'other'.[4] Thus, though Robert Wedderburn complained of the collusion between English and Scottish borderers, at the same time he emphasised the differences between the two peoples. An overemphasis on cross-border similarities has led to the underestimation of any commonalities between the Scottish Borders and the Lowlands, and the physical, mental, governmental and personal connections between the two. Such connectivity was symbolised by the passes of Fala and Soutra, that allowed a horseman from Edinburgh to be in Peebles within a day, and it was facilitated by a common language, Scottis.[5] These provided conduits for the cross-fertilisation of social, economic, religious and cultural practices, and identity, the transmission of government between Edinburgh and the Borders, and the involvement of Scottish borderers in the life of the political nation. The underestimation of the more positive linkages between the Scottish borderer and crown is due, in part, to an under-appreciation of the effectiveness of government in the Scottish Borders and an imposition of English models of the difficulty of Tudor governments' relationships with their borderlands, onto Scottish circumstances.[6] But, in a very real way, the fifty miles from Jedburgh to Edinburgh could link a borderer to his royal government in a potentially more beneficial relationship than that between the English borderer and the English court, the latter prejudiced by the alienating 300 miles from Hexham to London.

The dominance, however, of the concept of a cross-border mentality has come to downplay the very significance of the Anglo-Scottish frontier line. If this was true of the days before union, how much more so after 1603? Then, as James VI and I wrote, the island of Britain was 'separated neither by Sea, nor great River', so that the borderers 'cannot distinguish, nor know, or discerne their owne limits'. Neither James, nor subsequent historians, however, has taken full account of the enduring effects of hostility, the separate nature of two sovereign kingdoms and the differences between them. This failure is due, perhaps, to the anglo-centric assumption of the inevitability of a 'Great Britain', with only one meaningful frontier, that provided by the sea: this last, Colley finds, a 'glib and retrospective interpretation'. Instead, an acknowledgement is needed of the 'sense of paramountcy of inland frontiers – using that term to mean that which stands face to a real or imagined enemy, or at least to something that is considered alien in

---

[4] L. Colley, 'The significance of the frontier in British history', in W. R. Louis (ed.), *More adventures with Britannia: personalities, politics and culture in Britain*, London 1998, 13–29 at pp. 15–18.
[5] Old Scots, as a distinct language from English.
[6] This extent of this alienation is now questioned by Newton: 'the elites of the north-eastern reaches of the kingdom were not the isolated and backward quasi-feudal northern gentry of myth': *North-east England*, 43.

part – [which] persisted long after the Acts of Union'.[7] So two main themes emerge here: firstly to determine what similarities the Middle March did have with the other Scottish regions, which requires some contextualisation of social, economic and religious circumstances in the Scottish Borders, and a re-evaluation of the significance of the borderline itself.

I

Much has been made of an apparent ambiguity of the frontier line noting the continuation of dispute over the Debateable Land until a divide through it was agreed in 1552.[8] However, the overall line of the frontier, from the Solway Firth, along the border hills to the Cheviots and from there along the Tweed to Berwick, was set in the mid-thirteenth century and had been unchallenged since the fifteenth. Contention remained only in a small number of areas that straddled the frontier, such as the Debateable Land, ownership of which was variously claimed or disavowed by governments anxious to deny responsibility. The smaller disputes that rumbled on were more contested pasturage rights or property boundaries, between private landowners, than international disagreement over a frontier. Anthony Goodman notes the strength of feeling about the 'immutability' of this line. A general understanding existed of where the frontier line was and of its antiquity. Borderers may have chosen to ignore it when pasturing their livestock, or hunting with their neighbours, but that does not mean that they were unaware of its existence.[9]

Furthermore, no matter how pedestrian this may sound, administrative boundaries applied by both Scottish and English governments demarcated the entire region. The laws that affected the Scottish side of the border were those formed by a Scottish government. An inhabitant of this region may have been a borderer, but in terms of the law and government of his physical locality, he was a Scottish borderer. A march warden from one side of the border was not allowed by law to prosecute an offender from the other. Resistance after 1603 to the remanding of borderers to the country of their offence, when the frontier had supposedly dissolved, demonstrated an enduring understanding of its significance. The frontier was institutionalised within the framework of each country's law and administration.

These administrative regions helped to differentiate the Borders from the rest of Scotland, with their border-specific offices and extra layer of border laws. When these differences were combined with the militarisation of society necessitated by the defence of the border, historians, perfectly reason-

---

[7] Colley, 'Significance of the frontier', 17.
[8] CBP i, no. 76.
[9] RPC xii. 746; Goodman, 'The Anglo-Scottish Marches', 20.

ably, have identified the development of a 'frontier mentality'. For some, such as Alastair MacDonald, this included the borderers' increasing sense of alienation from their centre of government, in the sixteenth century. This may have contributed to a closer identification, of similar circumstances, between English and Scottish borderers. In contrast, however, Goodman concludes that, in the fifteenth century, the border lairds' political connections with the crown 'reinforced the tendencies among the border elites ... to make economic and financial ties away from the frontier, in and through the interiors of their realms'. Care is needed too, in the sixteenth century, not to discount the strength of these ties that continued to bind those on the geographical 'periphery' to Edinburgh. Indeed, the participation of some borderers in the highest levels of government, and their actions on behalf of the crown in the Borders, arguably could be seen as 'central' government taking place in a 'locality'. It is no longer so useful to separate the two, and this has led to some erosion in the value of the term 'frontier mentality'.[10]

What did all this mean to how the borderer thought of himself? Maureen Meikle concludes that the similarities between the Eastern Borderers manifested in a borderer's identity in which 'lairds and gentlemen tended to be Borderers first and foremost and Scots or English second'.[11] Cross-border fraternisation and cultural similarities might lead a borderer to identify more closely with his English counterpart than a fellow countryman. Some historians have pointed to cross-border marriages as evidence of this. Feverish report by English wardens of cross-border marriages led, in 1556 and 1583, to their prohibition by a border commission. In 1583 a generalised report on the 'riders' of the Borders listed a number of marriages between Scottish Elliots and Armstrongs and English Grahams and Fosters. Such marriages were blamed as the 'greatest occasion of the spoils and robberies on the Borders'. However, these marriages generally occurred at the lower socio-economic levels for which no marriage contracts exist. Reports of them were partly a result of English scaremongering and often linked to worries over the cross-border pasturing of livestock.[12] The only marriage contracts that survive are at the social level of the lairds and their families; amongst these no examples have been found, for between 1673 and 1614, of anyone from the Middle March marrying an English borderer. Those that did occur subsequently were often formed at court in London and not with English border ladies. Borderers may have had much in common, and friendships, with those on the other side, but, as Sizer concludes, 'Borderers themselves

---

[10] Goodman, 'Anglo-Scottish Marches', 19, 22–3, 29, and 'Introduction', 9; MacDonald, *Border bloodshed*, 201–2, 241; Goodare, *Government of Scotland*, 114–17.
[11] Meikle, *A British frontier?*, 3.
[12] CBP i, nos 6, 165, 197.

were rarely unified and seldom if ever conceived of themselves as a unified people.'[13]

One indigenous source of evidence of a contemporary mentality is the primarily Scottish border ballads: these do indeed show evidence of a cross-border frontier mentality, of shared heroic martial characteristics. However, there is also evidence of an heroic patriotism: the ballads about Otterburn were not just about Douglas/Percy rivalry, but also about being a Scotsman fighting an Englishman and winning.[14]

> The doughty Douglas bound him to ride
> Into England, to drive a prey...
> And he has burn'd the dales of Tyne
> And part of Bambrough shire;
> And three good towers on Reidswire fells
> He left them all on fire.

A ballad about the notorious Johnnie Armstrong, hanged with many of his surname in 1530 on a judicial raid by James V, mourns:

> But Scotland's heart was ne'er sae wae
> To see sae mony brave men die –
> Because they saved their countrey deir
> Frae Englishmen!

Citing his patriotism, Armstrong appealed unsuccessfully to James for clemency:

> Wist England's King that I was ta'en
> O gin a blythe man he wald be![15]

By themselves these ballads cannot prove conclusively the existence of a Scottish identity. What they do show, undoubtedly, is an understanding of the existence of a frontier line. Such a conclusion questions the comprehensive nature of a 'shared mentality' between the inhabitants either side of the border.[16]

Identity could, of course, take several forms: arguably the strongest was that which was closest, one's kindred. An Armstrong or a Turnbull probably identified more closely with his kinsmen, than his countrymen. But one person could have a number of overlapping, or perhaps concentric, identi-

---

[13] In 1614 Robert Ker, earl of Somerset, married Frances Howard, daughter of the earl of Suffolk, and, in the 1620s, Robert Ker of Ancrum married the daughter of the countess of Derby: Meikle, *A British frontier?*, 30–2; Sizer, 'Middle Shires', 282.
[14] Goodman, 'Introduction', 7–8, and Grant, 'The Otterburn War', 30–64; K. McAlpine, 'Proude Armstrongs and border rogues: history in "Kinmont Willie", "Jock o the Side" and "Archie of Cawfield"', in Cowan, *The ballad in Scottish history*, 73–94.
[15] Scott, *Minstrelsy*, i. 283, 286, 356–58.
[16] Goodman, 'The Anglo-Scottish Marches', 30.

ties.[17] So he could be an Armstrong, a Liddesdale man, an ally of the Scott surname, a borderer, a Scotsman. He might feel that he owed obedience to the chief of his kindred, Armstrong of Mangerton or Whithaugh, his landlord Scott of Buccleuch, the march warden Cessford, the sheriff Douglas of Cavers, and the king. And different borderers will have felt some affiliations to be more important than others. Within the marches themselves, there appears to have been differing degrees of 'bordererdom'. In the burgh of Peebles, the burgesses, though borderers themselves, feared the 'bordouris theivis and revaris' and were involved in the 'deidlie feid of the towne with the bordour'. What may be applicable generally to some borderers would not have applied to certain people and to some areas: though some borderers were involved in an active relationship with central government, there were others who acted with apparent indifference to the Scottish crown. It seems likely that the closer to the frontier a man lived, the less strong the link to the crown, and certainly the Liddesdale surnames of Elliot and Armstrong come in for the greatest censure. Crucially, also, it appears that, as MacDonald has found, there was a differing degree of integration with the Scottish crown within the social strata of the borderers, with greater cross-border fraternisation of the 'lesser' sort. But even amongst the 'wickit theivis of Liddisdaill', a borderer was a Scottish borderer, and someone who would have understood himself as such.[18]

Perhaps the most compelling evidence for the existence of a Scottish borderer identity is what happened in the Borders after the Union of Crowns had supposedly removed the significance of the border. Between 1605 and 1612 the mutual suspicion, verging on outright hostility, displayed in the dispute between English and Scottish commissioners over the remanding of criminals to the country of their offence, was that between one countryman and a foreigner. James's hopes that all inhabitants of his joined kingdoms would embrace the idea of a 'Great Britain' would not be realised within his lifetime. The effects of long-term 'warfare and hostile propaganda' on the attitude of one national to another were such that, as Jane Dawson asks, how could James have hoped 'to eradicate the long-standing enmity ... and so transform their deep-rooted hatred into an enduring amity'. As late as 1798 the historian John Dalyell observed the 'long and inveterate animosity ... hardly yet extinguished'. If this was the case on a kingdom-wide basis, how much more so would it be amongst the people that had suffered most from that enmity?[19] The strongest case for the continuing importance of the borderline is made by that which precluded full Union in James's lifetime.

---

[17] Newton makes a similar point for Northumberland and Durham: *North-east England*, 10–11.
[18] *Charters and documents relating to the burgh of Peebles, 1165–1710*, ed. W. Chambers (Scottish Burgh Record Society, 1872), 342, 356; MacDonald, *Border bloodshed*, 237.
[19] J. Dawson, 'Anglo-Scottish Protestant culture and integration in sixteenth-century

II

Work on the Borders has, inevitably, focused on what made them singular or different from the neighbouring Lowlands. Whilst it is important to keep border-specific circumstances in mind, the region also needs to be approached as any other in Scotland. Hostility and warfare impacted on the Borders, but so did more general social, demographical, economical and ecclesiastical developments common to elsewhere in Scotland. The themes of population growth, agricultural practices, landlord-tenant relations and Reformation were often similar to, and connected into, those experienced in the Lowlands.

It is however not surprising that accounts of the Borders tend to ignore these common themes, given the way in which contemporary portrayals differentiated the region: 'Our ancestors were savages, or they were but one degree removed ... In an cold and uncongenial time, luxury is of late introduction ... thus, the ancient barbarism of Scotland, perhaps, originates in the weather.' This was particularly so, Dalyell felt, in the Borders, as he recounts the journey of a papal delegate, Aeneas Sylvius, in the fifteenth century. On his arrival in the English Borders, he 'complains he could get neither bread nor wine ... Upon an alarm from the Scots, the men fled to a remote tower' leaving the cleric with one hundred women, sleepless, around a large fire.[20] A barren environment, lacking in victuals, plagued by violence and peopled by feckless men. In the mid-sixteenth century, John Leslie described the effects of war in the Scottish Borders:

> the ground albeit fertile anuich [but] feiring that schortlie the weiris oppresse thame, thay alutterlie contemne to tile [till]. Quhairthrouch cumis to passe that be steiling and reif, thay rather seik thair meit ... Upon fleshe, milke and cheis, and soden beir ... thay lyve. Thay have verie lytle use of breid, even as they have of gude beir, amaist na wine. Thair castelis and palices ar scheiphouses and luges, quhilkes thay commonlie cal pailes [pele towers ... and they lived in a mountainous landscape of] wildernes, bygates, kraigs and glenis.

As a result, 'thay are persuadet that all the gudes of al men in tyme of necessitie, be the lawe of nature, ar commoune to thame' and their 'maneris [are] frome the rest far diferrent'.[21] In the 1650s the map-engraver Joan Blaeu pictured Teviotdale, 'among the steep borders of hills and rocks ... inhabited by a warlike people'; Liddesdale, where 'there are no cornfields, all is pasture and moorland ... and around are many small towers of military men'; and Nithsdale and Annandale which 'nurture a warlike race of men'.[22] The image

---

Britain', in Ellis and Barber, *Conquest and union*, 87–114 at p. 91; Dalyell, *Fragments*, 23–4.
[20] Dalyell, *Fragments*, 3, 18.
[21] Leslie, *History*, i. 97–8, 101.
[22] Joan Blaeu, *Atlas of Scotland*, Amsterdam 1654, 30–1, 42–3, 46.

of the desolate remote 'wasteland', and the barbarous inhabitants it created, the subject, too, of miserable English reporting, continues to permeate most histories of the Borders.

But it was not all gloom and doom. Blaeu goes on to expound on the bounteousness of Tweeddale, where the

> land often swells into mountains; those which closely overlook the Tweed and the banks of the other rivers on either side are green, lovely and very suited for pasture ... some of them produce grain, some hay ... [and] an abundance of milk, cheese and butter. In the more low-lying places, where it comes closest to Selkirk, sheep have such healthy and dry pasture that, what scarcely occurs in other regions, they reach their fifteenth year ... Fuel in this Province is partly sods and peats, of which there is a great supply everywhere ... so that almost nothing is wanting in this Province, which is necessary for man for daily use, whether one considers food, or clothing, or hearth.[23]

The Tweed 'was an especially notable fishery [with] a great abundance of salmon, ascending it from the sea ... [and] a very abundant supply of fat and healthy trout and other river fish', whilst at Eddleston, by Peebles, 'the local people, gathered there for the fishing ... are sometimes scattered by the force of the fish as they burst out'. Unlike Dalyell, he thought 'the region enjoys a temperate climate and for the most part clear and quiet air'.[24] The importance ascribed to fishing can be seen in the contested ownership and protection of fishing rights, many in the hands of the abbeys, who rented them to local lairds.[25] Blaeu's *Atlas* of 1654, and Timothy Pont's maps of the 1590s, upon which it is based, reveal a plethora of stone tower houses following the lines of the rivers, which contrasts with the poorly settled wastelands described by English officials of their side of the border.[26]

What both these negative and positive images portray is the overwhelmingly rural nature of the region, whose agriculture was dominated by the rearing of livestock, the hunting of deer and game, and exploiting the rivers, rather than by the production of crops. Some wheat, but mostly oats, bear (barley) and peas were grown in the valleys in the east of the Middle March, around Melrose and Kelso, but where the land rises to the south and the west, arable gave way quickly to pastoral. Transhumance had been practised on the higher ground, with cattle being driven up in the summers, indicated by the existence of 'shiels' in many place names, and the wardens' reports of it. By the seventeenth century, however, Ian Whyte concludes that cultiva-

---

[23] Ibid. 33–4.
[24] Ibid. 33.
[25] Meikle, *A British frontier?*, 136.
[26] Blaeu, *Atlas*, 32, 34; Pont maps, NLS, Pont 35(2); I. C., Cunningham (ed.), *The nation survey'd: Timothy Pont's maps of Scotland*, Edinburgh 2001, 9–13. Julian Goodare notes that Pont was mapping a 'landscape of power' in the prominence that he gave to the lairds' houses. In which case Blaeu's maps indicated a considerable network of powerful figures in the Middle March: *State and society*, 251.

tion had expanded into previous shielings where there were now permanent farms. Thus Hawick Shiels, just south of Hawick, was producing grain in 1625, whereas the more marginal land at Foulshiels in Liddesdale was not.[27] The preponderance of livestock in the lairds' inventories attested to their interest in breeding and rearing, and the concentration of any wealth that they had in these live products rather than the 'insight and geir' to be found within their houses. A man's wealth was gauged in the numbers and quality of his sheep and cattle, and not the fanciness of his gaff. But in a Scottish economy that in the sixteenth century was dominated by the production of meat for the local market, and wools, skins and fells for export, this made sense. In the period 1460–1600, wool products amounted to around 60 per cent of all Scottish export revenues, with 75 per cent of it being exported through nearby Edinburgh. Whilst the export of raw wool was falling by the later sixteenth century, once trade recovered after the Rough Wooing of the 1540s, the export of woolfells, skins and cattle hides recovered, maintaining their levels into the 1590s. And, as Maureen Meikle notes, there was also a 'ready market' in the local burghs of Melrose, Kelso, Jedburgh, Peebles and Selkirk.[28]

But lest this give too thriving a picture of the Middle March's economy, it should of course be remembered that for most of its residents, those yeoman farmers and peasants who rented their small acreages from the lairds or the formerly monastic regalities, farming was to subsist, to feed their families and to pay their meagre rents in kind or pennies or service. In this they did not differ from the rest of Scotland, in which Whyte observes an 'underlying similarity in the organization of rural society over the country as a whole' that lasted into the eighteenth century.[29] Where they held arable land, they operated an infield and outfield system, but for many their land will have been pasture. They will have also depended on the grazing provided by the common lands in the moors surrounding the burghs, such as those of Peebles and Selkirk. Their diet was heavily weighted to meat and dairy, as was that in the Lowlands: there, however, population pressures on land meant that grains were beginning to replace the traditional diet.[30] There is perhaps a case for the borderers, who held onto land and livestock, retaining a more substantial diet despite their claims of poverty. Tony Goodman, however, cautions that there was probably, from the late fifteenth century, a 'growth in the settlement of the more marginal upland dales, in part stimulated by

---

[27] I. D. Whyte, *Agriculture and society in seventeenth-century Scotland*, Edinburgh 1979, 84; Buccleuch muniments, NAS, GD224/943/1.
[28] I. Guy, 'The Scottish export trade, 1460–1599', in T. C. Smout (ed.), *Scotland and Europe, 1200–1850*, Edinburgh 1986, 62–81 at pp. 62–4; Meikle, *A British frontier?*, 131–2.
[29] Whyte, *Agriculture*, 24.
[30] Idem, *Scotland before the Industrial Revolution: an economic and social history, c. 1050–c. 1750*, London–New York 1995, 113, 122.

an expansion of cultivation and grazing, and by population growth, in more fertile' areas. Both demographic and economic factors, he warns, may have helped to trigger the militarisation of these more vulnerable borderers when their less fertile lands failed and they turned to livestock theft.[31]

But added to the socio-economic factors, that affected the Lowlands too, there were in the Borders, of course, additional problems associated with the effects of Anglo-Scottish hostility. The English regularly relished burning their way through the Borders; but there is also evidence of the borderers' ability to recover relatively quickly after periods of warfare. After the disasters of Flodden and subsequent English incursions into the 1520s, Goodman concludes that 'there was a strand of optimism in Jedburgh about war with the English, and that it was not seen there as necessarily a dire threat to the continued prosperity of that vulnerable bastion of the middle march … on one of the principal English invasion routes'. Towns could take a few years to recover, but Jedburgh, in 1523, was prosperous according to Lord Dacre, with twice as many houses as Berwick. Such speedy recovery was less possible in the uplands of western Teviotdale however, where as Goodman also observes, 'campaigns in a region heavily dependent on stock-raising, probably drove families deprived of their essential cattle and sheep to commence or intensify their thefts'.[32] Thus, English incursions 'are likely to have had a destabilizing effect on parts of society in this march (in contrast to the east march), threatening the economy of fragile uplands and the livelihoods of marginal pastoralists and husbandmen'.[33] The destruction caused by subsequent large-scale English raids through the Middle March in the Rough Wooing of the 1540s, and in support of the king's party in the early 1570s, is trumpeted in the letters of the English captains and wardens, but such incursions were, by 1573, a thing of the past. Cross-border raiding of livestock continued, but the burning of buildings and crops was over. Large-scale raiding, too, was declining by the 1590s, despite the impression given by hysterical English wardens.[34] This did not, however, stop the burgesses of Jedburgh and Selkirk from continuing to attribute their poverty to long-term hostility into the 1620s, when questioned over their provision of poor relief or a sufficient tolbooth.[35]

In all this, the ordinary borderer will have been dependent on the good will of his landlord rather more than the depredations of the English. And, in contrast to the forced enclosures being experienced in England in the period,

---

[31] A. Goodman, 'The impact of warfare on the Scottish Marches, c.1481–c. 1513', in L. Clark (ed.), *The fifteenth century: conflicts, consequences and the crown in the late Middle Ages*, Woodbridge 2007, 195–211 at pp. 197, 207.
[32] Ibid. 198, 204, 205.
[33] Ibid. 206.
[34] P. W. Dixon, 'Fortified houses on the Anglo-Scottish Border: a study of the domestic architecture of the upland area in its social and economic context', unpubl. DPhil. Oxford 1976, 73–5.
[35] RPC ix. 714–15; xii. 173; xiii. 160–1, 484, 525, 619

the picture appears more benign in Scotland. Whilst some enclosure was happening in the sixteenth century, Whyte dates its increased rate from the later seventeenth, usually radiating out from the laird's house, in increasingly 'utilitarian' forms. The impression is that the Borders were no different, the exception being the very beginnings of some sheep parks after regnal union. In the Eastern Borders, Meikle found that the land management practices of the English gentry, busy engrossing lands and evicting tenants, contrasted sharply with those of the Scottish lairds.[36] In Scotland, in the sixteenth century, though many tenants will have lacked a written tack to their lands, and those that did may not have held formal hereditary rights of tenancy, customary landholding still predominated. Ian Whyte notes the 'enduring paternalism', into the seventeenth century, of most landowners, and 'the strength of custom probably ensured that continuity of tenure was normal'. In 1697 the Scotts of Buccleuch, faced by massive rent arrears accrued by weather-beaten farmers, did not evict those who had a good record, and had lived on these lands 'past memorie of man'.[37] Some security also, though not formalised, was to be found in the 'kindly tenancy', which recognised the significance of the occupation of the tenancy by several previous generations of the same family. As Margaret Sanderson observes, 'kindly tenancy was not *how* the tenant held but *why* he held', 'a firmly established principle of landholding, not simply folk-law but a recognized right'.[38] Thus the occupancy of the same families was perpetuated for generations, and this was as much the case in the Middle March. Despite the upheaval that war will have created, a rental roll of the lordship of Liddesdale, in 1541, shows that most had been occupied by the same families *in hereditate*, whilst, in 1591, Scott of Buccleuch issued a new tack to Gilbert Elliot and his heirs, as 'kyndlie rentallors' of Commonside, 'presentlie occupyit be him' in Liddesdale.[39] The emphasis on long occupation can be seen also in the disputes that kindly tenants brought before the barony court associated with the lands. The informal rights of kindly tenancy were subject to the landlord's will, but Sanderson has found that such rights could be upheld. She concludes that these actions suggested 'a measure of resource and opportunity such as we would expect to find behind an assertive rather than suppressed section of the community, and they tend to detract from the traditionally defenceless image of the kindly servants'.[40] With reference to the work of such as Steven Hindle, John Walter, Mike Braddick and Keith Wrightson, these

---

[36] Whyte, *Agriculture*, 130–2; Meikle, *A British frontier?*, 127–9.
[37] I. D. Whyte, *Scotland's society and economy in transition, c. 1500–c. 1760*, Basingstoke 1997, 41; Whyte, *Agriculture*, 158; NAS, GD224/935/3.
[38] M. Sanderson, *Scottish rural society in the sixteenth century*, Edinburgh 1982, ch. v, quotations at pp. 58, 60, and *A kindly place? Living in sixteenth-century Scotland*, East Linton 2002, esp. ch. i.
[39] W. Fraser, *The Scotts of Buccleuch*, Edinburgh 1878, ii, no. 159; NAS, GD224/1059/1.
[40] Sanderson, *Scottish rural society*, 62.

kindly tenants had some power to negotiate with their superiors, and to resist changes to their tenancies.

There were processes underway, however, that affected tenancies all over Scotland. The most significant of these was the gradual increase in the feuing, from the late fifteenth century, by cash-strapped bishops and kings of church and crown lands, which was running apace by the mid-sixteenth. The immediate financial windfall offered by initial payments for the feus, and the opportunity to raise the annual rents, proved irresistible to kings, churchmen and commendators alike. In the longer term, though, rents failed to rise with inflation to the benefit of the tenants. However, since a feu charter established a family's right to inherit, this eroded the customary rights of inheritance.[41] In the Middle March this was of relevance, particularly, in the crown forest of Ettrick, which, from 1503, formed part of the jointure lands of Margaret Tudor, wife of James IV, and in the abbacy lands of Melrose, Jedburgh and Kelso. Feuing provided income to replace abbatial revenues here which were being drained by taxes levied for defence, normal church maintenance and 'for money to repair damage done by the English', though the latter, as Sanderson comments wryly, may have been 'just the fashionable excuse for feuing'.[42] Whilst theoretically feus could be sold to anyone, they were often granted to existing occupants or those with existing associations to the land. Thus, in 1547, Scott of Branxholme was granted several feus for lands in Roxburghshire by the commendator of Melrose: the Branxholmes had been made hereditary 'baillie principal' for the abbacy of Melrose in 1519, which they did not resign until 1621.[43] In her comprehensive survey, Sanderson estimates that more than 60 per cent of feuars in Scotland were sitting tenants, of whom more than 80 per cent were resident occupants. This correlates with her figures for Melrose abbey which show 64 per cent of feus being granted to occupants almost all of whom were resident. Feus were not only given to the lairds, Sanderson finding that large numbers of feuars came from the strata below the lairds, and formed a 'wedge of new proprietors'. Whilst lairds and their kinsmen accounted for 29 per cent of feus from the late fifteenth and sixteenth centuries, Sanderson found that 44 per cent were taken up by those below them. She concludes that feuing 'did much to entrench the tenant class in many of those parts of Scotland which had been church estates', though this was subject to further change in the seventeenth and eighteenth centuries as feus were conglomerated during the increasing commercialisation of the land.[44]

It was a similar picture in the crown-owned forest of Ettrick, which was subdivided into the wards of its rivers, Ettrick, Tweed and Yarrow. Here, in 1501, commissioners re-let the existing leases for nine years (rather than the

---

[41] Ibid. 63, chap. vi.
[42] Ibid. 71.
[43] RMS iv, no. 2319; NAS, GD224/930/41, fos 1, 3, 5; Fraser, *Buccleuch*, ii, no. 126.
[44] Sanderson, *Scottish rural society*, 75, 77, 80–1, 99, 105.

usual three), but with increased rents. When these expired most of them were converted to feu-ferme or hereditary lease.[45] This provided an increase in annual revenue to the crown of more than 400 per cent by 1513 and a cash injection of three times the formal yearly rental. What is perhaps surprising is that Madden detects a 'high level of competition' reflected in some turnover initially of feus: the examples he uses, however, were all to local people, which does not suggest incomers trading feus. It does suggest, perhaps, some population pressure on the lands neighbouring on Selkirk. As a result, buying a feu, and retaining it, was not a cheap matter, though in the longer term declining real rental values benefited the feuar. Like Sanderson, Madden found that lands more often than not stayed in the same families: the feuars of thirteen of the fifteen steadings in the ward of Tweed were from the same families as the leaseholders in the 1480s, and more than three-quarters of the feus set by 1513 were in the same families in 1541. Where there was some alienation it appears that the local Scott kindred cleaned up. Of a total of 78.5 steadings, the Scotts had bought the feus of thirteen by 1513, which had multiplied to 24.5 in 1541. Lairds from the existing prominent local kindreds, the Scotts of Branxholme, who had been master currours in the Ettrick ward since 1455, the Murrays of Blackbarony, the Stewarts of Traquair and the Kers of Cessford and others held 45 per cent of the total. Others, below them, designated 'in', and those without designations, held more than 50 per cent of the feus, many of them members of the same kindreds as their more lofty neighbours. And, again like Sanderson, Madden concludes that this represented a large number of local small proprietors, new to hereditary possession, 'who were to become an important part of the social stratum of the border'.[46]

What is difficult to determine, however, from these charters is to what degree the lairds then sublet their lands to smaller farmers, or what the quality was of the relationships between landlord and tenant. The records for baronial courts, that might have shown complaints, are thin on the ground for this period, in the Middle March as elsewhere in Scotland, though the regality records for the abbey of Melrose are a useful exception. Tenants could also bring disputes, usually with their neighbours, before the local birlaw courts but records for these are almost non-existent. A tantalising glimpse is provided by the report of one at Kelso, in 1747, which assessed the damage done to the tenants' crops by the duchess of Roxburgh's carriage.[47]

---

[45] Though referred to as a forest, this was an old royal hunting forest, largely deforested and split into small farms: C. Madden, 'The feuing of Ettrick forest', *Innes Review* xxvii (1976), 70–84; J. M. Gilbert, *Hunting and hunting reserves in medieval Scotland*, Edinburgh 1979, 136–9.
[46] Madden, 'The feuing of Ettrick forest', 72–5, 77, 78–9, 82, quotation at p. 80; Gilbert, *Hunting and hunting reserves*, 158.
[47] *The records of the regality of Melrose, 1605–61*, ed. C. S. Romanes (SHS, 1914–17); Goodare, *Government of Scotland*, 183.

What is evident, however, from the private papers of prominent borderer families, such as the Scotts of Branxholme, and the Kers of Cessford, Ferniehirst and Ancrum, was the personal nature of landlord-tenant relations in this period, which recalls Mike Braddick's description of most early modern English administration as 'face-to-face'.[48] A typical phrase was used in Scott of Branxholme's tack to Gilbert Elliot, which, granting him his lease for his 'thankfull service', called him 'my lovitt frend and servitor'.[49] The personal ties of kinship are also evident in a qualitative impression of the numerous tacks and loans granted to members of the same or related kindreds. For instance, in 1500, Scott of Branxholme stood surety for money owed by his tenant Robert Scott of Allanhaugh, with the lands of Whitchester in the barony of Branxholme to be regranted to the said Robert on repayment of the loan. In 1569 another Scott of Branxholme discharged another Robert Scott of Allanhaugh from being his tutor and granted him the non-entries of Whitchester. Despite a subsequent dispute, in which an Allanhaugh Scott was killed, in 1585 Branxholme and Allanhaugh signed a settlement that acknowledged Branxholme as Allanhaugh's 'chief'. When in 1593 Allanhaugh felt obliged to obtain letters of ejection against his tenants there, because 'they daylie trubillis and oppressis him ... sua that is is nicht possibil to inhabite his awin landis', all the named tenants were Scotts. Whilst this last shows that kinship was not always the social adhesive it could be, all these examples demonstrate the significance of kinship in allocating tenancies. When Allanhaugh had calmed down again, in 1599, he entered another Scott into his lands.[50] The impact of kinship on socio-political relationships is a theme that will be returned to repeatedly in this work, but it is clear here that it impacted significantly on economic relationships too.

Descriptions of landlord-tenant relationships, however, tend too sharply to create a dangerous 'them and us'. In the Middle March, as elsewhere in Scotland, it is apparent that this stratification was more blurred. As the work of Madden and Sanderson suggests, the emergence of small proprietors in the sixteenth century was creating a level that was not lairdly, but did have some substance and security of tenure. And within the lairdly class, Meikle has identified several strata which muddy sharp socio-economic distinctions further: the 'greater' lairds with lands, jurisdictions and followings that equated them with the lower levels of the nobility; the 'lesser' lairds that might hold some baronial jurisdiction and local office, but could also include the feuars of larger-scale landholdings; and the 'bonnet' lairds, also designated 'of' but who held as little as two husbandlands (52 acres).[51] The yeoman farmers were below these. In the Eastern Borders, between 1540 and 1603,

---

[48] Braddick, 'Administrative performance', 171.
[49] NAS, GD224/1059/1.
[50] NAS, GD224/918/27, fo. 2; 224/887/5; Fraser, *Buccleuch*, ii, nos 194, 195, 202.
[51] M. M. Meikle, 'The invisible divide: the greater lairds and the nobility of Jacobean Scotland', *SHR* lxxi (1992), 70–87.

Meikle estimates that of the 307 laird families, fifteen were bonnet lairds, thirty-three bonnet or lesser lairds, 219 lesser and forty greater lairds.[52] In the Middle March, the greater lairds included the Kers of Cessford, Ferniehirst, Ancrum and Faldonside, Scott of Branxholme, the Murrays of Philiphaugh, Blackbarony and, subsequently, Elibank and the Pringles of Galashiels and of that ilk. The lesser lairds, often younger sons who had established cadet branches, were such as the Scotts of Tushielaw and Haining, the Pringles of Torwoodlee and Buckholm, the Rutherfords of Hunthill and Hundalee, the Kers of Little Newton and Oxnam, who are often spotted holding minor office or acting as deputies for their higher-ranking kinsmen. The bonnet lairds, a class operating almost below the radar in state records and difficult to enumerate, can be found in the business of the presbytery sessions and the lists of jurors at Roxburgh's sheriff court. These stratifications were not cut and dried, Meikle and others noting movements between them: the declining value of feu-ferme rents increased the capital value of those lesser and bonnet lairds who had secured such tenure, though others, such as the Scotts of Haining, seem to slip under.

But this work will also suggest that other forms of relationships, such as those provided by kinship and alliance, could cut through the horizontal layers of economic status, creating closer ties between those of differing wealth and landholding. There is a further point here: in the sixteenth century the lairds of the Middle March, even the greater lairds such as Branxholme and Cessford, were not very well off. Indeed, the English wardens used frequently to sneer at their poverty, which they said made them too dependent on their followers' co-operation to maintain the rule of law amongst them.[53] In 1586 the estate of Walter Ker of Cessford, the Middle March warden, was valued at £4,865 Scots, which equated to about £450 sterling. In contrast, in 1601, his English counterpart, Sir John Forster, a canny collector of land, left £1,020.[54] And the English might have put their finger on it: as a result of their impecuniousness, the Middle March lairds were probably closer in economic circumstance to their tenants. This may have differed, to some degree, to the situation in the Lowlands, where Whyte has found an increasingly 'huge gulf between those who owned the land and those who worked it' in contrast to larger numbers of small proprietors elsewhere.[55] In the Borders, the economic disparity between landlord and tenant, which became much more startlingly evident in the seventeenth century, was, perhaps, more muted in the sixteenth.

In Scotland as a whole, Keith Brown estimates that the average net estates of peers more than tripled between 1570 and 1637. A look at the testaments of the Scotts of Branxholme, subsequently the earls of Buccleuch,

[52] Idem, A British frontier?, 12–20.
[53] CBP ii, nos 265, 283.
[54] Meikle, A British frontier?, 137–8.
[55] Whyte, Scotland's society, 128.

shows a transformation in fortune replicated by the other 'winners' in the march, the Kers of Cessford, subsequently earls of Roxburgh, and the Kers of Ferniehirst and Ancrum, subsequently earls of Lothian and Ancram. In 1574 Walter Scott of Branxholme died leaving, after huge debts, £1,396. When his great-great granddaughter, Anna, countess of Buccleuch inherited in 1661, she was reputed to have an income of £100,000 Scots a year: Charles II leapt at the chance to offload the financial responsibility for his illegitimate son, the duke of Monmouth, and swiftly married him to Anna. Despite his execution in 1685, Anna was reputed to have been served by attendants on their knees, in the manner of royalty, at her newly extended palace at Dalkeith.[56] Meikle injects caution here by noting that some of the eastern borderers within the Middle March such as the Kers of Ferniehirst and Cessford, and the Pringles of Galashiels and Torwoodlee, were spending money on smart new houses, which was not reflected in their inventories.[57] Whilst feu-ferme rents effectively devalued, rents on fixed leases began to increase in the seventeenth century: by 1650 the rental of Ettrick forest had risen from £2,763 to £22,760, Whyte noting the additionally beneficial effects, after 1603, of access to the north-eastern England market for lamb. Until land use became more commercialised, the economic disparity between those of differing social status, in the Middle March as elsewhere, was less than it was to become.[58]

As a result, the links provided by kinship or alliance could blur or reduce the significance of the social disparity between landlord and tenant, kindred leader and kinsman. These links created a different kind of relationship, perhaps, between superior and inferior than that provided by a strictly economic relationship. This is not to negate, however, that such layers of social status did exist, and were understood to be of importance. Implicit in kinship was the recognition of a social hierarchy within a kindred, in which one man led the whole, others headed the various branches, and the rest acknowledged the authority of those above them. The obligations inherent in such hierarchies, and the use of them by government, are examined in the next chapter. Landlords, too, whether rich or poor, could always evict. But, where the effects of economic disparity are more muted, it is suggested that the dynamics of landlord-tenant and kindred leader-kinsman relationships may have been more mutually dependent, or interdependent, possibly more willingly co-operative, than the future riches of the greater lairds, and their more impoverished tenants came to allow. As Whyte observes, in the sixteenth century, 'there was a good deal of consensus in rural society

---

[56] K. M. Brown, *Noble society in Scotland: wealth, family and culture, from Reformation to Revolution*, Edinburgh 2004, 106–7; NAS, CC6/5/1, fos 86–7; NAS, GD224/930/38, fo. 9; 224/935/11; M. Lee, *The heiresses of Buccleuch: marriage, money and politics in seventeenth century Britain*, East Linton 1996, 13, 24, 59–60.
[57] Meikle, *A British frontier?*, 149–51.
[58] Whyte, *Scotland's society*, 33–4.

between landlord and tenant' until the effects of feuing, amongst other forces, increasingly commercialised and hardened relationships during the seventeenth century. As in England, whilst such interdependence existed in the structure of local society, the protection offered by custom, was gradually to be eroded.[59]

One of the other forces impacting on rural society in Scotland was population which, in the sixteenth and early seventeenth centuries, was substantially expanding. Population estimates for Scotland are notoriously tricky but in 1500 it was in the range of 500–700,000. Of this, the population in the Borders was around 50,000, that is roughly 10 per cent of the total. By 1700, and after the dearth of 1695–9 had reduced it slightly, the total population had increased to around 1.1 million.[60] Population density was inevitably lower in the Borders than the Lowlands, and the carrying capacity of land certainly half or as little as a third of that in the Lowlands.[61] There was a difference too between the numbers supported by the more fertile arable lands of the East March and the more extensive uplands of the Middle. Goodman has found demographic pressures probably pushing some into these less fertile areas. Where this was unsuccessfully pursued on previous wasteland, some borderers may have turned to what was held to be their traditional pastime, of relieving others of their livestock.[62] Evidence of this has to be balanced however by an appreciation of the relative stability of landholding amongst those with tacks or feus well into the seventeenth century.

This has been a picture of a hugely rural society. But, of course, the Middle March had a number of good-sized towns: the principal ones were Jedburgh, Peebles and Selkirk, the administrative centres of its sheriffdoms, and also Kelso to the east, Melrose towards the north and Hawick in the south. The population in both Peebles and Selkirk has been estimated at around 800, which meant that they were relatively sizeable towns for Scotland given that not many towns exceeded 1,000 people (excepting such as Edinburgh).[63] These burghs provided the location for markets of local goods, wappinschaws and musters, the meetings of presbyteries and kirk sessions, the courts of the

---

[59] Ibid. 29–34, 38–9; Wrightson, 'The politics of the parish', 22–5, 32–3.
[60] Percentage estimated in Wasser, 'Violence', 57–8; Whyte, *Scotland before the Industrial Revolution*, 113; M. Lynch (ed.), *The Oxford companion to Scottish history*, Oxford 2001, 487–8.
[61] Whyte, *Scotland before the Industrial Revolution*, 114–15.
[62] Goodman, 'Impact of warfare', 197, 207.
[63] T. Devine and S. G. E. Lythe 'The economy of Scotland under James VI: a revision article', *SHR* l (1971), 91–106 at p. 95; P. S. M. Symms, 'Social control in a sixteenth-century burgh: a study of the burgh court of Selkirk, 1503–1545', unpubl. PhD diss. Edinburgh 1987, 14. Blaeu's *Atlas* shows Selkirk as a sizeable walled town, and describes (pp. 33–4) Peebles as 'set in a very fine location ... famous for five threefold ornaments, that is for three churches, three bell-towers, three gates, three squares, and three bridges'.

sheriff and burgh, and occasionally for justice courts when kings and regents swooped down into the Borders. The church, shire and burgh records that do exist for the period give an impression of regular town life and administration ticking over, much in the way it will have done in the neighbouring Lowlands. Whilst business was badly disrupted during Anglo-Scottish hostilities, such incidents as the burning of Hawick, or Kelso, or Jedburgh, were, by 1573, never to be repeated in the less overtly hostile times of the late sixteenth century. The late sixteenth-century urban history of the Borders reads much the same as that of other parts of Scotland.

III

There were similarities too between the experience of the Borders and Lowlands in ecclesiastical matters after the Reformation; as elsewhere, the embedding of the Reformation took longer in some areas than others.[64] But where the Kirk was well-established, the chain of authority provided by the ecclesiastical hierarchy connected the religious life of the Borders into that of the kingdom and it was subject to the processes (and problems) underway throughout. As James Kirk remarked of that other 'remote' area, the Western Highlands, the Church's organisation there 'conformed, in all essentials, to the patterns which prevailed elsewhere in Scotland ... integration, not separation, remained a salient feature of the ecclesiastical structure'.[65] Much of the Middle March was in the diocese of Glasgow, but from 1581 presbyteries were gradually established to oversee parishes within their regions, and these were accountable to the regional synod. In 1581, when thirteen model presbyteries were set up, the list did not include any from the Middle March. In 1582 David Calderwood reported that the presbytery of Teviotdale (Selkirk) could not be erected due to the lack of qualified ministers. However, an unrealised proposal in 1583 to merge the presbyteries of Melrose and Peebles with those of Dunbar and Chirnside suggests that these presbyteries had been set up by then (though in 1592 the presbytery of Peebles was told that it 'was not as yit fully establischit', though operational). Thus a line of communication and responsibility ran from the ministers and kirk sessions of the Borders' parishes, through the ministers' membership of the presbyteries of Jedburgh and Selkirk to the regional synod of the Merse and Teviotdale,

---

[64] M. Lynch, 'Preaching to the converted: perspectives on the Scottish Reformation', in A. A. MacDonald, M. Lynch, and I. Cowan (eds), *The Renaissance in Scotland: studies in literature, religion, history and culture offered to John Durkan*, Leiden 1994, 301–43.

[65] This he compares to the disruption of the mid-seventeenth century and the resurgence of Roman Catholicism there: J. Kirk, *Patterns of reform: continuity and change in the Reformation Kirk*, Edinburgh 1989, 450, 487.

and the presbytery of Peebles to the synod of Lothian and Tweeddale, and from there to the General Assembly.[66]

There were problems however: in common with other areas, many parishes did not have qualified ministers, and most, until at least the early 1570s, in the Middle March were filled by readers who could not administer the sacraments. There was a spate of appointments in the mid-1570s, but more parishes were filled in the years leading upto the mid-1590s: by 1596 thirteen of Jedburgh presbytery's parishes had ministers, eight out of ten of Selkirk's, with similar figures for Peebles's.[67] Some of these ministers, however, were split between parishes and others were plain absent: William Fowler of Hawick's duties as minister were incompatible with his situation as secretary to Queen Anne in Edinburgh and then London, whilst Calderwood raged against John Abirnethie, minister of Jedburgh from 1593 to 1639, despite, from 1616, being bishop of Caithness, 'a diocie in the farrest north', though he seemed to spend most of his time in Jedburgh.[68] Parishes suffered from under-funding, their lands having been alienated into secular hands, but these were the difficulties causing friction over finances and patronage between crown and Kirk at the highest levels and were not confined to the Borders. In 1588 and in 1591 the General Assembly complained at the effective disposal of the crown's ecclesiastical patronages into the secular hands of nobles and lairds.[69] In Teviotdale, Meikle estimates that only ten out of thirty-eight parishes had not had their revenues appropriated.[70] Local landowners such as Buccleuch often controlled the teinds: he had, for instance, the tack of the teinds of St Mary of the Lowes, near Buccleuch, and in 1608 he granted the tack of the teinds of the parsonage of Hawick to his great friend, the future deputy treasurer, Murray of Elibank.[71] Partly as a result of this, many churches were ruinous and parishes vacant. In 1592 the presbytery of Peebles was rebuked by its synod for its 'ruinous' kirk and it was yet unbuilt in 1595.[72] In 1608 the General Assembly was still moaning that there were many kirks 'wanting pastors, and other misorders, speciallie in the Merse and Teviotdaill, Cathness and Sutherland', which underlined

---

[66] The seat of the presbytery of Selkirk was at Melrose until 1640 when it was transferred to Selkirk. Presbytery records exist for Peebles from 1596, Jedburgh from 1606 and Selkirk from 1607: NAS, CH2/295/1; CH2/198/1; CH2/327/1; *BUK* ii. 146–8, 187; D. Calderwood, *The history of the Kirk of Scotland*, ed. T. Thomson and D. Laing (Wodrow Society, 1842–9), iii. 521–2, 680–1; *The records of the synod of Lothian and Tweeddale, 1589–96, 1640–49*, ed. J. Kirk (Stair Society, 1977), 41.

[67] *Fasti Ecclesiae Scoticana: the succession of ministers in the Church of Scotland from the Reformation*, ed. H. Scott, J. Lamb and D. MacDonald, Edinburgh 1917, i. 268–300; ii. 98–145, 168–98.

[68] Calderwood, *History*, vii. 261–9.

[69] Kirk, *Patterns of reform*, 424–5.

[70] Meikle, *A British frontier?*, 211.

[71] NAS, GD224/930/43, fos 4, 8; GD224/930/38, fo.15; GD224/918/27, fos 4, 5.

[72] *Synod of Lothian and Tweeddale*, 38–9, 87.

continuing problems. A commission was given to John Spottiswoode, archbishop of Glasgow and others for the 'planting of the kirks that ar presentlie destituted of pastors' paying particular attention to the 'great necessite of the kirks' of Annandale, Ewesdale and Eskdale, just into the West March, which 'are altogether unplanted'. They were empowered to enforce the physical repair of churches and organise the uniting of parishes in order to make the parishes more viable.[73] In 1609 Jedburgh presbytery ordered two of its brethren to go to Edinburgh 'to seik owt some lawsuit and instruments to plant the kirkis ... destitute off pastours'. It was a recognised problem.

There were also problems associated with the patronage of the vicarages and parsonages, with several secular landowners having secured the rights of nomination to them. This could lead to dispute, such as in March 1607 when Buccleuch claimed that he had nominated a Mr William Clerk, by 'an frie presentatioun' to the kirks of Liddesdale, which the presbytery of Jedburgh seemed happy to accept. However, in May, it was challenged by a Mr Thomas Ballantyne, with the support of Home of Cowdenknowes, who had an 'ordinance of the Synod and craivit it micht be obeyit'. After a long period of argument over the patronage, Buccleuch's nominee seems to have been overcome and, in December, Ballantyne was admitted to the kirk at Castleton at the foot of Liddesdale.[74] In this we can perhaps see the sorts of friction between local kirk administration and the local nobility, which during the seventeenth century began to swing increasingly in favour of the presbyteries.[75]

The presbyteries' remit was not just confined to ecclesiastical administration but extended to wider social controls as part of the reformed Kirk's mission to impose a 'godly society' that went far beyond insistence on kirk attendance.[76] They held considerable powers over the enforcement of morality, including the threat of excommunication, the imposition of public penance and the refusal to administer the sacraments or carry out marriages. The records of Jedburgh's presbytery, in 1606 and 1607, reveal the trials of several men and women for incest, the tracking down of an alleged illegitimate child of the earl of Angus, and the repeated rebuke of Helena Cranstoun, Lady Newtoun, for failing to attend her kirk during a dispute with Turnbull of Bedrule over where she should sit. Miscreants were ordered to do penance at their kirk, on their knees, in 'sakcleith' or 'lineins'. John Rutherford 'gaif in his supplicatioun desiring his bluids done a twentie yeiris past micht be silencit by favour and to grant to him his marriage myt go fordwart', on which he was ordered to do penance in sackcloth. The use of

---

[73] BUK iii. 1061–2. Sadly the records for Spottiswoode's visitation are scarce.
[74] NAS, CH2/198/1, fos 28, 33, 36, 57.
[75] M. Todd, *Culture of Protestantism in early modern Scotland*, New Haven–London 2002, esp. ch. viii; J. Goodare, 'Scotland', in B. Scribner, R. Porter and M. Teich (eds), *The Reformation in national context*, Cambridge 1994, 95–110 at p. 102.
[76] Goodare, 'Scotland', 100–4.

shame by the presbytery to control behaviour would have been more keenly felt, probably, by those of higher social status whose authority rested on the popular acknowledgement of their superiority. Sentences such as the public repentance given to the laird of Bedrule for his adulterous behaviour would have done nothing for presbytery-laird relations.[77]

Presbyteries, however, were dependent on the support of the local elites when they made accusations against witches. Presbyteries could interview but not try a witch themselves, needing a commission from the high court or the privy council to do so. The commissions appointed were almost always constituted of the local lairds and the presbytery will have also needed the help of such figures to apprehend the accused.[78] In April 1608 the presbytery asked the Middle Shires commissioner Sir William Cranstoun to apprehend Meg Lyell in the Spittal by nearby Crailing 'suspect to be ane witche'. This may be the Marjorie Lyell who was tried at Jedburgh in 1613. The commissioners in this case were a roll call of prominent local lairds, Ker of Ferniehirst, Sir John Cranstoun of that ilk, George Douglas of Bonjedburgh and Nicol Rutherford of Hundalee. Another accused, Margaret Scott, was questioned by the Selkirk presbytery in 1607, after being slandered by another woman, but the case was dropped in 1609. There were no witches accused in Peebles in the period though there were spates of multiple accusations in 1629 in Selkirk and Peebles, and in 1649 in all three presbyteries here.[79]

The presbyteries were also subject to outside pressures, from the Kirk's hierarchy above, and from prominent local figures. The synod of Lothian and Tweeddale did not seem to esteem the presbytery of Peebles, ordering, in 1592, that if any 'wechtie mater cumis befoir thame that they returne the same to the presbyterie of Edinburgh' to decide: they were not allowed to admit ministers to parishes or deal with much other than adultery.[80] Additionally, the presbyteries were affected by broader processes such as James's re-introduction of the episcopacy from 1606 and from 1607 the imposition of constant moderators to oversee presbytery business. The General Assembly appointed Sir Robert Ker of Ancrum and Sir Andrew Ker of Ferniehirst to choose a constant moderator for Jedburgh, Lord Roxburgh for Selkirk and the Murrays of Elibank and Blackbarony for Peebles.[81] But as elsewhere in Scotland, such interference was resisted by some presbyteries. In March 1607 Lord Roxburgh insisted on his nominee, Mr James Knox, being accepted but the presbytery held out until May before submitting. Shortly afterwards,

---

[77] NAS, CH2/198/1, fos 11, 13, 16, 52, 53, 65.
[78] J. Goodare, 'Witch-hunting and the Scottish state', in J. Goodare (ed.), *The Scottish witch-hunt in context*, Manchester 2002, 122–45.
[79] NAS, CH2/198/1, fo. 67; *RPC* x. 28–9; NAS, CH2/327/1, fo. 4; J. Goodare, L. Martin, J. Miller and L. Yeoman, 'The survey of Scottish witchcraft', University of Edinburgh, http://www.arts.ed.ac.uk/witches/ (archived Jan. 2003).
[80] *Synod of Lothian and Tweeddale*, 41.
[81] *RPC* vii. 300–1, 344, 376, 401.

Ancrum and Ferniehirst attempted to insist on the acceptance of their ally, Mr John Abirnethie, by the presbytery of Jedburgh which included the stubborn Presbyterian Mr David Calderwood, the future historian. The dispute raged on for a year, and Abirnethie was not confirmed until July 1608, after Elibank was appointed to enforce the nomination. This led to Calderwood's suspension and the installation of a new minister that August. In March 1608 too, the privy council accused the synod of Merse and Teviotdale of disobedience 'upoun some passionat humour of their awne' in discharging their constant moderator. Calderwood and four others were put to the horn for also refusing to submit to a visitation to Teviotdale by the bishop of Orkney. The council thought that this was 'ane offence so heinous, as gif that it be not examplarlie punist, thair nedis no forder dewtye nor obedience to ony way expected' from ministers generally. They were banned from preaching and confined to their parishes, Abirnethie writing unsuccessfully on their behalf to the powerful Middle Shires lieutenant, the earl of Dunbar in August. In February 1609 the presbytery appealed to the council which refused to do anything until they knew James's opinion.[82]

But for all the problems, recusancy does not seem to have been the issue it was the other side of the border. As Meikle shows, whilst Northumberland was riven by confessional divides between the major families, only the Kers of Ferniehirst seem to have openly retained their Catholic sympathies: Andrew Ker of Ferniehirst after all had been a godchild of Mary Queen of Scots, and his father had fought on her side in the Marian Wars. Ferniehirst played host to several French priests in 1584, stirring up feverish speculation amongst the English wardens.[83] Other Marian supporters, such as the Scotts of Branxholme, had either converted or kept quiet about their religious affiliations, though Lord Eure suspected that Branxholme was a 'papist', 'mimitating the Spaniard'.[84] Ker of Ancrum's aunt, Alison Home, wrote anxiously to him at court in 1606 hoping that he 'stands fast to the faith he was brought up in' – it was unclear whether she feared the depravity of the court or Protestantism, but Ancrum was to become a noted psalm-writer.[85] However, superstition died hard, and whilst people seemed generally to have conformed, pilgrimages to shrines and wells persisted into the seventeenth century. Peebles was the site of a well-known shrine, and its synod complained in 1592 and 1596 that 'pilgrimaris [were] permittit to cum in pilrimag' every May, with 'the

---

[82] NAS, CH2/198, fos 33, 40, 42–3, 73, 75, 77, 99; *RPC* viii. 68, 102–3, 126, 128, 148, 508–10; Calderwood, *History*, vi. 706–12, 716; A. R. MacDonald, *The Jacobean Kirk, 1567–1625: sovereignty, polity and liturgy*, Aldershot 1998, 132–6.
[83] Meikle, *A British frontier?*, 210–14; *CSP Scot.* vi, no. 676; vii, nos 17, 19, 22, 24, 27, 33.
[84] *CBP* ii, nos 265, 283.
[85] Lothian papers, NAS, GD40/2/13, fo. 8.

picture of the crucifix [still] standing upoun the croce', which the presbytery seemed reluctant to destroy.[86]

IV

The years from 1573 to 1625 were a time of transition for Scotland, the last vestiges of a late medieval society fading: the bloodfeud was gradually being replaced by the public justice of the law courts, and James's reign began to take on the characteristics of early modern government, extending and intensifying the intervention of the crown in all areas of life.[87] Changes in landholding through the extensive feuing of church and crown lands were felt all the more after the Reformation, as the abbeys' regalities fell into secular hands. As crown and Kirk attempted to embed the Reformation, the whole of society felt the effects of the imposition of a 'godly' society. But all this was work 'in progress' and nothing changed overnight. Some things did not change at all: land-use continued much as it had done, the commercialisation and modernisation of farming a thing, largely, of the future.

One thing did change after 1603, irrevocably, as it turned out: Scotland, though still a sovereign kingdom, became part of a larger entity, the composite kingdoms of James VI and I. The burgesses of Edinburgh keenly rued the ending of James's proximity, whilst stroppy Presbyterian ministers probably relished his absence, but the people that were most significantly affected were the borderers, as the diplomatic significance of their southern boundary dissolved overnight. Scottish governments were never again to use instability in the Borders as a bargaining counter with England, and the government's attitude to the region changed accordingly. The diplomatic policies that had differentiated the Borders from the rest of Scotland were slowly removed, whilst cross-border hostility was replaced by a previously illicit livestock trade, which rapidly expanded to feed the northern English market.[88] However, the links that connected the Borders to the Lowlands endured, ensuring that the social, economic and religious processes underway elsewhere in Scotland continued to impact on the Borders as well.

[86] *Synod of Lothian and Tweeddale*, 38–9, 50, 94, 100.
[87] Brown, *Bloodfeud*, esp. ch. ix.
[88] J. C. Watson, 'Scottish foreign trade, 1597–1640', unpubl. PhD diss. Edinburgh 2003, 171, 192.

2

The Socio-Political Structure of the Middle March

James VI inherited a system of government from his late medieval forebears that was heavily dependent upon co-operative nobles and lairds governing their regions in line with crown policy. Such reliance did not necessarily mean, however, that government was less effective as a result, for the crown could secure the co-operation of regional elites with lands, titles and offices that further legitimised and underwrote the authority of these prominent figures.[1] It was a mutually dependent, and beneficial, relationship, and borderers, like lowlanders and highlanders, had much to gain from co-operating with the crown, as did the crown in retaining their co-operation. For this arrangement to work, however, sufficiently developed structures of authority needed to be in place in each region, and the authority recognised of those that headed them. This was as true of the Middle March as elsewhere in Scotland. Whilst the power of the Middle March's elite was legitimised by the crown, in terms of office and jurisdiction, at the same time it was dependent on the support of those whom they governed and the subordinates' acknowledgement of their superiors' authority. This chapter will investigate how the structures of authority were formed in the Middle March, who led them and how they exercised power, including their provision of good lordship: it will suggest that these socio-political structures, their inbuilt chains of authority and their associated obligations, provided a network of power that was itself part of a machinery of government. Formal office-holding is considered separately in chapters 3 and 4; this chapter is concerned primarily with the framework of authority that was formed by the social structures of the region.

The second main theme of this chapter is the impact of kinship upon such socio-political structures. Society throughout Scotland was stratified horizontally into nobles, greater, lesser and bonnet lairds, and those below. Cutting vertically through these layers, however, was the grouping formed by kinship, whereby one kindred could contain members of all socio-economic levels from the richest noble to the poorest tenant. By the sixteenth century, each kindred was identified by the surname of its members: in the Highlands these groupings became known as clans, in the Borders, as 'surnames', and

---

[1] J. Brown (Wormald), 'The exercise of power', in J. Brown (ed.), *Scottish society in the fifteenth century*, London 1977, 33–65.

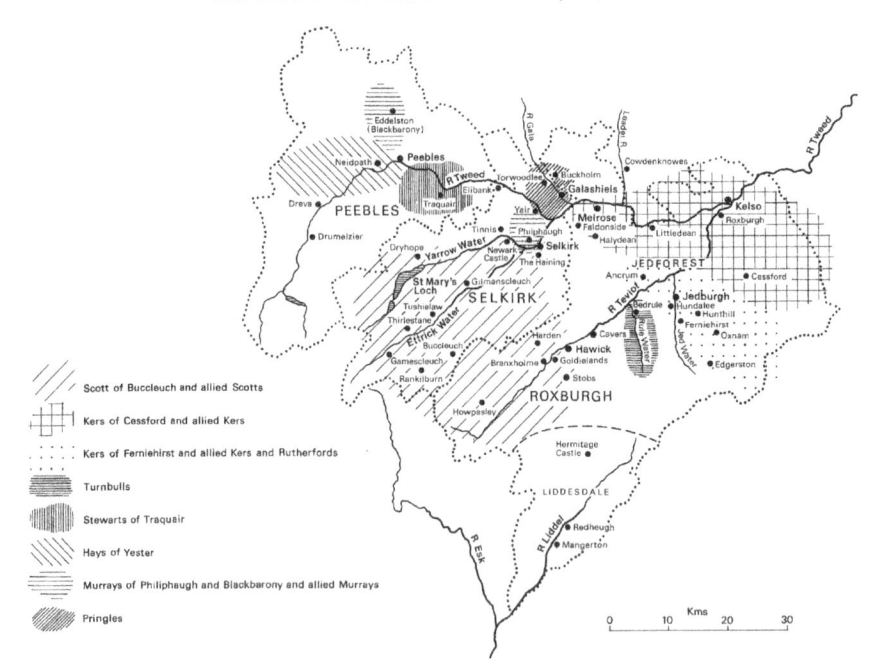

Map 3. Landholdings of the major surnames in the Middle March

everywhere as of their 'name'.[2] Blood ties bound these groupings but these were reinforced by understood obligations of service, obedience, maintenance and loyalty and a sense of common identity. These social relationships created social entities, within which individuals acted or saw themselves as part of a group; but they also formed networks of power within which the authority of the leader was recognised, a chain of authority established. The structure, ties and obligations of kinship helped to maintain the authority of the elite, and provided a framework of power that the crown could utilise to effect its policies within any region. The significance of kinship within society and government was widened further by alliances where blood ties were more distant, or missing, but which replicated the obligations and benefits of kinship. This chapter will consider to what extent social structures in the Middle March were affected by kinship and alliance, including the way in which marriage consolidated alliances, and how the crown was able to use the networks of power thus created to effect government in the Middle March.

[2] The first contemporary use of 'surname' to describe the kindreds of the Borders has been traced by Rae to 1498, although this was applied to an English kinship group: *Administration*, 5–6.

SOCIO-POLITICAL STRUCTURE

I

Throughout Scotland, the implications of the term kindred or kinship went far further than mere nomenclature. Kinship brought with it expectations of loyalty and unity based on a sense of common purpose and identity. But should this appear too communal, kindreds also contained a recognised social hierarchy in which the lesser acknowledged the superiority of their leader, of lairdly or noble status, and he would expect their co-operation with his decisions. There was a strongly paternalistic strain to their relations whereby the leader was meant to provide protection and maintenance, in return for the loyal service of his kinsmen. Mutual obligations existed between them. Of course, the bonds of kinship may have been, in some situations, more apparent than real: the laird and his kinsmen may have had differing objectives within a wider common agreement; there may have been other calls on their loyalty from government, religion or economic necessity; the strength of kinship may have been weakened by increasingly distant blood ties; kinship may have been more significant in rural areas than urban, and in some regions than others, and it may have been decreasingly important by the 1600s; and the significance of kinship probably lingered longer in the hilly Borders than the Lowlands.[3] But even here, the strength of kinship was subject to qualification: as Alison Cathcart rightly cautions (for the Highlands), whilst 'blood kinship lay at the heart of clan society', 'kinship alone was not enough to secure cohesion [so] it was reinforced through socio-economic manrent, political and military co-operation'.[4] For all this, government throughout Scotland continued well into the seventeenth century to identify individuals in relation to their families, as son of (or father or brother or wife etc.), whilst most private agreements or settlements of dispute named several members of each family involved. And tenancy agreements acknowledged the customary expectations of inherited occupancy through 'kindly' tenure. As Sanderson observes, the kin in kindly was not coincidental.[5] Kindreds formed the basis of the structure of local society; kinship was fundamental to the workings of that society.

The concept of kinship was so integral to Scottish society in the sixteenth century that where 'real' kinship did not exist, or was so diluted that its bonds were impaired, other relationships recreated many of the characteristics of kinship. 'Fictive' kinship, whereby alliances could be sealed with other more distant kinsmen, or different kindreds, could be achieved through marriages, tenancy agreements and bonds of manrent and maintenance, in which the latter detailed the mutual obligations of protection and service owed between

---

[3] Maureen Meikle notes, too, the significance of kinship networks in the Eastern Borders as throughout Scotland: *A British frontier?*, 25, 45; Wormald, *Court, kirk and community*, 29–30, 40.
[4] Cathcart, *Kinship and clientage*, 90–1, 93, 213–15.
[5] Sanderson, *A kindly place?*, 7.

a superior and his 'fictive' kinsmen. Jenny Wormald has shown that bonds of manrent were made by those who wanted to 'become as kinsmen to one another'. In general these bonds were not made between kinsmen, because the obligations that they spelled out were inherent in kinship and therefore unnecessary to formalise in writing. Cathcart, however, has recently found that sometimes they were used where existing bonds of blood kinship were not felt to be strong enough.[6] This is an important qualification to any assumption of the cohesive nature of kinship, as the internal feuds of the various Ker families would attest. None the less, the mutual support expected of kinship underwrote relations between kinsmen, and those with whom they aimed to be similarly associated.

The aspirations of 'fictive' kinship can also be seen in the expectations of 'good lordship'. Both Jenny Wormald and Michael Brown identify links between kinship and lordship where the mutual obligations between lord and adherent replicated those between kinsmen of differing social status. Jenny Wormald observes that the 'fundamental bonds of society were forged not through land but through kinship and personal lordship' and that the bonds of manrent show that 'lordship was seen in terms of kinship'.[7] And, as with kinship, for lordship to be credible it had to show that it was not a one-way street: whilst the subordinate had to acknowledge the authority of his superior or lord, so too did the superior have to appear, at the very least, to be looking after the interests of those below him. For James Scott, this was the maintenance of a public transcript of a 'dominant ideology of paternalistic lords and faithful retainers' where the lords had to be seen to act in accordance with the expectations of lordship. This gave those subordinates, subconsciously at least, some power to negotiate the terms of the exercise of power over them. As John Walter observes, 'power holders have to negotiate means of legitimating their authority and thereafter successfully represent their actions as falling within the terms of legitimacy', where the 'protection of the subject [was] its primary responsibility', a 'doctrine of stewardship'. There was, indeed, 'an inevitable tension between the ideal of good lordship', 'the personal nature of their relationship with their tenants ... and the actual practices of landowners'.[8] But cynical manipulation of a public discourse of power or not, the realities of life in a society where official means of coercion were limited, meant that the lord needed to retain the co-operation of his kinsmen, dependants and tenants in helping him fulfill his official and private duties. A significant degree of interdependence could therefore be seen as providing for a dynamic relationship both between superior and subordinate, and between superior and the crown.[9]

---

[6] Cathcart, *Kinship and clientage*, 79–80; Wormald, *Lords and men*, 76.
[7] Wormald, *Court, kirk and community*, 29–30.
[8] Scott, *Domination*, 11–12, 102; Walter, 'Public transcripts', 123–5, 135.
[9] Similarly, for England, Keith Wrightson notes the 'areas of relative interdependence

Throughout Scotland, these ties of lordship and kinship created structures of authority that provided the government with a mechanism that it could use to impose policy in any region, including the Borders, if it chose so to do. These localised dynamics were also part of a broader structure of power in the kingdom keeping those in the Borders connected into the highest levels of government. In this the Borders were no different from the Lowlands. Co-operative local elites, backed by their extensive networks of kinship and lordship, could act for the crown in their own regions.

In the Borders, during the fourteenth and fifteenth centuries, the prominent lords had been the earls of Douglas and their fortunes demonstrated the way in which lordship and kinship could work to the benefit of the crown, the landed elite and their subordinates. Until the mid-fifteenth century the Douglases effectively acted as well-rewarded crown agents in the Borders, organising border defence and conducting the internal administration of the region. Their power was based, according to Michael Brown, on the 'kindred, men and adherents' that they attracted to their allegiance through the exercise of 'good lordship'.[10] The effect of the forfeiture by James II of the 'Black' Douglas earls in 1455 dramatically altered the structure of power in the region; its effects could still be seen in the Middle March in the later sixteenth century. James granted the wardenship instead to the Douglas earl of Angus and also the forfeited Ewesdale, which, with Angus's existing lands of Jedforest, significantly increased the 'Red' Douglases' authority in the region: James had successfully replaced a disaffected Douglas magnate with a loyal one. In the 1500s the Douglases of Cavers were the hereditary sheriffs of Roxburghshire and the Douglases of Drumlanrig continued to hold power around Hawick. At the same time James II was careful to retain the loyalty of the other local kindreds such as the Kers, Scotts, Pringles, Murrays and Rutherfords, investing them in land and local offices from the forfeited forest of Ettrick where they were already resident.[11] By the mid-sixteenth century, some branches of these families had prospered to the extent that they could be termed greater lairds; these people were themselves the leaders of large kindreds, exercising lordship over significant followings and extensive lands. The emergence of such families, including the Scotts of Branxholme, the Kers of Cessford and Ferniehirst, the Murrays of Philiphaugh (formerly Falahill) and Blackbarony, the Stewarts of Traquair and the Hays of Yester, filled any potential power vacuum following the demise of the Black Douglases. The same families were still in place in the late 1500s, rewarded for their co-operation by a grateful crown. James II had cleverly

---

within the structure of society to remind the dominant in household, manor or parish of the contingent nature of social heirarchy': 'Politics of the parish', 10–46, 32.
[10] Brown, *The Black Douglases*, 38, 167, 179.
[11] RPS, 1455/8/3, accessed 24 June 2009; Brown, *The Black Douglases*, 294–6, 300–1, 317, 331; Gilbert, *Hunting and hunting reserves*, 136–7, 158.

avoided concentrating too much power in the hands of one kindred, and James VI was to benefit from this diffusion of power in the Middle March.

This march presented a more cohesive picture of society at the time than was evident in the West March. Here the picture was much more fractured, the huge spread of forfeited Douglas landholdings fought over by the Maxwells and the Johnstones into the late sixteenth century, both kindreds vying for the wardenry and supremacy, whilst successive kings brought in outsiders to command its strategic, previously Douglas, castles. In contrast again, Maureen Meikle's study of the lairds of the Eastern Borders identifies a greater degree of continuity of landholding and office in the Eastern Borders than amongst their more troubled Western neighbours. The tenacious rise of the Eastern lairds in the sixteenth century was somewhat at the expense of the Lords Home, but the continued dominance of the Home kindred in the East March meant that it was one kindred, the Homes, whose authority prevailed there.[12] This was in direct contrast to the more even distribution of office and landholding amongst the various kindreds, or surnames, of the Middle March, where a spread of power amongst several surnames remained evident. Exploring the structures of these surnames forms one of the most useful methods of evaluating the exercise of authority in the Middle March.

II

The surnames were social organisations that had many points of similarity with the kindreds of lowland Scotland where the differences between the two may be only in the degree of significance that kinship exerted in socio-political relationships. The surnames were similar too to the Highland clans.[13] 'Surname' was not the only term used however to designate a Borders kindred: an assurance by Ker of Cessford and Scott of Branxholme in 1545 referred to 'thair kyn'; but in 1577 a subsequent Cessford referred to a band of assurance made by Walter Scott of Goldielands on behalf of Branxholme and the 'utheris of his surname'.[14] Such terms would have been used throughout Scotland, but in the latter half of the sixteenth century the 'surname' was a widely used, Borders-specific term whose meaning was usually understood. It appears in countless government papers and English reports, which were often derogatory. As a result, the surnames were associated with a certain notoriety, particularly by the English. There was, for instance, an inherent correlation between surnames and disorder in a report,

---

[12] Meikle, *A British frontier?*, 19, 64.
[13] Here, however, there were discernable differences, particularly in the nature of landholding: there was no direct association between the surname and the lands held by its individual members, in the way that there was, perhaps, an assumption of lands held for a clan in some parts of the Highlands (though this in itself is contentious).
[14] *RPC* i. 22; ii. 643-4.

of 1582, by Sir John Forster, the English Middle March warden: 'there is greate feedes and slawghters risen amonge the surnames of the Borders of Scotlande, which cawseth great disobedience there'.[15] However, in Scotland, in this period, the term 'surname' was also used frequently to describe a kindred in charters and assurances, as in 'I am bound and obliged' for my 'surname'. The term therefore was not necessarily associated with criminal behaviour. Historically, the misunderstanding of the difference between the English and Scottish use of the word has had an unfortunate impact on the subsequent assessment of the Scottish surnames.

Occasionally confusion did seem to exist about what a 'surname' was in Scotland. An English report on the 'gentlemen and surnames' of the marches distinguished between the two in England, but termed the Scottish surnames 'gentlemen' as if Scottish gentlemen were not part of the surnames.[16] Similarly, the Scottish government sometimes showed some confusion, or perhaps a tendency to correlate the clans and surnames: an act of 1587, 'for the quieting and keeping in obedience of the disorderit ... of the bordoris hielandis and Ilis', was addressed to the 'capitanes cheiffis and chiftanes of all clanis alsweill on the hielands as on the bordouris'. The terming of the surnames as 'clans' was revealing for it was this act that for the first time equated the Highlands and the Borders within legislation. During the sixteenth century the crown's perception of the inhabitants of Scotland's peripheries had worsened. Unfortunately for the border surnames, they were being increasingly bracketed with clans, with the result that government's association of clans with disorder was being extended now to the surnames.[17] Border surnames were also associated with the looser confederations of 'riders and ill doers', 'clannis of theiffis', operating mainly in the outlying areas of the marches, and more accurately termed 'gangs' by Rae.[18] Each of these units may have been dominated by one surname, such as the notorious Armstrongs or Elliots, but not exclusively so. Ridpath described the 'gang' of mainly Armstrongs attacked by Sir Robert Carey in 1598 as 'a tribe of banditti'.[19] This was to the detriment of the perception of the 'surname' both then and now.

---

[15] *CBP* i, no. 120.
[16] *CBP* i, no. 166. The Scottish government tended to refer to Scottish gentlemen as the 'lairdis' or 'lards' with the designation 'of' the place that they were from (rather than 'in' which indicated an inferior social status), as in the 'laird of Buccleuch'. All so designated were landed. The 'greater' amongst these lairds were nearer in status to the nobility than their lack of title might suggest, the fluidity between nobles and 'gentlemen' or lairdly class being in contrast, as Maureen Meikle observes, 'to the stratification of the English gentry [which] was rigid and separate from the nobility': *A British frontier?*, 11.
[17] *RPS*, 1587/7/70, accessed 9 Oct. 2009; Goodare and Lynch, 'Scottish state and its Borderlands', 204ff.
[18] *CBP* i, no. 197; Rae, *Administration*, 7.
[19] Ridpath, *Border history*, 478.

The attribution of disorder to the surnames as a whole has also obscured the differences between the various surnames: not all surnames, or all members within the same surname, will have behaved in the same way all the time. They were not a homogenous group and should not be treated as such. Alison Cathcart makes a similar and convincing plea for the reputation of some highland clans in comparison to others.[20] Contemporarily, certain surnames in certain areas were specifically targeted by government. The band of 1569, by Teviotdale men to aid the regent Moray in suppressing the 'rebellious people' inhabiting Liddesdale, Eskdale, Ewesdale and Annandale, referred 'in speciall to all personis of the surnames of Armestrang, Ellot, Niksoun, Crosar, Littill, Batesoun, Thomsoun, Irwing, Bell, Johnnestoun, Glendonyng, Routlage, Hendersoun, and Scottis of Ewisdaill, and uther notorious thevis'.[21] Of the dales only Liddesdale falls administratively within the Middle March, the others lying in the West, and it is these names that seem to have been most frequently of concern. Middle March borderers of course also regularly appeared in government complaints, but the impression given by the men of the dales in the West March should not unnecessarily prejudice any assessment of the behaviour of the men in the Middle.

The main surnames here were the Kers, Rutherfords, Douglases and Turnbulls in Roxburghshire, the Scotts, Pringles and Murrays of Falahill (Philiphaugh) in Selkirkshire, the Stewarts, Hays, Murrays of Blackbarony, Veitchs and Tweedies in Peebleshire and the Armstrongs and Elliots in Liddesdale. Within surnames there were often several branches of those that had descended from the original families, sometimes known as graynes. These widened both the base of the membership of the larger surnames and the area of each surname's landholdings. The branches remained interlinked with each other not only through proximity but also through ties of kinship, marriage and connections of obligation to the leaders of their surnames.

The surname leaders that were resident in the march were generally of greater laird status before 1600, though several, including Cessford and Branxholme, were ennobled soon after this. Their authority derived partly from their family's landholding and the manpower that this brought them, and partly from their status as leaders of kindreds, who could expect the loyalty of their kinsmen, including those who did not hold land directly from them. Leaders were usually determined according to rules of primogeniture, particularly in the case of the more powerful surnames, where the family held more extensive lands.[22] The act of 1587 that listed these leaders in the Middle March included the earls of Bothwell and Angus (who were

---

[20] Cathcart, *Kinship and clientage*, 5–7, 22–3, 29.
[21] *RPC* i. 651–3.
[22] In the families of the Scotts of Branxholme/Buccleuch, Kers of Cessford and Ferniehirst, the Murrays of Blackbarony and Philiphaugh, leadership of the surname was always determined by primogeniture in the sixteenth century, excepting when that person came into that position during his minority. Then a senior member of the family would act as

not resident) and the lairds Ker of Ferniehirst, Scott of Branxholme, Turnbulls of Bedrule and Hallrule, Scott of Howpasley, Ker of Littledean and Douglas of Cavers, the sheriff of Teviotdale.[23] Though representative, this list was not comprehensive: other prominent surname leaders included Hay of Yester, Stewart of Traquair, Ker of Cessford, the Rutherfords of Hunthill and Hundalee, the Pringles of Torwoodlee and Galashiels, the Murrays of Blackbarony and Falahill (subsequently Philiphaugh).

There were also lesser or cadet branches of some of the larger surnames, which had their own heads, such as the Scotts of Harden, Haining and Goldielands, who owed their allegiance to the principal leader of their surname, Scott of Branxholme, later known as of Buccleuch, and who often acted as tutor or deputy for him. These were the 'dependent lairds' identified by Meikle as 'linked to greater lairds by bonds of kinship or through the political bond of manrent'. These lesser lairds extended the power base of the surname leaders, enhancing their status and authority.[24] Over time, whilst some lesser branches were absorbed into the greater surname, others began to act independently. For instance, within the Ker surname the Cessfords (subsequently earls of Roxburgh) were predominant, but through the sixteenth century two other main branches were established, the Kers of Ferniehirst and of Newbattle (subsequently Lothian). Thomas Ker, known as 'first' of Ferniehirst (d. before 1484), was the third son of a Cessford, but by the 1560s the Ferniehirsts were acting independently of the Cessford. Similarly, Mark Ker, commendator of Newbattle, was a second son of Sir Andrew Ker of Cessford (d. 1526) who became an influential privy councillor. His son, Mark, was created first earl of Lothian in 1606.[25] In general, however, by the beginning of the seventeenth century, leadership of almost all the surnames had settled in a specific family.

A surname leader could expect allegiance from those of his surname. Ian Rae described the intense loyalty of borderers to their surname and its leader, in which their 'devotion to him exceeded the cold feudal allegiance of a vassal, being tinged with something of the warmer feeling of the clansman'.[26] Historically, there has been something of an assumption of this loyalty: the reason, however, why a kinsman acknowledged the authority of his leader and co-operated with him needs to be examined further. What was in it for the kinsman? Could the loyalty associated with kinship be merely an act, part of a public transcript in which kinsman and leader were playing formulaic roles? This public discourse perhaps obscured a hidden transcript

---

leader or 'tutor', as Scott of Goldielands did for Scott of Branxholme from 1574 until he reached his majority.

[23] RPS, 1587/7/70, accessed 24 June 2009.
[24] Meikle, *A British frontier?*, 17, 19.
[25] In 1565 Ferniehirst refused to sign an agreement between the Scott and Ker kindreds brokered by Cessford: Fraser, *Buccleuch*, i. 139.
[26] Rae, *Administration*, 7–8.

in which both almost certainly had different objectives. Perhaps the lesser kinsman was secretly muttering discontent over his rent or physical well-being in the alehouse.[27]

There were two different loyalties going on here: one to the leader, to whom the kinsman was related (no matter how distantly), and the other to the kindred as a whole. This hidden transcript is of course extremely difficult to detect; largely illiterate borderers leave no written reminiscences. However, there are clues in the many reports of kinsmen, with their leaders, riding together on raiding expeditions, in one kindred's feud against another, and in their battle cries 'A Douglas' or 'A Turnbull' that ring out through the ballads. Clearly the kindred offered a sense of identity but, more than this, action was being structured by the surnames. Taking action as part of a kindred offered greater protection, and chance of success, than operating alone. The surname as a whole often allied in the pursuit of a common dispute, providing armed support as needed. Thus in 1597, when Robert Scott of Thirlestane attempted to bar the burgh of Peebles from the disputed lands of Cademuir, he was assisted by Sym Scott of Bonnington, John Scott of Hundleshope and his brother Thomas, William Scott in the Glack and Walter Scott in Bowhill 'with braid aixis and swerdis ... in hostile and weirlyke maner'.[28] And this loyalty to the kindred was the source of the loyalty to a leader, in which he was trusted to direct the protection offered by a larger unit. That he did so, further secured his kinsmen's support, and reinforced his own authority. When, in 1585, Scott of Allanhaugh promised to 'serve, manteine, and defend my said chief', Scott of Branxholme promised to 'fortifie, manteine and defend' Allanhaugh and his kin 'as ane cheif aucht to do to his surname and freindis'.[29] This was an overt acknowledgement of the mutual obligations that governed the interaction between leader and kinsman, and the loyalty that was expected between them. It played perhaps to the public transcript, but, for all that, it demonstrated expectations of maintenance and protection, service and loyalty that were generally understood throughout Scottish society. Similarly, Cathcart parallels the 'reciprocal obligations' between clansman and chief with the bonds of manrent and maintenance that Lowland society too embraced.[30] The romance of a clansman's loyalty should not hide the pressing realities of a society in which violence was prevalent, on the border, in the Highlands, and 'inland', that necessitated such personal bonding.

So, the surname leader was expected to provide protection to those of his name, to maintain 'good lordship'. In 1602 an English report claimed that the actions of the Scottish wardens were limited by their need 'to maintain their private greatness by working a dependency of such persons as

---

[27] Scott, *Domination*, 4–9, 24–5.
[28] RPC v. 373–4.
[29] Fraser, *Buccleuch*, ii, no. 202.
[30] Cathcart, *Kinship and clientage*, 85.

will the rather at any time follow their Wardens in all their private quarrels'.[31] In English eyes, Branxholme's rescue of his follower Armstrong of Kinmont from Carlisle castle in 1596 was the most notorious example of this. Branxholme, however, would have felt that he was fulfilling his duty to protect a dependant. It was also important for Branxholme to uphold his personal honour (which had been violated by the English breaking of a day of truce in their capture of Armstrong), for this directly impacted on his status; loss of honour potentially undermined his authority and his entitlement to be leader. Furthermore, martial prowess, of which this incident was a fine example, was also seen to be honourable. It was expected of lordship in sixteenth-century Scottish society in general, and in particular on the border with England.[32] To English chagrin, Branxholme's actions were lauded, William Bowes complaining that both Branxholme, and Cessford, 'have got great reputation with the inland lords and gentlemen, for their valorous defence of their charges'.[33] Branxholme's 'honourable' actions displayed his martial prowess, boosted his reputation amongst his allies and the political elite, fulfilled his obligations of lordship and as keeper, all thus helping to legitimate his offices and leadership.

The 'defence' that Branxholme supplied was part of the lordship that a kinsman expected of his kindred leader. In 1608 Walter Scott of Synton, dying prematurely, nominated his 'werie guid lord and cheif' Lord Buccleuch as 'protector and defendar of my wyfe and bairnis that they incur na wrang'.[34] In practice, good lordship often meant interceding on a dependant's behalf in any form of dispute, either in court, or privately with the contender. A surname leader could also arbitrate in an internal dispute within his surname. In 1528 Scott of Branxholme was the 'ovirman' in a private arbitration of a dispute between John Scott of Borthwick and his brother Walter. The list of 'arbiteris and amicable compositoris' chosen by each of the brothers were all of the Scott surname; all of them promised to abide by Branxholme's decision. His authority was acknowledged: having someone superior gave the kinsmen a recognised mechanism with which to settle their dispute, which both parties would recognise.[35] A leader might also intervene in a criminal case initiated by the crown. Thus, in 1606, Scott of Buccleuch used his association with Sir Gideon Murray of Elibank to attempt at privy council level to overturn a death sentence on Andrew Scott, 'ane commoun rydar' convicted of horsestealing.[36]

A leader was also expected to provide maintenance: he might rent his kinsmen lands, he might employ him in a private capacity on his lands,

---

[31] *CSP Scot.* xiii/2, no. 828.
[32] For similar concepts of honour in England see Braddick, *State formation*, 71–2, 189–90
[33] *CBP* ii, no. 595.
[34] NAS, CC8/8/45, fos 150–3.
[35] Scott of Harden papers, NAS, GD157/162.
[36] *RPC* vii. 714–15.

or in his undertaking of public office; and he was expected to dispense his patronage in his kinsmen's favour. Thus it is significant that nearly all of the Kers of Cessford's deputies as wardens, from at least 1583 to 1602, were Kers. Similarly, in 1608, Scott of Buccleuch granted the vicarage of St Marie of the Lowes to Mr James Scott, whilst his son's armed guard, as triumvir in the Borders in 1622, included three of the Scott surname.[37] In the old raiding days, a leader would have distributed a share of the proceeds to his accompanying kinsmen, and on his death he may have re-distributed his wealth to include his kinsmen. Goodman uses the example of David Scott of Buccleuch, in 1491, willing goods to forty recipients, fourteen of whom were called Scott.[38]

In return, a kinsman's service often took the form of armed attendance on his leader, either in his private dispute, or on behalf of the surname, or in fulfillment of his official duties as warden or keeper or sheriff, or as part of a national muster. When Branxholme rode to rescue Kinmont Willie, he was accompanied by numerous Scotts, including the doughty Harden and Goldielands.[39] A kinsman would also be expected to support his surname leader in any time of difficulty. For instance, in 1621, when the earl of Buccleuch had severe financial problems, Walter Scott of Harden intervened with seventeen of Buccleuch's creditors giving 'his personall bond for their releif'. Subsequently, Harden was entrusted with the running of Buccleuch's estates during his absence abroad. On his death, in 1633, Buccleuch 'was so confident of [the Scotts of Harden's] affection to his family, that he made the three Harden brothers curators to his children.[40] A kinsman was also expected to co-operate with any decision made by his leader, as Branxholme's position as oversman demonstrated. Such expectations of co-operation, service, loyalty and protection together created a structure of obligations that was recognised by kinsmen and leader alike, whilst the fulfillment of these duties reinforced the authority of the leader. And such obligated relationships were not peculiar to the Borders – they were characteristic of Scottish society.

Similarly, the obligations within a surname, like kindreds throughout Scotland, helped to determine allegiances and responsibilities within a feud; the kinship element was significant in determining the pursuit of a feud. One kindred was often pitted against another in a common vendetta. A kindred leader would be expected to organise retaliation within a feud, and he would expect the active, often armed, support of his surname. Similarly, he would be expected to negotiate any resolution of a feud on behalf of his surname and then to enforce the settlement. A statute against the resump-

[37] A. Groundwater, 'The Middle March of the Scottish Borders, 1573 to 1625', unpubl. PhD diss. Edinburgh 2007, 100; *RPC* xii. 695–6; *RMS* vii, no. 270.
[38] Goodman, 'Impact of warfare', 207; Fraser, *Buccleuch*, ii, nos 92–4.
[39] *CBP* ii, no. 252.
[40] NAS, GD157/3071.

tion of the Scott-Ker feud in 1577 recalled the contract of 1565 between Scott of Buccleuch and Ker of Cessford. In this both had, 'on behalf of his surname', promised to reconcile.[41] Kindreds could provide the framework for bloodfeud; equally, the obligations of kinship could provide the mechanism for its resolution. For Wormald, kinship was therefore a force for stability underwriting 'good lordship' within the locality.[42] The traditional view of the troublesome nature of the surnames, notorious for their feuds, has underestimated the stability that could be fostered by their ties of kinship.

The usefulness of such structures of obligations was recognised by the crown, which frequently utilised them to exert its own authority in the region. If the crown wanted to raise an army, on an unpaid forty-day basis, it could oblige the surname leader to bring those in his allegiance to a muster. This was particularly pertinent to the Borders, since such retinues formed the basis of defence against English incursions. Of more daily significance, however, the crown could implement an ordinance within a locality by calling on the leader to ensure that it was carried out within the territory of his surname or to mobilise his surname to assist him in its implementation. Again, this method of government was not specific to the Borders; the crown used such mechanisms to impose its will throughout Scotland. Increasingly, the responsibility of a surname leader for his adherents, and his obligations to assist the crown, were formalised in the subscription of a 'general band'.[43] Both Rae and Goodare, whilst uncertain over the band's exact provenance, concur on its existence from the early sixteenth century and the prevalence of its usage in the government of the Borders. Such bands, and further ordinances for upholding them, were issued in this period in 1572, 1573, 1574, 1576, 1599 and 1602. They were not confined, however, to the Borders: one, for 1574, was registered in 1576 on the day after a similar one subscribed by the gentlemen of Aberdeenshire.[44]

By signing such a band, a surname leader was obliged to take the often uncomfortable responsibility for the actions of those in his allegiance, or risk a fine or forfeiture. The crown could also use it to make the leader himself behave. In 1524 a general band had been subscribed promising to keep 'good rule' on the Borders; in 1540 Walter Scott of Branxholme, in return for his release from ward, promised the privy council to uphold the 'band maid of befoir at Jedburgh' to the same 'grete effect'.[45] The leaders of the local surnames dominated the lists of subscribers, such as the one for the band

---

[41] RPC ii. 643–4, 665.
[42] Wormald, Lords and men, 1–2, 5, 9–10, 13, 33, 77, 160, and Court, kirk and community, 36.
[43] Balfour recorded a typical form of general band: Practicks of Sir James Balfour, ed. P. G. B. Neill (Stair Society, 1962–3), ii. 574–6.
[44] Goodare, State and society, 258–60; Rae, Administration, 62, 116–19; RPC ii. 117, 370–3, 547–52; vi. 45–6, 435–6.
[45] Fraser, Buccleuch, ii, no. 158.

signed, in 1569, by the 'baronis, landit men, gentilmen, inhabitantis of the sherefdome of Berwik, Roxburgh, Selkirk, Peblis' at Kelso. The wording of this band was typical: the undersigned found themselves 'bundin and obleist ... to the Kingis Majestie our Soverane Lord' to be 'obedient subjectis ... and professit inymeis to all thevis'. If they failed in this 'or revelis nocht the contravenaris of this band gif we knaw thame, we ar content to be puneist thairfoir according to the generall band and panis contenit thairin'. In this endeavour, they promised that they 'specialie sall assist the Laird of Bukcleuch and utheris Lairds'. The band was 'invoilabillie to induir, to ... effect a perpetuall and perfyte ordour'.[46] Similar heads of surnames signed the 'Band of Roxburgh', in 1573, 'conforme to the generall Band'. A band could also oblige him and his surname to assist the crown against English thieves raiding or against overt English hostility in wartime. In this period, however, England and Scotland were supposedly at peace; rather than calling for assistance against England, the band of 1569 was followed by a statute promoting 'the peace and amytie' by criminalising Scottish cross-border raiding.[47]

Government also used the obligations of kinship through the pledge system to enforce the compliance of surnames.[48] This was not specific to the Borders, but it had been frequently used there, both for internal and cross-border justice. A human pledge was surrendered by the surname, often its leader, either to the crown or to the opposing warden, to ensure the good behaviour of specific surname members. They were also pledged to ensure that offenders turned up at cross-border days of truce and at Scottish internal judicial courts. For instance, seven Elliots were pursued, in 1574, for the 'pledge of Liddesdale'. If those they were pledged for did not appear, in theory the pledge would be subject to the penalties that would have been applied to the offender. In 1579 the English reported of the Liddesdale surnames that their 'sureties are like to hang, for so the King has commanded' for their non-compliance.[49] There were several problems with this system, not the least being that the onus was on the pledge to surrender himself to the place of custody, and in the 1570s regent Morton attempted to tighten up the system, with a series of ordinances on the transport and keeping of pledges.[50]

As a result, leaders were forced increasingly to assume responsibility for the good behaviour of their surname. In 1587 the Act anent the Borders and Highlands made the principals of the kindreds accountable for the rest of their name.[51] When Buccleuch surrendered himself to English custody,

---

[46] *RPC* i. 651–3.
[47] *RPC* i. 651–3; ii. 548–9, 549–52.
[48] A standard form of missive sent to the keepers of pledges of 1577 is in the Cuninghame of Caprington papers, NAS, GD149/265, fos 12, 13: Goodare, *State and society*, 260.
[49] *RPC* ii. 367–73; *CSP Scot.* v, no. 446.
[50] *RPC* ii. 271–3, 282, 367–70, 477–8. James also tried to reinforce the pledge system in the Act Anent Pledges of 1598: *RPS*, 1598/12/4, accessed 9 Oct. 2009.
[51] *RPS*, 1587/7/70, accessed 9 Oct. 2009.

in October 1597, it was ostensibly for the non-appearance of his surname's pledges at a day of truce. James VI noted that Buccleuch 'being a gentleman, entered only for his pledges' and that he needed to be released to apprehend the fugitives, who were 'unable to be trapped for delivery but by himself'.[52] In 1599 Buccleuch was absolved from acting as cautioner and chief of the Scott surname in a civil case against Walter Scott of Harden, since the general band only referred to criminal offences. During Buccleuch's absence abroad, in 1602, Robert Scot of Haining acted as his 'governor', assuming the burdensome responsibility for the Scott surname. As a result he was summoned before the privy council for numerous Scott offences, including a raid by Scott of Whithope on Traquair's lands at Blackhouse.[53] In the same year Ker of Cessford, now Lord Roxburgh, was pursued for the offences of the Kers in Morebattle and Heughhead.[54]

Increasingly, however, the general band and the pledge system came to be seen as insufficient and, from the 1570s, acts of caution were used in an attempt to enforce the good behaviour of specified individuals. In these the obligations of kinship were reinforced by monetary penalties where specified individuals became obliged to their cautioners, who could incur a fine for their non-compliance. They were often imposed to prevent the further escalation of dispute so that arbitration could take place peacefully. To some extent they had a similar function to the system of binding over in England, whereby monetary sureties were imposed to forestall violence, and the wording of the English complaint 'that he standeth in Fear of his Life or of some bodily Hurt' was similar to that of the Scottish cautions.[55] Thus, in 1604, Murray of Elibank acted as cautioner for his kinsmen, the Murrays of Falahill and Eddleston, not to harm Sir William Stewart of Traquair with whom they had an ongoing feud. The numbers of these cautions increased exponentially in the 1590s and early 1600s.[56] Acts of caution were not a border-specific device, the crown vigorously encouraging men from all over Scotland to subscribe such assurances. They should therefore be seen also as part of James's broader policy of increasing the intervention of the crown in private disputes everywhere, drawing the processes of justice within its own remit. This was to be most visible in James's particular interest in the suppression of the bloodfeud, which reached its apex in the 1590s. James was using the obligations of kinship, reinforced by monetary penalties, in order

---

[52] *CSP Scot.* xiii/1, nos 86, 88, 89. Branxholme's surrender was more to do with the changing diplomatic situation. See chapter 7 below.
[53] *RPC* vi. 372–3, 376–7, 395.
[54] *RPC* vi. 387.
[55] S. Hindle, 'The keeping of the public peace', in Griffiths, Fox and Hindle, *Experience of authority*, 213–44 at pp. 217, 220–2; M. Dalton, *The countrey justice* (1618), repr. London 1742, 267–8.
[56] *RPC* v. 561–748; vi. 607–834; vii. 556

to address an embedded problem, which in itself was largely delineated by the affiliations of kinship.

From the poorest member of a surname, to his immediate family head, and the head of that branch to the surname leader himself, all were involved in a mutually beneficial and mutually burdensome matrix of obligations, in which there was a significant degree of interdependence. It is ironic, given the government's increasingly tainted view of the surnames, that this was the mechanism that government continued to use in the imposition of its authority on the region. In the 1580s it was still the ties of obligation through kinship that government relied upon to govern its regions. In addition, the very men employed by the crown's officers to help them to fulfill their duties were often kinsmen. The structure of the surname thus formed part of the base of the framework of national government.

III

Whilst the surnames provided the most significant element in the social structure of the Middle March in this period, they can only be fully understood by a study of the interaction between branches of a surname and of one surname with another. This could take the form of alliance, often through marriage, which was consolidated either by the leasing of lands, lending of money or the taking of responsibility for others' behaviour. Interaction also occurred in the context of enmity, and enmity was often the catalyst for the formation of rival surname alliances. The persistence of some feuds in the Middle March, such as that between the Kers and the Scotts, throughout the sixteenth century might give an impression of a static framework of alliance and enmity. However, feud could be resolved and alliance result. The enmity between the Scotts and the Elliots of the 1560s evolved into alliance in the 1590s.[57] The frameworks of alliance and dispute had significant implications for government in the region given the crown's dependence upon its agents securing the co-operation of those whom they were supposed to govern.

An overview of the alliances within and between surnames can be derived from a map of the Middle March.[58] A pattern emerges: those of the same surname, and often of those in alliance, hold lands in proximity to each other. Conversely, where the lands of two rival surnames adjoined, the map illustrates the possible areas and reasons for friction between them. Broadly speaking, the map shows that the Kers and their allies, the Rutherfords, predominated in the eastern part of the region, particularly in Roxburghshire, and surrounding the towns of Jedburgh, Kelso and Melrose. The huge Scott kindred dominated the middle and south of the region, particularly

---

[57] Fraser, *Buccleuch*, i. 142–5.
[58] *See* map 2.

Selkirkshire, and the areas around the towns of Selkirk and Hawick; through its alliance with the Murrays of Blackbarony this area extended north into Peeblesshire. The rival Stewarts of Traquair and Hays of Yester were the other most prominent landholders to the west in Peeblesshire, where they had their own affiliates, respectively, the Veitchs and Tweedies. Significantly, the position of Tinnis near Selkirk and Buckholm near Galashiels on the blurred frontline of the lands of the Kers, Scotts, Pringles, Murrays and Stewarts led to much dispute.

Where alliances were made between different kindreds, they were held together by ties of obligation that replicated those of kinship, and the provision of good lordship by a surname leader to those in his allegiance. The latter were referred to, both officially and privately, as 'dependaris', 'adherentis', 'partakeris' and 'allyis'. The leader was supposed to provide for his followers, intervening in judicial processes on their behalf, physically in armed dispute against their enemies and securing patronage for them. Alliance too could be detected in the responsibility that a leader assumed for the good behaviour of his adherents, evident in pledges, acts of caution and privy council ordinances. In return, the physical support that these followers gave to their leaders is apparent in the prosecutions against and the remissions given to them, and the despairing reports of the English wardens, whilst adherents acknowledged their obligations to allied kindreds and their leaders in bonds of manrent and agreements to behave. Finally, the connections made consciously between and within surnames motivated numerous marriage contracts and tenancy agreements.

One of the most tangible ways in which alliances were maintained within and between surnames was through landholding. The Scott surname was one of the largest landholders in the Middle March, with extensive lands in Selkirkshire, Roxburghshire and, following the forfeiture of the earl of Bothwell in 1594, in Liddesdale. The heads of the more senior branches of the surname were in a position to rent lands to surname members. Thus the Scotts of Branxholme rented land to their tenants the Scotts of Allanhaugh throughout the sixteenth century, and they had similar agreements with the Scotts of Howpasley, Synton and Thirlestane. Control of the lands was kept within the Scott surname, whilst the ties of obligation between the surname members and their leader, Branxholme, were maintained. The Ker surname also held extensive lands, with several branches of the name in the Middle March. The principal branch throughout the sixteenth century was that of Cessford, and, as Meikle observes, the Cessfords 'were obsessive about their lands remaining in their kinsmen's hands' making repeated entailments to the other Ker branches of Newbattle, Faldonside, Littledean, Primsideloch, Mersington, Linton and Gateshaw.[59] With the lands held by the other major

---

[59] Meikle, *A British frontier?*, 27.

Ker branches, such as Ferniehirst and Newbattle, this established a network of Ker influence and landholding throughout Roxburghshire.

One way of keeping the lands in the surname was by marrying within it. Isabel, granddaughter of Thomas the 'first' Ferniehirst, married Sir Walter Ker of Cessford (d.1581), whilst Thomas's grandson, Sir John Ker of Ferniehurst (d. 1562) married Catherine, daughter of Sir Andrew Ker of Cessford. In 1614 Margaret, daughter of the first earl of Lothian, married Andrew, eldest son of Sir Andrew of Ferniehirst. Then, in 1631, Anna, countess of Lothian, daugher of the second earl of Lothian, married the head of another important branch, Sir William Ker of Ancrum, and the title of Lothian stayed in that branch. William was the son of Robert, first earl of Ancram, who was descended from Sir Andrew Ker of Ferniehirst (d. 1545). Subsequently, the titles and lands associated with Lothian, Ferniehirst and Ancrum were consolidated into one family following the failure of the male line in the Lothian and Ferniehirst families and intermarriage between these branches.[60] Endogamous marriage within the wider surname was not unusual. It consolidated alliances within surnames where the kinship ties were becoming more distant. The absence of parish records in this period makes it difficult to assess just how common this practice was, but there are examples of it within the Scott family too, including Margaret the daughter of Walter of Branxholme marrying Robert of Thirlestane in the 1560s, Walter of Harden married Mary, daughter of John of Dryhope in 1577, whilst famously, the eleven-year-old Mary Scott, countess of Buccleuch, married her kinsman Walter, son of Scott of Haychesters, in 1659.[61]

Similarly, marriages outside the surname could foster alliances, widening the networks of allegiance within the region. They did not however guarantee friendship, particularly when a marriage was contracted as part of the resolution of a feud. For example that between Walter Scott of Branxholme and Margaret, sister of Robert Ker of Cessford, in 1586, did little to resolve the Scott-Ker feud. Marriages were usually contracted between people within the same locality.[62] However, from the late sixteenth century, the greater lairds were beginning to marry outside the Borders and into the nobility. This had political advantages. In 1580 Sir John Forster, noting the marriage of Margaret, sister of William Ker of Cessford, to Lord Home and the marriage of a daughter of that union to the Earl Marischal's son, observed how these links had strengthened the Cessford's position in the march.[63] Robert Ker of Cessford, Lord Roxburgh, married firstly the niece of the chancellor, and his new neighbour, John Maitland of Thirlestane, but his second marriage, in 1614, was to the sister of the earl of Perth. Similarly,

---

[60] *The Scots peerage*, ed. P. J. Balfour, Edinburgh 1904–14, v. 51, 60–78, 454–71; vii. 332–46.
[61] NAS, GD157/1540; Lee, *Heiresses of Buccleuch*, ch. iii.
[62] See chapter 1 above.
[63] CBP i, no. 70.

the marriages of his children, from 1613, were mostly into the non-borderer nobility.[64]

More normal, however, for the sixteenth century were marriages made locally to enhance alliances within the region. The close relationships between the Murrays and the Scotts were a good example of the benefits that marriage and alliance between surnames could bring. In 1551 a marriage was agreed between Andrew Murray of Blackbarony in Peeblesshire and Grisel Beaton, widow of William Scott of Kirkurd, in which Scott of Branxholme, her father-in-law, paid her tocher, and Patrick Murray of Falahill acted as witness.[65] This joined the Murray branches of Blackbarony and Falahill in an enduring alliance between them and the Scotts. Grisel and Andrew went on to have at least three sons, one of whom was Sir Gideon Murray of Elibank. Elibank was, therefore, a half-brother of Walter Scott of Branxholme, who died young in 1574, and uncle to Walter Scott of Branxholme, afterwards Lord Buccleuch. In 1573 Scott of Branxholme, acting as curator, agreed to a contract of marriage for John Murray of Blackbarony, son to the late Andrew; John's co-curators included Patrick Murray of Falahill. In 1590 Blackbarony agreed, on behalf of Branxholme, the resolution of a dispute with Sir Andrew Ker of Ferniehirst.[66] The Murrays of Falahill (subsequently Philiphaugh), the hereditary sheriffs of Selkirkshire, were cousins of the Murrays of Blackbarony and often acted as witnesses and curators to them. In 1585 Blackbarony stood caution for Elibank for the sum of £5,000.[67] Around 1580 these links were consolidated further by the marriage of Agnes, Blackbarony's sister to Patrick Murray of Falahill.[68] She was the mother of John Murray of Philiphaugh – thus Murray of Elibank was also an uncle to Philiphaugh and Philiphaugh was a first cousin to Scott of Branxholme, first Lord Buccleuch. These links cemented the alliance between both branches of the Murrays and the Scotts of Branxholme.

Gideon Murray of Glenpoint, afterwards Elibank, was the third son of Andrew Murray of Blackbarony, and an example of a younger son in a cadet branch who successfully established himself and his successors as heads of their own name. His close relationship with his nephew Buccleuch was beneficial to both. In the 1590s Buccleuch acted several times in a series of contracts on behalf of Gideon and his elder brother John. In 1591 Elibank agreed to the reversion of the lands of Eldinghope to Buccleuch; in 1597 he promised to pay Buccleuch the profits from lands he was renting from Hay of Yester; subsequently Buccleuch borrowed 800 merks from Elibank.[69] As Elibank's career progressed, they were both able to help each other, both

---

[64] *Scots peerage*, vii. 345–7.
[65] Elibank papers, NAS, GD32/2/2.
[66] RMS iv, no. 2351; NAS, GD32/2/3; 40/2/9, fo. 81.
[67] RPC iii. 728.
[68] NAS, RD1/xx/383.
[69] NAS, GD224/887/8/2; GD224/906/25, fos 1, 2, 4, 5; GD224/341/1; GD224/930/39,

personally, and to fulfill their official duties in the Borders. Elibank was appointed a Middle Shires commissioner from 1605, became a privy councillor in 1610 and treasurer depute from 1613. In 1606, at Buccleuch's 'ernest sute', Elibank, as commissioner, attempted to intervene in a case against a thief named Scott 'on promissis of [Buccleuch's] grit offices in the advancement of this our service, and the presenting of sum to justice mair notorious'.[70] Buccleuch showed his appreciation consenting, in 1608, to a tack by the vicar of Hawick of the teinds and kirk to Elibank for his lifetime. The connection endured after Buccleuch's death, and in 1617 the second Lord Buccleuch acted as cautioner to Elibank, now treasurer depute, for a 40,000 merk loan from an Edinburgh burgess.[71]

Buccleuch was not the only Scott with whom Elibank had such mutually beneficial relations. In 1592 Elibank received a commission to destroy the fortified towers of Harden and Dryhope belonging to Walter Scott of Harden. He does not seem to have fulfilled his duty, apparently using the commission to protect the buildings on behalf of his friend. Then, in 1599, Elibank and Harden together received a remission under the great seal for the burning of houses in Liddesdale. In 1611 Elibank married his daughter Agnes to William, apparent of Harden. In 1617 Elibank interceded with James VI on behalf of William's father Walter in his feud with Scott of Bonnington in which Harden's other son, Essinsyde, had been killed possibly whilst acting as a deputy on the border guard. Also, in 1616, Elibank had secured a pardon from James VI for another Scott, John of Tushielaw, for the slaughter of a brother of Robert Scott of Thirlestane.[72]

The Murrays and the Scotts were also linked to the Kers of Ferniehirst through the marriage of Janet Scott, half-sister of Blackbarony and Elibank, to Sir Thomas Ker of Ferniehirst. She was the mother of Robert Ker, the future earl of Somerset. Thus Elibank was an uncle and Scott of Buccleuch was a cousin to Somerset, James's court favourite from around 1608 to 1615, and Andrew Ker of Oxnam, the captain of the border guard from 1613. Elibank acted as Somerset's agent in Scotland and was to receive substantial grants of land from him.[73] Links between the Murrays and Kers of Ferniehirst were strengthened further when Robert Ker of Ancrum, captain of the border guard until 1613 and a close cousin of the Ferniehirsts, married Elizabeth, daughter of John Murray of Blackbarony; in 1607 Blackbarony acted for

---

fo. 3. Elibank was described as Buccleuch's chamberlain in the 1590s: A. C. Murray, *Memorial of Sir Gideon Murray of Elibank and his times, 1560–1621*, Edinburgh 1932, 35–6.
[70] RPC vii. 714–17.
[71] NAS, GD32/20/19; GD224/918/27, fos 4–5; Mar and Kellie papers, GD124/10/151, fo. 3.
[72] Agnes was the 'muckle-mou'ed Meg' of Borders legend: RPC iv. 769; NAS, GD157/1419; 32/2/7; GD157/1544; GD124/15/29, fo. 14; GD32/1/8; NLS, Denmilne, Adv. MS, 33.1.1, vol. 8, fo. 33.
[73] RPC ix. 232; RMS vii, nos 613, 754.

Ancrum in his absence abroad.[74] Ancrum went on to become an influential gentleman in Prince Charles's Bedchamber. The duties of Elibank, Ancrum and then Oxnam in the Borders were facilitated by their alliance, and the support of their Scott, Ker and Murray kinship networks, whilst Buccleuch, Oxnam and Elibank served also on the privy council. The position of their ally, Ker of Ancrum, meant that they were connected too with the highest levels at court. Alliance could provide additional support for a surname and its leader whilst extending to the alliance the protection and patronage that a surname leader could provide. It could also provide a network of obligation that government could utilise in the Borders, and secure the service and co-operation of a widespread alliance in the region with government policy.

Marriage and kinship were not the only ways to cement an alliance. Alliances between a surname leader and those of a different surname could be formalised in a bond of manrent, whereby the dependant was 'bundin and oblissit' to provide the leader with his service and loyalty to the exclusion of any other, excepting the king. In return, the leader was obliged to protect and 'maintain' the dependant, replicating the obligations of kinship. Manrents could be made for a variety of reasons, Cathcart usefully distinguishing between bonds made for socio-economic reasons, and those for political reasons made by a leader aligning with a superior.[75] A political bond was subscribed, in 1574, by Sir Thomas Turnbull of Bedrule with the Turnbulls of Hallrule, Barnhills and Minto to Archibald eighth earl of Angus. Though they held land in Angus's regality of Jedforest, this bond was particularly timely given the ascendancy of the Douglas kindred during the regency of James Douglas, earl of Morton. Bedrule, noting that his forbears 'of a langtyme hes servit and dependit upon the hous and erlis of Angus, as oure kyndlie gude lordis', promised to 'trewlie serve the said erll, ryd and gang, and tak anfald, trew and plane part with him'. The named Turnbulls subscribed this 'oure band and faithfull promise' on behalf of 'our selffis, oure kin and freindis of oure surnames'. When Morton was overthrown, the council ordered the discharge of this bond.[76] Sometimes bonds included agreement over a tenancy of land, but not usually. However, such ties were often implicit; the dependants involved were often tenants, and Cathcart terms these socio-economic bonds. For instance, in 1595, the Bateys of Eskdale subscribed a bond of manrent to Scott of Buccleuch, who was their landlord. They 'bindis and oblissis us' to Buccleuch and that they 'salbe reddy at all tymes to do our said maisteris service'.[77]

---

[74] Lothian papers, NAS, GD40/2/13, fo. 1.
[75] Cathcart, *Kinship and clientage*, 87–9, 117.
[76] W. Fraser, *The Douglas book*, Edinburgh 1885, iii, no. 214; *RPC* iii. 368.
[77] From the Middle March, for the period from 1573, Wormald lists bonds of manrent to Ker of Ferniehirst, Scott of Branxholme and the earls of Angus. She estimates that only 10 per cent of bonds included a reference to land: *Lords and men*, 53–4, 66, appendix A at pp. 323–4, 354–5; Fraser, *Buccleuch*, ii, no. 213.

Overlapping, and possibly conflicting, spheres of obligation, of kinship, lordship and tenancy, had existed for some time. The government recognised this in the clause of 1587 that called for the surname leaders to assume responsibility for those tenants who 'dependis upoun the directionis the saidis capitaneis cheiffis and chiftaines (be pretensis of blude or place thair duelling) althocht aganis the will oftymes of the lord the grund'. The act listed the 'clans' in the Middle March that depended upon their 'chiftanes ... oftymes aganis the willis of thair landislordis': these included the Elliots, Armstrongs, Nicksons and Crosiers. However, though their landlords may not have been of the same surname and they had their own surname leaders, tenants could be allied with another surname.[78] In 1591 Scott of Buccleuch rented land to Gilbert Elliot 'his friend and servitor', and, in 1599, Buccleuch was the arbiter in a dispute between Redheugh, Gilbert's brother, and a Martin Elliot, son of the late Sym Elliot, who held land in Buccleuch's lordship of Liddesdale. As landlord, Buccleuch, though of a different surname to the Elliots, was fulfilling the obligations of an allied surname leader.[79] Thus the leaders of surnames who rented lands to adherents of a different name increasingly incurred a responsibility for the behaviour of tenants outside their kindred. In addition, surname leaders also acted as cautioners, lent and borrowed money and interceded in judicial processes on behalf of those in their allegiance. Leaders of surnames were regularly ordered to assume responsibility not just for those of their surname, but also for those 'freindis, men, tennentes, allia, and part takaris'.[80] The 1587 act called for landlords and baillies to assume responsibility for 'thair men, servandis and induellaris within thair bailleries', whilst another of 1594 attempted to reinforce this by ordering these landlords to find surety for the good behaviour of their men.[81]

The adherence of troublesome surnames could be, therefore, a burden to a landlord or surname leader. Sometimes the leader tried to protect himself against such a responsibility. In 1594 Scott of Buccleuch was granted the lands of Liddesdale from those forfeited by the earl of Bothwell. This brought him the responsibility for his tenants including such notorious figures as the Elliots of Redheugh, Braidley and Gorrumberrie. In 1599, as 'the principillis of oure brenche', these Elliots signed a bond promising to relieve Buccleuch of his responsibility for any of their offences.[82] A similar bond by Lancie Armstrong of Whithaugh and Sym Armstrong of Mangerton in Liddesdale agreed to relieve Buccleuch for any penalties for their offences for Buccleuch

---

[78] *RPS*, 1587/7/70, accessed 9 Oct. 2009.
[79] NAS, GD224/1059/1; GD224/906/68, fo. 4.
[80] *RPC* i. 22.
[81] *RPS*, 1587/7/70; 1594/4/48, accessed 24 June 2009.
[82] NAS, GD224/906/5. There are at least nine such bands made to Buccleuch by the inhabitants (mainly Elliots) of Liddesdale in 1599, which were witnessed by Robert Scott of Haining. In 1602 Elliot of Redheugh 'as chief of the Ellots within Liddisdaill' was declared by the privy council to be answerable for Will Elliot of Fiddiltoun 'conforme to the general band': *RPC* vi. 476.

'be vertew of the generale band, hes fund caution and bund and oblist him that the haill inhabitantis of the boundis of Liddisdaill ... sall be ansuerable to the Kings Maiestie and his lawis'.[83] Sadly, this did not prevent the crown proceeding against Buccleuch in 1600 for raids between 1598 and 1600 by Mangerton and Whithaugh since they 'hes gevin thair bandis to him, com[ing] ... under his standart and baner'. Similarly, in 1602, Robert Scott of Haining, Buccleuch's deputy, was forced to assume responsibility for the troublesome Armstrongs following a raid by Whithaugh.[84] Buccleuch also took responsibility for those in his alliance who were not necessarily his tenants but who were in his allegiance. In 1607 he took the 'burding upone him for all his kin ... in speciall for Charles Geddes of Rauchane and haill surname of Geddes thair kin freindis assistaris pairtie and partakeris' in a settlement with Sir Alexander Jardine of Applegarth on behalf of his 'haill surname', to resolve the murder of two Jardines by the Geddes's.[85] The crown was utilising the obligations of lordship and allegiance in order to exert its control over these borderers, through the co-operative action of Buccleuch, and exploiting the co-operation that he expected of his tenants and followers.

The crown also used the responsibilities of alliance between members of different surnames in the acts of caution that it increasingly insisted upon. These were predominantly to stop the escalation of feuding, and were often reciprocated by the disputant, but were also used to compel obedience of specific orders: in 1587 William Hume of Lessudden and others became 'actit and oblist conjunctlie and severalie as cautionaris and souritie for Gawin Ellott of ye Stobbis That ye said Gawine suld entir and present Robert Ellott of Reidheuch personalie befoir us [the council] ... under the pane of tua thousand pundis', whilst in 1606 James Gledstanes, younger of Ormiston, stood surety for Robert Elliot of Lauriston, and *vice versa*, not to hunt in the Cheviots.[86] Alliance could be burdensome, and the crown did not hesitate to use these obligations.

The alliances between surnames could extend further through alliance to political factions, which meant that political rivalry at court had ramifications in the Middle March. Thus the social structure of a locality, founded on kinship and adherence, was part of a wider political as well as governmental framework. Alliance between a surname and a prominent figure could bring benefits to that surname in the locality, whilst the person receiving such patronage was then in a position to support his superior in the locality. For instance, Margaret Douglas, the mother of Scott of Branxholme, widowed in 1574, was the sister of the earl of Angus and thus allied Douglas and Scott interests in the Middle March. From 1572 Angus's uncle, James Douglas

---

[83] Fraser, *Buccleuch*, ii, no. 216.
[84] RPC vi. 179–80, 494–5.
[85] NAS, GD224/906/60, fo. 3.
[86] NAS, PC10/3/iv, fo. 16.

earl of Morton was regent and he made Angus lieutenant in the Middle March. John Carmichael of that ilk, a close relation of Angus and Morton, was made keeper in Liddesdale. Morton also needed to contain the power of the incumbent warden of the Middle March, William Ker of Cessford (Branxholme's long-term enemy). To do this he split the wardenry between Cessford and his kinsman William Douglas of Bonjedburgh, who became warden 'bewest the strete' (Dere Street). This arrangement ended with the decline in Morton's position from 1578.[87] The Douglas-Scott alliance was counterbalanced by that between the Kers and the Homes with the earl of Argyll, and subsequently the earl of Lennox. Subsequently, following the rise to power of the earl of Lennox, his ally, Cessford, was re-appointed to the full wardenry in 1581.[88] Also in 1581, following the decline of the Douglas position at court, the privy council found it necessary to discharge the bonds of manrent made by a number of Middle March families to Angus, including one by Scott of Goldielands acting for the young Branxholme.[89] Alliance and dispute at local level could replicate that at court and assume a more overtly political significance.[90]

Apart from these external political alliances, the connections between the Scotts, the Murrays and the Kers of Ferniehirst typified many alliances within the Middle March, which were predominantly formed within the locality. When alliances were formed outside the locality, these were generally in an eastwards direction. The ease of communication between the East and Middle Marches provided by the Tweed basin meant that it was probably inevitable that the Kers would have looked eastwards to the Homes for support. The physical barrier of the hills and dales of Eskdale westwards precluded much alliance in that direction and the Scotts of Branxholme's alliance principally came from within Roxburghshire and Selkirkshire. However, the marriage of Branxholme's sister Margaret, in 1571, to Sir John Johnstone of that ilk in Annandale brought them the alliance of that prominent West March family. This was not without its disadvantages, for with the Johnstone friendship came the enmity of their rivals, the Maxwells: in 1593 the Scotts accompanied Johnstone at the battle of Dryfe Sands against the Maxwells.[91] Kinship and alliance could bring huge benefits to a surname and was useful to the government in enforcing the responsibility of the surname leaders for their men's behaviour. Alliance however inevitably brought with it dispute.

[87] CSP Scot. v, nos 284, 315, 446; Fraser, *Douglas*, iv. 215–16.
[88] CSP Scot. v, nos 432, 471, 584; RPC iii. 344–6.
[89] RPC iii. 368.
[90] Keith Brown puts more emphasis on the effect of 'local alliances and animosities' in 'shaping court politics' though he also notes that 'the reverse was often just as true': *Bloodfeud*, 108.
[91] Fraser, *Buccleuch*, i. 139, 152–5, 177.

IV

Kinship was the glue of many an alliance whilst the kindred formed the social structure upon which much interaction was based. In the Middle March, where the kindreds were generally termed the surnames, this could be taken to indicate that Middle March kindreds were somehow different to the other kindreds of Scotland. However, the implications of the kinship element of the surnames were much the same for the Middle March as they were elsewhere. The protection expected by a member of the Scott surname from his surname leader, Scott of Buccleuch, in Selkirkshire was the same as that expected by those of the Maule surname from Maule of Panmure in Angus. Similarly the support expected by Buccleuch from an allied surname, such as the Elliots in the 1590s, was the same as that expected by Panmure from the Strathaquhins of Balwysse.[92]

The importance of kinship for this study is that it formed one of the main mechanisms of government in the Middle March as elsewhere in Scotland. At a basic level the surnames provided the manpower which local officials used to fulfill their duties, their deputies almost always coming from their own surnames or kindred. More than this, however, the kindreds formed a social structure in the localities, and a framework of obligation and accountability, which the government used when it exerted its authority in the region. The surname was the unit for which the government held the surname leader responsible under the general band and acts of caution. Conversely, alliances within and between surnames provided a network of obligations that members of a surname could use in their own interaction with government at both local and national levels. Kinship and alliance thus dynamised a system of government in which personal contact was crucial: they were part of the framework of government throughout Scotland. And when James's government began to exert increasingly direct control in all its regions, it continued to use the framework of the obligations of kinship and alliance, in the Middle March, as elsewhere.

The crown's utilisation of these obligations as a mechanism of government in the Middle March presupposes a defined network of kinship and alliance there. This there clearly was. Crucially, however, for the successful implementation of government policies, there had to be an underlying stability in the social structure provided by kinship and alliance. What is remarkable about the Middle March is the social continuity evident in the lasting importance of the region's main surnames throughout the period from 1573 to 1625. Indeed, this continuity can be detected as far back as the mid-fifteenth century. Furthermore, the only significant forfeiture in the Middle

---

[92] Bonds of manrent by the Strathaquhins to Maule of Panmure in 1570 and 1602: Wormald, *Lords and men*, appendix A at p. 332.

March in the late sixteenth century, that of the earl of Bothwell, did not cause a significant upheaval in the patterns of landholding and alliance. The Scotts of Branxholme and the Kers of Cessford, already two of the most significant surnames in the march, merely consolidated their position by acquiring Bothwell's lands. A similar social continuity existed in the East March but the picture in the West March is more confused. Here the instability caused by the continuing Maxwell-Johnstone feud, the forfeiture of John, Lord Maxwell, in 1609 and his execution in 1613, was evident in the number of acts of caution registered after 1603. Repeated reports of disorder in the West March, enduring into the 1620s, outlasted government concern over the Middle March. Whilst stability and the resolution of disputes could be fostered through strong links within and between kindreds, such alliances could also trigger dispute.

3

The Administrative Structure of the Middle March

The surnames, and their associated obligations of kinship and alliance, provided a framework for the exercise of power within the Middle March, as elsewhere. The socio-political structure of the march was also subject to external influences: the effects of the Reformation, socio-economic change and, of course, Anglo-Scottish relations. Predominant, however, amongst these was the impact of the government of James VI, which, from 1586 onwards, was determined to strengthen its presence throughout Scotland. The 'fitted carpet' of crown authority was unfurling to include not just the 'lawlands' of the centre, but also Scotland's periphery, the 'outcuntrey'.[1] The mechanisms that James was to use were similar to, or an extension of, those that had been in existence before and so were the people involved. This was not surprising: the crown was dependent upon prominent figures in each region with sufficient authority, known contemporarily as a 'strang hand', to effect government policy. They were operating, however, in a changed environment by the end of the period. Increasing numbers of people were participating in local government: Julian Goodare estimates that the number of local office-holders in Scotland quadrupled between 1560 and 1625.[2] And, throughout Scotland, the crown was showing a newly consistent intolerance of violent crime, increasingly drawing the resolution of dispute into its remit. In the Middle March the effects of this were intensified by a sea-change in Anglo-Scottish relations during the 1590s. Perhaps it is surprising that very few office-holders in the Middle March fell by the wayside.

Office-holding in the region was largely undertaken by the lairds, usually the leaders of their surnames and of its branches; Maureen Meikle calls the lairds of the Eastern Borders 'the backbone of local administration'. In 1573 the only resident noble was Lord Yester, near Peebles. In addition there was the non-resident, but occasionally present, Lord Home, as the secular commendator of the regality of Jedburgh abbey, and the earls of Angus and Bothwell. On a day-to-day basis, effective authority lay within the hands of those 'greater' lairds whose lands and followings gave them a status that verged upon that of the nobility, and the 'lesser' lairds who deputised for

---

[1] Goodare and Lynch, 'Scottish state and its Borderlands', 187, 201; Goodare, *State and society*, 214–15, 239.
[2] Goodare, *Government of Scotland*, 216–19.

them. The crown was powerless to enforce its policies unless these lairds chose or could be made to co-operate.[3] A grateful crown granted them the fees and jurisdictions of office-holding, and lands to reward loyal service. Whilst securing co-operative governors, simultaneously the crown legitimised the lairds' authority and gave them the patronage and power associated with office. It could be a mutually beneficial relationship as attested by the prospering fortunes of the Scott and Ker lairds during the suppression of crime in the early 1600s. In 1622, for instance, Buccleuch was appointed by the council to the triumvirate of Middle Shires commissioners as one of those 'special persones of power and freindschip' in the region, being sufficiently 'armid with power, freindschip, credit and meanis' to suppress crime there.[4] Buccleuch's effectiveness lay in the manpower that was provided by the huge Scott kindred, their allies and his many tenants, and the mutual obligations that characterised their relations. His authority rested upon his adherents' recognition of his leadership, which, in turn, was dependent upon his ability to fulfill the functions of good lordship.

Thus for these local governors to be effective, they needed more than the status given to them by office. In the absence of a standing army or even a guard, official means of coercion were limited. For early modern office-holders in England, too, as Michael Braddick shows, their legitimacy 'rested not just on legality but on the assertion of a wider claim to authority', which had to be secured through their actions as office-holders: 'their credibility depended on the reception of their performance'.[5] At the same time, office-holding, both public and private, gave such as Buccleuch the power associated with the specific office and the ability to reward or protect adherents. This enabled him to maintain his obligations to his subordinates and thus retain the legitimacy of his authority. A mutually beneficial relationship between the crown and its agent underwrote the authority of that agent within the region, and the exercise of his power on behalf of the crown, whilst allowing him to meet his adherents' expectations.

Crown appointments included both border-specific offices, in particular those of lieutenant, march warden and the keepership of Liddesdale, and those similar to the rest of Scotland, the most senior being that of sheriff (though the sheriffdoms had become hereditary in the sixteenth century). The crown also granted offices within crown lands such as the captaincy of Newark castle in Ettrick Forest. The surname leaders' power was further reinforced by their private jurisdictions, in baronies and regalities, and as bailies for greater absentee lords, which brought them into direct contact with many small tenant farmers in the region. Surname leaders also had either the formal right or the effective power to nominate provosts in the

---

3   Meikle, A British frontier?, 53, and 'The invisible divide', 70–1; Goodare, *Government of Scotland*, 120–4.
4   Goodare, *Government of Scotland*, 175; RPC xii. 675–6.
5   Braddick, 'Administrative performance', 171.

burghs of Peebles, Jedburgh and Selkirk, influence over nomination of ministers to parishes and the ability to appoint bailies to their lands. In this period these powers were augmented in the Middle March, as elsewhere in Scotland, by the formalised admission of lairds to parliament in 1587, attendance at the privy council in the 1590s and the creation of the Justices of the Peace in 1609. In addition, some borderers benefited from their appointment as commissioners for the Middle Shires from 1605.[6]

I

Throughout the Scottish regions, the sheriffs were the principal judicial and civil administrators in each shire and acted as the crown's agents there. In the Borders, there was the added layer of officialdom, that of the march wardens and the temporary lieutenants, occasioned by the proximity of the region to the border, and the necessity, in the past, to organise the defence of the kingdom. The day-to-day administration of the Middle March, however, remained in the hands of the sheriffs of the three shires of Roxburgh, Selkirk and Peebles. They held sheriff courts, were responsible for the collection of taxes and were meant to implement council ordinances and central court judgements.[7] The sheriff court of Roxburghshire, the only court in the Middle March for which records are available in this period, met regularly, on average at least thirty times a year, its business dominated by the proving of testaments, complaints over debts and arbitrations over spulzie, that is 'borrowing' without the consent of the owner. Violent crime may have been recorded separately.[8]

All the sheriffdoms were heritable and, in the Middle March by 1573, had been in the same families for several generations. Roxburghshire had been held by the family of Douglas of Cavers since 1412, following a grant by James I. Sir William Douglas, sheriff from 1558 to 1589, was the sixth Cavers to have inherited the office in a direct line of descent. His son Sir James presided over the sheriff courts at Jedburgh from 1590 to 1612, and James's son William, feuar of Cavers, took over officially in 1610.[9] The sheriffdom

---

[6] Goodare, *State and society*, 64, 74, 290; RPS, 1587/7/143, 1609/4/26, accessed 24 June 2009.
[7] For a general discussion of sheriff's duties see C. A. Malcolm, 'The sheriff court: sixteenth century and later', in *An introduction to Scottish legal history* (Stair Society, 1958), and Goodare, *Government of Scotland*, 175–81. Extracts of the sheriff courts of Dumfries and Lochmaben, in the West March, are printed in 'The sheriff court book of Dumfries, 1573–83', ed. P. Hamilton-Grierson, *Transactions of Dumfriesshire and Galloway Natural History and Antiquarian Society* xii (1926), 126–224, and *The Lochmaben court and council book, 1612–1721*, ed. J. B. Wilson (SRS, 2001).
[8] NAS, SC62/3–7. Sheriff court records are not available until 1636 for Peebles and 1652 for Selkirk: NAS, SC42; SC63.
[9] NAS, SC62/3–7; RSS v, no. 577.

of Peeblesshire (sometimes also known as Tweeddale) was held by the Hays of Yester, who were also sometimes provosts of Peebles, and substantial landholders there.[10] The fifth Lord Yester was sheriff from 1556 until his death in 1586, when he was succeeded by his son William, and then by William's brother James until his death in 1609. James was succeeded as sheriff by his son John, the future first earl of Tweeddale.[11] In Selkirkshire the sheriffdom was granted, in 1509, by James IV to the Murrays of Falahill. It encompassed the jurisdiction of the crown-owned Ettrick Forest, in which the Murrays had held the Forestership since the 1460s.[12] The Murrays held lands at Falahill in the north of the march but also at Philiphaugh near Selkirk. Patrick Murray of Falahill was sheriff from 1543 until his death in 1578, his son Patrick from then until 1601. He was succeeded by Sir John Murray of Falahill, subsequently known as Philiphaugh.[13] Occasionally there was dispute between the burgh of Selkirk and the sheriff over shrieval jurisdiction in the burgh; in 1540 the burgh was allowed by James to elect their own provost as sheriff.[14]

All the sheriffs were significant local landholders and linked into wider allegiances in their shires through kinship and alliance. All of them, too, used members of their kindreds or alliance to carry out their duties. The Cavers sometimes employed their sons as deputies, but they also relied on the good burgesses of Jedburgh to preside over the sheriff courts there. These were often Turnbulls and Rutherfords who were themselves related to powerful local families. William Douglas, a bailie in Jedburgh, was deputy in 1601, as was a James Douglas in Cavers in 1602. From May 1603 William Douglas, younger of Cavers, increasingly took over the role of depute eventually becoming sheriff principal until at least 1624. He shared the responsibility with the burgesses John Alensone and Mr John Rutherford (who was sometime provost of Jedburgh and was the younger brother of the neighbouring Rutherford of Hunthill).[15] The support of these local networks of allegiance gave the Cavers both the manpower, and the authority, that the office of sheriff required to be effective. Likewise, in Peeblesshire, the Yesters used the local Murray of Romanno as their deputy from 1574, which also therefore tied in the support of the powerful Murray of Blackbarony surname, which held extensive lands to the north of Peebles.

There were a number of difficulties facing any sheriff. In particular, he had to carry out his duties in the face of complicated alliances and enmi-

---

[10] Rae, *Administration*, appendix 1, 235.
[11] *Calendar of writs preserved at Yester House, 1166–1625*, ed. C. Harvey and J. Macleod (SRS, 1930), 235; *RPC* iv. 25; *RSS* iv, no. 3126; *RMS* v, nos 1830, 1872; *ER* xxi. 114.
[12] Rae, *Administration*, appendix 1 at p. 235; T. Craig-Brown, *The history of Selkirkshire*, Edinburgh 1886, 338.
[13] *RPC* ix. 55, 205; *RMS* vi, no. 1461; Pringle of Torwoodlee papers, NRAS, NRAS482/31, fos 12, 14.
[14] *RMS* iii, no. 2207; Symms, 'Social control', 23–4.
[15] *RSS* v, no. 577; *RPC* xii. 222; *RMS* viii, no. 592.

ties in the locality, and the obligations that they brought. In 1586 letters of horning were issued by William Ker of Woodhead against William Douglas of Cavers, as sheriff of Teviotdale, for his failure to have Ker admitted to the lands of Bedrule, forfeited by the Turnbulls, who were Douglas allies. Cavers was forced to stand surety of 5,000 merks for Sir Thomas Turnbull of Bedrule and, in 1587, was ordered to find caution with the earl of Angus that he would submit himself, and those for whom he was bound, to justice by the English warden.[16] Thus, in addition to his responsibilities as sheriff, he was accountable, with monetary pain, for those allied to him. Feuding too could compromise a sheriff. In Jedburgh the bailies were not able to help Cavers in the action against Turnbull because of the 'deidlie feidis standing unreconsilit' there, so that they 'can nawayes gif obedience to the said charge without the perrell and dangear of thair lyveis'. The Yesters, as sheriffs of Peeblesshire, were affected by their long-term feuds, such as that with the Stewarts of Traquair, who were major local landholders, and other related feuds. In 1586 William, master of Yester, was denounced rebel for not subscribing a mutual band of assurance with Traquair. In the same year the council ordered that those holding office, such as a sheriff, should not be obeyed until they had settled their affairs. In May 1587 a justice court was held at Peebles for the sheriffdoms of Peebles and Selkirk at which all those attending had promised to stay their disputes, yet the following month William, now Lord Yester and sheriff, was warded in Edinburgh for refusing to resolve his feud with Traquair. In 1599 Yester was accused by the council of not apprehending Tweedie of Drumelzier, one of his adherents and was denounced, similarly, by Mr Archibald Douglas, parson in Peebles, for failing to arrest his kinsman John Hay of Smithfield. Douglas was at feud with the Horsburghs, allies of Yester.[17]

As a result, throughout James VI's reign the sheriffs were criticised increasingly for inefficiency and partiality, and for being 'falteis or negligent in the executioun of thair offices'.[18] In 1596 James Douglas of Cavers, as sheriff, was summoned by the Lords of the Exchequer to account for the taxes owing from Roxburghshire.[19] In 1599 the sheriffs of Roxburghshire, Selkirkshire and Peebleshire were castigated by the council for being 'altogeddir cairles and unmyndful of the dewtifull discharge of thair officeis' in failing to apprehend long lists of offenders. Murray of Falahill was censured for his failure to hold any head courts in Selkirk between 1586 and 1599. The sheriffs of the Middle March, however, were not the only ones targeted by the government: in the same month, a commission was formed to consider ways to make sheriffs more effective throughout Scotland. The accusations against the Middle March sheriffs should be seen within the context of a more

[16] *RPC* iv. 57–8, 63–4, 82, 189, 191.
[17] *RPC* iv. 57–8, 68, 70, 71, 156–7, 186, 210; vi. 58.
[18] *RPC* vi. 57.
[19] NLS, Douglas of Cavers papers, Acc. 6803, Box 9, fo. 2.

general governmental attempt to improve judicial systems. A charge in 1601 to all sheriffs to post a list of offenders unrelaxed from horning, from 1596, did not include any from the Middle March.[20]

But James's particular ire was reserved for the hereditary nature of the sheriffs' office which he viewed as an obstacle to the effective imposition of law. From 1610 onwards James was to concentrate on persuading, with limited success, specific sheriffs to surrender their heritable offices in return for compensation.[21] In 1617 a commission looking into heritable office recommended that sheriffs should be encouraged by 'ane competent satisfactioun in honoure and utherwayis to be gevin to thame'. Thus Elibank, on James's behalf, entered into negotiations with Douglas of Cavers, in 1620, over the payment of £20,000 Scots for the surrender of this office. This was unsuccessful, and a Douglas of Cavers was still referred to in 1711 as the 'Heretable Sherriff of Tiviotdale'.[22] James had more luck, after lengthy bargaining, with the Murrays of Philiphaugh: in 1615 Lord Binning wrote to James that he, with Elibank, had 'with difficultie' persuaded Philiphaugh to resign his office in return for 20,000 merks. Cunningly, payment was arranged in the conversion of a yearly fee of £500 that he was already receiving, as a commissioner for the Middle Shires, into a liferent pension: the crown thus retained Philiphaugh's services 'in all tyme cuming', whilst the 'ease of his pryce might be ane argument to bring others who might be herefter delt with for renunciation of the lyke offices'.[23] Philiphaugh finally resigned in 1619, but he continued to hold public office in the region as a commissioner for the Middle Shires and held courts of justiciary in Selkirkshire in 1622.[24] Subsequently, the crown appointed the sheriffs of Selkirkshire on a yearly basis. However, since local support was essential if a sheriff were to be effective, the crown necessarily had to appoint the sheriff from a limited pool of those with local authority. As a result, the list of subsequent appointments was dominated by the Murrays of Philiphaugh and their allies. Pringle of Torwoodlee was sheriff in 1620. Sir Walter Scott of Harden gave his oath as sheriff in August 1621 but, a month later, following a letter sent to James about his 'insufficiencie' for the office, Sir Robert Scott of Thirlestane was sworn in instead. Sir James Pringle of Galashiels was sheriff in 1622 and Pringle of Torwoodlee again in 1624. Philiphaugh was reappointed in 1623 and 1625, and a Philiphaugh was sheriff of Selkirk in 1690.[25] The Murrays

---

[20] RPC vi. 56–9, 68–9, 329.
[21] Eight sheriffships were surrendered by 1625, including those of Dumfries, Selkirk and Berwick in the Borders: Goodare, *Government of Scotland*, 187–190; RPC 2nd ser. i. 659.
[22] RPS, 1617/5/38, accessed 24 June 2009; RPC xii. 289–90; Douglas of Cavers papers, Acc. 6803, box 9, fo. 2; Acc. 6991.
[23] NLS, Denmilne, Adv. MS 33.1.1, vol. 6, fo. 22.
[24] RPC xi. 586–7; xiii. 333; Craig-Brown, *Selkirkshire*, 342.
[25] RPC xii. 322, 567, 570, 575; xiii. 43, 333, 592, 789–90; Walter Mason papers, BA, Hawick, WM11/102.

may have surrendered their hereditary office but the crown still depended upon their goodwill in Selkirkshire.

Given the difficulties that the crown encountered in securing the surrender of heritable appointments, one way of increasing central control over judicial processes in the shires was for the crown to appoint prominent local figures to new offices there. Envious of the English system of Justices of the Peace, James drove through their introduction into Scotland in 1609, with the first appointments in 1610. In tandem with crown concern over feuding, the act of 1609 hoped that the 'ungodlie barbourous and brutall custome of deadlie feadis' would be overcome by the appointment of 'some godlie wyse and vertuous gentlemen' to 'trye and prevent all sic occasionis as may breid truble and violence' in each shire. At the same time, the crown replicated some of the sheriff's powers in the JPs' commissions, and their area of jurisdiction was the same. Here there might have been potential for conflict: however, most sheriffs also became JPs. Moreover, as it turned out, JPs' duties did not usually compete with those of the sheriffs, being more concerned with local socio-economic matters, such as the management of poor relief. A certain blurring of duties did happen: in 1623 Sir James Pringle of Galashiels in his capacity as sheriff of Selkirkshire convened a meeting of the local lairds to set in place measures for poor relief. He was also a JP. In general the office seems to have been introduced relatively harmoniously alongside existing jurisdictions.[26]

There was, however, nothing new about the names of the JPs in the Middle March, because for them to have any effect, they had to have existing authority there. As a result, the appointments reflected the existing *status quo* within the shires. With the act's objectives over feuding in mind, it is interesting to note that the JPs in each shire included lairds from opposing sides in previous or existing feuds and it would be difficult to describe many of them as either 'godlie' or 'vertuous'. In Roxburghshire, for instance, the long-term enemies, Buccleuch and Roxburgh, were appointed whilst in Selkirkshire JPs included Robert Scott of Haining, himself still in dispute with the burgh of Selkirk, as was another, Andrew Ker of Yair. However, the commission for the peace provided a new structure in which existing and former combatants were meant to work together in implementing crown policies. It was in their interests to do so, and also benefited the crown. The new JPs, Goodare suggests, were 'to extend the authority of the crown further down the social scale', to include the lesser lairds in formal office, and caused a 'dramatic expansion' of local administrators.[27] The government was then able to use these lairds' networks of allegiance to effect judicial processes. In 1611, at a justiciary court held at Jedburgh by Elibank, a Scott affiliate and JP, the assize was dominated by the surnames of Scott

[26] RPS, 1609/4/26, accessed 24 June 2009; RPC ix. 75–6; xiii. 789; Goodare, *Government of Scotland*, 204–7.
[27] Goodare, *Government of Scotland*, 203.

and their allies: it also included a Roger Scott, captain of Hermitage castle, whose office put him in a position to effect the apprehension of offenders on behalf of the JPs.[28] There were few changes to those appointed JP by 1625. In 1623 a renewal of the commissions of the peace confirmed them in the hands of those who had held them since 1610, with the addition of a few lairds of the lesser variety, such as Scott of Sandelands and Pringle, younger of Whibank.[29] However, separate commissions of justiciary continued to be issued for specific cases, such as that in 1615 to the sheriff of Roxburgh and deputies, and the provost and bailies of Jedburgh, for the apprehension of two offenders.[30] In 1618 Buccleuch, despite his appointment as both JP and commissioner for the Middle Shires, was issued with a separate commission for the apprehension of some fugitives, though possibly since their surnames were Scott, it was felt necessary to underline his duty in this case.[31] The system of JPs was established in legal terms, though it was perhaps not as fully functional as James would have wished.

The position of the Middle March from 1603 within a specially designated area, the Middle Shires, in which border-specific types of jurisdiction existed, further complicated the picture. In 1611 James granted commissions to his 'weilbelovit' Cranstoun and Elibank to be Justices within the bounds of the sheriffdoms of the Middle Shires: both of them were already commissioned JP. These new commissions gave them jurisdiction in a wider area, the whole of the Scottish Middle Shires, rather than just the respective shires to which as JPs they were limited. The commissions also gave them 'full pouir, frie libertie and auctoritie' to try pleas of the crown at justice courts and power of life and death.[32] Clearly, the need for the formalised registering of this widened jurisdiction reflected government perception of the difficulties caused by differing levels and areas of jurisdiction: such clarification in the Middle March was particularly needed, given the overall jurisdiction invested in the commission of the Middle Shires which transcended local jurisdictions.[33]

II

This extra layer of border-specific officialdom in the Middle March potentially complicated the administration of justice. The duties of the lieutenant and wardens had gradually evolved from the organisation of defence into primarily judicial duties, organising the redress of cross-border crime

---

[28] *RPC* ix. 708.
[29] *RPC* xiii. 445–6; xiii. 331, 342.
[30] *RPC* x. 332.
[31] *RPC* xi. 452–3.
[32] *RPC* ix. 194–6.
[33] See ch. 7 below.

and, domestically, imposing fluctuating crown wishes upon the miscreant borderers. There is not, however, any evidence of a clash between sheriff and warden, though records are frustratingly limited here: there seems to have been an understanding of the border-related nature of offences for which the warden was responsible.[34] Instead, the office of warden, and his deputies could also be seen as an opportunity for more prominent locals to be involved in public office. The wardenships lapsed on James's succession to Elizabeth's throne in 1603, though a new office, of commissioner of the Middle Shires, was created two years later to effect the pacification of crime. Border-specific appointments were particular to the region: however, like other officials, they were as dependent on their networks of kinship and allegiance for their effectiveness, and as such a reflection of their existing local status.

The most senior office in the Borders was that of lieutenant. The crown made limited-term appointments to the post, usually of one year, normally in response to heightened concern about law and order there. Sometimes the appointment was for just one or two marches but, particularly in the case of longer terms of office, the lieutenancy could cover all three. Lieutenants were almost always nobles and, in the case of the Middle March, they usually had close connections within it through landholding or kinship. The lieutenancy, such as the one granted to the earl of Angus in 1598, always included the powers of justiciar. Angus had 'full power and commission' to hold courts anywhere within the specified marches. In support of this office, he was to charge the borderers to 'convene thame selffis in armes at all tymes and occasionis for accumpanying him to the ... dayis of trew or persute of thevis'. Some commissions, such as that to Angus in 1586, specified wages to be paid monthly to his armed retinue: 100 merks to the captain of horse, horsemen at £20 and footsoldiers at £6.[35] But the lack of a permanent armed guard was a perpetual complaint, which was not fully addressed until the establishment of one in 1605. This perhaps suggests that the funding of it had not been seen as a priority until after Union. The lieutenant could however call on the services of his alliance within the marches.

This was particularly relevant to the Douglas earls of Angus as lieutenants in the Middle March. Between 1573 and 1603 the lieutenancy was filled intermittently for around seventeen years, the principal holders being the earls of Angus, who held it for more than nine years.[36] The Douglas family's historical landholding in the regality of Jedforest gave them a significant foothold in the march. Others of their surname were still landholders in the Middle March, such as the Douglases of Drumlanrig and Bonjedburgh; Douglas of Cavers was, of course, sheriff there. This meant that the Anguses had a network of kinship in the march and existing powers of jurisdiction in their own lands there. These networks were extended through other

---

[34] Meikle, *A British frontier?*, 62–3.
[35] *RPC* iv. 111; v. 464.
[36] Rae, *Administration*, appendix 4 at pp. 254–6.

surnames in their alliance: these included the Carmichaels, Turnbulls and Scotts, especially of Buccleuch, Margaret Douglas, the sister of the eighth earl, being the mother of the 'bold' Buccleuch of this period.[37] Undoubtedly the crown will have recognised the benefits of these in effecting the lieutenancy.

In July 1574 Archibald eighth earl of Angus was appointed lieutenant of all the marches. The appointment sprang from the hopes of the new regent, James Douglas, earl of Morton, of concluding an alliance with England. This resulted in a sustained effort, between 1573 and 1578, to impose order in the region, the most consistent attempt to do so before 1597. Morton was consciously using the networks of Douglas kinship and adherence to support him in this. But whilst Morton depended on Angus in the Borders, Angus was similarly dependent on Morton for office: Angus was dismissed in March 1578, following Morton's deposition as regent.[38] Following the renewal of negotiations with the English over the League in 1586, however, Angus was again appointed lieutenant in the East and Middle Marches. He took part in at least two judicial raids to the Middle March between 1586 and 1588.[39] James's increasing concern from 1597 over the English succession triggered a more consistent approach to imposing justice in the marches, leading to the appointment of William, tenth earl of Angus, as lieutenant in June 1598. He was still in office in 1600 and took part in at least two judicial raids to the region, in 1599 and 1602.[40]

The short-term nature of their role, their involvement in central government, residency elsewhere and the temporary prioritisation of border affairs by government meant that the effectiveness of lieutenants was short-lived, often hampered by local allegiances. For instance, Angus was warded for a couple of weeks in early 1587 as a pledge for the entry of those accused by the earl of Arran, despite having been reappointed lieutenant only five days before.[41] Additionally, the lieutenant's appointment with powers of jurisdiction and resources superior to those held by the wardens could lead to resentment since it amounted to 'the temporary eclipse of the warden altogether'.[42] Co-operation between lieutenant and warden depended on existing ties: as lieutenant from 1574 to 1578, Angus, who was uncle to Scott of Branxholme, was unlikely to have garnered much support from the warden, Ker of Cessford, though he would have had more luck with Douglas of Bonjedburgh, whom regent Morton had appointed warden of the west side of the Middle March from 1576 to 1578.

[37] Sir Walter Scott of Branxholme, subsequently Buccleuch (c.1565–1611).
[38] RPC ii. 572–3, 613, 678–9.
[39] RPC iv. 84–5, 111, 124, 146, 156–7, 271.
[40] RPC v. 464, 466; vi. 76, 467–6; CSP Scot. xiii/1, no. 170; Rae, Administration, appendix 6 at pp. 265–71.
[41] RPC iv. 156–7, 157–8.
[42] Rae, Administration, 111.

In contrast, the permanent appointments of the wardens were perhaps of more significance in the long-term imposition of justice. The role of warden had evolved into the policing of the Borders, with particular responsibility for liaising with the warden of the opposite English march. By this period, the warden normally received the powers of justiciar with his commission and this enabled him to try the four pleas of the crown.[43] In the Middle March the wardens were all resident, and, in the sixteenth century, the wardenship was held almost exclusively by the Kers of Cessford. Like the lieutenancy and the sheriffdom, the wardenship was dependent on the support of local networks of allegiance. Unusually, it was granted by regent Arran to Scott of Branxholme in 1550, following Cessford's brief dismissal for treating with the English during the Rough Wooing. Branxholme's commission committed him to answer for his affiliates to both 'Scottis and Inglis, and to mak redres for thame at dayis meting on the bordouris' with the English wardens.[44] This recognised that his kinsmen, allies and tenants lived within the bounds of the march and that he was answerable for them, but, similarly, it was understood that they would give him support there. Branxholme proved only a short-lived appointment being murdered by his Ker enemies in 1552. After a short time, while Mary de Guise attempted to find a replacement that was not of the Ker surname, Walter Ker of Cessford was re-appointed. The Cessfords then held the wardenship, with only two short interruptions, until it lapsed in 1603. Mary de Guise's failure to find an alternative speaks volumes about the necessity for the warden to have extensive local support: Branxholme left only a tiny grandson as heir, and there was no one else from the Scott surname at that time whose authority was sufficiently recognised in the march to be effective as warden. It was a similar picture in the other marches: in the East March the warden was usually from the great landholding Homes with their extensive networks of power through their large kindred; in the West it ricocheted between the rival families of Maxwells and Johstones, both large kindreds, and to one or the other of whom most inhabitants were allied.

The crown's dependence on the Cessfords' networks of power meant that there were few exceptions to them as warden. During his regency Morton attempted to regain some crown control over the office, in 1576 appointing his adherent Douglas of Bonjedburgh to the western half of the wardenry. Bonjedburgh did not survive the end of Morton's regency in 1578.[45] Factionalism at court again led, during the short-lived ascendancy of the earl of Arran, to the appointment, from November 1584, of Sir Thomas Ker of Ferniehirst for eight months. He, too, did not outlast his benefactor, being

---

[43] See ibid. 42–73 for details on the office of warden. In 1586 a statute declared that Cessford should not be burdened as warden 'with ony actioun criminale or civile ... saulffing in materis tuicheing redress of [border] attemptatis': *RPC* iv. 46.
[44] Fraser, *Buccleuch*, ii, no. 176.
[45] *CSP Scot.* v, nos 284, 315.

dismissed on Arran's fall.[46] From 1594 some recognition was given to the increasing power of Walter Scott of Buccleuch, following the forfeiture of the earl of Bothwell and Buccleuch's acquisition of his lands in Liddesdale. With this, he received the associated keepership of Liddesdale, and, subsequently, was considered effective warden of the west side of the Middle March. Sir William Bowes complained that Cessford could not answer for the whole of the march 'but must seeke' to two others he was at feud with, Buccleuch and Ferniehirst, for their parts.[47]

The wardenship was supposed to be a remunerated position, but the sums involved were small and not always paid.[48] After 1588 the payments to Cessford came from the newly erected barony of Roxburgh, and, after 1595, from the barony of Ernecleugh too.[49] This did not stop Cessford complaining in 1598 that he had never been compensated for his services. In 1600 he received a charter to the bailiary of Kelso, worth 650 merks a year, in recognition of his services.[50] The English wardens often noted the poverty of their counterparts, finding in it one of the main reasons for their ineffectiveness. In 1596 Lord Eure wrote that Cessford's 'meane estate of lyving' 'forces him to befriend his clan, overlook outrages, and support lawless men about him who serve him without charge'.[51] They had a point: almost without exception Cessford's deputies were of the Ker surname, and Robert, the future earl of Roxburgh, was deputy for his father William in 1590 and 1592.[52] Andrew Ker of Faldonside 'being a speciall man by whome [Cessford] is advised' appeared with him at a day of truce in 1583 and was his deputy in 1590.[53] In 1583 James Ker of Greenhead was Cessford's deputy and, between 1597 and 1602, Andrew Ker of Heiton and Andrew Ker of Greenhead were deputies for Robert, along with John Mowe of that ilk, a local laird, linked with the Ker family.[54] Most of these, including Robert, featured repeatedly in English complaints about cross-border raiding.

English wardens ascribed the ineffectiveness of their Scottish counterparts to their involvement in their adherents' disputes: they were 'extraordinarilye addicted to parcialities, favour of theire blood, tenantes and followers'.[55]

---

[46] RPC iii. 699; iv. 4; CSP Scot. viii, no. 80; NAS, GD40/2/9, fos 70, 75; GD40/2/11, fos 48, 49, 50.
[47] RPC v. 178; CBP ii, no. 171.
[48] For payments of wardens' salaries see Rae, Administration, appendix 3 at pp. 250–3.
[49] RMS v, no. 1521; vi, no. 318.
[50] Roxburgh papers, NRAS, NRAS1100/728.
[51] CBP ii, no. 410.
[52] CBP i, nos 736, 750.
[53] Ker of Faldonside was married to the earl of Arran's sister and advised Cessford to join with Arran in 1583, advice Cessford clearly ignored, which led to his temporary replacement by Ferniehirst: CBP i, nos 90, 190, 659.
[54] CBP i, no. 245; ii, no. 1382; RPC vi. 440–1.
[55] CBP ii, no. 323. This was hypocritical given that the English wardens were also involved in feuding. In 1596 Lord Eure, for a short time Middle March warden, complained that he

The principal feud to affect the wardenry was that between the Cessford wardens and the Scotts of Branxholme, and their alliances. Cessford was also compromised by his feud with the Kers of Fernichirst. In 1590 Sir Andrew Ker of Ferniehirst, and his allies Thomas Ker of Cavers and Robert, brother of the late William Ker of Ancrum (who had been murdered by Robert Ker of Cessford), were granted exemption from Cessford's warden court.[56] In 1584, whilst warden, Ker of Ferniehirst received some guidance from Arran that since 'thair may be many greit exemptiounis' as a result of 'that bipast affection to his hienes present rebellis', he should convict offenders on 'sum furthir pruif'. It was clearly felt necessary for extra measures to be taken to ensure support for Ferniehirst's wardenship: his allies Branxholme, the Rutherfords of Hundalee, Edgerston and Hunthill and William Douglas of Cavers subscribed a bond to assist him in his office.[57] The networks of alliance that supported any warden in office could simultaneously prove an impediment.

The influence of court factionalism, and local alliances, was felt too in the other border-specific office, that of the keepership of Liddesdale. Though Liddesdale was technically part of the Middle March, its keeper held the same powers of jurisdiction there as the warden did elsewhere and he was not subordinate to Cessford. Sometimes the keepership and the wardenship were held by the same person, but always with separate commissions. The lordship of Liddesdale was held by the earl of Bothwell until his forfeiture in 1594, when it passed to Scott of Buccleuch. The keepership and the lordship, however, did not necessarily go together. But, as the crown was to recognise, in the same way as wardens relied on their networks of authority, so could the keepers. Prior to 1573, keepers appointed from outside the region and lacking local alliances or landholding were generally short-lived and deemed ineffective. In 1574, as part of regent Morton's initiative in the Borders, John Carmichael of that ilk was appointed, until 1581, and the demise of his patron.[58] Ostensibly, Carmichael was an outsider and might have been expected to fail. However, he was married to Margaret Douglas, Morton's sister, and commanded considerable support both from central government and from the Douglas and Scott affinities in the Middle March. With the passing of Morton, Ker of Cessford's position recovered and he was appointed keeper conjointly with his wardenship from 1581 to 1583. Ker of Ferniehirst held the keepership similarly conjoined during his brief period in the sun from 1584 to 1585.[59] Subsequently Bothwell was keeper intermittently, based on his ownership of the lordship of Liddesdale, until

---

had 'so many such ennimies' amongst the Carey, Widdrington and Forster faction: *CBP* ii, nos 432, 441.
[56] NAS, GD40/2/11, fo. 56.
[57] NAS, GD40/2/9, fos 69, 72.
[58] *RPC* iii. 47, 344; *CSP Scot.* iv, no. 788; Rae, *Administration*, 240.
[59] *RMS* iv, no. 2570; *RPC* iii. 344–8, 574, 699; *CBP* i, no. 103.

his rebellion in 1591.[60] Over the next three years, as court favour swirled, the keeper was Buccleuch, then Cessford, then Lennox with Ferniehirst as his deputy, and then Cessford again.[61]

In 1594, however, Liddesdale and its keepership were resigned by Lennox on an hereditary basis to Buccleuch, a dubious honour for which Buccleuch apparently paid 2,500 merks.[62] The grant recognised that Buccleuch was the surname leader with the most authority in the region; his surname's vast landholdings lay at the northern head of the valley.[63] Buccleuch strengthened the authority that his landholdings gave him in Liddesdale by getting his Armstrong and Elliot tenants there to subscribe bonds promising to be answerable to him for the redress of any offences.[64] This meant that he could be effective, if he chose. A letter of indemnity to Buccleuch in 1608 lauded him as a 'man of energy, prompt in cousel and action, powerful in fortune, force, arms and following … in punishing malefactors and refractory and rebellious persons'.[65] Buccleuch also had the support of his large Scott kinship to act as his deputies in Liddesdale: Walter Scott of Goldielands and Robert Scott of Haining did so before 1603; Robert Scott was captain of Hermitage castle in 1599, when he witnessed a number of bands by the men of Liddesdale to Buccleuch.[66]

The English wardens found the status of the keeper difficult to understand, equating it more with the keeperships of Tynedale and Redesdale, which were subordinate to the authority of the English warden. This meant that they were unsure with whom to deal for effective redress when offences were committed by men of Liddesdale.[67] In 1596 Eure complained that he could not get any redress from Buccleuch for Liddesdale for most of its inhabitants were joined with him 'by oath and scripte'.[68] Buccleuch himself was clearly implicated in a number of cross-border raids, particularly into Lord Scrope's West March, and was described by Scrope as 'the chief enemy … to the quiet of the border'.[69] The most notorious of these exploits was his release, in 1596, from Carlisle castle of Kinmont Willie, an Armstrong and tenant in Liddesdale for whom Buccleuch was responsible. It may have been a convenient way to satisfy his country's honour, and an enjoyable snipe at his foe, but for Buccleuch it was important that he should be seen to be protecting his adherents. It did his image a world of good, the 'honour-

---

[60] *RPC* iv. 197–8, 432; *CSP Scot.* ix, no. 436. R. G. Macpherson, 'Francis Stewart, fifth earl Bothwell, c.1562–1612', unpubl. PhD diss. Edinburgh 1998, 238–46.
[61] *RPC* iv. 649, 668; *CSP Scot* x, nos 581, 623, 640, 652, 695, 765, 779; xi, no. 157.
[62] *RPC* v. 178; Fraser, *Buccleuch*, i. 174–5, 178; ii, no. 211.
[63] See map 3.
[64] Fraser, *Buccleuch*, i. 227–9; ii, nos 216, 217; NAS, GD224/906/5.
[65] Fraser, *Buccleuch*, i. 230–2.
[66] *RPC* vi. 179; NAS, GD224/906/5.
[67] Rae, *Administration*, 36.
[68] *CBP* ii, no. 232.
[69] *CBP* ii, no. 253.

ability' that Braddick identifies as a necessity for English office-holders here being upheld. These obligations were, however, seen by the English as detrimental constraints on his office.[70] James, however, did not seem to find much problem with this situation until around 1597 when increasing concern over his still-unconfirmed succession to Elizabeth's throne prompted a change in his attitude to the region.

James's fears, however, proved unfounded, with, in 1603, his peaceful accession to the English crown. In theory, this removed the international nature of the frontier that had necessitated the extra layer of border-specific officialdom. The office of warden lapsed, but the administration of the new Middle Shires continued to include additional officials, with the creation of other border-specific institutions to prosecute James's now permanent intolerance of crime there. The people employed, however, came from those families that had traditionally been involved in governing the region: this was not surprising since the 'strang hand' needed of any official, let alone one who was meant to root out all violent perpetrators of crime, still rested in the authority that they held through their networks of alliance and power. But there were added advantages to border-related office after 1603, most obviously that it was more directly remunerative in terms of substantial fees and, eventually, titles. Crucially, also, it gave its officials the patronage of further offices to dispense to their adherents within the judicial framework of the Middle March: this provided the patron with the manpower and co-operation that he needed to fulfill his onerous duties, whilst simultaneously rewarding that support. And, finally, the lieutenant and commissioners of the Middle Shires appear to have been more tightly controlled by, accountable to and in communication with, the council in Edinburgh, than the wardens had been. This in itself was a reflection of James's new determination to suppress crime there but it also allowed those borderers who were allied to the new officials increased access to the highest levels of power in Scotland. This was to the mutual benefit of all those included in such networks and to the crown. Those, such as the Armstrongs, who did not heed the warning signs of the late 1590s, were not so happy.

The continuation of disorder in the marches was most frequently attributed to the lack of a paid armed force to maintain the impetus of judicial raids.[71] One of the first measures taken in the pacification from 1605 was the creation of a border guard with twenty-five horsemen under the captaincy of Sir William Cranstoun. Cranstoun was to be paid one hundred merks a month, his horsemen forty merks each.[72] It was a difficult job, which involved liaising with both Scottish and English commissioners, who were not always in agreement, and covered the entire Scottish Borders. In 1606 Cranstoun tartly told the English commissioners that 'If you will needs be commanders,

---

[70] CBP ii, nos 237, 252; Braddick, 'Administrative performance', 172, 185–6.
[71] The formation of one under Angus in 1586–7 was short-lived: RPC iv. 111.
[72] RPC vii. 704.

I desire that your discretion may appear as well as your authority. Think not that my body can be everywhere to do all your services [in apprehending miscreants north of the border].'[73] His enthusiasm for the job is reflected in the numerous indemnities that he received, such as one, in 1609, where the king recognised his 'verie good and acceptable service' having 'exponit himself to mony perrillis and hazertis' and 'incurrit the malice of sic as haittis oure peace'. A commission in 1611 lauded his 'singular wisdom, forsight and dexteritie'.[74]

Cranstoun was a minor laird, the son of Cranstoun of Morriston, but had married Sara, the heiress of John Cranstoun of that ilk, from whom he appears to have inherited the designation. Cranstoun was tied into the kinship networks of the Middle March: Sara Cranstoun's sister Margaret was married to Sir James Douglas of Cavers, sheriff of Roxburghshire, and in 1616 his son John married Elizabeth Scott, daughter of Walter Lord Buccleuch.[75] This brought him the support of one of the principal local administrators and the connections of the powerful Scott surname, whilst his deputies were mostly of his own name, including his sons John and James, his brother Alexander of Morriston, and another two John Cranstouns.[76] The rewards associated with the captaincy were not merely monetary. In 1609 William was created Lord Cranstoun of Crailing and, in 1610, James granted him the lands, fortalice (presumably a fortified tower), manor and fishings of Langholme, recently forfeited by Lord Maxwell, and now erected into the free barony of Langholme. More lands followed in Esk, Wauchopedale, Roxburghshire and Lauderdale.[77] This would have brought him the power associated with landholding in the heartlands of his jurisdiction to buttress the authority that he held through his captaincy. His success was recognised by additional office: in 1608, being known as 'affectionat to his Majesties service', he was appointed provost of Annan in place of Lord Maxwell and, in 1610, he was made a JP for Roxburghshire; on the earl of Dunbar's death in 1611 he replaced him as lieutenant of the whole Middle Shires.[78] Later in 1611 he was joined by Elibank and two others in a reconstituted commission of the Middle Shires with an annual fee of £500, to which he was reappointed in 1613 and 1618. Most significantly he was admitted to the privy council in August 1611 on which he served until at least 1624.[79] Cranstoun epitomised the way in which local authority and influence at a national level could be combined in one person to his own benefit and to

---

[73] HMC, *Muncaster*, 250–1.
[74] RPC vii. 286–7; viii. 37–8, 278; ix. 129.
[75] Dalrymple (earls of Stair) papers, NAS, GD135/1028; RMS vii, no. 25.
[76] RPC viii. 279, 420; ix. 1–2, 40–2, 155, 166, 305–6; NAS, GD40/7/29.
[77] RMS, vii, nos 169, 214, 217, 223, 659; RPC viii. 471.
[78] RPC viii. 36–7; ix. 75–6, 129, 244.
[79] RMS vii, no. 505; RPC ix. 244; x. 164; xi. 345; xiii. 552

that of the crown. Cranstoun could effect crown policy in the Middle March whilst the crown underwrote his authority in his locality.

Following his admission to the council, Cranstoun resigned his captaincy to Sir Robert Ker of Ancrum, who had been nominated by James. Ancrum, it was said, was known for his 'sufficiency and mony worthie pairtis', which would enable him to fulfill his office. His 'sufficiency' was based on his status as an important laird near Jedburgh, who could also rely on the support of those in his kinship, in particular the neighbouring Kers of Ferniehirst. By 1611 he had the bonus of the blossoming favour in which his cousin, Robert Ker, future earl of Somerset, was held. He was well remunerated and had the additional patronage brought by a subsequent increase in the numbers of the guard to forty.[80] In turn, this enabled him to be more effective. In 1613 Ker of Ancrum nominated in his place Ker of Oxnam, Ferniehirst's heir, Somerset's nephew, and his cousin. Ancrum appears to have held the captaincy of the king's guard too for, in April 1614, Oxnam replaced him in this as well.[81] The captaincy of both the king's and border guards was combined from then on: in 1618 Oxnam received another commission as captain of the guard in Scotland. Oxnam remained captain until the guard's disbandment in 1621, James feeling that 'oure kingdome is reduceit to suche quietnes as thair is no necessitie ane ordinarie Gaird within the same'.[82] Oxnam seems to have been extremely active, receiving a number of indemnities, including one which conveniently excused him and his father for the slaughter of various Turnbulls in the years before his captaincy.[83] Like Cranstoun, he was admitted to the council, becoming a formidable figure in the Borders and a physical link between central and local administration.

Rewards for his service came not only with further office but were also monetary: in 1613 Oxnam was granted the keepership of the castle of Dumfries; in 1618 he was granted a pension of £200 sterling; and in 1622 the privy council was moved to continue his pension for his lifetime, commending his 'singulair wisdome, foirsight, courage and dexteritie' and for accepting the disbandment of the guard with a 'most submissive maner'. He clearly knew how to play the game.[84] Oxnam had a lieutenant, who, in 1615, was William Ker of Grange and, in 1619, William Scott of Harden. All his deputies came from the alliance between the Scott, Ker of Ferniehirst (not Cessford) and Murray surnames.[85] For all his power in the region and on the council, however, success in all arbitrations was not guaranteed: in 1619 he

---

[80] RPC ix. 244–5, 248, 289–90
[81] RPC x. 176, 184, 231.
[82] NAS, GD40/7/35; RPC xii. 582–4. Goodare notes that 'in effect the Border guard was transformed into a new "king's guard"'. However, the guard was still being called the 'Gaird upoun the Bordouris' and 'Border Garrison' in 1617: *State and society*, 150; RPC xi. 217.
[83] NAS, GD40/7/31.
[84] NAS, GD40/7/30, 36; RPC xii. 657–60.
[85] NAS, GD40/13/43; RPC xi. 546–7.

lost an action against an alleged 120 men raiding the turfs on his moor at Oxnam.[86] Unlike Cranstoun and Ancrum, fears over Oxnam being too busy as captain of the border guard did not seem to preclude, in 1613, his admission to the council and appointment as commissioner of the Middle Shires.[87] Arguably, the concentration of several offices within one man underlined his authority, coordinated action and more directly linked the fulfillment of policy in the Borders with its creation in Edinburgh and London.

The office of march warden lapsed with the union of 1603,[88] but the opportunistic cross-border raiding of the 'Ill week' showed James the necessity of maintaining an overseer in the Borders. Lord Home was appointed lieutenant over all three Scottish marches in July 1603, with Sir William Cranstoun as his deputy.[89] By 1604, against the background of failed union negotiations, this was felt to be insufficient permanently to suppress offenders and, in March 1605, the council announced the creation of the commission of justiciary for the Middle Shires. Five commissioners were appointed with 'full power to hold courts of justiciary in the said shires for the trial and punishment of offenders', and with immunity for any 'mischance or inconvenient' in execution of their commission. A similar commission was created in England, but neither had jurisdiction on the other side of the border. The Scottish commissioners were to have the assistance of the border guard and the sheriffs. In November 1605 their powers of justiciary were extended to allow them to act individually and also to impose fines, for which they were accountable to the Exchequer, in addition to warding offenders. They were accountable directly to the council and were supposed to submit a report on their proceedings every two months: whilst this was over-hopeful, there was evidence of much contact, the commissioners asking the council for advice on specific cases. Appointments were not made for a fixed term, but were occasionally renewed. All the initial five Scottish commissioners continued in office for some time through the various permutations of the commission: four of the five were appointed to the conjunct commission of 1618. Whilst their powers were similar to those of the wardens, the commissioners' jurisdictions were not confined to one march and covered the whole Scottish Borders. Significantly, the assistance of a standing guard meant that the commissioners could maintain their effectiveness over a prolonged period, whilst an annual payment of £500 each encouraged their commitment. Both the guard, and the compensation, may have reduced their dependence on the unpaid support that, previously, had been felt to compromise the wardens.[90]

---

[86] RPC xii. 21.
[87] RPC x. 164, 170–1, 200.
[88] As each appointment as warden was by commission, and not a statutory office, it did not have to be formally abolished, merely not reissued.
[89] RPC vi. 833–4; vii. 19.
[90] RPC vii. 701–4, 714–17, 717–20; viii. 15–16; ix. 287; xi. 345.

For all that these appointments demonstrated a newly coordinated approach to the Borders, almost all the commissioners originated or had very strong connections there: those that were the 'most meit and able to execute the charge comittit unto thame' and 'quhais former behaviour and actionis assures us of thair fidelitie and eirnest affectioun'. They were tied into existing networks of kinship and alliance in the region, with proof of co-operative service prior to 1605. They included Gideon Murray of Elibank, who became one of the longest serving.[91] Success in the Borders brought further advancement: in 1610 Elibank was admitted to the privy council and was named a JP for Selkirkshire. In 1611 he was appointed to a reconstituted commission along with the now ennobled Cranstoun, holding three justiciary courts at Jedburgh that year.[92] In 1612 he was made deputy treasurer and in 1617 his heavy workload was recognised when his nephew, Sir John Murray of Philiphaugh, replaced him as commissioner. The support of the local kinship networks of the Murrays of Philiphaugh and Blackbarony and of the Scotts of Buccleuch provided him both with manpower and the status in the locality to effect command.[93] His allies benefited from his protection and access to the privy council: in 1606 he petitioned the council in a case against Andrew Scott at 'the ernest sute of ... young Buccleuch, with sindry utheris of the name of Scott, upoun particular promissis of grit offices in the advancement of this our service, and the presenting of sum to justice mair notorious'.[94] And he does appear to have had the cooperation of Buccleuch, who himself, in 1608, received an approbation for his services in the Borders.[95]

In December 1606 James VI wrote to his commissioners that 'we do not find so good success of your proceedings as we expected ... We have therefore appointed the earl of Dunbar, who is a councillor in both our kingdoms and likely to be often at Berwick, to resolve any difficulties that may arise in the execution of your service'. As the senior commissioner he was to hold 'supreme authority in all matters requiring dispatch ... with power to apprehend outlaws and put any of them to trial and execution' and jurisdiction on both sides of the border, the only official ever to do so.[96] Dunbar was the recently ennobled George Home of Spott, a long-time servant of James's and since 1601 treasurer of Scotland. From 1603 to 1606 he was also chancellor of the exchequer in London. His devotion to James and tirelessness in his service enabled him to fulfill his offices in both countries. He had been active in the Borders from at least August 1605 when he was involved with a justice court held by the commissioners at Hawick. In May 1606 he directed

---

[91] RPC vii. 702.
[92] RPC ix. 54, 75–6, 194–6, 705, 708; x. 331.
[93] RPC ix. 504; xi. 11. Elibank's sister Agnes was Philiphaugh's mother.
[94] RPC vii. 714–17.
[95] RPC viii. 205; RMS vi, no. 2165.
[96] HMC, *Muncaster*, 266–7; HMC, *Salisbury*, xviii. 371.

a search for fugitive Grahams on both sides of the border and held a justice court at Peebles that August. He remained the supreme commissioner until his premature death from illness in 1611.[97]

Dunbar was, in many ways, ideally placed for such a commission: he was a member of the extensive Home kindred in the East March, and had been granted the lands of Greenlaw, Redpath, Foulden and Lochend in Berwickshire and in Northumberland at Norham.[98] This meant that his self-interest tallied with that of the government in the region. Crucially he had the ear of both James and the earl of Salisbury, conducting an intimate correspondence with the latter. In August 1607 he was given renewed powers of justiciary in the Middle Shires. This, combined with his other duties, which included quelling recalcitrant Presbyterians at the General Assembly, must have kept him away from the Borders for considerable periods.[99] When he was there, however, he made his mark, repeated reports of his success and severity going south.[100] He was well rewarded for his efforts: in 1606 his lands with the castle of Dunbar were erected into the free barony of Dunbar and, in 1610, he was granted lands worth £350 rent annually, £3,000 in money and bonds for £6,000. Dunbar's passing was acknowledged by the council, who thanked him posthumously for reducing the Borders to a 'wounderfull obedience' and to 'ane perfyte and setle peace'.[101]

This assessment of the Borders was premature for later, in 1611, a new commission of the Middle Shires was appointed. Its commissioners had the 'sufficiencie, knawlege, and experience in punishing of vice and the committaris thairof, and of thair willingnes to sie justice florishe'. This description certainly applied to Elibank and Cranstoun.[102] With the addition of Ker of Oxnam in 1613, Cranstoun and Elibank remained commissioners until at least 1617, concurrently with being privy councillors and JPs in their shires. All three had significant support in the Middle March from their kinships and alliance and Murray of Philiphaugh, Elibank's kinsman and replacement in 1617, was no different. He was also a JP and sheriff of Selkirkshire. This combination of office coordinated their efforts in the pacification, reinforced their powers of jurisdiction and facilitated lines of communication.[103]

---

[97] HMC, *Salisbury*, xvii. 410; xviii. 368–71; HMC, *Muncaster*, 255, 260. For Dunbar's career see J. Sizer, 'The good of this service consists in absolute secrecy: the earl of Dunbar, Scotland and the Border (1603–1611)', *Canadian Journal of History* xxxvi (2001), 229–57 at p. 233; M. Lee, *Government by pen: Scotland under James VI and I*, Urbana 1980, 61–111; and N. Cuddy, 'Anglo-Scottish Union and the court of James I, 1603–1625', *Transactions of the Royal Historical Society* 5th ser. xxxix (1989), 107–24 at pp. 108–10, 115, 118.
[98] HMC, *Salisbury*, xvi. 78.
[99] Ibid. xix. 31, 164, 247, 254, 320, 350; RPC vii. 728–9.
[100] RPC viii. 37–8.
[101] RMS vi, no. 1773; HMC, *Salisbury*, xxi. 212; RPC ix. 129.
[102] RPC ix. 194.
[103] RPC x. 164, 170, 176, 200; xi. 11.

Renewal of central government concern over the Borders amid reports of the resumption of disturbance following James VI's journey north in 1617, led to the formation of the rather different 'conjunct commission' of 1618.[104] This unwieldy body of thirty commissioners each, from Scotland and England, was an attempt to widen the participation in the pacification of local figures: most of the commissioners already held office as JP or sheriff in the Middle Shires. In many ways it reflected a judicial framework already in place in the borders: from the Middle March, in addition to Cranstoun, Oxnam and Elibank, it included the earl of Roxburgh, Lords Buccleuch and Yester, the sheriff Douglas of Cavers, Sir John Ker of Jedburgh, Douglas apparent of Bonjedburgh and Sir Robert Stewart of Shillinglaw, Traquair's heir. Most of these had the previous September appeared before the privy council to swear responsibility for their adherents under the terms of the general band of 1602.[105] The council was continuing to use the traditional accountability for their adherents of an enduring group of Middle March surname leaders, alongside granting these leaders new powers as commissioners. In 1619 some of the commissioners were ordered to list 'all idill personis, maisterles men, and vagaboundis' in their localities: Yester and Shillinglaw were to be responsible for Tweeddale, the Douglases of Cavers and Bonjedburgh for Jedburgh Forest, Buccleuch for Liddesdale and Eskdale and Roxburgh, Cranstoun, Oxnam and Cavers for Teviotdale. The structure of authority in the march had changed little.[106]

Despite disbanding the guard in 1621, the council was faced with calls for its revival following the reported increase in theft in Annandale, Eskdale and Ewesdale.[107] On the advice of the resident elite there, it was decided to appoint a triumvirate of persons of 'power and friendship' within the Middle Shires to 'have oversight of all these schyris ... [to] procure the assured peace'. The triumvirate consisted of the earl of Buccleuch, the Maxwell earl of Nithsdale, and John Murray of Lochmaben, subsequently earl of Annandale. They were to nominate ten men to act under them.[108] Buccleuch, a man with a 'strang hand' in the troublesome dales, predictably formed his list of deputies from his surname and allied tenants. Subsequently, he felt the need to nominate a further six since 'the chairge is so spatious and wyid as hardlie can the ten persones gevin up be him discharge that poynt of dewtie'. They included his tenants, the Armstrongs of Whithaugh and Kinmont and an Elliot.[109] It was characteristic of the way in which pacification had been undertaken that the names of Whithaugh and Kinmont, synonymous with cross-border raiding before Union, were now deputies in the suppression

[104] *RPC* xi. 291, 344–8, 386–7.
[105] *RPC* xi. 218, 225–7.
[106] *RPC* xii. 149–51, 219–22.
[107] *RPC* xii. 583–4, 775; Goodare, *State and society*, 131–2, 150.
[108] *RPC* xii. 672–9.
[109] *RPC* xii. 695–6; xiii. 17–18.

of such activity: the poachers turned gamekeepers. Concern, however, over engrained habits prompted the exemption of the Johnstones of that ilk and Westraw from the jurisdiction of the triumvirate due to the presence on it of their former Maxwell enemy, since 'the hairtburning betuix thair frendis and followeris is not yit fullie extinguishit'.[110] By this point the 1618 conjunct commission seems to have disappeared.[111] However, most of the commissioners of 1613 remained in place, in a subordinate role in support of the triumvirate. In July 1624 Lord Yester and Sir John Stewart of Traquair were added to the triumvirate being found advantageously resident and, in 1625, the earl of Angus and Yester were adjoined to what appears to have been a renewed commission for the triumvirate to Buccleuch, Nithsdale and Annandale.[112]

The crown was continuing to use the surname leaders, and lairds, several now ennobled, and their affiliates to effect the pacification. Simultaneously, the commissioners' offices gave them both status in the locality and also access to central government through their direct accountability to the privy council. For Elibank, Oxnam and Cranstoun their co-operation with the crown led to their inclusion in the highest levels of government, tightening the connections between the local administration and Edinburgh.

III

The offices of warden, lieutenant, keeper and commissioner were all specific to the region. However, as elsewhere in Scotland, the distribution of power there associated with landholding, kinship and alliance, affected elective offices too. For instance, any local alliance between surnames was reflected in those appointed to office in the local burghs. Evidence of this lies in the names of local officials in Jedburgh, Selkirk, Peebles and Hawick. Whilst ostensibly these were elected by the burgesses, their names indicate links with families living outside the town but holding lands in its vicinity. The provostship reflected the status of both the man himself and also the strength of his connections. In Jedburgh, the Rutherfords often appear as provost. They were closely related to the Rutherfords of Hunthill and Hundalee who held lands just outside Jedburgh and were allied with the local Kers of Ferniehirst and the Douglases of Cavers.[113] Similarly, in Selkirk, the Scotts of Haining traditionally held the post of provost; they held lands just outside

---

[110] RPC xii. 673–5.
[111] Watts notes the resurrection of the English side of the 'virtually defunct' commission in 1619 which continued functioning until around 1624. No superior commission, such as the triumvirate, was appointed in England: *From Border to Middle Shire*, 200–1.
[112] RPC xiii. 68–9, 542–3, 553; xiv. 677–92; 2nd ser. i. 193.
[113] Rutherfords were listed in 1552, from 1569 to 1581, and in 1592, whilst Mr John Rutherford, was provost in the early 1600s: *RMS* vi, no. 1803; *RPC* iii. 368, 600; v. 13.

Selkirk, but also had the ownership of the mill there and tenements within the burgh. Robert Scott of Haining was provost during the 1590s and again in 1614, despite a dispute with the burgh. The Hainings were allied to the Scotts of Branxholme, major landholders in Selkirkshire, Haining acting as Branxholme's deputy in the 1590s. Branxholme also occasionally appeared as provost, and, in 1598, Haining, was listed as deputy provost.[114] Unsurprisingly, the names of the bailies also reflected the influence of the local surnames: in 1608 a James Scott was bailie in Selkirk and another James Scott was bailie in Hawick.[115] A provost's authority could be augmented by additional office, sometimes temporary, such as sheriff depute, which was usually thanks to his alliance: thus from 1610 until at least 1615 Mr John Rutherford often acted for Cavers as sheriff depute of Roxburghshire.[116] Haining's authority was further substantiated when he acted for the Scott surname on behalf of Buccleuch during his absence in the early 1600s. Haining received commissions as sheriff *in hac parte* to deal with specific matters, as in 1604 when he granted sasine to James Veitch of lands in Ettrick Forest, in Selkirkshire.[117]

The situation was slightly different in Peebles, where the sheriffs, the Hays of Yester, were provosts in the burgh too in the 1570s. A convention of estates in 1590 protested against crown endorsement of nobles in burgh office and Yester stepped down, but the Hays retained their influence as councillors. They did not treat this office as a nominal position, appearing at the burgh head courts in the tolbooth, and using it to intervene in Peebles's affairs. This was not necessarily to the detriment of the burgh since they repeatedly lobbied on its behalf at central courts.[118] There were bailies to carry out the day-to-day work of burgh officials. Burgesses included kinsmen of the surnames holding lands near the burgh, the Veitchs, Tweedies and Horsburghs. Gilbert Tweedie was burgh treasurer in 1575 when he witnessed a sasine with his kinsmen, Alex Tweedie of Dreva and Walter Tweedie, reader at Broughton.[119] After the Yesters, the bailies took over the provostship, probably helped by the legislation of 1609 inhibiting nobles from holding local office. These bailies had additional authority as the burgh's representatives at parliament.[120]

---

[114] BA, WM3/21; 4/20/1; 11/61, 79; 12/7, 65, 88; RPC v. 450; x. 793; BA, SC/S/12/33/1; Symms, 'Social control', 66.
[115] RPC v. 450; vii. 669–70; BA, WM3/12.
[116] NAS, SC62/2/6–7; RPC xi. 156.
[117] NRAS482/31, fo.10; RPC vi. 372–3.
[118] Keith Brown notes that 'many burghs were content with the security a powerful local lord could guarantee them': 'Burghs, lords and feuds in Jacobean Scotland', in M. Lynch (ed.), *The early modern town in Scotland*, London 1987, 102–24 at p. 103; M. Lynch, 'Introduction', and 'The crown and the burghs', in Lynch, *Early modern town*, 1–35 at pp. 20–1, 55–80 at pp. 64, 65; *Peebles charters*, 329–30, 345, 356.
[119] *Yester House writs*, 218.
[120] *Peebles charters*, 342, 361, 364; RPC x. 686; xi. 156; xii. 352.

But for all the legislation to protect the independence of burgesses from external influences, it continued to be difficult to hold office without the support of the local landholders. Where burghs did try to elect their own officials in the face of opposition from outside the town, conflict occurred. This was particularly the case in Jedburgh, surrounded as it was by the lands of the Kers of Ferniehirst and Cessford and the Rutherfords of Hunthill.[121] Throughout the period, the provostship was under pressure from all three powerful families, difficulties that were exacerbated by the feud between the Cessfords and the Ferniehirsts. In 1581 Ferniehirst was briefly made provost, which antagonised Cessford, and in 1590 the burgesses elected a Rutherford, a Ferniehirst ally, in defiance of a ruling by James VI in favour of Cessford.[122] In 1603 Sir Robert Ker of Ancrum was appointed provost: his family was at feud with Cessford over the murder of his kinsman, but he had the support of Sir Andrew Ker of Ferniehirst. The affair came to blows on the streets of Jedburgh, and at least one Ferniehirst kinsman was killed.[123] In 1617 the bailies and council of Jedburgh charged Ferniehirst to appear concerning complaints against him over a recent election of town magistrates.[124] In 1619, in an attempt to resolve this, James VI ordered that the provost of Jedburgh should be chosen with the advice of Ferniehirst and his son, Ker of Oxnam, an ordinance repeated in 1622. This decision reflected the enhancement of Ferniehirst's position following Oxnam's success as a privy councillor and captain of the border guard.[125] In many ways, however, James was merely recognising the structure of power in the locality.

IV

The socio-political structures formed by the surnames provided a framework for the exercise of power within the Middle March, as elsewhere. These structures were not, however, confined the public sphere, but existed also within the private jurisdictions associated with landholding in regalities and baronies, either within their own lands, or as bailies on behalf of lay or temporal superiors. Baron and regality courts dealt with all tenancy matters, could settle civil disputes and try cases of slaughter and theft: though some of these powers were assumed by the central court of session in this period, those with baron's jurisdiction, like Angus in his regality of Jedforest, or

---

[121] See map 3.
[122] CBP i, no. 111. Both Maureen Meikle and Keith Brown detail the intricacies of the friction: A British frontier?, 60–1; 'Burghs, lords and feuds', 108–9.
[123] NAS, GD40/13/34; GD40/2/11, fos 55, 56; RPC v. 273; Ancient criminal trials, ii/2, 378–81.
[124] NAS, GD40/13/47.
[125] NAS, GD40/13/39, 56.

Douglas of Drumlanrig in his Dumfriesshire lands, continued to assert these rights into the seventeenth century.[126]

The erection of baronies, which escalated in the later 1500s, as vigorously pursued in the Borders as elsewhere, was to give their owners these powers of jurisdiction within their consolidated landholdings.[127] Typical was that by Scott of Branxholme: in 1577 the lands at the heart of Buccleuch territory were described as the barony of Branxholme, to which were added lands in the lordship of Ettrick forest and the barony of Minto; in 1599 a *de novo* erection called Branxholme consolidated his older landholdings with his more recent acquisitions, in particular those resulting from the forfeiture of the earl of Bothwell.[128] Within these baronies some holders held the superior jurisdiction associated with burghs of barony. Such baronies erected in the Middle March in this period included those of Ker of Littledean, Pringle of Galashiels, Viscount Haddington, Murray of Darnhall and of Kelso, in 1614, for Lord Roxburgh.[129]

The power associated with private jurisdiction was jealously maintained and distributed only to those in the holder's alliance. In 1515 the earl of Angus appointed the Kers of Ferniehirst bailies in his large regality of Jedforest, near Jedburgh, an appointment which later became hereditary. The grant of the bailiary in itself acknowledged the *de facto* authority of the Ferniehirsts as significant landholders nearby.[130] However, by 1600, a dispute had arisen between the two families over the rights to hold bailie courts in Jedforest. From 1601 Angus repeatedly tried to use his rights of repledging cases before the sheriff court at Jedburgh to his regality court, including a failed attempt to get Ferniehirst brought under his jurisdiction. In 1612 the dispute escalated, Angus and Ferniehirst both making 'great convocation of the lieges in arms for holding courts at Lintellie in the Lordship of Jedburgh Forest', where 'both parties were resolved to hold the same'. Ferniehirst and his heir were temporarily warded but released following a letter from James to the council. Both parties were publicly reconciled during the council which decided in Angus's favour.[131]

If a landholder did not own a regality himself, then the next best thing was to be appointed a bailie of one. In the Middle March the Church, as a major landowner, with the abbacies of Dryburgh, Kelso, Jedburgh and

---

[126] *RPC* ix. 372–4; NLS, Denmilne, Adv. MS 33.1.1, vol. 10, fo. 112.
[127] *The burghs of Scotland: a critical list*, ed. G. S. Pryde, London 1965.
[128] NAS, GD224/479/1; GD224/918/12; *RMS* vi. 956.
[129] *Burghs of Scotland*, 61, 63, 64, 65.
[130] Papers relating to the regality courts of the earls of Angus including for Jedforest, 1579–1620: A. O. Curle and J. Curle papers, NAS, GD111/1/7; 40/7/1. Angus's regality of Jedforest was confirmed in a charter of 1602, held for one red rose: *RMS* vi, no. 1283.
[131] This dispute was despite the marriage between Ferniehirst's eldest son, Andrew of Oxnam, and Angus's daughter in 1600: NAS, GD111/1/26; *Ancient criminal trials*, ii/2, 378–81, 509–11. Angus had appeared with three or four hundred armed supporters: *RPC* ix. 372–4, 394, 398, 400; NAS, GD40/13/41.

Melrose, was happy to dispense these powers to a local. These bailiaries tended to become hereditary within a family that already held significant lands itself and was of a sufficient status for its authority as bailie to be recognised in the locality. For instance, the Kers of Ferniehirsts also held the bailiary of the neighbouring abbacy of Jedburgh from 1528, with power to hold courts within it, repledge cases and appoint deputies, for which they were paid £10 a year from the fermes of Newbigging. Following the Reformation, the abbacy passed into the hands of the Lords Home, but the Ferniehirsts' position as bailie was confirmed in 1616.[132] Similarly, the Scotts of Branxholme were made hereditary 'baillie principall' for the regality of the abbacy of Melrose in 1519. Branxholme was granted 'full and playne power' to hold courts within the regality's lands, to appoint officers such as clerks, and had 'justice to minister, trespassouris to pwynis, ward and dome to gif in' and the 'malis ... and otheris our deweteis' to lift. He swore that he and all his 'men and frendis' would obey all the abbot's commands. A charter of 1524 made clear the extensive lands involved, for not only were they around Melrose, but also at the heart of Buccleuch territory at Ettrickhead, Rodonoland and Eskdalemuir; in granting the bailiary, the abbot was recognising what was to some extent already in effect the case.[133]

It was a profitable arrangement: there were several instances of the Scotts receiving the tack of regality revenue, such as a grant in 1588 of the tack of teinds of the parishes, towns and kirks of Hassendean and Cavers by James, commendator of Melrose, to Scott of Buccleuch and his heirs for nineteen years.[134] Buccleuch was also able to distribute lands from the regality to his kindred. In 1615 he assented to a sasine for Scott of Thirlestane's son in Eskdalemuir.[135] Buccleuch did attend regality court sessions but usually had his nominated deputies to act for him. They were usually from his kindred. In 1568 this was Thomas Scott of Haining and, in 1608, a deputy bailie was Walter Chisholme of that ilk 'descendand from the said hous of Bukcleugh'.[136]

Buccleuch's bailiary powers were of advantage to his allies. In 1608 the council remitted an action by Murray of Elibank against a portioner at Blainslie in the regality to the bailie court there; fortuitously Elibank was a Scott affiliate. The occupiers of Blainslie protested against Elibank's advantage, claiming there could be 'na proces in respect of the consanguinate standing betuix ... Bukcleugh, and the said Sir Jedeane, beand full sister and brother bairnes, and also betuix the said Sir Jedeane and Walter Chisholme of that ilk, principall bailie deput'.[137] The court found in favour of Elibank

---

[132] NAS, GD40/7/4, 33.
[133] Fraser, *Buccleuch*, ii, nos 126, 127, 131; papal confirmation of bailiary in 1525, no. 132.
[134] NAS, GD224/930/43, fo. 2.
[135] Napier papers, NAS, GD430/208.
[136] RMS iv. 1819; *Regality of Melrose*, i, pp. xlix, 12, 32, 41.
[137] *Regality of Melrose*, i. 41.

and again in another against the occupiers of Elibank's lands at Langshaw.[138] When, in 1618, the regality of Melrose was included in the the barony of Binning granted to Thomas Hamilton, the future earl of Melrose, Elibank's lands at Langshaw were excluded from the new barony.[139] Buccleuch resigned the heritable bailiary in favour of the earl of Melrose in 1621, but reserved that office in his lands of Rodonoland, Ettrickhead and Eskdalemuir.[140]

As a result of the gradual alienation of church lands through feuing throughout the sixteenth century, prominent landholders such as the Scotts of Buccleuch and the Kers of Cessford and Ferniehirst had accumulated numerous tacks of teinds, feus of the lands associated with the parish kirks and thus influence over nomination to these parishes. Not only did the Branxholmes have the tack of the teinds of Hassindean and Cavers from Melrose, but also those, from 1553, of Lessudden from Dryburgh.[141] The advantages of connections between surnames was evident: in 1590, and again in 1603, William Scott the chanter of the Chapel Royal of Stirling granted the tack of the teinds of the parish of St Marie kirk of the Lowes (near Buccleuch) to Branxholme.[142] And, of course, Buccleuch pursued his rights of nomination to the kirks of Liddesdale, and in 1608 agreed the tack of the teinds of the parsonage of Hawick to his old friend, Elibank.[143]

Where valuable rights of nomination and the assignation of teinds were involved, inevitably there was dispute. The Ferniehirsts, for instance, claimed ownership of the teinds of the kirks of Innerleithen and Little Newton. In 1586 these teinds were claimed by the commendator of Melrose abbey, in which the parishes lay, and Ferniehirst and Rutherford of Hunthill were denounced rebel for armed interference with the teinds.[144] In 1596 Buccleuch, who had presumably controlled the teinds as bailie of Melrose, assigned the teinds of Innerleithen to Ferniehirst's heir, Ker of Oxnam, in settlement of a fatal brawl between Ferniehirst and Buccleuch adherents.[145] In 1602 Ferniehirst wrote to his son to ensure that their enemy Lord Roxburgh did not include these rights in the erection of his barony of Roxburgh. The dispute was still ongoing as late as 1616 when the council was charged to suspend a claim by Roxburgh on the teinds of Little Newton which would have been to the prejudice of Ferniehirst.[146]

The restructuring of the Church after the Reformation brought changes in its administration at a local level. From 1581 presbyteries were gradually established to oversee the parishes within their areas and were account-

---

[138] Ibid. i. 41–2, 56–7, 62–3; Sir William Fraser charters, NAS, GD86/379; 111/1/27.
[139] RMS vii, no. 1915.
[140] NAS, GD224/930/41, fo. 11; RPC xiii. 549.
[141] NAS, GD224/930/43, fo. 1.
[142] Ibid. fos 4, 8; GD224/930/38, fo. 15.
[143] RMS vii. 270; NAS, CH2/198/1, fo. 33; GD224/918/27, fos 4–5.
[144] RPC iv. 115.
[145] NAS, GD40/2/9, fo. 86.
[146] NAS, GD40/2/12, fos 4, 44.

able to regional synods.[147] Membership of a presbytery mostly consisted of the relevant local ministers. They were however subject to external pressures, both lay and of their ecclesiastical superiors. For instance, in Jedburgh, the minister, Mr John Abirnethie, was an ally of the Kers of Ancrum and Ferniehirst and, in 1607, Ferniehirst supported his nomination as constant moderator of the presbytery.[148] At Selkirk presbytery too, in 1607, there was resistance to interference in the nomination of the constant moderator: Lord Roxburgh appeared several times at its meetings between March and May 'charging the burcht be vertew of his commissioun to guid thereupoun' to admit his nominee Mr John Knox, minister of Melrose. Finally, in May, Archibald Ker clinched it for Roxburgh requiring the presbytery to admit Knox, as charged by the king, and the presbytery finally acquiesced.[149] Roxburgh's power over the presbytery had received James's backing: disobedient Presbyterians were not popular with the king.

The other major landholder in the region was the crown, and here too was a useful source of employment and power, through the crown's appointment of men to manage or protect its properties. The two most significant of these were Ettrick forest and the castle of Newark, which lay within it. Appointments to the posts of forest ranger or currours, bailie of the forest and the captaincy of Newark reflected the existing distribution of power amongst local families. Their status was reinforced by the offices' control of the tacks of the lands involved, the related jurisdiction and the patronage of the offices of their deputies. In the fifteenth century the Pringles, Homes and Murrays were currours in the Tweed and Yarrow wards of the forest whilst the Scotts had 'something of a stranglehold' in the Ettrick ward.[150] Craig Madden, tracing the amassing of lands within the forest by prominent locals, notes that they 'were attracted to these royal feus as a means of extending their territorial influence and prestige within their particular locality'. In 1514 Queen Margaret's grant of extensive lands to James Murray of Falahill included those of Philiphaugh, which was to become the centre of this branch's domain. In 1541 the Scotts held the feu of twenty-four and a half steadings in the forest, whilst ten were held by the Kers of Cessford, Linton, Greenhead and Ferniehirst.[151]

The Scotts of Branxholme, however, filched the juiciest plum when, in 1543, the crown appointed Branxholme to the captaincy of Newark castle 'with power to make deputes and constables'. This office was combined with the duties of bailie and chamberlain of the lordship of Ettrick Forest.[152]

---

[147] BUK ii. 482–7, 636. See chapter 1 above.
[148] Abirnethie was subsequently bishop of Caithness and was still asking for Ancrum's favour in 1623 over the bishopric of Moray: NAS, GD40/2/13, fos 1, 32.
[149] NAS, CH2/327/1, fos 3, 4, 5, 8.
[150] Gilbert, *Hunting and hunting reserves*, 136–9, 149.
[151] Madden, 'The feuing of Ettrick forest', 80, 82; Craig-Brown, *Selkirkshire*, 338.
[152] Fraser, *Buccleuch*, ii, no. 162.

Although it was not technically heritable, it seems that it was effectively so: Branxholme's grandson and heir Walter was confirmed in the captaincy and bailiary by Mary, Queen of Scots, in 1565 and by James VI in 1573, as was his son, Walter.[153] As bailie, Branxholme was granted full power to hold bailie and chamberlain courts, where he was to punish trespassors, and poind goods from offenders, and had the 'privilege and fredome of the said baillie and chalmerlane courttis, to ... replege' inhabitants of the forest from 'quhatsumeuier juge or jugeis, spirrituale or temporale'. This meant that he could, in theory, rescue his adherents, resident in the forest, from trial by another jurisdiction. As the queen's chamberlain there he was expected to arrange the collection of all duties; in return he was granted the duties from the lands of Carterhaugh, Whitilbra, Auldwark and Huntly. In 1595 Branxholme still had these mails of £120, 'assignit of auld to the keping of the said castell'.[154] Equally important, however, was the patronage that the office brought him. In 1592 James Scott of Newark was Branxholme's chamberlain there and, in 1617, when Buccleuch had the 'chief commandiement within the haill boundis of the cuntrey of the Forrest', Walter Scott of Harden and his son William were his chamberlain and bailies.[155] Buccleuch was able to reward adherents at the same time as staffing his offices, to his benefit and to that of his royal employer.

V

The English sneered at the dependency of the Scottish wardens on the support of their kindred and allegiances. They however underestimated the way in which government was able to use the obligations of kinship and alliance, and the manpower provided by adherents, to staff local administration and impose its will in the locality. Cessford's deputies in his wardenship were almost always Kers, whilst Buccleuch used Scotts in his offices in Liddesdale, Melrose and Newark. Furthermore, such prominent local figures could count on the support of those in their alliance: such were the links between the Kers of Ferniehirst and the Rutherford provosts of Jedburgh, and Buccleuch and the Murrays of Philiphaugh in Selkirkshire. The strengthening intrusion of central government, for instance through the appointment of JPs, might have been expected to undermine the significance of kinship and alliance in the framework of local authority. By the end of the seventeenth century this was probably the case: however in the early seventeenth century, in the Middle March, central government was still using largely traditional methods of imposing its policies. The new institutions or offices of govern-

---

[153] Ibid. ii, no. 191; NAS, GD224/890/10, fo. 20; *ER* xxiii. 63.
[154] Fraser, *Buccleuch*, ii, no. 162; *ER* xxiii. 63.
[155] Craig-Brown, *Selkirkshire*, 323; *RPC* v. 25; xi. 100.

ment, such as that of the JP, were developing alongside, and to some extent utilising, traditional frameworks of authority and reflected the existing *status quo* in the region. The rhetoric associated with kinship was certainly overblown; kinship may have been becoming less significant in the face of a government after control of judicial systems, but it still mattered.

This pattern of local office-holding in the Middle March differs somewhat from the dominance of the Homes over office that Meikle has found in the East March. At times, both the offices of East March warden and the sheriff of Berwickshire were held by the fifth and sixth Lords Home. They used their Home kinsmen to help them in their public offices and as bailies within their landholdings.[156] The existence of several kinships holding office in each shire of the Middle March meant that no one family came to dominate the march as a whole. Though the Kers of Cessford were (usually) wardens, they never held the sheriffdom of Roxburghshire in which the majority of their landholdings lay. The picture in the West March was more muddled: the wardenship was constantly in dispute, swapping hands repeatedly between the Maxwells, Johnstones, Herries and others. In contrast, in the Middle March, the continuity of the same kindreds and their allies in local offices demonstrated an underlying stability in the frameworks of authority there. Friction between the surnames could lead to dispute but, at the same time, the alliances of surnames acted as a counter-balance to any one surname's power.

This account of local office-holding in the Middle March has demonstrated the existence of a comprehensive framework of government in the locality. The individual shires of the march had the same institutions of local government as elsewhere in Scotland: furthermore, the position of the shires within the march meant that there was an additional superstructure of border-specific offices. As Julian Goodare notes, the nerve-endings of central government were exceedingly alive in this locality as a result of the 'over-government' of the Borders. The system of government in the Scottish Middle March was, perhaps, more cohesive and responsive to central government than was possible in the more confused situation in its English counterpart. The warden of the English Middle March suffered from the interference of the garrisons at Carlisle and Berwick and the outsiders brought in by the later Tudor governments. Mervyn James has illustrated how 'the agents of the government frequently showed a greed and aggressivity offensive to the northern communities'. Typical of these was Thomas, tenth Lord Scrope, warden of the English West March, whom Spence describes as an 'inexperienced outsider'.[157] Such a situation did not exist across the border in Scotland where local authority remained in the hands of the region's indigenous

---

[156] Meikle, *A British frontier?*, 62–3.
[157] Goodare, *State and society*, 257–8; James, *Society, politics and culture*, 3; Spence, 'Pacification', 69.

leading figures. As part of the process by which the Scottish crown was able to increase its control over local government, by including within government those whose authority it had harnessed, so the Scottish government was able to retain the service of its men in the Middle March.

4

Middle March Men in Central Government

In the latter part of the sixteenth century there was a movement towards more centralised control of the administration of justice. What was remarkable was the apparent lack of local resistance to the intensifying presence of the king's government. The crown had made the regional elites feel part of this evolving structure of government by including them within it, not only in their own regions but within government at its highest levels as well. This seems particularly true of the Middle March. This chapter looks at how figures from the region participated in the government of the kingdom, and how they themselves embodied the governmental connections between Edinburgh and the march. Traditionally, such men were used to being involved in government in Edinburgh in a representative or advisory capacity, in being called to account by the privy council and the admission of some to the council itself, as representatives to parliaments, or as allies of court factions, or as members of the royal household. A number of them owned townhouses in Edinburgh. As Julian Goodare observes, the participation of the political elite of the borderers in national politics was noticeable, even though it may have been less than that of the elite of the central Lowlands.[1] But these men were not merely operating at the 'centre' of government: they were providing a direct link between that centre and their 'localities', the regions in which they already held authority and continued to do so.

Political or court life was therefore not alien to the lairds of the Middle March. The march's proximity to Edinburgh, and the routes provided by the rivers of the Tweed basin, enabled relatively easy communication.[2] The West March was not so accessible, being significantly further from Edinburgh, with the hills separating Nithsdale, Annandale and Eskdale impeding communication across the region. Of the two main places used by the crown for musters or judicial courts in the Middle March, Peebles was only a day's ride, whilst Jedburgh was less than fifty miles from Edinburgh. In 1576 the council met in Edinburgh on 8 November and at Jedburgh four days later. A messenger sent on a round of the East and Middle March towns was paid virtually the same as one sent to St Andrews or Perth.[3] Whilst these lines of communication could be used by the crown aggressively on a judicial raid, they equally facilitated the lairds' involvement with central government.

---

[1] Goodare, *State and society*, 257–8.
[2] *See* map 1 above.
[3] TA xiii. 224.

And, as Maureen Meikle has also found, the lairds of the Eastern Borders embraced the political opportunities that this access gave them: in the 1590s, indeed, she notes a 'turnaround' where the lairds were increasingly becoming influential courtiers. This was due partly, she says, to a conscious decision by James to establish a 'safety net' of lairds, loyal to his service, but it also formed part of the more general inclusion of such figures throughout Scotland that the admission of the lairds to parliament in 1587 represented. Such inclusion substantiated the connections between central government and local administration: Goodare emphasises the crucial role that the nobility played in maintaining the links between the two, but it seems here that the lairds and kindred leaders of the Middle March were equally willing participants in James's evolving government.[4]

From 1603 the involvement of men from the Middle March became even more significant when James departed for London, leaving the privy council to carry out government in his name. Whilst the deluge of directives from London was to drive policy in Scotland, the Scottish council was able to resist unpopular or unworkable directives and was to continue to issue many of its own.[5] By effectively allowing the council some discretion, James avoided the alienation that the imposition of a vice-regal type figure might have caused, and retained the co-operation of the Scottish governing elite. James could look to Europe for similarly sensitive treatment of elites within the multiple kingdoms of the Iberian peninsula and the Polish-Lithuanian alliance, where a degree of self-government in the less powerful kingdom eased relations between the different regions of these unions: this could give, as J. H. Elliott concludes, 'the most arbitrary and artificial of unions a certain stability and resilience'. These more cordial relations were reversed when Philip IV of Spain's minister, Count Olivares, abruptly changed policy towards Portugal in the 1630s, seeking a greater degree of integration and conformity, which alienated some of the Portuguese elite, a weak background to the Portuguese revolt in 1640.[6] The appointment of those from the Middle March to central government, especially on the council, and within the royal household at Whitehall, secured their co-operation in their homelands, at the same time

---

[4] Meikle, *A British frontier?*, 53, 63–4, 279; *RPS*, 1587/7/143, accessed 24 June 2009; Goodare, *Government of Scotland*, 118.

[5] An instance of this was the council's carefully worded evasion of proposals for the transportation of offenders to the colonies in 1618: *RPC* xi. 291, 353–4. Goodare notes that 'there was still only one privy council. Not only did it not move to London, but no second council for Scottish affairs was established there': *Government of Scotland*, 142. The council, he says (p. 138), was able to make its own decisions, that it '*was* the government, or at least the daily central government'.

[6] J. H. Elliott, 'A Europe of composite monarchies', *Past and Present* cxxxvii (1992), 48–71 at pp. 54–6; E. Opalinski, 'The path towards the commonwealth of the two nations', in MacInnes and Ohlmeyer, *The Stuart kingdoms*, 49–61; M. Greengrass, 'Introduction: conquest and coalescence', in M. Greengrass (ed.), *Conquest and coalescence: the shaping of the state in early modern Europe*, London 1991, 1–24 at pp. 11–13, 16–17.

as giving them the power of the office itself, the patronage associated with it and facilitated access to the king.[7] The benefits accruing to the adherents of the office-holders, either in terms of being able to get something done, or in the pensions that could be recommended, ensured their support further down the scale and in their localities. This underwrote the authority of the surname leaders both at central and local level. Simultaneously, the crown was able to use the framework of relationships, from the highest to the lowest levels, as a chain of command and a conduit for the transmission of orders, from London to the Borders. Thus the crown, its official elite and their adherents mutually gained from an inclusive system of obligation, service and reward.

In the 'new world' of James's 'united' kingdoms, these connections represented a much-needed cohesive between the separate sovereignties of the English and Scottish kingdoms, as a counter-balance to the tensions evident in the regnal union.[8] These tensions were played out in the Middle March, now part of the Middle Shires, where, despite the disappearance of the international nature of the frontier, cross-border distrust continued. General resistance to any merging of English and Scottish law was felt all the more keenly in a cross-border region where two separate jurisdictions remained. Border-specific institutions continued to differentiate the region from elsewhere. But these problems aside, border-specific appointments gave the wily lairds of the Middle March a further opportunity for political advancement and material gain, at the same time strengthening governmental links between Edinburgh and the Borders, and indeed London.

I

As elsewhere in Scotland, the Borders had been represented in parliaments and conventions of estates for centuries by nobles and clerics, either resident or with landed interests there, and by burgesses. From the Middle March, the main noble representatives were the earls of Angus and Bothwell and Lord Yester. The Church was represented by the commendators of the abbeys of Kelso, Dryburgh, Melrose and Jedburgh: also attending was the bishop of Glasgow, who as head of the diocese that encompassed the march, had interests in the area, as did the Ker commendator of Newbattle. Burgesses were sent from the burghs of Jedburgh, Selkirk and Peebles and from Lauder on the edge of the region. Given the often-lengthy intervals between parlia-

---

[7] Neil Cuddy details the involvement of Scotsmen within the patronage system at James's English court: 'The revival of the entourage: the Bedchamber of James I, 1603–1625', in D. Starkey and others (eds), *The English court: from the Wars of the Roses to the Civil Wars*, London 1987, 173–225, and 'Anglo-Scottish Union', 107–24.

[8] G. Burgess, 'Introduction: the new British history', in Burgess, *New British history*, 1–29, 17.

ments, the same burgess did not tend to reappear at the next, with the odd exception such as Thomas Henderson who represented Jedburgh in 1587, 1593 and 1594. Some names reappear however such as the Mitchelhill family, burgh commissioners for Selkirk in 1579, 1612 and 1617 and the Rutherfords for Jedburgh in 1584, 1612, 1617 and 1621. The last two were Mr John Rutherford, a man with powerful local contacts and in whom, typically, a number of roles were combined: a burgh commissioner, occasionally provost of Jedburgh, often sheriff depute for the Douglases of Cavers and connected to the Kers of Ferniehirst.[9]

The biggest change in parliamentary membership in this period was the appearance of lairds. Though lairds had been attending conventions and parliaments in increased numbers since the Reformation Parliament of 1560, their admission was not formalised until the act of 1587, which called for a shire electoral system.[10] Before 1606 almost all the lairds recorded from the march, such as Traquair, Cessford and Buccleuch, were already members of the council. From 1606 commissioners were listed for each of the shires of Roxburgh, Peebles and Selkirk. They were drawn from a pool of prominent local surname leaders: these figures were already familiar to government, taking responsibility for their kindreds under general bands, and as local office-holders. Typical of these were the Murrays of Blackbarony who appeared regularly for Peeblesshire, whilst, in 1612, Murray of Elibank appeared for Selkirkshire accompanied by his cousin Philiphaugh, the sheriff there. Other prominent Selkirkshire representatives included Scott of Thirlestane and the Pringles of Torwoodlee and Galashiels. Galashiels was a JP and also sheriff in 1622. Similarly, the sheriffs of Roxburghshire, the Douglases of Cavers, often represented the shire at parliament. These people were part of the existing 'backbone' of local administration and their involvement in parliament represented a physical connection between 'local' and 'central' government. Indeed, they were functioning as part of both.[11] Conversely, other lairds from the Middle March attended parliament and conventions as a result of office within central government and not as shire representatives. These included John Carmichael of that ilk, who had been involved with the region from his keepership in the 1570s and who, in 1590, had served on a short-lived council subcommittee for the Borders, and Sir John Maitland of Thirlestane, chancellor from 1587. Opportunities existed, for those borderers that chose, to participate fully in national political life.[12]

---

[9] Groundwater, 'Middle March', appendix K.
[10] From 1573 to 1587 only one laird from the Middle March was recorded as attending either convention or parliament: J. Goodare, 'The admission of lairds to the Scottish parliament', *EHR* cxvii (2001), 1103–33 at pp. 1110–12, 1115–16; *RPS*, 1587/7/143, accessed 7 July 2009.
[11] Goodare, *Government of Scotland*, ch. v.
[12] Idem, *State and society*, 232.

Contact between Edinburgh and the Middle March was maintained outside the times of the irregular meetings of parliament. Sometimes the council came to the Borders on judicial raids and summoned borderers to meet it there, but throughout the period prominent borderers were either in office in Edinburgh or were summoned to appear before the council. They were asked to advise on border affairs and arbitrations of local feuds, to subscribe to general bands and to stand surety for members of their adherences. Thus, in 1573, 'close writings' were sent to Douglas of Bonjedburgh, Rutherford of Hunthill and others of Teviotdale to appear before regent Morton to give 'advis for quieting of the cuntrey'. Another summons, in 1600, by the council for a meeting with 'certane speciall barounis of the Bordouris' was 'for ordoure-taking anent the setling of the present disordouris of the Bordouris and repressing of the insolence of the rebellious thevis', which needed to 'be solidlie deliberat and advisit upoun and the ordoure to be tane'. Having deliberated, James and his council decided that a cause of disorder was the non-residence of certain prominent borderers, and they ordered Mark Ker, commendator of Newbattle, to stay at Neidpath castle by Peebles and the Tweedies of Drumelzier and Veitch of Dawick in their own castles nearby.[13] James was using local leaders with power in the region to advise him and then to implement policy in the region, but at the same time this allowed those leaders access to James and underlined their authority to their subordinates.

Such two-way communication became all the more important after James's departure for London, both to inform James and to avoid alienating the regional elites. Astutely, James was to continue to use borderers to advise him and the Scottish council on the situation in his infant 'Middle Shires'. In 1606 the Shires commissioners composed some questions to the landlords of the marches and then presented their answers to the council which agreed with their suggestions.[14] In 1618, when the commission was temporarily expanded, thirty borderers were appointed to it, the roll call of names from the Middle March making familiar reading. As ever, the council expected these officials to provide local knowledge, as well as having the power in the Shires to continue the pacification.[15] In 1622 letters were sent to the nobles, barons and gentlemen of the Middle Shires to attend a meeting of the commission in Edinburgh for 'consulting and advysing upon the best and reddeist meanis how the foder grouth of ... evellis may be stayid' in Annandale, Eskdale and Ewesdale: their protests against the disbanding of the border guard the previous year, and their advice to appoint some of 'power and friendship' in the region, led to the formation of the triumvirate of the three earls holding lands in these dales.[16]

---

[13] TA xii. 359–60; RPC vi. 136–8, 152–5.
[14] RPC vii. 720–1.
[15] RPC xi. 344–8.
[16] RPC xii. 650, 671.

The names of those advising James on the Borders remained much the same, from the 1570s to the 1620s. In 1600 Cessford, Ferniehirst and Scott of Haining (who was Buccleuch's representative) were amongst those whose counsel was thought worthy, and in 1619 Cessford (now Roxburgh), Ferniehirst's son Oxnam and Buccleuch appeared. The list of those summoned in 1622 was almost the same as for those who appeared four years before. The crown was continuing to use the region's frameworks of power and those with local knowledge to implement policy there: these advisers were men whose families had a tradition of being involved with central government.[17] This partly reflected the crown's heightened concern, particularly at times of more amicable Anglo-Scottish relations, in the mid-1570s, around 1586 (despite Mary's execution) and from the late 1590s onwards. But it also was the result of the march's proximity to Edinburgh.

This proximity also meant that the council could hold its officials and local leaders more easily accountable. Landlords from the Middle March were sometimes asked to present lists of fugitives within their lands and of those for whom they were accountable. For instance, in 1605, all lairds, lords and officers in the Borders were ordered to 'gif up on writing a speciall accompt upoun thair othis of the nowmber, quantitie, qualite, and names of all thair tennentis or inhabitantis within thair severall officeis ... in quhatmaner, forme or trade of lyf they leve or mantene themeselffis': those listed without surety or obvious employment were to be deemed of criminal tendency.[18] Again, in 1606, the commission ordered all landlords to present any who were fugitive or did not have surety and, in 1619, the commissioners were told to survey 'all idill personis, maisterles men, and vagaboundis' in their localities: Yester and Shillinglaw were to be responsible for Tweeddale, the Douglases of Cavers and Bonjedburgh for Jedburgh forest, Buccleuch for Liddesdale and Eskdale and Roxburgh, Cranstoun, Oxnam and Cavers for Teviotdale.[19]

Being ordered to help the council could, however, be something of a double-edged sword; appearance at the council underlined these borderers' importance within the locality and gave them access to the council. All too often, it also involved them is having to find monetary surety for their own good behaviour or that of their adherence.[20] In 1586 a summons to various Kers to answer before the council 'tuicheing gude reule and quietnes to be observit on the Bordouris' was accompanied by the order to find surety for their appearance: the amounts involved were significant, Andrew Ker of Greenhead and John Rutherford of Hunthill having to find £10,000, Will Ker of Ancrum, 10,000 merks, and his brother Robert and James Ker of

[17] RPC vi. 136–7; xii. 650.
[18] RPC vii. 707–9.
[19] RPC vii. 722–3; xii. 149–51, 219–22.
[20] Rae, Administration, 115, 124–6.

Lintalee, 5,000 merks.[21] A similar summons in 1587 was made to Scott of Buccleuch, Ker of Ferniehirst, Douglas of Cavers, Elliot of Redheugh, Turnbull of Bedrule and the Rutherfords of Hunthill and Edgerston. Scott of Haining had to stand surety of 5,000 merks for Buccleuch's appearance and another for Turnbull of Bedrule to supply redress for all cross-border offences by him and those for whom he was responsible. Both of these summonses were for the 'weill and quietnes of the bordour'.[22] As the 1590s progressed, such summonses to the lairds of the Middle March declined in frequency but continued for those in the West March: in particular to Lord Maxwell, who in 1600 was pronounced rebel for his non-appearance to answer for 'himself and those for whom he is answerable'.[23]

These summonses were not necessarily triggered by government concern about border-specific crime, but formed part of a more general crackdown on violence, in particular the crown's growing intolerance of feuding. Combatants in feuds from all over Scotland were increasingly being asked to appear before the council for resolution of their feuds, and to find surety to stay the further escalation of violence.[24] The crown sought greater control over judicial systems, drawing the private resolution of feud into the public arena. In the Middle March the most notorious of the feuds was that between the Kers of Cessford and the Scotts of Branxholme, which had existed from at least 1526, and resurfaced in 1577. In January 1578 the council summoned both sides to appear with twenty men each before Morton. Morton (the Scotts' ally), and his council ordered the unlucky Kers to pay £1,000 for the non-fulfillment of a marriage contract of 1565 between the two sides.[25] In 1587 Buccleuch was ordered to attend the 'amicable decision of the King and his Council', alongside the opposing party, Tweedie of Drummelzeir, 'both parties now [becoming] bound to stand by the decree ... and in the meantime assure each other against harm'. In the same year James VI staged his legendary 'love banquet' at which he attempted to reconcile the entire Scottish nobility by getting them to hold hands and feast on wine and sweetmeats. Buccleuch's adherents, sadly, were not listening and, in 1591, whilst he was abroad, Scotts from the Goldielands, Harden and Burnfoot branches invaded the Drummelzeir and Dreva lands of the Tweedies, for which they were summoned before the king. Poor Edmonstone of that ilk, who had acted as cautioner for Buccleuch in this feud, was found liable to pay the monetary surety when the Scotts failed to appear.[26]

But some communication was stimulated by border-specific issues, particularly at times of increased amity in Anglo-Scottish relations. This often

---

[21] *RPC* iv. 77, 82.
[22] *RPC* iv. 183, 189, 191.
[23] *RPC* vi. 121, 240.
[24] For discussion of feuding see chapter 5 below.
[25] *RPC* ii. 643–4, 665.
[26] *RPC* iv. 169n., 709, 721.

resulted in the surname leaders of the march being ordered to meet with the council during a judicial raid into the Borders. This was especially the case during the regency of the anglophile Morton, when the Middle March experienced at least four such raids.[27] A proclamation would be made in advance, typically charging all 'Erllis, Lordis, baronis, Frehalderis, Landit Men, Gentilmen, and Substantious Yeomen' of the Borders to attend the council, such as one issued to those of Roxburgh, Selkirk and the bailiary of Lauderdale to meet the council at Jedburgh in October 1575. Sometimes specific individuals would be named.[28] A proclamation and raid in 1576 resulted in the council being recorded at Jedburgh from 12 November until at least 6 December. Each day was set aside to deal with the business of separate regalities and parishes and at the end a roll of fugitives was drawn up. All local leaders, wardens and sheriffs were charged to pursue those rebels.[29] Whilst, of course, the primary objective here was for the crown to impose its wishes in the region, its presence there provided an opportunity for those local leaders to make contact with the highest levels of government. They would certainly have felt in touch with it.

II

But some were more in touch than others, in particular those that managed to get themselves admitted to the membership of the privy council. Nominal membership of the council was large, varying between thirty and fifty councillors, but its normal business was usually undertaken by a core inner group, principally officers of state, and those attending seems to have settled in a small group especially after James went down to London. In 1610 the council was reconstituted, slimmer and more professional, and formalised appointments made to it. This too was found 'exceeding grite', however, and in 1621 another restructuring brought the membership down to ten councillors.[30] Such appointments underlined the status of these prominent figures to their kindreds and allegiances in the march. Council membership also provided tangible connections between these adherents and central government, enabling direct access to the most powerful decision-making institution in Scotland and a line, furthermore, to the crown. Goodare notes the sustained frequency of council meetings at around every three days, which ensured almost constant contact with the highest levels of government.[31]

---

[27] G. R. Hewitt, *Scotland under Morton, 1572–1580*, Edinburgh 1982, 131–3.
[28] RPC ii. 460.
[29] RPC ii. 554, 566–73; CSP Scot. v, no. 241.
[30] Goodare, *Government of Scotland*, 133–5, 137; R. R. Zulager, 'A study of the middle-rank administrators in the government of King James VI of Scotland, 1580–1603', unpubl. PhD diss. Aberdeen 1991, 116, 146–7.
[31] Goodare, *Government of Scotland*, 132; Groundwater, 'Middle March', appendix O.

Reversing the direction of linkage, central government was able to use its councillors' networks of power to implement policy in the Borders, where all the councillors from the Middle March held local office. Throughout this period there was a consistently high degree of involvement of prominent borderers in the council, which was often out of proportion to that of members from the rest of the country. Whilst this may have been a factor of their residential proximity, it was also a reflection of crown concern about the Borders region: simultaneously, however, this concern gave those prominent borderers a foothold at the centre of policy-making in Scotland, and the ultimate decision-maker. Of the three marches, the largest number of councillors came from the Middle: from the East the Lords Home occasionally attended, and from the West, the Lords Herries and Maxwell were similarly infrequent, with the exception of Robert Lord Maxwell who attended from 1619. An exception from the East March was George Home of Spott, earl of Dunbar, who appeared regularly from 1592 until his death in 1611.[32]

The appointment of some of the councillors was almost certainly prompted by border-specific concerns, particularly at times of amicable Anglo-Scottish relations, and increasingly so as the 1590s progressed. One of the principal of these councillors was Sir John Carmichael of that ilk: though originally from the West March, he had strong kinship links within the Middle March through the Douglas-Scott alliance and held the keepership of Liddesdale in the 1570s. He was admitted to the council in November 1588, having been appointed West March warden two months before, replacing his brother-in-law the earl of Angus, who had just died, and in the aftermath of the border legislation of 1587. He was clearly a trusted figure, accompanying James on his journey to Denmark in 1590.[33] From 1591 to 1598 he averaged at least eighteen appearances a year at council, with more frequent attendances in 1592 and 1596. Arguably these were years of greater government concern in the Borders following Bothwell's rebellion and the Kinmont Willie episode.[34] However, there are not many examples of Carmichael's presence occasioning greater discussion of the Borders. In 1599 his attendance at council peaked at fifty-three times: this coincided with James's urgent pre-occupation with the succession, which he did not want to be prejudiced by border incidents.[35] Similar concerns probably ensured the membership of all the earls of Angus

---

[32] Alexander Lord Home attended thirty-four times between 1591 and 1597 and then not at all until 1607. Neither he nor his successor attended between 1610 and 1625. The Homes were suspected of continued Catholicism, Alexander being subject to pastoral supervision in 1602 and his successor was confined in 1615 following a dispute with the archbishop of St Andrews: *RPC* vi. 477n.; NLS, Denmilne, Adv. MS 33.1.12, vol. 15, fo. 30; Zulager, 'Middle-rank administrators', 77–8, 109–10.
[33] *RPC* iv. 322, 326, 768; D. Moysie, *Memoirs of the affairs of Scotland, 1577–1603* (Maitland Club, 1830), 84; Zulager, 'Middle-rank administrators', 75, 114–15
[34] Branxholme's rescue of the notorious Kinmont Willie Armstrong from Carlisle castle antagonised Elizabeth. See chapter 6 below.
[35] *RPC* vi. 33, 66, 117.

during this period, all of whom, before 1603, held the lieutenancy. There is no record of William, the eleventh earl's attendance until he appeared at a convention of council and nobles in 1621 but, as a noted Catholic, he spent much of his time abroad. The vigorous disputes of the tenth and eleventh earls with the Kers of Ferniehirst over their bailiary of the Angus-owned regality of Jedforest demonstrated their personal interest in the region: James was able, therefore, to combine the benefits of the service that the earls could give him on council and in lieutenancy, with the control that their landholding in the region gave them.[36]

The other principal border-specific officials in the Middle March were the Ker of Cessford wardens, and Scott of Branxholme, as keeper of Liddesdale after 1594 and effectively in control of the west side of the march. Both Cessford and Branxholme attended the council in December 1594, appearing occasionally but not with any frequency until 1599 in the case of Cessford, and 1607 in the case of Buccleuch.[37] There is, however, record of them being at court in the intervening period, and evidence of their popularity with the king. In 1596, following the rescue of Kinmont Willie from Carlisle castle, the English complained that Buccleuch 'openly says the King has freely remitted his deed ... as good service to him and his comune wealth'.[38] Branxholme appeared twice on the council that year, and at the convention of nobles and council in 1597, and that October James asked Elizabeth to release Buccleuch early from ward.[39] Cessford seems to have been a more politically agile courtier than Buccleuch, becoming quickly involved in central government and reaping the rewards that it brought. In 1598 William Bowes noted that Cessford was 'well befriended by a stronge faction' at court which secured him James's protection from English complaints. Lord Eure thought Cessford's 'naturall dispositione ...wyse, quicke spirited, perfecte in Border causes, ambitious, [and] desyrous to be greate'.[40] So a combination of personal interest and, from the late 1590s, the king's increasingly consistent strong line in the Borders ensured Cessford's inclusion in the council and his frequent attendance from 1599. In 1600 a grateful king created him Lord Roxburgh and confirmed an annual pension of 650 merks for Cessford's services as warden and as his 'domestik servitor and counsallor'.[41] The appointment of Buccleuch and Cessford to the council recognised their significance in their locality, whilst the increasing frequency of their attendance reflected their growing involvement in central govern-

[36] *RPC* iii. 23; iv. 365; v. 466; xii. 404.
[37] *RPC* v. 197, 557; vii. 340.
[38] *CBP* ii, no. 302.
[39] *CSP Scot.* xiii/1, no. 86.
[40] *CBP* ii, nos 343, 909.
[41] NRAS1100/728.

ment and secured their co-operation with it. This coincided with, or was part of, their greater commitment to the imposition of justice in the Borders.

In 1594 another borderer, Sir William Stewart of Traquair, from the Middle March, had been admitted. Ried Zulager concludes that the appointment of Carmichael and Traquair to the council was 'quite clearly an effort to involve influential local men in the decision-making process of the central government, though they were also sent back to the borders to implement those policies'. He compares such inclusion to the 'broad geographical base' of James IV's government.[42] Traquair, unlike his enemy Yester who appeared only very occasionally, attended the privy council frequently between 1595 and 1603, peaking in 1599 when he was present at least forty-one times. Like Carmichael, Cessford and Buccleuch, Traquair's inclusion was almost certainly a reflection of James's concern to maintain good relations with England by using these prominent local officials and their networks of power in the march, particularly in the late 1590s, as Elizabeth aged. Their power in the region will have helped when, in October 1602, the council was at Dumfries and Peebles for nearly two weeks during which judicial courts were held: Traquair was sitting throughout.[43]

The presence of a few men from the Middle March on the council had more to do with their administrative talents, but this too was of benefit to their kindreds. Two such were Mark Ker (Lord Newbattle), commendator of Newbattle abbey, second son of Ker of Cessford, and his son, Mark, who inherited the commendatorship and became first earl of Lothian. Newbattle sat regularly on the council from 1579 until his death in 1584 when he was replaced by his son who remained on the council until his death in 1609. The latter was appointed vice chancellor in 1604. He was first cousin to William Ker of Cessford and in 1614 his daughter Margaret married Andrew, eldest son of Ker of Ferniehirst: he was thus tied into the Ker kinship and no doubt this strengthened the position of the Kers at court.[44] But the Kers were also strengthened by their alliance with another councillor with extensive lands in the Middle March, John Maitland of Thirlestane. The marriage of his niece Margaret Maitland to Robert Ker of Cessford in 1587 (in spite of James's disapproval) linked him firmly with that principal branch of the Ker surname. Maitland's closeness to James protected Cessford from the king's wrath over his marriage, his killing of William Ker of Ancrum in 1590 and from English accusations over cross-border raiding, Zulager observing that Maitland was 'both the most successful product and manipulator of secondary social patronage'.[45] Like Lothian, he made his career in James VI's

---

[42] Zulager, 'Middle-rank administrators', 116.
[43] *RPC* vi. 467–72.
[44] *RPC* vii. 15; viii. 272n.; xiii. 453n.; Zulager, 'Middle-rank administrators', 61, 68, 89, 90.
[45] NRAS1100/987; Meikle, *A British frontier?*, 232; Zulager, 'Middle-rank administrators', 149.

service on the council and as chancellor from 1587 until his death in 1595.[46] But, as Rae noted, 'although a man devoted entirely to the central government, [he] was a man with border ancestry', strengthened by his ties to other border families, and this 'undoubtedly coloured his entire border policy'.[47] He was well rewarded with lands in Lauderdale and elsewhere, laying the foundations for his son's future Lauderdale earldom, and his great-grandson's political prominence.[48]

After 1603 membership of the council meant being part of the chief organ of arbitration and executive power resident in Scotland. As Goodare emphasises, the council 'could do things on its own account, without the monarch', whilst the 'king operated within the options set by his ministers'.[49] This gave those ministers significant powers over arbitration, patronage and office-holding and discretion over the implementation of crown policy. In the Borders, this policy was dominated by the suppression or pacification of crime, both cross-border and internally. Of the Middle March men previously involved, both Cessford and Buccleuch eventually reappeared on the council. Buccleuch spent several years serving in the Low Countries, but in 1606 he became Lord Scott of Buccleuch and, in 1607, was listed on the council. In 1608 he sat eighteen times at council, whilst also helping in the pacification of the Borders, being granted an approbation by James for his service there that December. Central government's formation of policy, and the local execution of it, was physically linked in the person of Buccleuch, whilst his networks of power, framed by his many adherents and extensive landholdings in the region, gave him the authority and the manpower to effect the pacification. Buccleuch was succeeded on his death by his son, also Walter, who appears to have taken his place on the council in 1615, sitting on average around sixteen times a year.[50] He too was directly involved in the pacification, formal recognition of the usefulness of his 'power and friendship' in the region encapsulated in his appointment, in 1622, as one of the triumvirate of commissioners. In 1624 an apparent attempt by Robert Elliot of Redheugh to murder his 'superiour and landislord' Buccleuch was treated by James with the utmost severity considering 'the qualite of the persone whome they intendit to haif murthoured being a nobleman, a counsellor, [and] our comissionar'.[51] Buccleuch was also on a commission to discuss the export of Scottish wool to England, along with several other borderers with extensive grazings, whose own interests like Buccleuch's were affected.[52]

---

[46] M. Lee, *John Maitland of Thirlestane and the foundation of the Stewart despotism in Scotland*, Princeton 1959.
[47] Rae, *Administration*, 209.
[48] RMS v, nos 1305, 1306, 1346, 1392.
[49] Goodare, *Government of Scotland*, 140.
[50] Fraser, *Buccleuch*, i. 230–2; RPC x. 464.
[51] RPC xii. 675–9; xiii. 486–7.
[52] RPC xiii. 70, 106, 141.

Buccleuch's inclusion in the council left him in a position to protect his own and his followers' interests in the Middle March. At the same time, the crown was able to use his authority over his surname and his landholdings in the region.

Cessford was similarly involved when he was not playing at court: in 1610 the opulence of a list of his clothing gives an idea of the kind of life he was leading there. His second wife Jean Drummond was governess to James's children until 1617, and their wedding in 1614 was paid for by the queen. Both Buccleuch and Cessford were reappointed to the reconstituted council, Roxburgh in 1610, and Buccleuch in early 1611, both sitting very regularly that year.[53] Roxburgh was a particularly frequent member of the council for the rest of James's reign: from 1599 and 1621 his attendance was between fifteen and twenty-four times a year, rising after 1621 to around fifty times in 1624. This could be said to be very regular given that the yearly average for council meetings was just over a hundred.[54] In 1617 he was appointed to the commission for the Plantation of the Kirks, in 1619 to Prince Charles's Scottish Council (along with Sir Robert Ker of Ancrum and Sir Gideon Murray of Elibank) and in 1623 to the commission anent Manufactures.[55] After the office of warden lapsed in 1603, Roxburgh did not hold any border-specific office, except in 1618 when he was named as a commissioner of the Middle Shires. He did, however, hold public office when, in 1610, he was appointed JP for Roxburghshire.[56] Like Buccleuch he provided a physical link between central and local government, securing for the crown the co-operation of much of his Ker kindred in the Borders, at the same time as maintaining Ker interests in Edinburgh.

A possible linkage between the execution of the pacification and membership of the council was even more greatly evident in the renewed appearance of the earl of Dunbar, from 1606 lieutenant in the Borders, and in the admission of several of the pacification's principal officers, Murray of Elibank in 1610, Lord Cranstoun in 1611, and Ker of Oxnam in 1613.[57] All of these were men whose careers, status and wealth were built in the service of James VI and I and who were dependent on his favour. Whilst they all came to own lands in the region, their power there initially was legitimised by office but effected through their kindreds and alliances, all having connections with the Scott, Ker, Murray and Douglas kindreds in the Borders. Grants of lands to them rewarded their services, whilst maintaining their vested interests in the region and extending their power bases. Membership of the council facilitated the representation of their alliances

---

[53] NRAS1100/1227; *Scottish peerage*, vii. 346; *The letters of John Chamberlain* (American Philosophical Society, 1939), i. 487, 507; *RPC* viii. 469; ix. 138–9; Birrel, *Diary*, 41.
[54] Goodare, *Government of Scotland*, 132.
[55] *RPC* xi. 169; xii. 59–60; xiii. 291–2.
[56] *RPC* ix. 75–6; xi. 345.
[57] *RPC* ix. 54, 244; x. 170–1.

at the centre of government and helped to secure the co-operation of these borderers.

Elibank, a commissioner and JP, was also, in 1611, named lieutenant of the Middle Shires following the death of Dunbar, and was to become the most prominent of these councillors. In 1612 he became deputy treasurer possibly as the result of Somerset manoeuvering before his own admittance to the council as treasurer.[58] He was a diligent member, his attendance averaging more than fifty-seven times a year, whilst continuing to be directly involved in the continuing pacification. Such was the weight of his council duties, however, that he was replaced as commissioner in 1617 by his nephew Murray of Philiphaugh.[59] Elibank's long career brought him lands and pensions, whilst his offices brought him the associated patronage with which to reward his kin and the power with which to intervene on their behalf. As a younger brother, Elibank did not inherit much, but, in 1595, his acquisition of the lands of Elibank, in the lordship of Ettrick, formed the nucleus of what would become an extensive landholding.[60] By 1608 he was the proprietor of Langshaw in the regality of Melrose and, in 1617, he was granted a charter of his lands of Elibank, Glenpoint and others in Tweeddale in the centre of his official jurisdiction in the Middle March.[61] His deputy treasureship came with a yearly salary of £1,500, which was increased in 1616 to £2,400 a year for his lifetime; after his death it was to be split between his sons.[62] His success established the foundations of his branch of the Murray surname as one of the senior in the Borders: in 1615 his son Patrick of Langshaw was granted an annual pension for his lifetime of £100; in 1623 the treasurer was ordered to pay Elibank's heirs all annuities due to them and, in 1643, Patrick became Lord Elibank.[63] Elibank's reliance on the king was dramatically demonstrated at the end of his life. When, in June 1621, he heard that James had withdrawn his favour, he was said to have died of melancholy shortly afterwards.[64]

The combination of border-specific and council offices held by Elibank meant that he could help those in alliance with him from the Middle March. Thus, in 1616, he secured a pardon from James for Scott of Tushielaw for the slaughter of a brother of Scott of Thirlestane and, in 1617, he intervened with James on behalf of Walter Scott of Harden in his feud with the Scotts of Bonnington; Harden's son was married to Elibank's daughter. He wrote that, as deputy treasurer, he had already given the escheat of Bonnington's land to his son-in-law and asked James to uphold the grant. In 1616, in a dispute

---

[58] *RPC* x. 54, 128–9, 194, 504; x, p. vii
[59] *RPC* x. 164; xi. 11.
[60] NAS, GD32/12/15–20.
[61] *Regality of Melrose*, 38; NAS, GD86/443; *RMS* vii, nos 1661, 1854, 1915.
[62] NAS, GD32/1/6; GD86/433; *RPS*, 1617/5/65, date accessed 12 Oct. 2009.
[63] NAS, GD32/1/9, 16, 18; GD124/10/264.
[64] *RPC* xii. 509n.

over the office of comptroller of the ordinance, Elibank admitted that he had already 'disponed' it to a nephew, James Murray. In addition, he was able to use his mutually beneficial working relationship with Murray of Lochmaben, the future earl of Annandale, for the benefit of himself and his kindred. Lochmaben, as a member of James's household in London, had access to the king, but also needed the information that Elibank as councillor could send him and Elibank petitioned him on behalf of his kindred. In 1616 Elibank sent his 'earnest request' for Lochmaben's support for compensation to their cousin James Murray of Kilbaberton, the king's master of works in Edinburgh.[65] Like Elibank, the first captain of the border guard, now Lord Cranstoun, combined border office with regular attendance at council. Though he resigned the captaincy, he continued as a commissioner of the Middle Shires. He, too, used his position to help himself and his family: in 1611, for instance, he wrote to James asking for his continued favour in a dispute over some of his lands and, in 1615, he wrote to Murray of Lochmaben on behalf of his nephew Douglas of Cavers.[66] He was rewarded with lands from the forfeiture of Lord Maxwell, and in 1617 he was able to use his councillorship to defend himself in an arbitration over them: here he claimed that he had already 'disponit a pairt of these landis amangis his freindis' demonstrating how office-holders were able to dispense the rewards associated with their office to secure the co-operation of their adherents.[67]

The linkage between membership of the council and the pacification can be most happily seen in the appointment of Ker of Oxnam as captain of the border guard and commissioner around the same time as his councillorship was proffered.[68] In 1613 Oxnam was also granted the keepership of the castle of Dumfries from the luckless Maxwell, which made him even happier, and well supported, in the region of his duties.[69] Oxnam was also clearly the beneficiary of kinship connections, surviving his uncle Somerset's plummet from grace in 1614 when he was protected by his cousin Ancrum in Prince Charles's household. Lacking the huge accumulation of lands of Roxburgh and Buccleuch, he was more dependent on the benefits associated with involvement in central government. When the guard was disbanded in 1621, Oxnam's pay as captain was continued for his lifetime.[70] Oxnam's frequent attendance at the council, an average thirty-four times a year to 1625, meant that he was able to intervene on his family's behalf; in 1616, the council suspended an action in favour of Lord Roxburgh which would have

---

[65] NAS, GD124/15/29, fo. 14; NLS, Denmilne, Adv. MS 33.1.1, vol. 7, fos 9, 32; vol. 8, fo. 33.
[66] RPC ix. 244; NLS, Denmilne, Adv. MS 33.1.1, vol. 3, fo. 58; vol. 6, fo. 47.
[67] RPC x. 164; xi. 59.
[68] RPC x, pp. vi–vii, 164, 170–1, 200.
[69] NAS, GD40/7/30.
[70] RPC xii. 582–4, 657–60.

removed the ownership of the teinds of Little Newton from Ferniehirst.[71] Office transformed Oxnam's position both financially and socially. Before 1610 he had failed in an attempt at court in London to resurrect his family's parlous circumstances, but in 1622 his father was created Lord Jedburgh, to which title Oxnam was heir. And James was a grateful monarch to those aiding the pacification at the heart of his newly 'unified' kingdoms.[72]

In 1617 John, viscount Lauderdale, the late chancellor's son, was admitted to the council on which he appeared regularly, almost weekly, for the rest of the reign of James VI and I. Whilst this meant that he covered business that was usually unrelated to border affairs, he sat frequently with other borderers such as Oxnam, Elibank, Cranstoun and the earl of Lothian, and often with Roxburgh or Buccleuch.[73] Though no correlation can be made between the presence of the borderers at council meetings and recorded border-related business, they coincided regularly with each other at meetings. It is perhaps not too fanciful to infer that this resulted in a more co-ordinated approach to dealing with the Borders. There was evidence before 1603 of councillors with significant connections in the Middle March coinciding at sittings: in 1586–7, and in 1590–1, the earls of Angus, Maitland of Thirlestane, Ker of Newbattle and Home of Cowdenknowes, and, from 1590, Carmichael of that ilk, predominated in privy council attendance at a time when the number of those appearing was usually between four and ten members. From 1592 another borderer, George Home of Spott (later Dunbar), from the East March attended council regularly. The attendance of men from the East and Middle March was not replicated by those of the West March, Lord Herries attending only infrequently. During the early 1590s this meant that attendance by men with strong connections in the East and Middle Marches was disproportionate to that by councillors from other Scottish regions.[74] It is difficult to determine whether this was a conscious policy on James's part, to include those with influence in a region deemed of concern, either to suppress perceived disorder, or to manage events there as part of a diplomatic leverage against England. An expansion of the privy council in the later 1590s, arguably at a time when it was of greater importance to James to secure stability in the Borders during discussions over the succession, meant that the predominance of borderers decreased. This perhaps reflected a decrease in the usefulness of the region as a bargaining counter with the English. After 1603 the continued regularity of attendance by Newbattle (soon Lothian) and increasingly by the Lords Roxburgh and Buccleuch maintained Middle March representation on the council and directly connected the council to those responsible for implementing the pacification. This became even more so with the admission after 1609 of Cranstoun, Elibank and Oxnam. So,

[71] NAS, GD40/2/12, fo. 44.
[72] RPC xii, pp. cviii, 679; NAS, GD40/2/12, fos 15, 20.
[73] RPC xi. 214.
[74] Meikle, *A British frontier?*, 77–82; Groundwater, 'Middle March', appendix.

whilst it is difficult to discern the precise motivation behind James's employment of the men from the Middle March, the fact remains that at all times there were close links between council and their region: prominent figures from the Middle March were not alienated from central government; they sat at its table.

III

Privy councillors and those employed within the royal household were rewarded for their service and were also in a position to pass these benefits onto their kin and allies. Indeed their support system was maintained by the patronage that they could provide. As Zulager notes, the 'redistribution of patronage to kinsmen and friends was at the core of Scottish politics'. It was expected of prominent figures. 'This is where the real give-and-take of Scotland's kin-based society impacted upon the institutions of State and shaped the particular methods of Scottish government'.[75] Goodare observes that 'the characteristic pattern of authority within the early modern state was one of patronage and clientage', noting the power of patronage inherent in an appointment to a royal office. A senior official 'stood at the head of a network of clients ... who staffed the lower levels of administration'.[76] Government was still conducted predominantly through personal relationships, embodied in the personal style of James's government. Access to the king or his heir was, therefore, of great significance. It could be obtained through official governmental office or through membership of the royal household or through connections with someone who had access.

Some of those who attained high governmental office started their careers in the household where, as Zulager observes, the importance of 'introduction and endorsement' cannot be overstated.[77] Amy Juhala's survey of James's household until 1603 reveals the early careers of subsequently prominent figures and indicates the significance of kinship in obtaining office. For instance, from at least 1590 to 1599, George Home of Spott, the future treasurer, was master of the wardrobe as well as appearing on the privy council, whilst his wife, Elizabeth Gordon, was a gentlewoman of the queen's Bedchamber in 1591. From the Middle March, Carmichael of that ilk was principal master stabler from around 1585 to 1593, and captain of the guard from 1592 to 1596. Mark Ker of Prestongrange, Lord Newbattle from 1591, was master of requests in 1578 and 1581, and was a gentleman of the Bedchamber in 1580. The same year, Ker of Cessford was an extraordinary gentleman of the chamber and, in 1593, his son Robert was principal

---

[75] Zulager, 'Middle-rank administrators', 146–7.
[76] Goodare further notes that clients who were ineffective in office, or did not hold posts in the administration, were of no use to the patron: *State and society*, 81–2.
[77] Zulager, 'Middle-rank administrators', 149.

of the king's guard as well as acting as warden. Ker of Ferniehirst was a gentleman of the Bedchamber in 1592 and, from around 1598 to 1603, his half-brother Robert, the future Somerset was a page of honour. However, apart from the numerous examples of Kers throughout the royal household there were few other surnames from the Middle March.[78] The Kers seem to have had a particularly felicitous relationship with the court, not matched by, for instance, the possibly less refined Scotts.

In 1603 the court moved south to London and inevitably the arrival of a Scottish king at Whitehall led to changes in the composition of the royal household there. Whilst James retained most of Elizabeth's councillors, introducing only a few Scotsmen, and split the privy chamber equally between Scotsmen and Englishmen, he introduced a new chamber, the Bedchamber, physically positioned between himself and the privy chamber, which was no longer so privy. This he filled with Scotsmen. For Neil Cuddy, the Bedchamber from 1603 was integral to the way James governed and 'continued to be of central political importance during the reign', with the numbers of signatures to English signet warrants procured by the Bedchamber growing from about a sixth of the total in 1614, to nearly one half by 1624. Given the predominance of Scottish courtiers in the Bedchamber, this gave them significant control over the distribution of patronage, grants of monopolies, offices, lands and titles, whilst their 'intimate, institutionalized access' to the king gave their alliances back home in Scotland a proven route to royal favour or intercession.[79] But the benefits were not all one-way: James was able to use the routes of communication provided by these relationships to transmit policy, staff the offices that his objectives necessitated, utilise the manpower and obligations that the regional elites could generate and, crucially, keep himself informed and advised. Some courtiers were also in very regular contact with individual councillors in Edinburgh, their correspondence enabling an informal cross-fertilisation of information between senior Scottish ministers and those with intimate knowledge of the king's wishes and the opportunity to influence his decision-making. Thus a courtier told the chancellor, Dunfermline, that 'I have wreittin these lynnes to yr honor by his majesties derectione to lett yow understand' the latest news from London, and asks, about a dispute in Scotland, 'what yee wald have hes majestie doe in it let me knowe'.[80] Communication was thus maintained between the king and those administering for him in Scotland, its elites

---

[78] A. Juhala, 'The household and court of James VI of Scotland, 1567–1603', unpubl. PhD diss. Edinburgh 2000, appendix 1, 'Royal household'; appendix 2, 'Bills of household'.
[79] Cuddy, 'Revival of the entourage' 177, 187–8, and 'Anglo-Scottish Union', 110–11, 118–19. See also K. M. Brown, 'The Scottish aristocracy, anglicisation and the court, 1603–38', HJ xxxvi (1993), 543–76.
[80] NLS, Denmilne, Adv. MS 33.1.1, vol 5, fo. 50.

could be kept happy, and the crown could secure their co-operation in the implementation of policy in their regions.

In the Borders the suppression of crime remained a preoccupation, primarily driven by a newly consistent intolerance of cross-border and internal raiding of livestock at the heart of the infant united kingdom. Several councillors were involved in the pacification: courtiers, too, were to facilitate it, through the routes of communication, command, patronage and information controlled by several borderers in the royal households. Here, of the borderers, the Kers continued to dominate: Robert Ker, earl of Somerset, the king's favourite from around 1608 to 1615, Robert Ker of Ancrum in Prince Henry's and then Prince Charles's households, and Robert Ker, now Lord Roxburgh, through his wife's closeness to the queen. As John Chamberlain sniped in 1613, 'nothing of any moment is don here but by [Somerset's] mediation, and sure yt is a marvaylous straunge fact that three Roberts of the same surname shold be so greate and powerfull, about the King, Quene and Prince, all [at] one time'.[81] From the former West March, but with strong connections in the Middle, John Murray of Lochmaben, too, was to become an extremely influential gentleman in James's household. All of these figures were involved to some extent in the pacification, though less directly in the case of Somerset. For those that were connected to these men, by kinship or alliance, they provided direct access to James, or his sons, being able to present petitions on their behalf at the right time: as the Scottish chancellor, the earl of Dunfermline, emphasised to Lochmaben, 'if yie that ar daylie attendentis, domestic, and hamelie with his Sac: Ma:, can not: move his Ma:', then who could? At the same time, Lochmaben, for instance, was dealing directly with Douglas of Drumlanrig over the pacification, Drumlanrig reporting, in 1616, his 'tryall and punischment thair of [of offenders] to the deith for the wrang that is alredis done: ... to terrifie all other malefactoris from attemping the lyk heirefter'.[82] James would have approved.

The significance of Somerset's influence from an English perspective has been the subject of some debate, but there has been no consideration yet of what his spell in the sun meant for the transmission of policy to Scotland, and for his Scottish connections.[83] In terms of the Borders, there is a clear connection between the favour that he was shown by James, the patronage that he distributed and the implementation of the pacification. Somerset, a *protégé* of Dunbar, became a groom of the Bedchamber in 1603 and a gentleman of the Bedchamber in 1607. In 1608 he was granted the

---

[81] *Chamberlain letters*, i. 510.
[82] NLS, Denmilne, Adv. MS 33.1.1, vol. 5, fo. 143; vol. 7, fo. 4.
[83] P. Croft, 'Can a bureaucrat be a favourite? Robert Cecil and the strategies of power', and L. L. Peck, 'Monopolising favour: structures of power in the early seventeenth-century English court', in J. Elliott and L. Brockliss, *The world of the favourite*, New Haven–London 1999, 81–95, 54–70; Cuddy, 'Revival of the entourage', 209–13.

sizeable pension of £800.[84] In 1610 he was granted extensive lands, mainly in Dumfriesshire, from the forfeiture of John Lord Maxwell. Following Dunbar's death in 1611, the Venetian ambassador reported that 'everybody is endeavouring to secure [Ker's] favour and goodwill'.[85] Ker was created viscount Rochester in May 1612 and elevated to the earldom of Somerset in November 1613. At the same time, whilst acting *de facto* as the English Secretary following the death of the earl of Salisbury, he was admitted to the Scottish council and appointed treasurer of Scotland.[86] In 1614 he managed to get his nephew William Ker appointed a groom of the Bedchamber, a position he maintained until at least 1625. He was also responsible for the secondment of his cousin Ker of Ancrum to the household of Prince Henry, and then of Prince Charles.[87] As James observed to Somerset 'Do not all court graces and place come through your office as Chamberlain ... And have you not besides your own infinite privacy with me, together with the main offices you possess', your kinsman, Ancrum, 'who loves not to be idle in my son's Bedchamber'.[88] But Somerset's patronage was not confined to the offices he could secure for his kinsmen at court but was also used to effect James's policy in the Borders, and, as part of this, secure the position of his Ker kindred there.

Immediately beneficial to the impoverished Ferniehirst Kers was Somerset's distribution of the lands that James had granted him from Maxwell's forfeiture. Andrew Ker of Oxnam's journey to court in London, in 1609, was not successful and he had returned 'barren of hopes and friends'.[89] The rising fortune, however, of his uncle Robert prompted hope: in 1610 Robert wrote that James was willing to give the title of Lord Jedburgh to his brother Fernie–hirst, but first had to have proof that the estate was fit to support it, so, in 1612, Robert, now viscount Rochester, transferred Maxwell lands to Ferniehirst.[90] The same year Rochester sent Ferniehirst other 'helpes' which he had 'procured from the king ... with promise of furtherance in anything that may contribute to the preservation of the house of Ferniehirst'.[91] The following year, Rochester's (now Somerset's) nephew Oxnam was admitted to the privy council and appointed to the commission of the Middle Shires and the captaincy of the border guard. Somerset was providing James with the manpower and the authority of the Ker kindred to effect the pacification, whilst making sure that the additional authority that these offices gave remained within his family.[92] In 1622 Ferniehirst was finally granted the

---

[84] Cuddy, 'Anglo-Scottish Union', 115–16.
[85] *RMS* vii, no. 217; *CSP Venetian* xii. 135.
[86] *RPC* x, pp. vi–vii, 157.
[87] Cuddy, 'Revival of the entourage', 213.
[88] *The letters of James VI and I*, ed. G. P. V. Akrigg, Berkeley 1984, 340.
[89] NAS, GD40/2/12, fos 14, 15, 20.
[90] NAS, GD40/2/12, fos 20, 22; *RMS* vii, no. 786.
[91] NAS, GD40/2/12, fo. 34.
[92] *RPC* x. 157, 170, 176, 200.

title Lord Jedburgh. As significant to the pacification, however, were Somerset's grants from the Maxwell forfeiture to his uncle Murray of Elibank, the most prominent Shires commissioner, and privy councillor. In 1611 Elibank, acting as Ker's agent for his affairs in Scotland, brought a case before the council against the bailie of Caerlaverock, the lands of which had been granted to Ker. In 1612 Ker granted the castle of Caerlaverock, an important Dumfriesshire stronghold, to Elibank's son, Langshaw, and further lands in the Borders to Langshaw and Elibank, thus securing Elibank's support for the Ferniehirsts on the council and for the pacification in a region where he now had significant vested interests, and power.[93] However, what court success brought to a kindred could be endangered by the favoured one's fall from grace. Both Oxnam's and Elibank's positions were threatened by Somerset's ruin in 1615, Elibank beseeching Lochmaben's help at court with James, since Oxnam's enemies would not fail 'to seik his harme and skaithe at this tyme'.[94] Subsequently, Elibank wrote a deeply thankful letter to James for his 'extraordinarie' favour, despite the 'ruyne of my unhappie kinsman'.[95] That Oxnam and Elibank continued to prosper says much for their diligence in office and their usefulness to James, but perhaps, too, was thanks to the influence of another kinsman at court, Ker of Ancrum, himself a *protégé* of Somerset.

When, in 1613, Ancrum went to London he nominated his cousin and friend Oxnam to replace him as captain of the border guard. Direct contact was being maintained between the court and the imposition of the policy of pacification, Ancrum's immediate family serving in the guard, whilst securing the co-operation and power of the wider Ker kindred.[96] This sphere of influence widened further through the Kers' connections with John Murray of Blackbarony, Elibank's older brother, reinforced through Ancrum's marriage to Blackbarony's daughter Elizabeth. Ancrum nominated Blackbarony to manage his affairs in 1607, during his continental travels.[97] Ancrum was to remain a gentleman of the Bedchamber for Prince, and then King Charles, until the late 1540s.[98] In 1621 Prince Charles recommended him to the countess of Derby as suitable for marriage to her daughter, reassuring her that 'what hee wants in meanes hee hath in neerness about my person'.[99] Ancrum's service in the household of James's heir, and the longevity of it,

---

[93] *RPC* ix. 232; *RMS* vii, nos 636, 754.
[94] NLS, Denmilne, Adv. MS 33.1.1, vol. 6, fos 51, 52.
[95] Ibid. fo. 57.
[96] *RPC* x. 176.
[97] NAS, GD40/2/13, fo. 1.
[98] NAS, GD40/2/13, fos 13, 15. He survived a short period of disfavour, in 1620, over his involvement in a fatal duel with Charles Maxwell of Terregles. Ancrum was convicted of manslaughter but pardoned six months later: *Correspondence of Sir Robert Kerr, first earl of Ancram and his son William, third earl of Lothian*, ed. D. Laing (Bannatyne Club, 1875), p. xiv.
[99] NAS, GD40/2/19/1, fo. 8.

guaranteed him constant access to Prince Charles. In 1619 the importance of this increased further when Charles began to take more interest in Scotland and his own Scottish council was appointed. This meant that it was beneficial for anyone who wanted office or something done in Scotland, and especially in the Borders, to find favour with Ancrum. Both Ancrum and Lord Roxburgh were appointed to the prince's council. In 1623 Roxburgh found himself having to beg Ancrum, the son of the man he had killed in 1590, to assure Prince Charles of Roxburgh's 'treu haert ... reddie to his service'.[100] Ancrum was well rewarded: he was granted the earldom of Ancrum in 1633 and manoeuvred to acquire the earldom of Lothian for his son.[101]

A wealth of surviving letters to Ancrum demonstrates recognition of the significance of his influence at court.[102] At the most basic level was what he could secure for his kindred. As early as 1606 his aunt Alison Home wrote asking Ancrum to give his friendly advice to her son who wanted a post in London. Already noted were the benefits of Ancrum's protection to Ferniehirst and Oxnam, and in 1617 Somerset's sister Anne, Lady Balmerino, wrote to Ancrum asking for his approval of her petition to James on Somerset's behalf. Ancrum was able to secure some favour for Lord Balmerino, since in 1621 Balmerino acknowledged his obligation to him.[103] A letter from Margaret Lady Ochiltree in 1621, signed 'your most affectionat mother', thanked Ancrum for furthering her suit with Prince Charles and asked him to remind the prince to prompt Elibank, the deputy treasurer, to pay her pension.[104] The longer Ancrum remained at court, the wider the circle of supplicants became. After Elibank's death in 1621, which left a vacancy on the prince's council, the earl of Lauderdale amongst others asked Ancrum to influence Prince Charles into appointing him.[105]

The Kers were certainly the most notable beneficiaries and manipulators of court patronage from the Middle March, but the Murrays of Lochmaben and Elibank also benefited from such patronage, and both were intimately involved in the pacification. Lochmaben, whilst remaining a gentleman in James's Bedchamber, became one of the triumvirate for the Middle Shires in 1622 and was rewarded with the earldom of Annandale.[106] At the same time, given his absence in London, he was able to use the gratitude of his borderer allies to look after his interests there.[107] But he was not solely preoccupied with borderers or border business, being one of the chief founts of informa-

---

[100] NAS, GD40/9/8, fo. 1; *RPC* xii. 59–60.
[101] NAS, GD40/2/13, fos 48, 53; 40/7/47.
[102] NAS, GD40/2/13. Some of these letters are in the *Correspondence of Robert Kerr*.
[103] NAS, GD40/2/13, fos 8, 12, 29.
[104] NAS, GD40/2/13, fo. 20. She was not his mother. Her daughter Anne was married to Ferniehirst.
[105] NAS, GD40/2/13, fo. 28.
[106] NLS, Denmilne, Adv. MS 33.1.1, vol. 5, fo. 68; vol. 6, fos 51, 52.
[107] Ibid. vol. 5, fos 139, 141, 145.

tion within James's household and in very regular contact with the Scottish council. Weekly, the chancellor Dunfermline kept Lochmaben aware of the wintry summer of 1614, whilst Dunfermline acknowledged himself 'mair bound to your kindnes and guid will, nor eiver I can have meanis to acquite, or in onye maner to recompense'.[108] Contacts such as these between councillor and courtier, courtier and members of regional elites fostered cohesive relations between those exercising power in Scotland with the policy-makers in London, whilst in the Borders, such as Ancrum, Oxnam, Elibank and Lochmaben benefited from a self-perpetuating cycle of patronage, whilst their further redistribution of lands and offices secured the co-operation of their wider kindreds and alliances in the pacification.

IV

Kinship and allegiance continued to influence appointments and to provide the support for those offices. As Dunfermline reminded Lochmaben, in his gratitude, 'alwayis I wish yiow knaw all the guid offices yiow doe to me, are done to a freind, to ane kinnisman': even if this was merely rhetorical, he was voicing the expectation that the mutual obligations implicit in kinship underlay their relationship. And these relationships continue to characterise governance. Additionally, it is notable that the names of those from the Middle March in office in the 1570s were remarkably similar to those expanded numbers in office in 1625. Through a careful combination of stick and carrot, James VI and I had managed to retain the loyalty of the borderer elites despite the crown's encroachment on their existing authority. The importance of patronage, both as part of a system of reward and as a means of staffing government, if anything increased in this period. After James's accession to the English throne, and the treasure pots of London, the scope for reward was much widened. The grant of governmental office, from the Borders to the highest level, involved nobles and lairds within a newly invigorated and extended framework of authority that could help to impose crown policy in the regions. The crown and its officers mutually benefited in a cycle of service and reward, whilst the connections within these patronage networks provided conduits for information and much-needed adhesive between the separate components of the newly unified kingdoms.

What is evident from all this is that borderers were not alienated from central government; they were part of it. It would be a mistake to think of the Middle March as a remote peripheral region in the way that historians have identified Cumberland and Northumberland in relation to the centre of government in London. Ellis, Spence, Watts and James have all variously noted the sense of alienation of English borderers from their

---

[108] Ibid. fos 48, 103.

national government and lack of involvement in it: for instance, in 1601, the northern counties of England were represented by only sixteen out of a total of 462 MPs in the House of Commons, while Scottish borderers may have accounted for as much as 25 per cent of any council sitting in the 1610s. The English northerner's alienation was exacerbated by the use, by successive Tudor governments, of outsiders in the marches as wardens and in the two garrisons at Carlisle and Berwick, whilst the English border officials were answerable to the Council of the North at York, a body which impeded contact between the English borderers and their central government.[109] There was no such blockage between the borderers of the Scottish Middle March and the council in Edinburgh. Or rather, the opportunities existed for those borderers who so wished, to embrace involvement with central government. For those that did not, or who did not have the access to higher authority that the patronage networks provided, James's evolving government will have seemed less amenable. The effects of such exclusion were exacerbated after James's departure for London, when the good burgesses of Scotland, in 1604, regretted 'the lois sustenit be Scottis men be his maiesteis absence, and thairfoir to desire [th]at this majeste may remayne in Scotland yeirle ane quarter of the yeir and sie justice administratt'.[110] Where the connections between regional elites, government in Edinburgh and James in London were weakened, lay, perhaps, the seeds of the future breakdown in communication between these elites and James's son.

---

[109] Spence, 'Pacification', 65, 71; Ellis, 'Tudor state formation', 62; Watts, *From border to Middle Shire*, 35–6.

[110] *Records of the convention of royal burghs of Scotland*, ed. J. D. Marwick, Edinburgh 1870, ii. 190.

5

Crime, Feud and Violence

The networks of power in the Middle March and their direct linkage to central government could provide the crown with a system with which to fulfill its objectives in the region, including the suppression of crime, if it had the will to do so. There can be little argument that widespread crime did take place: there was report enough of theft, reset,[1] feud, violence and cross-border raiding from both English and Scottish sources. Many of these crimes, particularly feuding, were common to the rest of Scotland. The march's proximity to England, however, occasioned specific types of crime and there were areas close to the border that appeared to be beyond the limits of government control. To the government then, and to subsequent historians, the border-specific nature of crime was what caused extra concern over the region and is the subject of much of this chapter: but this concern should be placed within the context of the crown's increasing intolerance of violent crime and the evolution of judicial systems throughout the kingdom. So whilst border-specific offences need to be addressed, this chapter will also assess how crime in the Middle March compared to that elsewhere, and how the region was affected by a shift in the crown's attitude to crime and justice in general.

The latter part of the sixteenth century and the early part of the seventeenth saw the criminalisation of many activities previously tolerated, such as firearm-bearing, witchcraft and, peculiar to the Borders, hunting in the Cheviots.[2] But perhaps of most significance was the crown's changing attitude to feud, which was criminalised in 1598.[3] This chapter examines the structure of feuding in the Middle March, necessarily drawing on the impact of kinship and alliance on the origins, escalation and any resolution of dispute – and how James VI's government increasingly intervened. Such intervention formed part of processes underway throughout Scotland, and the suppression of feud was itself part of broader developments in the way government was effected. By the 1590s the private settlement of dispute was deemed no longer acceptable as the crown began to draw judicial processes within its remit. Nobles, heads of surnames and lairds were encouraged to bring their disputes, or those of their affiliates, to Edinburgh for arbitration by the court of session

---

[1] Reset was the receipt of stolen goods or harbouring a criminal.
[2] *RPC* v. 274–5, 321–2; vii. 41–2, 707–9.
[3] 'Act Anent Removing and Extinguishing of Deidlie Feuds', 1598, repeated 1600: *RPS*, 1598/6/2, 1600/11/44, accessed 12 Oct. 2009.

or in some cases by the privy council. Theoretically at least, arbitrations could then be imposed by the crown, either directly at council or through a warrant sent to the local sheriff or through holding a cautioner accountable for his charge. For this process to work the crown needed the co-operation of prominent figures. Much has been made of the nobility's acquiescence, but for it to be effective in each locality, the co-operation of the lairds and their kindreds was crucial.[4] The effect of the suppression of feuding was felt throughout society and government. The replacement of private justice by state-controlled judicial processes led, as Goodare observes, to the ending of both 'autonomous noble power' and its 'machinery', a noble's 'network of armed local lordship'.[5] There was no longer the need for armed retinues. Bonds of manrent, the adhesive of lordship, swiftly died out after 1600, and in 1604 there was an ordinance against the making of private assurances.[6] Moves towards government monopolisation of justice should also be put within the context of broader governmental policies which involved greater direct intervention in many facets of life in pursuit of, for instance, a 'godly' society; a widening base of those with official authority in local administration, such as the JPs and the kirk session elders; and the evolution of non-judicial administrative structures throughout Scotland.

The ending of feuding affected the Middle March as much as anywhere else in Scotland. Numerous borderer lairds, including the surname leaders, were forced to submit their differences to arbitration by the council and to find surety for the good behaviour of their kinsmen and allies. The increase, nationally, in the numbers of such acts of caution registered by the council from the 1580s, dramatically peaked during the period 1600 to 1610 as the crown showed its determination to suppress feud. In the 1620s the number of such sureties being registered for the Middle March was greatly reduced. This suggests that the incidence of feud there had lessened since it no longer troubled the council so much. The inclusion of such veteran combatants as the bitter enemies Roxburgh and Buccleuch in central government rewarded the ending of their own feuds. At the same time, public office as commissioner, councillor or JP was beginning to transform the responsibility of these prominent individuals for their kinsmen and tenants from lordship to that of policemen. By the 1620s little dispute was recorded from the East March too, where the acts of caution had always been significantly less than in either the Middle or West Marches. The suppression of feud took longer in the West March where as late as 1622 James Johnstone of that ilk was granted an exemption from the jurisdiction of Robert Maxwell, earl of Nithsdale, one of the triumvirate, since 'the hairtburning betuix thair frendis and followeris

---

[4] Keith Brown notes that feud was pursued not only by the nobility but by the landed elite as a whole which included 'the barons, clan chiefs, and lairds': *Bloodfeud*, 8, 241–3.
[5] Goodare, *State and society*, 76.
[6] Wormald, *Lords and men in Scotland*, ch. ix, 'The end of bonding'; *RPC* vi. 594–6.

is not yit fullie extinguischit': the leaders may have reconciled but it would take longer for the changes to filter down through their affiliates.[7]

The suppression of feuding was one of the most significant achievements of James's reign. Michael Wasser's survey of the cases of violent crime coming before the council and central justice courts between 1603 and 1638 concludes that there was a detectable decline in violence in this period, which was linked to the ending of bloodfeud and the more frequent resolution of dispute within the courts. But it was a slow process. The private justice of the feud was being drawn into the public courts, but predominantly through private prosecutions rather than the crown's imposition of exemplary punishment.[8] The suppression of violent crime was an on-going process throughout the sixteenth century, and into the seventeenth, in the Middle March as well as in the central lowlands of Scotland.

I

There is no denying, however, the border-specific nature of much of the crime in the marches that caught the government's attention and continued to differentiate the region from its lowland neighbours. If anything, this peculiarity led to more intensified government in the Borders, where an extra layer of border laws had evolved over the centuries of Anglo-Scottish hostility, which supplemented the usual domestic law and judicial systems. Both domestic and border law were applicable here, whilst an international element was lent to judicial proceedings at meetings between Scottish and English march wardens during which an agreed set of laws was implemented. On a domestic level the overlapping jurisdictions of the border warden and the sheriff were potentially problematic, though this appears not to have caused too much dispute. Additionally, the Borders were subject to competing public and private jurisdictions whereby a landholder with baronial rights could repledge an offender from a public court to his own. But in this the Borders were no different from elsewhere in Scotland. There is some debate over how detrimental to justice such overlapping may have been, but as Goodare points out Scotland could be seen to have benefited from an integrated network of jurisdiction. This study suggests something between the two views.[9] There was certainly a judicial framework in the Middle March, which could be effective if government chose to use it. At the same time, though, disputes over jurisdiction, such as that between the earl of Angus,

---

[7] In June 1623 the privy council forced a formal reconciliation between Nithsdale and Johnstone and Johnstone's exemption was lifted: *RPC* xii. 673–5; xiii. 261–2.

[8] Wasser, 'Violence', 1, 57–8, 293–301.

[9] Catherine Ferguson is particularly concerned with the repledging of tenants from other courts: 'Law and order on the Anglo-Scottish Border, 1603–1707', unpubl. PhD. diss. St Andrews 1981, 28, 109, 240, 264, 320.

the Ferniehirsts and Jedburgh, hindered legal processes and led to further violence. Such contretemps, however, should not be ascribed solely to the situation in the Borders, and could occur anywhere. But the governmental concern that they prompted has highlighted crime in the Borders giving a confusing impression of judicial difficulties as being a particularly Borders problem.

The body of border laws had evolved through custom and during cross-border negotiations between Scottish and English commissioners over previous centuries. Record of them was made often as part of treaty negotiations but occasionally an official would attempt to clarify them. In 1448, for instance, William, earl of Douglas, drew up the known articles of border law at Lincluden to which Sir James Balfour acknowledged his debt in his summary of them in the 1560s.[10] Contemporary problems in defining march law occurred partly because of the diverse ways in which it had evolved. Whilst some had been drawn up to deal with specific times of peace and war, many articles had been established by custom. Balfour thought that 'all uther thingis that are not put in writ, that ar pointis of weir, and usit of befoir in time of weirfare' should be left to the warden's judgment, with the advice of 'the eldest maist worthie bordoureris, that best knawis the auld use of marche'. There was also an inherent problem with laws, devised in times of hostility, which were meant to operate also in times of relative peace. Despite the attempts at clarification, the privy council noted, in 1576, 'be dailie experience quhat harme and inconvenient occurris upon bordouris of bath the realmis throw ignorance of the lawis and lovabill custumes thairof' and, as late as 1597, an Anglo-Scottish border commission collated all known march laws into a new treaty, suggesting that confusion still existed.[11] This meant, therefore, that there was scope for endless argument, exemplified by the dispute, in 1596, between Lord Scrope and Scott of Branxholme: this centred on the legality of the capture, by the English, of Kinmont Willie on the Scottish side of the border during a day of truce in violation of the customary immunity, and his rescue by Branxholme. It became an issue of national sovereignty. A convention of estates endorsed the legitimacy of Branxholme's actions but typically referred the matter to a meeting of Anglo-Scottish border commissioners, whilst the council upheld

---

[10] *Balfour practicks*, ii. 590–613. See also Sir Robert Bowes's record in 1551 of March law in J. Raine, *The history and antiquities of North Durham*, London 1852, pp. xxii–xxvii; R. Bell, *Book of Marches* (1604), in J. Nicolson and R. Burn, *History of Westmorland and Cumberland*, London 1777, i, pp. xxiii–xxv; W. Nicolson, *Leges Marchiarum*, London 1747; G. Neilson, 'The March laws', in T. I. Rae (ed.), *Miscellany* (Stair Society, 1971), i. 11–77. For a comprehensive collection of laws see Tough, *The last years*, pp. xi–xx, chs vi, vii. For the development of English border law to 1502 see C. J. Neville, *Violence, custom and law: the Anglo-Scottish Border lands in the later Middle Ages*, Edinburgh 1998, pp. x–xiv.

[11] *Balfour practicks*, ii. 600; *RPC* ii. 523–4; *CBP* ii, nos 621–3.

Branxholme's position since Scrope's deputy had himself transgressed border law.[12]

The region was subject also to the changes underway in domestic law that affected the whole country. Some laws, however, were targeted specifically at the Borders. These were not usually, however, to manage cross-border relations, but principally the result of the government's general intrusion into legal processes being applied to a specific region. The act of 1587 for the quieting of the Highlands and the Borders was an example of this. However, the continued use until 1603 of the border laws meant that the Borders remained marked out as a peculiar region, even after the subsidence of the hostility that had inspired the original laws. So too did the ordinances of 1605, related to the pacification. This underlined the perception of the unique nature of the Borders and influenced the way in which government and the judicial system responded to the area.

II

The registering by the council of numerous acts of caution and crime-related ordinances in the late sixteenth century reflected the contemporary priorities of the government, and its increasing concern over crime. These provide a qualitative, if not a reliable quantitative, record of the types of crime in the Middle March and of government reaction to it. The preambles to many Borders-related ordinances repeated a litany of domestic offences: the 'band of Roxburgh' in 1573 listed 'the innumerabill slauchteris, fyre rasingis, thifts, reiffis, heirschippis and utheris detestabill enormiteis, dailie comittit', whilst the act of 1587 reiterated the problems of 'reiff, thift or ressett of thift, depradationis opin and avowit fyre raising upoun deidle feidis'.[13] In 1573 a muster at Peebles was intended to deal with the 'disorderit people' there who were harming the innocent by 'ransoming of thair personis, and constraning thame to pay blak maill, quhairby divers gude and proffeittabill landis ar utterlie herreit and laid waist'.[14] Ordinances were also made against cross-border crime at times of increased government concern over relations with England, and this was increasingly the case as the childless Elizabeth I grew older. One of 1587 ordered that no borderer was 'to ryde in England in weirlike maner, or to rais fyre, mak depredationis, or committ slauchtar, reif, thift, or ressett thairof, upoun quhatsumevir personis, inhabitantis of the realme of England' under pain of death.[15]

---

[12] CBP ii, nos 237, 252; RPS, A1596/5/9, date accessed 12 Oct. 2009; RPC v. 290n., 298–9, 300n.; CSP Scot. xii, no. 195.
[13] RPC ii. 548–9; RPS, 1587/7/70, accessed 12 Oct. 2009.
[14] RPC ii. 242–3.
[15] RPC iv. 209.

The rhetoric used in such threats reflected the government's perception of the Borders, which appeared to be worsening throughout the sixteenth century as government priorities in the region changed.[16] Perpetrators of crimes in the Borders were often described as 'disorderit and wickit personis', and in 1573 the council thought that the borderers' actions were 'to the greit hurt of the commoun weill' of Scotland. The act of 1587 thundered against their 'wicked inclinatioun ... delyting in all mischeiffis and maist unnaturallie and cruellis waistand flayand heryand and distroyand' to the detriment of their 'awin neighbouris'. Their offences were the 'maist barbarous cruelties and godless oppressionis'.[17] Godless crimes did not sit well within a supposedly 'godly' society. Moreover, these miscreants were not mere common criminals but, in 1587, were seen as 'tratouris and malefactouris' 'aganis the gude peax and amytie standing betuix the twa realmes': crime in a region of sensitivity, was increasingly thought to prejudice the security of the whole realm and to be traitorous to the king.[18] Such condemnation increased through the 1590s, when it was becoming ever more important to James to maintain peaceable relations with Elizabeth. Thus, in 1599, the council ranted against the 'disordourit and brokin men of the Bordouris, enemyis to the publict peace and quietnes betuix the realmes, [who] hes of lait committit divers insolenceis and enormities in hostile and weirlyke maner within the realme of England, to the evident prejudice and violating of the peace and amitie'.[19] Evident in its rhetoric was the warping of governmental concern over crime in the Borders occasioned by its deteriorating perception of the borderers. Such descriptions were stereotypical and generalised. Government records such as these cannot, therefore, be used as an accurate depiction of reality but they colourfully illustrate the crown's changing attitude to the region.

One of the most common complaints concerned theft. Theft was variously termed 'thift', the illegal removal of someone else's goods; 'spulzie', the removal or borrowing of goods without someone's permission, either with intent to return or claiming them as their own; 'heirschip', theft with violence, often used to describe raiding; and 'reif', also used to describe raiding, in particular theft of livestock. In the Borders the theft was usually of cattle or sheep, predictably, because they constituted the subsistence and wealth of the borderers. It was seen as particularly significant that livestock theft provided subsistence, and, increasingly from the late 1580s, government felt that such theft had replaced farming or other honourable employment as a way of life in the Borders. Theft, it was thought, struck at the core of society, impeding normal agricultural practices and was deleterious to 'peace, quyetnes, and gude ordour' in the region. It had to be exemplarily

---

[16] Goodare analyses a similar trend in government's perception of the stereotypical highlander: *Government of Scotland*, 222, 233–5.
[17] RPC ii. 242–3, 558–9.
[18] RPC iv. 188.
[19] RPC vi. 13.

punished with 'immediate remeid', and, in 1605, the new commissioners of the Middle Shires were ordered to expel 'all idle vagaboundis quhais meanis to leif and sustene thameselffis being unknawyne caryis ane presumptioun of thair unlawfull mantenance'.[20]

Livestock theft was sometimes accompanied by the theft or ruining of crops and could escalate into violence. Such crime was usually associated with dispute over ownership of the lands involved and such cases often formed the origins of feuding. In 1601 William Paterson, portioner of Windylaws, brought a case against Andrew Pringle, also portioner there, for slaying several sheep on his lands over the previous year, harassing his servant, stripping 'his haill claithis of him, strak and dang him, and left him naked, and schortlie thairefter invadit and persewit [Paterson] ... for his slaughter' and then 'pasturit his guidis upoun [Paterson's] ... growand cornis'. Similarly, in 1602, Jackie Laidley of Antrop accused the Rutherfords of the Toftis for scaring him off his lands, throwing his corn into the river Jed, burning down his house and theft of his goods and animals throughout 1601. Increasingly the government intervened and here the Rutherfords, failing to appear before the council, were denounced rebel.[21] Many complaints described the 'hostile and weirlyke maner' of the offenders, such as Scott of Thirlestane and his allies who, in 1597, 'with braid aixis and swerdis ... cuttis five plewis pertening to the inhabitants' of Peebles, and 'with bendit pistollettis and uthir armis persewit the said complanirs of thair lyveis'.[22] Such violence was often a feature of dispute and extreme violence sometimes resulted in slaughter. But such crimes in the Middle March should not be viewed as something that was a regional characteristic: in the late sixteenth century feuding was a national phenomenon.

When the theft was cross-border it aquired an extra dimension. The opprobrium attached to it depended upon the state of Anglo-Scottish relations at the time. As Julian Goodare notes, if relations were bad 'far from being punished, the criminals would be encouraged'.[23] However, from 1586 to 1587, and from 1597 onwards there was a detectable increase in government condemnation of raiding across the border. Problematically, however, the reporting of such raids survives mostly in the English wardens' records of theft by Scots in England: those of the Middle March reflected raiding into Tynedale, Redesdale and north-east Cumberland. For instance, in July 1596 Sir Robert Carey enumerated recent raids into the English East March reporting 296 cattle, forty-three horse and 1,055 sheep taken 'by our unruly neighbours of Tyvidale'. The value of spoils taken from its Middle March was estimated, in 1596, by the English at £15,876 sterling.[24] All these figures

[20] *RPC* vii. 701–4.
[21] *RPC* vi. 224, 331–2.
[22] *RPC* v. 373–4.
[23] Goodare, *State and society*, 220.
[24] *CBP* ii, no. 323.

have to be considered with some caution. It was often in the English warden's interest to inflate them, either in an attempt to get compensation from the Scots, or to emphasise the importance of his office to the English government. Lord Scrope, the English West March warden, certainly exaggerated his figures when he complained that Branxholme was 'ready with 3,000 men on the border side to invade us' in August 1596, though he was happy to admit to an English raid into Branxholme's territory that had brought back 400 sheep.[25]

It was the larger scale raids that gave them their notoriety but the size of raids varied. Peter Dixon's survey of raids between 1526 and 1603 shows a decline in the average size of recorded raids through the century, with a slight rise in their frequency from 1591, which was probably the result of increased reporting by wardens. Raids by between fifty and 200 men represented more than 47 per cent of the raids recorded between 1550 and 1585, declining to 22 per cent of the raids between 1586 to 1590, whilst, after 1585, over half the numbers of raids were accompanied by under ten men. Between 1580 and 1585 thieves from Liddesdale dominated the league table, accounting for 80 per cent of raids, dropping to 22 per cent for the next period to 1590, a slack taken up by the Grahams of the West March. Bills against men of Teviotdale in the Middle March accounted for an average of 22 per cent between 1586 and 1603. Most of the rest are accounted for by the West March. Over the period from 1510 to 1604 it was claimed that more than 50,000 cattle had been stolen. This sounds bad, but English offences are under-represented in the lesser survival of Scottish bills of complaint, whilst overestimation of losses was common to both English and Scottish wardens. Both Rae and Dixon conclude that the levels of raiding remained fairly constant from the 1570s to the late 1590s. It was government objectives in the region that were changing.[26]

Sentencing policy on theft reflected contemporary concern about it. In 1597, in fear that a 'publict weare' would result from the raid of July, James declared that he would pursue the miscreants 'with fyre and swerd, with all rigour and extremitie, to the ruteing oute of thame, thair race and posteritie'. That November the privy council ordered that no longer was mercy to be granted to thieves who were to be 'puneist … to the deid'. In 1599, to prevent the 'violating of the peace and amitie quhilk sa happelie hes continewit betuix the realmis', James was resolved 'to punishe with all rigour the disturbaris' of the peace.[27] By 1605 the government's view of theft, as one of the root causes of disorder in the whole cross-border region, prompted a

---

[25] CBP ii, nos 332, 336.
[26] Piers Dixon's figures are based on reports in CBP. He attributes the rise in the number of recorded raids after 1585 to a greater frequency of reporting, as a result of increased government interference on both sides of the border, and not an increase in numbers of raids: 'Fortified houses', 73–5; Rae, Administration, 220.
[27] RPC v. 404–5, 422–3; vi. 13.

severe sentencing policy on anyone stealing goods across the border. Those taking cattle valued at more than twelve pence were to be sentenced to death. In contrast, attacking an Englishman with a weapon was punishable only by twenty days in jail: if harm was involved, the offender was to be jailed until some form of satisfaction could be given.[28] The reset of theft, which gave safe harbour to offenders, was viewed as similarly heinous because it was thought to encourage criminals: this was particularly so in relation to any cross-border crime, where offenders could escape over the border. In 1576 the council claimed that 'the cheif cause of all the stowthis and utheris disordouris ... is the resett supplie consort and ayd gevin to the fugitives rebellis and outlawis'; it ordered that resetters were to be punished in the same way as if they had committed the crime themselves.[29]

Cross-border crime was certainly extensive. It should, however, be viewed within the context of cross-border relations and separately from internal crime within the march. And such domestic crime in the Borders should be viewed within the context of crime throughout Scotland. A survey of the violent crime, and related acts of caution, registered by the council between 1573 and 1599 shows a significant increase nationally in the record of violence from about 1587. Scottish society was not necessarily, however, becoming more violent, this rise mainly being accounted for by the dramatic proliferation of assurances as the crown began to draw the resolution of private dispute into its remit. Over the period, violent crime in the Borders represented about 20 per cent of the total figures for Scotland. If the population there was about 10 per cent of the national figure, this percentage would suggest a higher incidence of violent crime within the Borders in relation to the Lowlands.[30] Wasser's quantification of cases appearing before the central criminal courts between 1603 and 1638 found similarly, concluding that the Borders had 'an ongoing severe problem with violence'.[31] But violence, according to Wasser, was not a 'regional phenomenon'; crime in Scotland was 'serious, extensive, and frequently practiced by the landed elite' and the borderers were no different in this. Caution is needed with such quantitative assessments: for instance, there were almost no assurances from the western Highlands, and no one would suggest that these highlanders were lived in peace and harmony. This meant that violence in the Highlands was misleadingly under-represented in national percentages and, as a result, that in the Borders, almost certainly, over-represented. This was partly due to the greater proximity of the Borders to Edinburgh but also, crucially, because of the greater development of the apparatus of government in the Borders than in the Highlands. As Goodare notes, the 'nerve-ends' of government were particularly sensitive in the Borders; Wasser, too, concludes that these

---

[28] RPC vii. 707–9.
[29] RPC ii. 476–7.
[30] RPC ii–vi; Groundwater, 'Middle March', appendix G.
[31] Wasser, 'Violence', 57–8.

figures were more a demonstration of how well the region had become 'integrated into the machinery of central government'.[32] Once the crown began to insist on the central resolution of feud, it was relatively easy to encourage the borderers to subscribe assurances. Registering of crime was thus perhaps more a reflection of a sensitive framework of government in the Borders, and its changing priorities, than an accurate representation of crime.

The East March accounted for significantly less record of internal violence than the Middle and West Marches where figures were roughly equal. The similarity between the Middle and West was due possibly to the higher frequency of cautions being subscribed by men from the Middle March who were physically closer to Edinburgh than their western counterparts. This could also suggest that governmental structures were more effective in the Middle March. And whilst the record of violent crime was more frequent in the Borders, violence was common in Fife as well as Roxburghshire. The extensive reports of cross-border crime, however, probably gave a misleading impression of crime within the region. Furthermore, it also appears that the incidence of cross-border crime was greater in the West March than in the Middle, particularly if the figures for Liddesdale are excluded. Government, however, tended to describe crime in any part of the Borders as endemic in the entire region. As a result, events in the West March tended to colour the impression of the Borders as a whole. Concentration upon offences in the Borders should also not preclude the consideration that, though cattle raiding was less frequent in the Lowlands, other offences occurred there which caused similar concern, such as counterfeiting, treason or feuding. Equally, the theft of livestock was bound to dominate in Borders where it was the main form of wealth. Maitland was talking about the whole country when he lamented that

> In Scotland gritter miserie
> grit ewill in to this land we se
> As slauchtir hirschep thift and reiff
> Distructioun of all polecey
> and all manner of maist mischeiff.[33]

III

Violent crime was often the playing out of feuds, and in this period the crown was growing intolerant of such behaviour. In 1595 James having considered the state of the 'commounweill, altogidder disdordourit and shaikin louse be ressoun of the deidlie feidis and contraverseis standing amangis

---

[32] Goodare, *State and society*, 258; Wasser, 'Violence', 13, 21, 56, 58, 62.
[33] Sir Richard Maitland, 'Lament for the disorderis of the cuntrie', in *Maitland folio manuscript*, i. 317–20.

his Hienes subjectis of all degreis ... calling to mynd quhat unnaturall slauchtaris, bludeshed, barbarous cruelteis and inconvenientis hes occurit' decided to 'purge this land of the proude contempt'.[34] He ordered a number of outstanding feuds to be brought for resolution before him and his council, so that by his own 'panes and travellis', 'perfyte reconsiliatoun and aggreement' would be had amongst all the lieges. This led to the explosion in the numbers of acts of caution; and in 1598 he pushed the Act Anent Feuding through a convention of estates.

Contemporarily, feuding was seen as particularly prevalent in the Borders, a preamble in 1599 attributing 'the cheiff and onlie caus of the grite misreule and unquietnes of the West Bordour' to 'the deidlie feidis and querrellis standing betwixt the principall noblemen and barronis' there and that it could not be 'quieted and settled ... unless the saidis feidis be removeit'.[35] English wardens concurred, in 1596 describing the 'deadly foed, the word of enmitye in the Borders, implacable without the blood and whole family distroied'.[36] They repeatedly attributed crime in Scottish Marches to the 'greate feedes' among the surnames 'which cawseth greate disobedience there'.[37] In 1602 Sir Robert Cecil thought that 'the disorders alleged to arise from the abuses in the [Scottish] Wardens government in pursuing particular quarrels in blood', were prevented in the English Borders by the employment of outsiders as wardens, free of 'those particular respects of blood and kindred'.[38] The English marches were no stranger to feud, however; Forster's criticism of Scottish feuding turned a blind eye to his own involvement, with the Widdringtons, in a feud against Lord Eure in Northumberland.[39] English reports of feud should also be put into perspective: the wardens' proximity to, and primary interest in, the Scottish Borders meant that their reports did not consider feuding in the rest of Scotland.

But by the 1590s feuding was seen by government as a kingdom-wide problem. For instance, in 1595, when James ordered the settlement of several feuds, of the thirty-four nobles and lairds listed as in dispute, only six were from the Borders.[40] Between 1604 and 1610, 1,965 acts of caution were registered in Scotland, which were predominantly related to feud. Of these, around 330 (17 per cent) were for the Borders. Out of these around a third originated in the Middle March, with very many fewer in the East March and around a half from the West March.[41] The preponderance of feuds

---

[34] RPC v. 248.
[35] RPC vi. 46.
[36] CBP ii, no. 323. Wormald challenges this excessively wide definition of feud encompassing whole surnames: *Court, kirk and community*, 37, and 'Bloodfeud', 70–1.
[37] Sir John Forster, the English Middle March warden, to Francis Walsingham, 1582, CBP i, no. 120.
[38] CSP Scot. xiii/2, no. 828.
[39] CBP ii, no. 432; Meikle, 'A godly rogue', 126–63.
[40] RPC v. 248–9.
[41] RPC vii. 545–697; viii. 629–733.

from the West March in the figures for the Borders was largely accounted for by the persistence of the Johnstone-Maxwell feud. But feuding was a phenomenon of sixteenth-century Scottish society and Keith Brown's enumeration of feuds suggests that it was spread more evenly throughout the whole country than might have been expected. Whilst he found that feuds in the Borders numbered around 23 per cent of the national total, those from the Lowlands south of the Tay accounted for 40 per cent.[42] Cases from the Borders were almost certainly over-represented in these figures given the combatants' proximity to the central courts in Edinburgh. Prior to the work of Wormald and Brown, historians thought of feud as a 'specific cause of turbulence on the borders' where 'border society was turbulent by nature', without acknowledging contemporary concern over its incidence elsewhere. Ian Rae's excellent summary of the government's increasing channeling of the settlement of feuds in the Borders through central law courts, did not go on, however, to include the legislation of 1598 on something seen as a national problem.[43] Feuding was happening in the Middle March but not at a rate that far outstripped that in the rest of Scotland. When James's government decided to outlaw feuding in 1598, it was with the whole country in mind.

There was much report of dispute, however, in the Middle March.[44] The origins of such feuds are now often obscured by the lack of records, either in terms of judicial arbitrations or private settlements, and what was classed as feud is not always immediately obvious. Where the dispute is only evident through territorial settlements, it is not always possible to determine whether violence has occurred. Dispute therefore may or may not have escalated to feud, if feuding is classified as necessarily violent. The Act Anent Feuding of 1598 recognised this problem, attempting to determine feud as where 'thair is ather na slauchter upon nather syde/ or slauchter upon ane syde/ or ells slauchter upoun bath sydis'.[45] But, as Keith Brown observes, 'a clear definition of feud is still not really possible'.[46] He found it difficult, too, to assess the average duration of a feud: often, record of a feud was made only during the time that it was being resolved and that time was usually fairly short.[47] The example of the Scott-Ker feud in the Middle March, record of which existed from at least 1526 to 1597, would challenge any definition of feud as a short-term phenomenon. And, as Brown observes, 'revenge had a long memory'.[48] In the Middle March there was certainly much dispute, but, as elsewhere, the blurring of the line between dispute and feud means that its

---

[42] Brown, *Bloodfeud*, 6–7, 277.
[43] Rae, *Administration*, 10, 126, 211.
[44] List of feuds in the Middle March in Groundwater, 'Middle March', appendix F
[45] Brown, *Bloodfeud*, 3–5; RPS, 1598/6/2, accessed 12 Oct. 2009.
[46] Brown, *Bloodfeud*, 8.
[47] Ibid. 277.
[48] Ibid. 27.

origins can be opaque. A feud may have started over a minor incident, or a disagreement over land, but have been perpetuated by the escalation of the feud into violence, whereby the injury or slaughter of one party may have legitimised the further escalation of the feud. The violence itself had become the reason for the persistence of a feud. Any resolution, therefore, had to take into account both the original hurt and that sustained along the way.

A number of reasons may therefore have existed for any feud, though some types of dispute were more prevalent. Dispute often arose over territorial boundaries, and in the voicing or prosecution of such a dispute it could achieve a degree of enmity, which escalated into violence. Such feuds mostly remained within the locality in which they began.[49] Feud could also result from its principals supporting opposing sides in a political dispute at a higher level, particularly if this had led to slaughter. But the feud was subsequently shaped predominantly through the social structure of the region: given the importance of kinship within social groupings, dispute was often conducted by opposing kindreds and their allies. Jenny Wormald, whilst underlining the significance of kinship within a feud, cautions that kinship was sometimes more of rhetorical or symbolic importance. People might be paying lip-service to the values of kinship, whilst utilising them as a justification for their own actions.[50] Disputes over landholdings were clearly important: lines of potential friction can be readily pinpointed between areas where specific surnames dominated landholding (see map 3). Landholding may have been at the heart of a dispute, but the widening support for each side in the pursuit of a feud was usually on the basis of kinship or alliance.

An analysis of some of the Middle March's feuds demonstrates the ways in which feud operated and how the obligations of kinship and alliance, which had helped to shape the feud, also provided mechanisms for its settlement. Recent work on the feud emphasises the importance of this process of settlement in which an informal but generally understood code provided mechanisms, including compensation and reconciliation, which were, as Wormald found, 'a force for peace': there was a 'widespread acceptance of the principle of compensation rather than retribution', a means thus to stall the spiral into further violence.[51] The most notorious of the Middle March feuds was that between the Scotts and the Kers. It has been endlessly recounted, romanticised and vilified, and above all presented as an indictment of the destabilising effect of feud in the Borders. But its progress certainly demonstrated repeated attempts to contain it. The long-term failure of these attempts, however, was attributed to the inability of the crown generally to control its greater lairds in their own regions, and in particular the crown's impotence in the Borders.[52] But, in many ways, the gradual disappearance of this feud

[49] Ibid. 7.
[50] Wormald 'Bloodfeud', 66–8.
[51] Idem, *Court, kirk and community*, 36–7, and 'Bloodfeud', 66–71.
[52] Rae, *Administration*, 75–6, 91, 126, 160, 221.

exemplified the way in which James VI suppressed feud throughout Scotland with the co-operation of the nobles and lairds, who had been involved in feuding, in its extinction.[53] As such, the Scott-Ker feud could therefore demonstrate the crown's ability to impose its authority on a region historiographically held to be effectively outwith the government's control.

A summary of the Scott-Ker dispute through the sixteenth century illustrates some of the complexity of relationships involved. In 1526 Sir Andrew Ker of Cessford was killed at Melrose by James Elliot, an adherent of Sir Walter Scott of Branxholme, as the Scotts attempted to rescue the young James V from the earl of Angus and his allies, who included the Kers. Here, the Scotts and the Kers were being sucked into magnate politics at the highest level. In 1529, as part of a settlement of the feud that resulted, Branxholme married Janet Ker of Ferniehirst, cousin to the slain man.[54] Marriage was a common means to consolidate a settlement, usefully marrying off the unlucky spinsters of the family. Such arrangements, however, were not always successful, and here the feud did not cease, resurfacing during the Rough Wooing of 1543–8. In 1548 Elizabeth, widow of Walter Scott of Branxholme (d.1504), but born a Ker of Cessford, was killed when her Ker kinsmen burned down the Scott-owned Catslack tower. In 1549 the Scotts complained to the council that the Kers had broken an agreement to resist the English by assisting the earl of Sussex in the burning of Scott lands in Teviotdale. Mary de Guise, recognising Branxholme's loyalty to the Stewarts, in 1543 appointed him to the captaincy of Newark castle in Ettrick, an appointment reconfirmed in 1545. In 1550 she appointed Branxholme as warden of the Middle March, a post traditionally held by the Kers of Cessford and from which, in 1544, Cessford had been discharged. This was guaranteed to antagonise the Kers, and in retaliation, in 1552, affiliates of the Cessford and Ferniehirst Kers murdered Branxholme on the streets of Edinburgh.[55]

Branxholme's heir was a grandson and still infant, but as he grew up an attempt was made, in 1565, to resolve the feud. Cessford agreed to ask Branxholme's forgiveness at St Giles's in Edinburgh in a public display intended to broadcast the reconciliation to all their kinsmen. The agreement was to be consolidated through the proposed marriages of the murdered Branxholme's daughter Janet to George, son of Ker of Faldonside, and his granddaughter Elizabeth Scott to Thomas Ker of Ferniehirst. Neither of these marriages took place, but another of the granddaughters, Janet, did marry Ferniehirst in 1569. In 1577, when Regent Morton's council complained that 'the said feid is newlie gevin up ... deidlie hatrent and grudge proclamit, quhairupoun

---

[53] Brown, Bloodfeud, 269–70.
[54] In a contract of 1530 both sides agreed to go on four pilgrimages and daily masses were to be said for each family: Wormald, Lords and men, 128.
[55] NAS, GD40/2/16/Add. 1; Fraser, Buccleuch, i. 118–22; ii, nos 151, 162, 163, 164, 166, 169, 173, 176, 181, 182, 185.

forder inconvenient is liklie to follow'. Since the contemporary Branxholme was still a minor, it is clear that the dispute had radiated outwards from its principals to include members of the wider Scott and Ker surnames. Cessford and the Scott representative, Scott of Goldielands, were summoned to appear at a council arbitration of the dispute. Reflecting the alliance between the Douglases and the Scotts, and the strength of the Scotts' position during Morton's regency, the Cessfords were forced to pay £1,000 in compensation to the Janet whose marriage had not been fulfilled.[56] The incendiary mixture of local rivalry and court factionalism could not have been more evident.

By the 1590s, despite the attempts at resolution, and the marriage of the murdered Branxholme's great-grandson, also Walter Scott of Branxholme, to Margaret, sister of Robert Ker of Cessford, the feud seemed to be as strong as ever. In 1596 there were reports of Cessford challenging young Branxholme to a combat.[57] These two feisty men were jousting for position in the Middle March: Cessford was his father's deputy as warden, but they were rivals for the keepership of Liddesdale, which after 1594 fell into Branxholme's hands. Branxholme now effectively held control over the west part of the march, and was pretty much Cessford's equal. Both had profited from the forfeiture of Branxholme's step-father, the earl of Bothwell, an affiliation that will have exacerbated their personal enmity. By 1597, however, the favour at court of both Branxholme and Cessford had slipped, as James sought to persuade the English of his suitability for the succession by insisting on their temporary warding in England. As Branxholme lay in captivity in Berwick, letters between them spat their venom, Branxholme angrily signing himself 'Your brother in na termes', accusing Cessford of plotting against his life.[58] But the two were canny enough to note the winds of change and their personal feud never troubled the privy council again. James recognised their co-operation by ennobling them soon afterwards.[59]

This feud of course had wider ramifications than a personal dispute between Cessford and Branxholme: as heads of their surnames, members of that name usually followed them in dispute. The head of Cessford's cadet branch, John Ker of Ferniehirst, was named by Branxholme in his case against the Kers in 1549, and again in the indictment for the murder of Branxholme in 1552. Other Kers accused with Cessford included those of Hirsel, Primsideloch, Caverton and Linton. In 1565, however, Ker of Ferniehirst was excluded from the protection of the contract to redress the murder because he refused to sign it with Ker of Cessford with whom he seems to have fallen out. He was again excluded from another Ker settlement with Branxholme in 1569, but later that year agreed to marry Janet, Branxholme's sister. Ferniehirst and Branxholme were allied through the Marian wars, and both retained the

[56] Fraser, *Buccleuch*, i. 136–42; ii, no. 192; *RPC* ii. 643–4, 665.
[57] NAS, GD224/1059/17; Fraser, *Buccleuch*, ii, no. 204; *CSP Scot.* xii, nos 197, 224.
[58] *CBP* ii, nos 265, 842.
[59] *CSP Scot.* xii/1, no. 443; Fraser, *Buccleuch*, ii, no. 219.

support of the Kers of Littledean and Cavers. Whilst the principals may have been friends, their followers continued to take sides, and a resumption of this branch of the Ker and Scott feud was threatened, in 1591, when two of Ferniehirst's servants were killed in a brawl in Edinburgh with Branxholme's men. Both sides acted quickly to contain further escalation of the dispute, subscribing bonds of assurance not to harm each other. In 1596 the affair was resolved on Branxholme's assignation of the teinds of Innerleithen, which had probably been disputed, to Ferniehirst's heir, Andrew Ker of Oxnam.[60] Similarly, whilst Branxholme and Cessford may have not been overtly at feud after 1597, the disputes of their affiliates were not so quickly settled. In 1608 Sir Andrew Ker of Greenhead successfully pursued Robert Scott of Haining, a particularly combative individual, for an armed attack on the Ker-owned mill of Selkirk, the rights to which Haining disputed.[61]

The framework of feuding in the Middle March was further complicated by feuds amongst branches of a surname. The Kers of Ferniehirst and Cessford are a particular example of this. Maureen Meikle attributes their enmity to each attempting to assert its ascendancy over the other throughout the sixteenth century. In 1590 they clashed over the right to nominate the provost of Jedburgh.[62] In 1602, fearful for the stability of the border, James instructed Ferniehirst to sign a bond of assurance with Cessford, now Lord Roxburgh.[63] In the same year, Ferniehirst wrote to his son, Oxnam, to ensure that Roxburgh's erection of the barony of Kelso did not include Ferniehirst's title to the kirks of Innerleithen and Little Newton.[64] Both branches then made great efforts to keep the peace: in 1613 Roxburgh wrote to Ferniehirst inviting him to his daughter's wedding to the earl of Perth, thanking him for his attendance at his mother's burial. The teinds of Little Newton remained contentious, however, and, in 1616, an attempt by Roxburgh to divert them, to the prejudice of Ferniehirst, was suspended by the council. But when in 1619 a fight occurred between their affiliates, in which a Ferniehirst man was injured, Roxburgh wrote to Ferniehirst offering to take such measures as Ferniehirst desired 'to teach them to live more civilly and quietly'. Both Roxburgh and Ferniehirst were keen to assist in the suppression of feud between their surnames and enjoyed the benefits of their co-operation with the crown: Roxburgh was a prominent member of the council and Ferniehirst was shortly afterwards created Lord Jedburgh.[65]

The Scott surname could be similarly divided. In 1609 the council registered an act of caution, 'a variance having lately fallen out', for a mutual

---

[60] Fraser, *Buccleuch*, i. 139, 152–5, 171; ii, nos 173, 185; NAS, GD40/2/9, fos 80, 83, 84, 86.
[61] RPC viii. 134.
[62] Meikle, *A British frontier?*, 37, 60–2, 69, 71, 75, 77, 80–1.
[63] NAS, GD40/9/3.
[64] NAS, GD40/2/12, fo. 4.
[65] NAS, GD40/2/12, fos 44, 46, 50.

assurance between Robert Scott of Thirlestane, his brothers and bairns and Scott of Tushielaw. By March this list had lengthened to include in Thirlestane's alliance the Scotts of Goldielands, Whitslaid, Headshaw and Hundleshope and the Stewarts of Tinnis, when they were all asked to subscribe the assurance. Things had not been resolved by 1610 when the Scotts of Thirlestane were accused of bearing 'deadly hatred and malice against Walter Scott of Tushielaw and his sons, and intend to pursue them for their lives'. Thirlestane and Tushielaw were forced to subscribe another assurance. The Scotts of Headshaw and Whitslaid were cautioners for Thirlestane and also stood surety for each other, whilst Robert Scott apparent of Tushielaw stood surety for his father Walter.[66] This did not stop the feud, for in 1616 Tushielaw was granted a pardon for the slaughter of Thirlestane's brother.[67] The Scotts of Bonnington and Harden were also at feud, probably over the lands of Erniscleugh in Ettrick forest. Harden's ally Elibank interceded on his behalf with the council in 1617 and 1619. Bonnington appears to have lost the dispute, since William Scott, apparent of Harden, was granted in 1617 a great seal charter of the grant of Erniscleugh, formerly held by the Bonnington family, from the Kers of Cessford.[68]

The enmity between the Scotts and Kers was not confined to those of their immediate surnames. The links of alliance with other surnames drew them into the orbit of the Scott-Ker dispute. Differences within surnames and local territorial disputes meant that the Scotts or the Kers would not inevitably have had the backing of specified allied surnames. However, a loose framework can be made of alliance and feud in the Middle March. In general the Kers had the affiliation of the Rutherfurds, Pringles and Hays of Yester, whilst the Scotts normally had the support of the Stewarts of Traquair, Turnbulls, Murrays and Douglases and latterly the Elliots and Armstrongs. In return, surname heads supported adherents in their disputes: thus Branxholme supported the Turnbulls, in 1595, in their action against Cessford. The feud between Yester and Traquair fitted into this framework, as did the Traquair-Rutherfurd dispute over the lands of Edgerston.[69] But it was not set in stone. In the 1560s the Elliots would have been more likely to side with the Kers, but by the 1590s they were sworn adherents of Branxholme, many of them now his tenants. Similarly, in 1552, Douglas of Cavers was indicted for the murder of Branxholme, but Margaret Douglas, sister of the earl of Angus, married Branxholme around 1665 and Douglas of Bonjedburgh was allied with the Scotts during the Morton regency.[70]

Apart from the Scott-Ker feud, one of the other long-running feuds in the march was that between the Hays of Yester and the Stewarts of Traquair.

---

[66] RPC viii. 246, 255–6, 271, 435, 695–6, 724–5.
[67] NAS, GD32/1/8.
[68] NAS, GD157/189,190; GD157/1246; GD124/15/29, fo. 14.
[69] Rutherford papers, NLS, Acc.7676A, bundle iv.
[70] Fraser, *Buccleuch*, ii, nos 185, 206, 217.

This was brought before the council several times in 1586 and 1587.[71] That their lands adjoined each other, dominating the upper reaches of the Tweed, indicates where dispute might have arisen (*see* map 3), and Yester's superior jurisdiction as sheriff of Tweeddale probably exacerbated the friction between them. This feud was widened by a notorious one between their affiliates, respectively the Tweedies (Yester) and the Veitchs (Traquair), who held lands south-west of Peebles. The Tweedie-Veitch feud then extended further since the Tweedies had the support of the Murrays and, in 1605, Tweedie of Drumelzier stood surety for Murray of Eddleston (Blackbarony) not to harm Andrew Veitch portioner of Stewarttoun.[72] The origins of these disputes are unclear, territorial, political or merely personal, but they had become entrenched in, defined by and extended through the structures of the kindreds and alliances in the region.

This combination of disputed lands and the ramifications of the original disagreement being taken up by the wider kindreds and alliances was seen in the feud between the Traquair Stewarts and the Pringles over the lands of Buckholm and Tinnis. These lay on the same line of friction on the outer edges of both surnames' territories. In 1606 Pringle of Torwoodlee was cautioner for Pringle of Buckholm and his men not to molest Sir Robert Stewart of Shillinglaw, tutor and uncle to Stewart of Traquair, whilst the Stewarts of Shillinglaw and Tinnis promised not to harm the Pringles of Buckholm.[73] Stewart of Tinnis, a 'cadet of the house of Traquair', was murdered by a Pringle of Tinnis; a brother of Murray of Philiphaugh had been present. Though both Shillinglaw, on behalf of Traquair, and Philiphaugh tried to prevent any escalation of the dispute by making assurances in 1601 and 1604, the matter was still unresolved in 1618, when Shillinglaw complained that the murdered man's son was obstructing the issue of a letter of slains that would finalise the settlement. Shillinglaw complained that Traquair's old friendship with the Murrays was threatened by the continuation of the feud over the lands at Tinnis.[74] Though the incidence of feuding was much decreased by this time, the threat of its resumption could still encourage its resolution.

But kindreds and their allies were not the only embodiment of feuding parties. Some families were involved in feuds with local burghs: these disputes were predominantly about territorial rights, particularly over common land and mills, but could also be related to the burgesses' resistance to a local family's political power. Attempts to resolve them, in the Middle March, showed the increasing involvement of the crown in forcing an arbitration and settlement.[75] Rights over the common lands of the burghs were particu-

---

[71] *RPC* iv. 68, 186, 210.
[72] *RPC* vii. 601.
[73] *RPC* vii. 631–2, 655–6, 669.
[74] NAS, GD40/5/6; *RPC* vii. 556; xi. 337.
[75] Brown, 'Burghs, lords and feuds', 102–24.

larly contentious, dispute over them necessitating the potentially incendiary ridings of the boundaries that yearly took place to ensure their protection. Those at Selkirk generated many a dispute that appeared to lead to oppressive behaviour, and sometimes violence. A feud between the good burgesses and Andrew Ker of Yair and his four sons over the lands and mills of Yair and Cribs, that had begun before 1602, led to James VI ordering the burgesses in 1612 to 'forbear the riding of the marches ... [whilst] Andrew Ker should forbear pasturing his beasts' on the disputed common land because he understood 'trouble was likely'. This order was repeated in 1613 and Yair was ordered not to cut divots before the council had decided ownership. Both parties had been forced to find assurance not to harm each other, and were finally summoned to appear before the council, Yair writing hopefully to the burgesses that 'ye sall not be overt strait with me in this my sempill suit [before the council] for the awld freindschips hes being amang us'.[76] Robert Scott of Haining, sometime provost or deputy of Selkirk in the 1590s and early 1600s, was also in dispute with the burgh, from around 1606, over the mill and lands of Haining. In 1607 this led to Mr Patrick Shaw, the minister of Selkirk, and the burgesses, obtaining a letter of lawburrows against Haining to protect themselves against him. In 1608 Haining was summoned to appear before the privy council and ordered to remove himself from another mill on the lands of Heatherlee Green, but the ownership of the mill was still contentious in 1610.[77]

Often disputes within a burgh correlated with feuds between surnames from outside it, particularly where powerful families attempted to manipulate burgh elections. This was the case in Jedburgh where the right to nominate the provost was the subject of dispute between the Kers of Ferniehirst and Cessford in the 1580s and 1590s. In 1581, when Ferniehirst was briefly provost, the English noted that he and Cessford were 'at point of falling furth, and great enmytie is like to growe betwixt them'.[78] The provost was often from the Rutherford kindred, allies of the Kers of Ferniehirst. In 1590 the burgesses elected a Rutherford to the provostship in defiance of a ruling by James in favour of Cessford who was at feud with Ferniehirst.[79] In contrast, the Turnbulls of Minto and Stanyledge were at feud with Jedburgh and the Kers of Ferniehirst. In 1601 Thomas Turnbull killed Ferniehirst's brother Thomas of Crailing and his servant in Jedburgh. When in 1603 another Turnbull was tried for a number of offences of murder and cattle-theft, James Waddell, a burgess of Jedburgh, was not allowed on the assize because 'thair is deidlie feid standand betuix the haill name of Trumbill, on the ane pairt,

---

[76] BA, WM3/11, 12; 4/16; 11/99; 12/44, 75, 79; *RPC* vii. 647, 651; ix. 453, 457–8; x. 127, 134–5.
[77] Selkirk burgh papers, BA, SC/S/12/33/1; WM4/20/1; 11/61, 79; 12/7, 65, 88.
[78] *CBP* i, no. 111.
[79] Brown, 'Burghs, lords and feuds', 108–9; Meikle, *A British frontier?*, 60–1.

and the Laird of Pharniherst, the haill Kerris, and the haill inhabitantis of the toune of Jedburghe, on the uther pairt, for the slauchter of Thomas Ker, brother to ... Pharniherst'.[80] Peebles was similarly affected by the feuds between its neighbours, the Yesters and their affiliates the Tweedies and the Horsburghs, and the Stewarts of Traquair and their supporters amongst the Veitchs, which repeatedly brought violence onto its streets. In 1590 the feud between the Tweedies of Drumelzier and Dreva and William Veitch of Dawick appeared before the council four times following the slaughter in Peebles of Patrick, son of William Veitch of Dawick.[81]

Feuds also existed with English surnames across the border, usually arising from long-running vendettas over past raids and slaughter. These too could draw in a wider circle of support and enmity. In 1579 it was reported that there were 'private quarrels between Herons [of Tynedale] and Carres involving other houses, who would rather overthrow each other than face the enemy'.[82] Sir John Carey, in 1595, reported the involvement of the March's main officers in similar cross-border feuds, the Kers of Cessford with the Storeys, and the Scotts with the Charltons of Hesleyside in Northumberland. In the course of the latter, Buccleuch was reported to have made 'a great rode' with an estimated 300 men into Tynedale and Redesdale 'wherein they took up the whole country, and did very near beggar them for ever'. In retaliation the Charltons 'did not only take their owne goodes agayne, but also hartned ... their neyghbors to take theirs, and not be afraide, which hath ever synce stuck in Bucclughe's stomach'. Carey traced the roots of this feud back to a 'long time synce, in a warr tyme' when the men of Tynedale men attacked Buccleuch's lands and 'tooke away hys grandfather's sworde, and would never lett him have yt synce'.[83] Such cross-border feuds were heightened by, or gained legitimacy through, the latent Anglo-Scottish hostility and demonstrate how external pressures might be acted out in the region.

Similarly, political struggles at court in Edinburgh were played out in the Middle March, where opposing kindreds allied with the noble factions and mirrored their enmity in the march. In 1579 the English reported 'the heat borne and hatred betwixt the Earl of Morton and the Carrs and Humes, who depend on Argyll' and 'the particular quarrels' between Carmichael and Ker of Cessford, Morton's enemy.[84] In 1580 Bowes wrote to Burghley warning that 'Lennox is already at Edinburgh strongly accompanied with sundry noblemen, the Carrs and Humes' and 'the flame of the fire likely to kindle' and 'come to hazard troubles on the Borders', where Morton was supported

---

[80] *Ancient criminal trials*, ii/2, 370–7, 419–21, 445; RPC vii. 44.
[81] RPC iv. 495, 496, 514, 551.
[82] CBP i, no. 41.
[83] The sword remains at Hesleyside. See Fraser, *Buccleuch*, i, 212–13; CBP ii, nos 77, 80.
[84] CSP Scot. v, nos 432, 446.

by the Douglases and the Scotts, the Kers' enemies.[85] Taking sides with the winning political faction could bring rewards of offices, but it could also exacerbate existing antagonism in the region. In 1587 Robert Ker of Cessford married Margaret Maitland, niece of the chancellor, Sir John Maitland of Thirlestane: this tied them in a mutually beneficial relationship providing patronage at court for the Kers, and Ker support for Maitland in the East and Middle Marches. However, Maitland's arch-enemy, the disdainful, and slightly mad, earl of Bothwell, married Scott of Branxholme's widow, Margaret Douglas, a daughter of the earl of Angus. Thus, when Bothwell was pursued by Maitland and James, from 1591, he was supported by the Scotts of Buccleuch, Harden and Whitslaid, this alliance paralleling the local feud between Buccleuch and Cessford.[86]

Feud was no longer to be tolerated throughout the kingdom, but it was particularly not to be tolerated where it might prejudice the newly amicable Anglo-Scottish relations. Feuding was as characteristic of life in the Middle March, as it was elsewhere, and when measures were taken to suppress it in the Borders, the processes of intervention were the same as those underway throughout Scotland. In this, the crown was supported by the acquiescence of the nobles and lairds. Roxburgh's attempts in 1619 to stifle the resumption of the Cessford-Ferniehirst feud amongst their affiliates was telling: this, from a man involved personally in several feuds in the 1590s, exemplified the way in which prominent figures everywhere had changed their attitude towards feud in line with government policy. The chief perpetrators of feud had become the agents of its suppression.[87]

IV

If the Borders were a diplomatically sensitive region, the valley of Liddesdale to the south-west of the Middle March, its southern boundaries forming part of the Anglo-Scottish frontier, was particularly sensitive. Raids locally by Liddesdale men often meant across the border, and therefore had the added dimension that they threatened Anglo-Scottish amity: in 1587 Forster worried that the 'oppin attemptatis and incursis committitt be Liddesdaill is lyklie to cause the haill Bordouris brek, gif spedie remeid be nocht provydit'. As a result of this heightened concern, Liddesdale had an additional official, the keeper, whose necessity R. B. Armstrong attributed to 'the extreme lawlessness' of Liddesdale's inhabitants. The levels of cross-border crime here were certainly higher in comparison to the rest of the march, given the

---

[85] *CSP Scot.* v, nos 471, 584.
[86] Fraser, *Buccleuch*, i. 171; ii, no. 209.
[87] NAS, GD40/2/12, fo. 50.

frequency with which they were mentioned in reports, though it is almost impossible to quantify them.[88]

The opprobrium with which borderers were viewed as a whole was multiplied in government reports on Liddesdale. A band by the men of the Middle March in 1569 committed them to assisting in the suppression of 'the rebellious people inhabitantis of the cuntre of Liddisdaill and utheris thevis: … having regaird to the innumerabill slauchteris, fyre raisingis, heirschippis and detestabill enormiteis dalie committit be thame upoun the peciabill' subjects, in particular by 'personis of the surnames of Armestrang, Ellot, Niksoun, Crosar, Littill, Batesoun' amongst others. It was enough to know that someone was an inhabitant there for their heinous nature to be understood. Voicing the court's perception of the region, Maitland's poem complained 'Aganis the Theivis of Liddisdaill':

> Off liddisdaill ye commoun thevis
> Sa peirtlie stelis, now and revis
> That nane can keip, hors nolt nor scheip
> Nor yit dar sleip, for thair mischevis …

> Thai have neir hand hirreit haill
> Ettrik forrest and Lawderdaill
> now ar thai gane, in lowthiane
> And sparis nane, that thai will waill.

He thought 'ye mekle deill thame gydis' and that all they had 'the deill ressaif'.[89]

The keepership often went with the ownership of the lordship of Liddesdale, which was in the hands of the Bothwells. On the forfeiture of Bothwell in 1594, the keepership was granted on an hereditary basis to Buccleuch as the new lord of the regality of Liddesdale. His jurisdiction there thus carried the authority of a crown appointee and that of a private jurisdiction.[90] The only superior jurisdictions were those of the crown and its occasional lieutenants. There were, however, discrepancies between the effectiveness of the keeper's jurisdiction and the consistency of his actions, and what was expected from him by the crown. The English complained in 1579 that the 'officers of Lyddisdale … had neither the authority nor assistance to do or execute their offices', whilst the 'particular quarrels betwixt Cesford [the warden] and [Carmichael the keeper] for the earl of Morton his master's causes … cannot but be a hindrance to justice'.[91] Personal feuds and political factionalism could prove obstructive to the fulfilment of a keeper's duties.

---

[88] *CBP* i, no. 514; R. B. Armstrong, *The history of Liddesdale, Eskdale, Ewesdale, Wauchopdale and the debateable land*, Edinburgh 1883, 10–11; Armstrong papers, NLS, Acc. 6110–20.
[89] *RPC* i. 650–3; Maitland, 'Aganis the theivis of Liddisdaill', 301–3.
[90] *RPC* v. 178, 191–2.
[91] *CSP Scot.* v, no. 446.

But the situation was complicated further by the mixture of personal and public responsibilities involved. In 1603 Sym Elliot of the Banks, 'ringleader of the thieves' who included three Armstrongs, was charged for armed theft and assault. At the request of the complainant, Buccleuch's deputy, Scott of Haining, agreed to refer the matter to the court of Lady Bothwell (Buccleuch's mother) at Liddesdale: though the accused was found guilty, Haining delayed in apprehending him and the complainant took the matter to the privy council. Haining was denounced rebel for failure to produce the accused and his own non-appearance. Both the Elliots and the Armstrongs were tenants of and adhered to Scott of Buccleuch. A number of Armstrongs and Elliots who 'hes given thair bandis to him [Buccleuch], comes under his standart and baner' and Haining as Buccleuch's 'governor' was forced to assume responsibility for them.[92] This left a situation where the official responsible for effecting justice in Liddesdale found himself being pursued by the crown to take action against his own men whom he had a personal obligation to protect.[93] The English Middle March warden in 1596, Lord Eure, complained that he could not get any redress from Buccleuch for Liddesdale, since all of Liddesdale are allied with him 'by oathe and scripte'.[94] This was often the case with the Ker wardens of the Middle March and their own Ker affinity, but in Liddesdale the problem was exacerbated by the conflicting responsibilities within the combination of Buccleuch's lordship of the entire area, his personal relationships with most of the inhabitants and the duties of his keepership. The crown's continuing use of a system of assurance to impose the law was inherently problematic, asking as it did for surname leaders to present to justice their own men on whom they themselves were dependent for support.

Whatever the problems in maintaining justice in Liddesdale, the crimes perpetrated by its inhabitants featured repeatedly in English reports, which inevitably highlighted their cross-border nature. A typical report was one by Scrope in 1597 of a raid by the Armstrongs with twenty-four men into the English West March, taking seventeen horses, ten pounds sterling of goods and killing two men. The same month William Bowes complained to Elizabeth of seventeen 'great attempts' by Liddesdale men since the Anglo-Scottish treaty of that May, which was meant to have stopped such incidents. The surnames of Armstrong and Elliot were particularly prevalent in English complaints. In 1597 the English demanded that pledges be surrendered from Liddesdale: the list included the Armstrongs of Mangerton and Whithaugh, Elliot of Lauriston, two other Elliots and a Nixon.[95] Liddesdale men were also, naturally, involved in crimes internally within the march. A complaint to the privy council in 1603 by Walter Scott of Tushielaw and his

---

[92] RPC vi. 179–80.
[93] RPC vi. 538–9.
[94] CBP ii, no. 232.
[95] CSP Scot. xiii/1, nos 13, 25; CBP ii, no. 666.

tenants listed theft of livestock and 'insight' from his lands near Ettrick by a number of Armstrongs of Liddesdale on five separate occasions in the course of a month in 1586. They were alleged to have taken a total of 2,800 sheep, 340 cattle and twenty horses. Even allowing for the massaging of figures by Tushielaw, these raids were of a sizeable nature.[96] The raiders of Liddesdale deserved their reputation: however, it was the cross-border crime that gave them their particular notoriety. And, as such, this cross-border crime should be viewed within the context of changing Anglo-Scottish relations and their effect on fluctuating government policy towards such crime. Liddesdale was a violent place, but these were violent and diplomatically unstable times.

V

When it came to the use of violence there was nothing more violent than the crown and its officials when acting in their execution of justice. This was nothing new, but by the later sixteenth century the crown was attempting to harness all violent methods of justice within its own control, progressing towards what Keith Brown has termed a 'state monopoly of violence'.[97] There was already a tradition of armed judicial raids by king, regent or lieutenant into the regions, when successive kings and regents had decided to make their authority felt. In the Borders this was usually during times of greater Anglo-Scottish amity. Musters were called to support them, those summoned being ordered to appear 'bodin in the feir of weir'. Common to all the proclamations of these raids was the intention to pursue miscreants with 'extreme rigour': the severity of the justice meted out in the raids was intended to be an exemplary deterrent. Sentencing policy at such courts was harsh, theft often punishable 'to the deid'. Judicial raids have left few records; in one of the few that do exist, for the court held at Jedburgh in 1587, at least sixteen were executed.[98] Crown officials also used violence out of court. Lieutenants and wardens were empowered to arrest, try and execute any offenders taken 'with the fang' and were granted indemnities for any summary justice that they had applied in the execution of their offices. This could lead to confusion. Cessford was the subject of a complaint that he had slain four men in England: his reply was that it was in the execution of his duty as warden, two being Scottish thieves. This was not clear to Scrope who complained that the 'greatest murderers are made the chief governors of the frontiers'. He included Buccleuch in this assessment.[99]

English suspicions were repeatedly to question the motivation of the Scottish government, which, whilst overtly professing its intention to suppress

---

[96] RPC vi. 538.
[97] Brown, *Bloodfeud*, 269.
[98] RPC iv. 146–8.
[99] CBP ii, no. 405; CSP Scot. xiii/1, no. 3; xiii/2, no. 640.

crime in the Borders, sometimes appeared privately to condone the illegal activities of its officials. A blurred margin seemed to exist between passive tolerance and active sponsoring of cross-border crime. In March 1587 Forster complained that the 'Kinge dothe write to the Lairde of Cesfurde to do justice, and yet in the meane tyme he appoynethe others to ryde and breake the borders, and dothe winke therat'. That November Lord Hunsdon, the English East March warden, questioned the point of James coming to Kelso on a judicial raid, when 'great oughtrages durst not be attempted by such men as hath done them, without the Kinges privitie', referring to the apparent approval that James had given to a cross-border raid by Buccleuch with 300 men who carried off goods to the Hermitage. In August 1596 Scrope railed against Buccleuch who he claimed was on the border with 3,000 men 'ready ... to invade us ... yet this man is thought fit by the King and Council to be still officer!' And in April 1597 Bowes wrote to Burghley of James's reluctance to 'bridle these wicked clandes' questioning 'whether it springe of too muche facilitie, or too little sincereitie': he concluded 'I consider their actions are done "by him or for him".' As Maitland acknowledged in his diatribe against those of Liddesdale, 'To se sa grit stouthe quha wald trowit/ onles sum grit man it allowit'.[100] Given James's recent and substantial grants of lands from the forfeiture of Bothwell to both Cessford and Buccleuch, the English suspicion is understandable.

VI

The English certainly thought that cross-border crime was partly attributable to James's policies in the Borders. His continued maintenance of figures such as Buccleuch and Cessford, despite their undeniable involvement in cross-border offences, was testimony to his use of the situation on the Borders in the conduct of relations with England. Cross-border crime disappeared fairly quickly after 1603, following concerted efforts by governments on both sides of the border, suggesting that if the will had been there, it could have been suppressed before.

Whilst Jenny Wormald has reassessed her downplaying of the violence in a feud, her overturning of a historical orthodoxy that viewed all violence as indicative of a powerless government has been invaluable in allowing a reassessment of government in Scotland.[101] The old orthodoxy indelibly permeated any assessment of violence in the Borders with an assumption that crime there was beyond the control of any government. But it is clear, from the huge numbers of assurances taken, and the gradual disappearance of feud in the Borders, that the government was able to effect its will when it was

---

[100] CBP i, nos 499, 560; ii, nos 336, 603; Maitland, 'Aganis the thevis of Liddisdaill', 302.
[101] Wormald, Lords and men, p. vi, and 'Taming the magnates?'

determined to, using the same mechanisms as elsewhere in Scotland. The Borders should be seen, therefore, within the context of developments in government attitude to crime and jurisdictions throughout Scotland. During the 1590s identifiable moves were made by the crown towards bringing the system of justice within its own remit and imposing the rule of law in the localities. There were several proclamations for the 'administration of better justice'. In 1590, understanding the abuse by lieutenants and others of their judicial powers, James ordered the discharge of all commissions of justiciary and lieutenantry. In 1600 a commission was ordered to consider the way in which sheriffs could be made more effective.[102] Insistence on a peaceful resolution of dispute was extended to other measures to prevent violence, such as the ordinances against the bearing of pistols and hagbuts, the subject of at least seven council proclamations between 1593 and 1597. Similarly, orders against feud proliferated, registered ten times between 1595 and 1597. A way of life, which previously had been tolerated throughout the country, was now subject to systematic review by government.[103]

But a final note of caution is necessary: such moves towards crown monopolisation of justice and violence were not concluded in this period. Michael Wasser found that the 'new was coexisting with the old' in terms of the continuation of the private pursuit of compensation well into the seventeenth century. However, this was now increasingly conducted through the courts rather than through the violence of feud. The use of courts was new, but the motivation behind it remained largely the same and dispute still included the use of violence.[104] The psychological attitudes of the whole community towards violence would take time to change. State prosecution of violent crime, with punishment as deterrent, was still in its infancy. This serves as a useful reminder that the growth in state power, which the increasing crown control of judicial processes represented, was underway but it was a work in progress.[105] The same should be said of its intervention in crime in the Middle March.

[102] *RPC* iv. 552; vi. 68, 233–4.
[103] *RPC* v. 90–1, 242, 247–9, 261–3, 273–5, 280, 303–4, 321–3, 392–3, 403, 437–8, 463, 497.
[104] Wasser, 'Violence', 271, 296.
[105] Goodare, *State and society*, 100.

6

The Road to Pacification, 1573–1597

The previous chapters have shown how the history of the Middle March from 1573 to 1625 should be seen within the context of developments that affected the whole realm: broader changes in crown policy towards its localities and in judicial matters, the evolution of kingship and government, the changing nature of lordship and the resultant gradual social evolution. The Middle March may have been on the periphery of Scotland but it was not an area separated from the kingdom. Its prominent figures were involved in central government and that government was able to make itself felt within the march if and when it chose to do so. Furthermore, given the fundamental importance of kinship in social and political frameworks at both local and central levels, factionalism at court had ramifications in the Middle March. But despite these connections, a variety of circumstances differentiated the region. These were occasioned principally by the proximity of the frontier with England and the changing nature of Anglo-Scottish relations during this period. For three centuries hostile governments had used the area as a diplomatic tool or military buffer zone. By the later sixteenth century, however, the conciliatory effects of the Protestant Reformation in both countries had softened Anglo-Scottish relations, and increasing amity was being consolidated by the likelihood of James's succession to the English throne. This meant that, by 1597, a region traditionally used as a buffer was now seen as a barrier to good relations. What had been an area occasioning sporadically direct intervention was now the subject of growing co-operation. By 1625 this had resulted in the more-or-less successful pacification of the Borders.

In 1573 the outlook had been very different. Scotland was emerging from six years of dynastic crisis and James was in his minority. Only four years before, English forces under the earl of Sussex had burned their way through the Scottish Middle March. By the end of the period, in 1625, the crowns of Scotland and England were united in the person of James VI and I and the international nature of the border had disappeared. James's succession, however, was neither confirmed nor inevitable. Similarly, the pacification of the Borders was neither guaranteed nor consistently pursued prior to 1603, enthusiasm for it fluctuating with successive regents, chancellors and monarchs. These next two chapters will trace the experience of the Middle March from 1573 to 1625 in the light of these diplomatic and political developments, through five main periods. This chapter covers the period until 1597: from 1573 to around 1578 during the regency of the anglophile earl of Morton; from 1578 until late 1585 through the years of court factionalism and vacillating diplomatic relations; and from 1585 to 1597, during James's emergent personal rule and through years during which amity with England was undermined by inconsistent crown policy in the Borders. The final chapter covers the origins of the post-union pacification in the period 1597 to 1605, when concern over the English succession and then the union prompted a novel consistency in border policy; and from 1605 to 1625 when the pacification was determinedly prosecuted in the newly created cross-border region, now renamed the Middle Shires. It was by no means a step-by-step progression, each phase being subject to reversal. 'Road to pacification' perhaps describes too smoothly linear a process: more accurately it should read 'the tortuous track towards less turbulent times'.

I

The beginning of this period was overshadowed by the preceding years of civil war, when the Middle March had been as divided as the rest of the country. Ker of Cessford had supported the king's party, whilst Ker of Ferniehirst and Scott of Branxholme had joined the Marian side: Branxholme had been raided by the English under Sussex in alliance with the Kers of Cessford. Though Cessford had been nominally warden of the march from 1570, for much of the time Ferniehirst had been acting as warden. The new regent, James Douglas, earl of Morton, of the king's party, was no friend of Ferniehirst, nor his son's godmother, Queen Mary. He immediately drove through Ferniehurst's forfeiture and exile, thus removing one of the few men who could challenge Cessford's authority in the Middle March, though relations between Cessford and Morton were not good either. The only other powerful enough figure in the march was Branxholme, but he died prematurely in 1574, leaving a young heir, the future Lord Buccleuch. The infant's mother Margaret was Morton's niece, and Angus's sister, solidifying the alliance between the Scotts and the Douglases. Though Branxholme's tutors managed his surname's affairs until he reached his majority in the mid-1580s, effectively there were few in the Middle March to counter-balance Cessford's power in the wardenship. Cessford commanded the support of several branches of the Ker surname, including those of Newbattle, Littledean and Faldonside, and a wider affinity which included such a prominent figure as Sir James Home of Cowdenknowes. The only other family that attempted to counter the Ker predominance in the 1570s was to be Morton and his Douglas surname.

Morton had secured his position with English military support and he intended to preserve this co-operation. A letter to Elizabeth in 1574 expanded on the measures needed to maintain the 'weale and increase of the amity betwixt both the realms', and his regency was to be characterised by relatively peaceful relations with England. Morton's attempts, however, to secure a formal alliance were unsuccessful.[1] The only exception to this was the Redeswyre crisis of July 1575 during which a kinsman of Sir John Forster, the English Middle March warden, was killed. Morton's preoccupation with preserving amicable Anglo-Scottish relations resulted in a concerted effort to suppress crime in the Borders, leading to nine judicial raids,[2] the tightening of the pledge system, measures to assist the wardens in redress of cross-border offences and the appointment of a lieutenant to oversee the enforcement of justice. In 1574 Morton emphasised his commitment by asking Elizabeth to urge her wardens to fulfill 'their duties in administration of justice, and such other good offices for the keeping of the peace and amity'.[3] His persistent efforts to maintain an efficient administration were admirable in the face of chilling relations between regent and English queen, and Elizabeth's reluctance to agree a formal alliance or pension. But Morton's judicial raids into the Borders should be seen, too, in the context of his efforts elsewhere to regularise Scotland's judicial system in the wake of the disruption of the civil war. Furthermore, the Scottish crown was broke, and judicial raids provided the much-needed funds that a tight-fisted Elizabeth was proving reluctant to supply.[4]

Morton's actions in the Borders were not, however, without self-interest, and their direction was largely determined by his personal circumstances and connections. This was unsurprising given the personal nature of sixteenth-century government and its reliance on familial obligations. As a result, the dynamics of kinship and alliance in the Middle March affected the appointments that Morton made to impose justice there. Inevitably, this introduced the enmities between kindreds and Morton was to alienate many outside his allegiance by filling offices in the Middle March with his own men. Morton, a Douglas, and allied to the Scotts, was reliant on the support of these surnames. Whilst, initially, his relations with the warden Cessford, the Scotts' enemy, were relatively harmonious, oiled by their common hatred of Ferniehirst, they soon deteriorated. In late 1573 Morton appointed his 'cousin and servant' Carmichael of that ilk, keeper of Liddesdale, with the intention that he would work with Cessford. Walsingham commented that 'Carmichael is one whom the Regent dearly loves'.[5] Next, Morton appointed his nephew, Angus, as lieutenant over all the marches. Then, in 1576, in a move guaranteed to antagonise Cessford, Morton appointed his kinsman William Douglas of Bonjedburgh warden of the Middle March west of Dere Street, thus reducing Cessford's area of authority. He then widened his kindred's authority by giving Angus the West March wardenship the

---

1 CSP Scot. v, no. 34; Hewitt, Scotland under Morton, chs vii, ix.
2 Rae, Administration, appendix 6.
3 CSP Scot. v, no. 34.
4 Goodare, State and society, 262.
5 CSP Scot. iv, no. 788; v, nos 172, 200.

following year.[6] None of these appointments outlasted Morton's downfall in 1580, though Angus played both sides for a while. The alienation that Morton thus stimulated was exacerbated by his pursuit of his personal vendettas: he was to target specific individuals, such as Ferniehirst, during his imposition of a rather partisan 'justice', though Rae noted the leniency with which he treated other opponents such as Lord Herries.[7] Melville felt that Morton committed 'dyvers wrangis and extorcions' under the pretext of administering justice and that his initial success as regent was because there 'was not another Erle of Mortoun to steir up the subjectis in factioun, as he used to do'. His position deteriorated, Melville said, once he alienated the nobility and became 'ingrat to all his auld freindis and sarvandis'.[8] Whatever Morton's personal intentions, they were in line with his public moves towards alliance with England until his authority was weakened in 1578.

In order to display his determination to stamp out crime to both the English and the borderers, Morton was to use judicial raids as an exemplar of judicial severity and sustained intent. Of the nine raids to the Borders, at least four were to the Middle March: the first in August 1573 was based in Peebles and Jedburgh and was repeated that November; in July 1574 there was a muster at Peebles and Selkirk; following the Redeswyre incident in 1575, a muster was called for Jedburgh but later postponed (one took place in Dumfries instead); and a judicial court was held at Jedburgh in November and December 1576.[9] Morton was present at all of these. The English were supposed to applaud, Morton writing to Burghley in 1573 that 'I have so travailed these days past with our disordered people inhabiting the frontier that I hope good fruits shall follow thereon to the comfort of the good people of both the countreis.'[10] Judicial raids were intended to make a lasting impression, too, on the 'thevis and disorderit people' of the region, but initially they dealt with those who had supported the queen's party, including Ferniehirst and his allies. The courts at Jedburgh in 1573 and 1576 were a calculated mixture of severity and leniency: so whilst the council was concerned at 'the evil exempill of utheris to do the like [steal] gif this be sufferit to remane unpunist', at Jedburgh in August 1573 'a greit part of [the thieves] hes enterit thair plegeis and maid suirtie for thair ... obedience in tyme cuming and reparatioun of thair bipast offenssis'. In 1576 'clemencie and pardoun for bigane offencis [was granted] ... on hoip to wyn the offendouris to obedience and bettir forme of leving heireftir'. Instead of physically punishing miscreants, the crown could replenish its coffers from fines, whilst

---

[6] RPC ii. 568–73; CSP Scot. v, nos 284, 315; Rae, Administration, appendix 2.
[7] Goodare, State and society, 262; Rae, Administration, 195.
[8] Memoirs of Sir James Melville of Halhill, 1535–1617, ed. A. F. Steuart, London 1929, 260.
[9] RPC ii. 242–3, 259–60, 274–5, 304–7, 384, 459–60, 476–7, 554, 566–73; TA xii. 352, 359–60; xiii. 17, 25.
[10] CSP Scot. iv, no. 723.

demonstrating its magnanimity: thus at Dumfries, in 1575, 'brokin men ... war puneist be thair pursis rather than thair lyvis', with courts in Jedburgh, in 1573, taking 'grit soumes of money' from the remissions granted, whilst offenders' 'guidis and geir salbe uptakin and intromettit with as escheit'.[11] The inhabitants of Selkirk paid £100, in 1573, when they came 'in the will of the King for assistance given by them' to Ferniehirst and a further £308 fine was paid later that year. The composition collected by the raid at Peebles in November 1573 was over £3,450 and that at Jedburgh, in 1576, exceeded £6,400 for Roxburghshire and Selkirkshire.[12] These were sizeable sums, intended to show Morton's commitment to suppressing crime.

Morton was determined to see this maintained in the long term by using pledges and assurances obtained during raids to secure future good behaviour: these were reinforced by the increasing use of mass subscription of bands. In January 1573 twenty-seven Teviotdale men appeared before the council in Edinburgh to swear that they would 'releif his Hienes and his Wardanis present and to cum at the handis of the Wardanis of Ingland'. They were obliged not to 'resset, supple nor intercommoun' with Ferniehirst 'or ony utheris declarit tratouris ... bot sall ryise, assist and serve his Hienes, his said Regent, Lieutenentis Wardane'. To ensure that they would do so, they agreed to 'takand the burding for thame selffis and utheris that thay have promissit for', by becoming cautioners for various named men, mostly members of their own surname. Those finding surety included the sheriff, William Douglas of Cavers, for whom William Ker of Caverton and Andrew Ker of Faldonside became cautioners, under pain of 2,000 merks.[13] This band was representative of several bands subscribed by men of the Middle March, earlier in April 1569, and then again during Morton's regency in August 1573, reiterated in June 1574 and repeated in August 1576. Though it was often used in the Borders, a band was not, however, a border-specific device: a similar band was subscribed by the 'Northland Men' of Aberdeenshire in August 1574, and repeated at Holyrood in May 1575.[14] What was different about the Teviotdale band was its specific obligation not to reset Ferniehirst and the targeting of certain surnames, such as the Rutherfords, to subscribe it and find surety, due to their alliance with the Kers of Ferniehirst and Cavers.[15] A band could be used for a specific objective and here Morton was using it to wreak personal vengeance on his opponents in the Marian wars.

Throughout his regency Morton was to attempt to tighten judicial measures. In particular, he addressed some of the problems of the pledge

---

[11] RPC ii. 274, 304–7, 476–8, 566–73. The composition of the Dumfries court was £1,968: TA xiii. 16.
[12] TA xii. 270, 272; xiii. 123.
[13] RPC ii. 179–80. It repeated the sentiment of the band subscribed at Jedburgh for the pursuit of Ferniehirst in February 1572: RPC ii. 116–18.
[14] RPC i. 650–3; ii. 452, 547, 548–9.
[15] RPC ii. 179–80.

system. In 1573 an ordinance made those with whom pledges were warded responsible for their non-escape and, in 1574, a number of Armstrongs and Baties were to be entered as pledges with various Maxwells and Johnstones on the West March. Warders were to 'become actit and oblist cautioneris for the personis plegeis'.[16] Similarly, lairds were increasingly asked to stand surety for the entrance to justice or good behaviour of their allegiance. For instance in December 1573, following a judicial ayre at Peebles, the Scotts of Thirlestane, Gamescleuch, Hartwoodmyres, Tushielaw, Branxholme, Birkenside, Deephope and Dryhope promised to ensure the entry of a number of Scotts and Littills to the Edinburgh tolbooth.[17] In June 1574 various lairds of the Middle March were ordered to register themselves in the books of the council as 'plegeis and souirteis for all ther personis inhabiting of thair landis'. These acts of caution were sometimes difficult to enforce. In June 1574 three lairds, bound under the pledge of Liddesdale for a number of Crosiers and Elliots, were fined the surety of 5,000 merks each for their non-appearance before the council to answer for their adherents' failure to appear. The same month it was directed that if any had not upheld the band against the reset of Ferniehirst, the lairds standing surety for them should 'hald thame, thair whiffis, bairnis, servandis and guides furthe of the saidis landis'.[18] Since, however, this was asking a laird to throw out tenants who were often of his own surname, to whom he had obligations of good lordship or kinship, and on whom he was dependent for support, this was difficult for him to carry out.

The obligations of kinship and alliance could be used by government to maintain order, but these obligations might stimulate problems too: nowhere was this clearer than in the existence of the bloodfeud, in the Middle March, as throughout Scotland. Since this was causing violence in an area that he wished to see peaceable, Morton increasingly ordered disputes to be brought to the council for arbitration. For instance, on 3 June 1575, in an attempt to resolve the long-standing and troublesome Pringle-Elliot feud, representatives of the two surnames were called to appear before the council on 24 June with their representatives. Those summoned to appear for the Pringles included Ker of Faldonside, and for the Elliots, the Douglases of Cavers and Bonjedburgh, Turnbull of Minto and two Rutherfords.[19] The list of supporters showed a neat delineation of alliances in the Middle March. It was to be expected that the Rutherfords would act with the Douglases against the Kers of Cessford and Faldonside and their affiliates: in 1576, when Ker of Cessford and Turnbull of Bedrule found assurance not to molest each other, Douglas of Bonjedburgh and Rutherford of Hunthill stood caution for Bedrule.[20] The

[16] Rae, *Administration*, 197; *RPC* ii. 272, 367–70.
[17] *RPC* ii. 306–7.
[18] *RPC* ii. 371–3.
[19] *RPC* ii. 453–4.
[20] *RPC* ii. 526–7.

council's intervention in feuds was also driven by Morton's pursuit of his own kindred's interests. In October 1577 the council intervened in the long-standing feud between the Scotts, Morton's allies, and the Kers of Cessford, which had resurfaced, summoning each side to appear with twenty men before the council. The weakened position of the Kers under Morton was reflected in the decision against them, the Kers being ordered to pay Janet Scott £1,000 for the failure of a son of Ker of Faldonside to honour a marriage contract. The feud continued, however, Robert Bowes noting in 1580 that 'little effect is come' of Angus's attempts to reconcile them.[21]

Similar attempts were being made by Morton's council to resolve feuds in other parts of Scotland, but in the Borders he was determined to prevent any disturbance that might disrupt peace with England. From 1573 until 1578 the only potentially disastrous cross-border incident was at a day of truce at Redeswyre on 7 July 1575, fabulously commemorated in the rollicking ballad, the 'Raid of Redeswyre'. An argument had broken out between Forster, the combative English Middle March warden, and Carmichael, acting for the Scottish march, which resulted in the killing of Sir George Heron, Forster's brother-in-law, and the capture of Forster and several Englishmen by Carmichael. They were warded immediately with Morton at Dalkeith in an effort to prevent further fighting.[22] Frantic Anglo-Scottish negotiations ensued, both sides fearing that 'peace or war hangs now by a twine thread' and that 'the broken men of the borders ... will draw on this sudden misadventure to great inconvenience and a dangerous consequence'. On 8 July Morton wrote to Walsingham for advice on how to proceed 'best for eschewing further breach and mischief', whilst Home of Cowdenknowes was sent to the border to request a meeting with the English emissary Killigrew. Huntingdon later noted that 'though the game was very injurious, yet good came thereof; for the Borders during that time remained quiet'.[23] Morton, in stopping the incident from escalating, showed himself able to control events within the Middle March. He issued a proclamation on 26 July reassuring the English of Scotland's continuing desire for peace on the frontier, to be read throughout the Borders towns, so that no borderer would disturb the 'good amytie'. Throughout, Morton continued to reassure the English of his good faith, reiterating that he had kept Forster in ward to calm 'the blood' and to maintain peace.[24] Though the English were not quite so conciliatory, Walsingham insisting that 'some severe punishment [is] executed on the offenders', both sides wanted to negotiate and a treaty was made between Morton and Huntingdon at Foulden in mid-September.[25]

[21] RPC ii. 643–4, 665; CSP Scot. v, no. 471.
[22] Rae, Administration, 199–201; Meikle, 'A godly rogue', 126–63; CSP Scot. v, no. 177.
[23] CSP Scot. v, nos 166, 169–71.
[24] RPC ii. 459, 460, 462–3; CSP Scot. v, no. 193.
[25] CSP Scot. v, nos 172, 175, 195, 196, 197, 206, 209.

One of the reasons for the subsequent cooling of relations between the two countries was Morton's failure to secure a pension from the English. Concern over this was prompted by the Scottish crown's financial insecurity, with poverty often said to limit the warden's effectiveness in the Middle March. As early as November 1573 Morton wrote to Elizabeth of his difficulties in retaining 'an ordinary force of horsemen and footmen for keeping the Borders in quietness', since 'state charges [have] been panefull and verie expensive for me'.[26] This was still the case in 1579, when an English memorial noted that Cessford had but £16 sterling a year 'yet his wardenries great and troublesome'. It further noted that a border guard and adequately compensated wardenries could be done for £3,000 sterling but that James could not afford this.[27] As a result the wardens were expected to organise any armed assistance from their own resources, and the lack of a paid armed force was often used as one of the reasons for the continuation of theft.[28] Morton occasionally alluded to such a force at work, in 1575 for instance, but it was not used continuously.[29] Indeed there was no record of the payment of such a force in the Middle March during Morton's regency, though subsequently both Cessford and Ferniehirst were thought to have been so assisted in the early 1580s.

Another of the problems facing wardens was the reset of thieves, both internally and cross-border, an ordinance of 1575 noting that reset was 'the cheif cause of all the stowthis and utheris disordouris committit within ayther of the realmes'.[30] In 1577 the threat of punishment of reset was to be proclaimed at Lauder, Selkirk, Peebles, Lanark, Dumfries and Jedburgh, so that none could claim ignorance.[31] Morton complained to Huntingdon over the reset of Scottish thieves in England, 'received in Tynedale' with 'Duke' Fenwick. He bemoaned Forster's failure in this respect, 'wherein their fugitives are ... received and maintained' and 'to the great encouraging of the wicked and disordered people'.[32] But this was one of the intrinsic problems that wardens faced in apprehending offenders; lack of co-operation on the part of the English warden would always undermine the efficacy of the Scottish warden (and *vice versa*). Forster's partisan execution of his duties was subject also to increasing English complaint and investigation.[33] Nor was the problem of reset confined to border thieves. Morton was made uneasy by the Scottish rebels lying just inside the English Borders following the end of the Marian wars. In 1574 he complained to the English that at the last day of

---

[26] *CSP Scot.* iv, no. 732.
[27] *CSP Scot.* v, no. 445.
[28] The privy council after Union certainly thought so, appointing a border force under Sir William Cranstoun as one of its first measures in the pacification: *RPC* vii. 709.
[29] *CSP Scot.* v, no. 209; Rae, *Administration*, 28, 85–9.
[30] *RPC* ii. 476–7.
[31] *RPC* ii. 620–1.
[32] *CSP Scot.* v, nos 55, 64, 111.
[33] Meikle, 'A godly rogue', 126–63.

truce, the English warden Forster had been accompanied by the rebel Ferniehirst. Not only was this potentially incendiary in a meeting with Cessford, but it had allowed 'sic of this cuntremen as plesit to confer with [the rebels] ... frie access sa to do'.[34] The continuing proximity of Marian sympathisers and their friendly relations with the English was a direct threat to Morton's own attempts to foster such relations and undermined the efficacy of cross-border redress.

In addition, problems associated with kinship and alliance impacted on the wardens' efficiency. All those holding office as warden or keeper were involved in networks of kinship and alliance within the march and, by extension, enmities. Robert Bowes thought that the Middle March wardens were 'parties to the factes' in the Redeswyre incident and 'much touched both in their own causes and for their friends'. He felt that justice would not be done by the wardens for fear of stirring up further trouble.[35] This was as applicable to cross-border alliances and enmities. The friendship between Forster and Ferniehirst, evident during the Marian wars and again at Redeswyre, was inevitably to the detriment of relations between Forster and Cessford.

Unfortunately for Morton, his efforts in the Middle March were undermined by his deteriorating position at court. His style of government had inspired increasing antagonism and, in March 1578, he was forced to stand down as regent by the alliance of the earls of Argyll and Atholl, with whom Cessford and Home of Cowdenknowes were joined, though by June he had managed to regain his membership of the council. Morton's dependence on his adherents in local office in the Borders now rebounded against him.[36] It had alienated Cessford, who remained too strong locally to be removed from office and, in 1578, as Morton's power decreased, Cessford regained control over the whole of his wardenship. There were few to stop his recovery. Ferniehirst was still in exile and the Scotts, the only other surname which could have challenged Cessford, were limited by the youth of their leader, Branxholme.[37] Morton's authority in the Borders was undermined further by the replacement of Angus by Lord Ruthven as lieutenant in March 1578. Despite Morton's initial efficiency, after 1578 he was able to do little more in the region.[38] In the end, the personal nature of Morton's intervention in the march, and his over-reliance on his adherents' support there, inevitably had alienated those outside his affinity. His rocky relationship with Cessford meant that once the tide had turned against him, Cessford and his adherents assisted in Morton's slide from power. The personal antagonism that Morton inspired was captured in Calderwood's description of another of Morton's

---

[34] CSP Scot. v, no. 54.
[35] CSP Scot. v, no. 197
[36] CSP Scot. v, no. 313; RPC ii. 667, 704.
[37] Rae, Administration, 203.
[38] Hewitt, Scotland under Morton, 206.

enemies, Ferniehirst, dressed in 'large ruffes, delyting in this spectacle' at Morton's execution in 1581.[39]

II

'the whole commonalty ... are ever apt for faction and tumult'.[40]

After 1578 the court descended into a lengthy period of factionalism until around 1585, during which time the leadership of the government changed several times. In the Middle March Morton's decline was evident in the strengthening of Cessford's authority as warden. In August 1578 Cessford and Cowdenknowes were sent for by James, at which meeting Cowdenknowes fell out 'in heich termes' with Morton.[41] This hostility had an impact on cross-border relations, an English officer complaining in December 1579 of 'such impediment and delays [to redress], notwithstanding the King's good inclination'. He thought that the problem was that 'Carmichael continues still Keeper of Lyddisdale' and that considering 'the particular quarrels betwixt Cesford and him for the Earl of Morton his master's causes ... [this] cannot but be a hindrance to justice'. The English seemed to approve of Cessford:

> Truly the Laird of Cesford has kept East Tivydale very well from any great attempt since the treaty in June last, and is willing to continue with goodwill if he might be assisted. It is ordered that Carmichael shall be answerable to him for Lyddisdale and most Tyvydale, but there will be devices to remove Carmichael, so that he be possessed in the whole office. The King likes well of Cesford, and wishes his fee to be augmented.[42]

The situation in the Middle March replicated the factionalism at court, disputes radiating outwards into the localities. In 1579 the English observed 'the heat borne and hatred betwixt the Earl of Morton and the Carrs and Humes, who depend on Argyll, Montrose and that fellowship'. Furthermore, Robert Bowes noted that Angus's failure to reconcile the Ker-Scott feud had irritated Morton 'with whom he has become disaffected and distanced'.[43] Then, in September 1579, the arrival of Esme Stewart, shortly afterwards created earl of Lennox, catalysed the opposition to Morton; in the Middle March those opposed to him were drawn to Lennox. In September 1580 Forster wrote that the Kers and the Homes (of East Teviotdale) were allied to Lennox since anti-Morton, whereas the men of West Teviotdale, the

---

[39] Calderwood, *History*, iii. 575.
[40] An English report in 1580: *CSP Scot.* v, no. 638.
[41] Moysie, *Memoirs*, 13–14, 17.
[42] *CSP Scot.* v, no. 446. Cessford was recommended for an English pension being 'of great power, constant, stout, valiant, greatly devoted to the Queen of England, and [he] hates the French': *CSP Scot.* v, no. 459.
[43] *CSP Scot.* v, nos 432, 471.

Scotts, Rutherfords and Turnbulls, were dependent on Angus and Morton. The same month, in Edinburgh, Lennox was reported to be 'strongly accompanied with sundry noblemen, the Carrs and Humes': the English feared that as a result 'the flame of fire [was] likely to kindle by the open dealing against [Morton] ... and peradventure, come to hazard troubles on the Borders, already disquieted'.[44]

Despite the crisis at court, Morton and the council continued to assure England of their good faith. An English report of December 1579 noted that 'The King is truly well affected to the Queen of England' since he thought that no 'good Scottish man ... will hinder the good amity betwixt the realms'. However, disputes at court proved an impediment to the efficacious judicial administration of the Borders, to the detriment of Anglo-Scottish relations. Another report noted that, following a number of complaints against Scots raiding into England, 'notwithstanding the King's good inclination', the 'causes being debated daily before the Council for *five weeks*, they could not bring the said offences to any conclusion'.[45] The tighter frontier control that Morton had been able to effect in his regency had lapsed as his support there declined. Morton's good relations with England were not to save him; Elizabeth prevaricated in showing support for him. Lacking this or local support, Morton was unable to resist an indictment by the council, in December 1580, for his involvement in the murder of Lord Darnley. Six months later he was dead, and Lennox was elevated to a dukedom.[46]

Despite his kinship with Morton, Angus had initially recovered his position following his removal as lieutenant in 1578. He was again offered the lieutenancy of the East and Middle Marches in 1580, though he hesitated before accepting it. In October 1580 Angus was able to summon five hundred men to prevent Lord Home from holding the Berwickshire justice court at Duns, whose office he now claimed on the forfeiture of Home's father. In January 1581, following the arrest of his uncle Morton, Angus was still in possession of Dalkeith, Morton's main property, when he resisted invitations to join the Lennox faction.[47] However, the Douglas position was deteriorating as Lennox's position strengthened. In the Middle March, Carmichael was discharged as keeper in January 1581, replaced by Cessford, Lennox's ally. Later that month Cessford and Ker of Faldonside were both sent to the Borders to re-establish a Ker dominance of Middle March office, both receiving parliamentary ratifications of their lands.[48] Carmichael was ordered to appear before the council in Edinburgh under pain of treason and, whilst

[44] *CSP Scot.* v, nos 584, 592.
[45] *CSP Scot.* v, nos 445, 446.
[46] Rae, *Administration*, 204–6.
[47] Moysie, *Memoirs*, 31–2; *CSP Scot.* v, nos 608, 614.
[48] *CSP Scot.* v, no. 670; *RPC* iii. 402; *RPS*, 1581/10/98, 102, accessed 7 Oct. 2009.

Angus held out at Dalkeith until June, he was forced then to flee to Carlisle with his adherents.[49]

Following these shenanigans, the men of the Middle March who were not allies of the Cessford-Lennox faction, were forced to change their allegiances. In March 1581 ten border lairds were obliged to sign a renunciation of 'all and quhatsomevir bandis of manrent or service made and subscrivit be thame in ony tyme by gane for the service of Archibald Erll of Angus'. The Rutherfords of Hundalee and Hunthill and Turnbull of Bedrule, who had just signed such bonds to Angus, were made to abandon him whilst George Douglas younger of Bonjedburgh also changed sides.[50] The same month, Randolph told Lord Hunsdon that

> one of the Traquairs came yesterday morning to the King and assured him that all the clans of the Scots, Trumbles, Rotherfords, and others of West Tiviedale belonging to the earls of Morton and Angus have offered their services to the King, notwithstanding their bands and promises made to Angus ... it is said that Traquair has brought this assurance in writing from them,

and that they were 'free of Morton'.[51] Later that year, Traquair was rewarded for this service with the gift of the parsonage of Bedrule in the heart of Turnbull lands. This patronage was excluded from the restoration, in 1581, of the lands of another of Morton's enemies, that of Ferniehirst.[52] Ferniehirst's recovery was sponsored by Lennox but, due to Cessford's strength in the Middle March, his position was still precarious. In September 1581 the English reported that Ferniehirst had been made provost of Jedburgh and that he and Cessford, the warden, were 'at point of falling furth, and great enmytie is like to growe betwixt them'. Ferniehirst did not survive Lennox's subsequent banishment.[53]

Inevitably, the changing political situation in Scotland had an impact on its relations with England. During the uncertainty following the arrest of Morton, the English felt that the Middle March had been left too much to its own devices. Hunsdon complained to Randolph about a raid in January 1581 from West Teviotdale into England by over a hundred men, done 'with open foray, as if it were open war'. He demanded that the Scottish council, 'if they mean the continuance of the amity', order the surrender of the offenders. It appears that he meant Cessford and Buccleuch, for it was commented that by the non-delivery of such as these, 'The King makes but a show of desire of quietness on the Borders'.[54] In January 1581 the English finally mounted a belated attempt to save Morton, amassing a military force

---

[49] *CSP Scot.* v, no. 756; vi. nos 32–3.
[50] *RPC* iii. 368; Fraser, *Douglas*, iii. 266–8.
[51] *CSP Scot.* v, no. 756.
[52] *RSS* viii, nos 379, 380; *RPS*, 1581/10/118, accessed 7 Oct. 2009.
[53] *CBP* i, nos 109, 111.
[54] *CSP Scot.* v, nos 680, 681.

on the Borders of about five hundred horsemen and two thousand footmen. In the confusion caused by Elizabeth's hesitant commitment, the Scots were unsure whether the English were going to invade in support of Morton.[55] Such distrust typified Anglo-Scottish relations throughout this period, James writing to Elizabeth that March to protest about an English force approaching the Borders in a time of 'so good peace'. He further requested a resumption of the wardens' meetings for the administration of justice.[56] Elizabeth, however, repeatedly delayed any such meetings, waiting for the outcome of Morton's trial, whilst James continued to reassure Elizabeth of his desire for 'the good amity and quietness betwixt us'.[57]

Tense Anglo-Scottish relations created a confusing situation in the Middle March, where Cessford, ostensibly sent by James and the council to organise redress, seemed unable to conclude anything with his opposite, Forster. Until their disbandment, the close presence of English forces alarmed Cessford, who wrote to Forster worrying that they planned to 'fire' his house.[58] Forster himself was constrained by Elizabeth's refusal to allow a meeting of the border commissioners, which could settle the more serious complaints.[59] In April, following the failure of English appeals to James on Morton's behalf, the majority of the English forces was disbanded. In June, after the execution of Morton, a Scottish force was dismissed 'seing the invasioun of England and thair forces from the Bordoures is removit'.[60]

Relations did not improve, however, during the ascendancy of the allegedly Catholic Lennox between 1581 and 1582. Lennox unnerved the English who distrusted his assurances that he would do nothing to change the Protestant Reformation in Scotland.[61] Against a background of fraught negotiations between Elizabeth and the captive Mary and Mary's correspondence with her French relations, English worries escalated over Lennox's alleged promotion of a revival of the 'ancient league' between the French and the Scots.[62] However, the situation changed in August 1582 following a coup, known as the Ruthven Raid, led by the Protestant earl of Gowrie, who seized the king.[63] The Raiders accused the deposed Lennox of having shown extraordinary favour to the exiled Ferniehirst, despite Ferniehirst being an 'enemy to this State'. In September Bowes reported that Ferniehirst, during

---

[55] *CSP Scot.* v, nos 652, 653, 666, 668.
[56] *CSP Scot.* v, no. 752.
[57] *CSP Scot.* v, nos 725, 764; vi, no. 10.
[58] *CSP Scot.* v, nos 732.
[59] *CSP Scot.* v, nos 725, 752, 764.
[60] *CSP Scot.* vi, nos 5, 9, 27; *RPC* iii. 392–3.
[61] *CSP Scot.* vi, nos 86, 121.
[62] *CSP Scot.* vi, nos 89, 121, 145. Walsingham wrote that England needed to secure 'the postern gate to any mischief or peril that might befall this realm' from Scotland: C. Read, *Mr. Secretary Walsingham and the policy of Queen Elizabeth*, Oxford 1925, i, 237, 417; quotation at ii. 149–50.
[63] Moysie, *Memoirs*, 41–3.

a reappearance in Scotland, appeared to be 'practisynge' to break the Borders by planning a provocative raid by Liddesdale men into England 'in daylight, that a war might arise between the realms'.[64] In November Ferniehirst was with Lennox besieging Edinburgh castle in an attempt to rescue James from the Raiders. The situation was complicated further by reports, in December, of a split between the earls of Arran and Lennox despite James's efforts at reconciliation, and in January 1583 Arran and his wife were described as being 'in full sway' at court. Lennox's subsequent banishment meant that his ally, Ferniehirst, was again forced to flee, asking Elizabeth for refuge at Alnwick.[65]

Against this background of shifting court politics, the situation in the Middle March remained confused. Despite protestations of friendship, there were recurring problems between wardens over delivery for violent crime. Slaughter was supposed to be referred to a meeting of the border commissioners for redress: Scottish wardens claimed that their 'private authority' was not sufficient to settle such serious offences. Probably due to a lack of direction from the council, Cessford appeared to be prevaricating. In April 1582 Cessford had written to Scrope that he was 'ready to cause deliver for any bills of "geir" filed ... since my acceptation. But for slaughter, I cannot "mell" with it, but "mon according to the aunciente custome referre the delivery hereof to the Princes and their commissioners"'.[66] In August 1582 one of the main charges against Lennox was that 'disorders on the Borders [had been] altogether neglected'. However, apparently things had not improved under the Ruthven regime. In October 1583 Scrope complained about the lack of redress since the downfall of Morton for Liddesdale from Cessford, in comparison to the good redress he had had with Carmichael. In three years he had had only one meeting with Cessford for Liddesdale and Cessford had refused to settle any complaints of 'hurts or mutilations', using, Scrope felt, spurious technicalities to obstruct justice.[67] The feeling appears to have been mutual, James complaining similarly to Elizabeth over Scrope's refusal to hold meetings. Elizabeth's response was to praise Scrope for his 'discrete dealing'.[68]

But the political situation at court was to change again, in June 1583, following James's release and the overthrow of Gowrie by Arran. This was of advantage to Ferniehirst who was to become close to Arran.[69] Cessford's

---

[64] *CSP Scot.* vi, nos 145, 160.
[65] Calderwood, *History*, iii. 635, 691; *CSP Scot.* vi, nos 288, 298.
[66] *CSP Scot.* vi, no. 107.
[67] *CSP Scot.* vi, nos 144, 678.
[68] *CSP Scot.* vi, no. 135.
[69] In 1584 Arran's niece Anne, daughter of Andrew master of Ochiltree, was contracted to Ferniehirst's heir Andrew with Arran's consent: NAS, GD40/2/10, fo. 57; R. Grant, 'Politicking Jacobean women: Lady Ferniehirst, the countess of Arran and the countess of Huntly, c.1580–1603', in E. Ewan and M. M. Meikle (eds), *Women in Scotland, c. 1100–1750*, East Linton 1999, 95–104 at pp. 96–7.

continuation as warden in the Middle March, and Lennox's fall from power in August 1582, had meant that Ferniehirst spent most of the early 1580s in exile. Despite his brief return to the Borders in 1581 and in late 1582, Ferniehirst was still in Paris in 1584.[70] However, even Cessford was vulnerable to regime changes. Arran's increasing power at court through 1583 and 1584 gradually eroded the position of Cessford's affiliation. In January 1583 Ker of Faldonside was warded, as was Cowdenknowes in April.[71] By May 1584 Cessford was 'indisposed to hazard himself in court, where he finds no surety'.[72] Ferniehirst returned in June and by October had replaced Cessford as warden and Cessford was warded. In November Ferniehirst was granted a force of one hundred hagbutters to assist him, paid for by the Treasury.[73] He was further granted £1,000 a year to repay him for the past 'wrak and ruyne of his leving ... quhairthrow he is not of power to retene and hold in hous his freindis or servandis'. His wife wrote thankfully of the family's restoration.[74]

Factionalism at court did not just affect the appointment of border officials but was replicated at local level by feuding surnames. In early 1581 the Scottish privy council, to prevent 'great deadly feuds amonst his grace's subjects in the Middle March', had suggested that Forster and Cessford should meet. Hunsdon wrily observed that he could not 'but marvel' how such a meeting would have any effect: his 'long experience' was that the borderers 'were never, nor are, at his Wardens' devotion'.[75] In 1584 Ferniehirst received his appointment as warden with some trepidation: 'He is in such fear upon entering into his office, that he has requested that the Laird of Cessford's men and other surname in East [Teviotdale] should lay in pledges to the King.' Cessford's warden-clerk Menteith refused to serve under Ferniehirst declaring he would 'rather refuse the realm of Scotland, than serve any but his old master'. As a result, Forster noted, 'there is great variance and contention like to grow, amongst them'. Cessford's decline was to the benefit of Ferniehirst's allies such as Buccleuch, the Rutherfords and the Douglases of Cavers.[76]

The lack of redress in the Middle Marches inevitably had a knock-on effect on Anglo-Scottish relations. Walsingham protested himself confused by James's assurances of amity. Whilst in Edinburgh in September 1583, he complained that a raid in August by the Scots into the English Middle March was so 'extraordinary' that it could not be left to the wardens to

---

[70] NAS, GD40/2/9, fos 65, 68; *CSP Scot.* vi, no. 676.
[71] *CSP Scot.* vi, no. 298; vii, nos 40, 77, 109.
[72] *CSP Scot.* vii, no. 113.
[73] *CSP Scot.* vii, no.180; *RPC* iii. 699–700; NAS, GD40/2/10, fos 51, 53, 56; GD40/2/9, fo. 75.
[74] *RPC* iii. 700.
[75] *CSP Scot.* v, no. 703.
[76] *CSP Scot.* vii, no. 411; NAS, GD40/2/10, fo. 55; GD40/2/9, fo. 72.

redress as James had suggested. Without James's own attention to this offence, Elizabeth should 'not but take it as a breach of the peace and amity ... There wanted nothing but banners displayed to have made it a plain act of hostility'. As he left for London, Walsingham thanked James for his list of good intentions in the Borders but regretted that Elizabeth would find them too 'ambiguous' to reassure her of his good faith.[77] The English also distrusted Arran, in particular for his links with Ferniehirst. In January 1584 English worries about a conspiracy by Mary, Queen of Scots, appeared to achieve some credence following the mysterious residence of some of Mary's envoys as guests of Lady Ferniehirst at Ferniehirst castle. Mary was godmother to one of the Ferniehirsts' sons and in correspondence with Lady Ferniehirst. Bowes feverishly reported the gratitude of the envoys to their hostess for her help in their negotiations with James as they departed for France.[78] In April there were warnings that Ferniehirst was to reappear from France with 12,000 crowns from Mary's French revenues. Ferniehirst returned in June but without the money.[79] In August 1584 Hunsdon wrote that despite the promises of redress made by Secretary Maitland, Scrope 'finds these to be but words' and that more than three hundred horsemen of Liddesdale, Ewesdale and Annandale had raided into the English Middle March.[80] For his part James also seemed to distrust Elizabeth's intentions. He answered English complaints sympathetically but blamed the lack of redress on Scrope as 'the chief occasion thereof' and, in February 1585, the Scottish demanded that Elizabeth organise 'the delivery of the traitors and rebels according to the league and amity'.[81]

The mixed signals coming from each country's government and wardens appear to have facilitated (if not actually encouraged) an increase in internal and cross-border raiding – or at least the report of it. The tenants of Ettrick forest complained of an English raid in January 1581 by eighteen men 'bodin in feir of weir' who had taken three prisoners, whilst in September 1583 Walsingham told the English council of the 'poor distressed people' of the English Marches recounting their 'grievous complaints of the great spoils and outrages committed on them by the Scots [principally from Liddesdale], some of them showing the bloody shirts of their friends and kinsmen slain'.[82] The increased number of reports of raids that occurred in the early 1580s certainly suggested an increase in raiding. However, it is likely this was partly a factor of increased reporting.[83] It is probable, however, that some increase in raiding did take place given the unsettled nature of central government

---

[77] *CSP Scot.* vi, nos 626, 628, 640.
[78] *CSP Scot.* vi, no. 676; vii, nos 17, 19, 22, 24, 27, 33.
[79] *CSP Scot.* vii, nos 58, 180.
[80] *CSP Scot.* vii, no. 271.
[81] *CSP Scot.* vii, nos 204, 549.
[82] *RPC* iii. 415–16; *CSP Scot.* vi, nos 653, 680.
[83] See chapter 5 above.

and the precarious nature of the warden's position, particularly that of Ferniehirst. Raids were not necessarily politically inspired but the political situation could facilitate them.

Despite the uncertainties affecting Anglo-Scottish relations in this period, both sides continued to protest their wishes to maintain the amity and there was some evidence of the Scottish council doing something to suppress cross-border raiding. In June 1584, for example, a muster was ordered to deal with the rebels and 'brokin men of the Bordouris' who intended 'to suscitat oppin weir' and 'thairby to dissolve the amitie ... betuix thir twa Crownes'.[84] In October 1581 James had urged parliament to approve attempts to secure an anti-Catholic league with the English and, in 1585, a Scottish request that Elizabeth uphold cross-border redress, as a 'league and covenant keeper', took place against a background of negotiations over such a league. The connection was made repeatedly, by such as the Secretary Maitland, between the successful conclusion of an alliance and the settlement of Border issues.[85] However, the necessity for co-operation between the wardens, combined with often contradictory indications by both governments, formed a potential stumbling block to successful negotiations. Exacerbating this was the continued factionalism at the Scottish court and Elizabeth's inability to resist meddling in the Borders.

Nothing typified these problems more than the slaying of Lord Francis Russell, eldest son of the earl of Bedford, at a day of truce between Ferniehirst and Forster in July 1585.[86] By this time court politics were in flux again: in May Walsingham was told that Arran 'has not as much of the King's power as he once had', and Cessford was 'feared likely to break his ward and make as great a "stimp stamp"' in the Middle March.[87] Though the Scots claimed that the Russell incident was an accident, both Arran and Ferniehirst were suspected of complicity, whilst Forster thought it was 'a pretended purpose to breake the amitie and peace between these two realmes'.[88] What makes Forster's allegations surprising was that he and Ferniehirst previously had always been friends. Forster had lent Ferniehirst money during his exile and written on his behalf to the English government.[89] However, tensions were high at such days of truce and perhaps it is more of a surprise that there were so few incidents where tensions turned into violence. James reacted quickly with an order that none was to harm any Englishman 'for staying of forder inconvenient' and Arran and Ferniehirst were eventually warded in Scotland. A muster was ordered for the Borders to prevent the 'brek of the

---

[84] *RPC* iii. 674.
[85] *CSP Scot.* vi, nos 72, 75; vii, nos 549, 653.
[86] W. C. Dickinson 'The death of Lord Russell, 1585', *SHR* xx (1923), 181–6.
[87] *CSP Scot.* vii, no. 621.
[88] *CBP* i, nos 330, 331, 336, 341.
[89] *CBP* i, no. 145.

gude peax' though, typically, Elizabeth prevaricated in accepting the Scottish assurances.[90]

Court politics then again intruded in the Middle March and Elizabeth plunged gleefully in. Angus and the other lords banished following the end of the Ruthven Raid were massing on the English side of the border, and it was noted that 'if the Queen will send them down, [the exiled lords] will be able to work wonders'.[91] Elizabeth delayed any decision about Angus until the border commissioners' meeting in early October about the Russell affair. However, the Russell incident was not resolved, the Scots refusing to deliver Ferniehirst.[92] In late October Forster, agreeing to a request by Angus, had 'taken order that none under my rule shall trouble the Borders, till these matters come to stay'. He noted that the earls had 'the hole force of the Borders with them' including Buccleuch.[93] Angus, Mar and the master of Glamis met at Cessford's residence near Kelso and were joined by 'the haill Merse and Hamiltonis'. Elizabeth's anger over the lack of redress for Russell's murder appears to have triggered her acquiescence in the lords' subsequent coup at Stirling on 2 November. Two days later the banished lords were welcomed into the council.[94] In late November Cessford returned to the Middle March from Stirling 'chosen warden and provost of Jedworthe and keeper of Jedworthe forest, and entered to divers commodities that Farnyhirst had'.[95] Carmichael was granted a remission and restored to his lands at Fenton and Dirleton.[96] Negotiations were resumed between the two countries and these formed the background to a more amicable beginning to 1586.

III

In the light of improved Anglo-Scottish relations and an apparent commitment by both governments to settle disputes, negotiations for an Anglo-Scottish league were continued from early in 1586.[97] These took place against the background of English concern, in 1586, over Spanish prepara-

---

[90] *RPC* iii. 759; iv, 4, 11, 13; *CSP Scot.* viii, no. 55.
[91] *The Hamilton papers*, ed. J. Bain, Edinburgh 1890–2, no. 521; *CSP Scot.* viii, no.133.
[92] *CBP* i, nos 355, 358, 359, 365. Fortunately for both English and Scottish governments, Ferniehirst died shortly thereafter thus honourably settling the matter: *CBP* i, no. 417.
[93] *CBP* i, nos 379, 382.
[94] *CBP* i, nos 387, 388, 398; *RPC* iv. 27, 30–3; Moysie, *Memoirs*, 53–5; *Melville memoirs*, 344, 348, 350.
[95] NRAS1100/633.
[96] *RPS*, 1585/12/45, accessed 7 Oct. 2009.
[97] There had been talks over a league in 1585 but these had been held up by the Russell incident: *CSP Scot.* viii, no. 81.

tions for an Armada and Elizabeth's desire to secure her northern frontier.[98] In the Middle March better relations were exemplified by Forster's description of a day of truce at Kelso at the beginning of April 1586 'where I gott very good enterteignment at the opposite wardens handes, and greater justice then ever I dyd see in my life', later commenting that 'the state of the Borders is as quiet as ever I knew'. In May the council ordered the compilation of all complaints for the forthcoming Border Commission, to facilitate an amicable meeting.[99] The same month James received the first £4,000 of his sparkling new English pension, and a greater amicability was evident in a letter that Elizabeth sent to James in June. Though she fell short of confirming James's succession to her throne, Elizabeth expressed the hope that she would continue to pay the pension and would do nothing to hinder his succession.[100]

Much was done to avoid any outbreak of cross-border trouble which could threaten negotiations. Various borderers, such as the notorious Robert Elliot of Redheugh, were ordered to enter some of their affiliates for past offences. A proclamation ordered those in the Middle March to assist the warden Cessford.[101] Several Kers from the Ferniehirst affinity found caution of sizeable sums to appear before the privy council in June, including William Ker of Ancrum who had to find 10,000 merks. A number of Rutherfords, Kers and Moscropes of Jedburgh stood surety for each other.[102] In June a council order prohibited anyone from attending a planned day of combat between the Burns of the Middle March and English Middle March men.[103] In these happier circumstances, the border commissioners met in June to discuss the Anglo-Scottish league and again in early July to arrange redress.[104] This was supported by the proclamation of a muster at Peebles to punish those who continued to commit offences 'aganis the subjectis of his [James's] darrest suster and cousing the Quene'. On 5 July 1586 a league was established between Scotland and England.[105]

The execution of Mary, Queen of Scots, in February 1587 should perhaps have undermined the new amity. The way in which both Elizabeth and James dealt with the aftermath said much about their desire to protect their alliance.[106] Initial threats of hostility by Scotland led to Scrope's muster of a defensive force on the West March. However, his observation of 'the great

---

[98] R. B. Wernham, *Before the Armada: the growth of English foreign policy, 1485–1588*, London 1966, 373, 380.
[99] CBP i, no. 421; RPC iv. 68.
[100] J. Goodare, 'James VI's English subsidy', in Goodare and Lynch, *Reign of James VI*, 110–25 at p. 115; CSP Scot. viii, no. 443; RPC v. 324–5.
[101] RPC iv. 46, 69–70.
[102] RPC iv. 77, 82.
[103] RPC iv. 81.
[104] Rae, *Administration*, appendix 5.
[105] RPC iv. 84–5, 92.
[106] Wernham, *Before the Armada*, 382–3.

brags given out by our opposite neighbours for revenge' remained unrealised, whilst Moysie wrote that 'The Inglishe ambassadour desired that the leage and amitie betuix the twa nationis micht be confermit, and inviolablie observit, because sayd he, the Queine wes werie sorie for taking' Mary's life.[107] Elizabeth immediately sent Robert Carey north 'to make known her innocence of her sister's death': James stayed him at Berwick for his own safety and to prevent any cause for offence to Elizabeth.[108] In fear, Forster had cancelled a day of truce, but a letter from Cessford reassured the English and their deputies appear to have met as early as March.[109] Suspicion continued however: in mid-March Forster wrote to Walsingham that 'the Kinge dothe write to the Laird of Cesfurde to do justice, and yet in the meane tyme he appoyntethe others to ryde and breake the bordors, and dothe winke therat', though in April Forster was able to write that 'the state of the Border is quiet'.[110] The general impression given by the records in the *Calendar of Border papers* in 1587 is that there was no major outbreak of raiding. If anything, despite the public 'brags' of revenge made, it appears that the council was trying to maintain the peace between the two countries. Indeed, a number of Middle March men were summoned before the council that June touching the 'gude reule and quietnes' there.[111]

The council's reaction to Anglo-Scottish relations should also be seen within the context of the political situation in Scotland. From 1586 Maitland, chancellor from 1587, brought to James's government his determination to establish an efficient administration and effective implementation of justice.[112] This inevitably impacted upon the Middle March where a desire to avoid upsetting the amity combined with Maitland's attempts to suppress any challenge to crown authority.

Traditional methods were used with a consistency not seen since Morton's regency to administer justice and to preserve good cross-border relations. In November 1586 the earl of Angus was appointed lieutenant with a waged force of two hundred men. In January 1587 a court held by Angus at Jedburgh reportedly hanged sixteen people, took pledges from others and ordered at least ninety more to find surety to enter themselves by March.[113] In June Robert Scott of Haining was made cautioner for Turnbull of Bedrule's entrance to the opposite wardens for all attempts committed by him and for whom he was responsible. He also stood surety of 5,000 merks for Walter Scott of Branxholme, who had now reached his majority, to 'underly sic

---

[107] CBP i, nos. 484, 485, 487, 490; Moysie, *Memoirs*, 60.
[108] *Carey memoirs*, 5, 7–8.
[109] CBP i, nos 489, 491, 497.
[110] CBP i, nos 499, 507.
[111] RPC iv. 183, 189.
[112] Goodare, *State and society*, 74–5; M. Lee, *Great Britain's Solomon: James VI and I in his three kingdoms*, Urbana 1990, 67–77.
[113] RPC iv. 111, 124, 132, 146–8; *RPS*, A1586/9/2, accessed 12 Oct. 2009.

ordour as salbe imputt for the weill and quietnes of the Bordouris'. A number of new cautions were made for the men of Teviotdale, including several by the earl of Angus for his affiliates including the sheriff William Douglas of Cavers and George Douglas of Bonjedburgh. Significantly, the caution obliged them to 'relieve his Majesty and his warden at the hands of the opposite wardens'. Maitland's concerns were not only internal. However, the fact that even Cessford, the warden, was himself forced to find surety showed the crown's continuing dependence on strong local figures, despite English complaints against them.[114] The English were bemused by the council's apparent ineffectiveness, complaining of nineteen Scottish raids into the English Middle March in May and June and fifteen in July, including one by Branxholme with (allegedly) 200 men into Redesdale.[115]

A couple of things were new however. Firstly, there was much greater involvement of the council in what previously would have been a matter of correspondence between the wardens. Maitland wrote in July 1587 to reassure Forster of the king's determination to stop further raiding. The wardens of the West and Middle Marches and Bothwell, as keeper of Liddesdale, were summoned before the council and made to promise to keep days of truce.[116] This intervention was partly the result of another novelty: in the late 1580s the way in which government perceived the Borders appeared to be worsening. The numerous English complaints to the Scottish king and council were a constant reminder of the Borders as a region of special concern. In addition such complaints were accompanied now by the threat to alliance and pension. Increasingly the region was equated with the problematic Highlands and similar measures to deal with both began to be promoted.[117] In July 1586 musters were proclaimed for both Peebles and Badenoch to deal with offenders 'inhabiting the cuntreyis ewest the Bordouris and the North and South Iles, and utheris Hieland cuntreyis' which was seen as endangering the amity.[118] Then, in July 1587, the act 'for the quieting and keeping in obedience of the disorderit subjectis inhabitantis of the bordoris hielandis and Ilis', 'delyting in all mischeifis', for the first time equated the regions in legislation.[119] Borderers were increasingly being seen by central government as 'godless' and 'barbarous' in the same way as the Highlanders had come to be seen over the previous two centuries. The act may have encapsulated a new attitude to the Borders but its articles contained largely traditional measures. It was a combination of domestic law applicable throughout Scot-

---

[114] *RPC* iv. 189, 191.
[115] *CBP* i, nos 522, 535.
[116] *CBP* i, no. 525; *RPC* iv. 92.
[117] Goodare and Lynch, 'Scottish state and its Borderlands', 201–4; A. H. Williamson, 'Scots, Indians and empire: the Scottish politics of civilization, 1519–1609', *Past and Present* cl (1996), 46–83.
[118] *RPC* iv. 92.
[119] *RPS*, 1587/7/70, accessed 7 Oct. 2009.

land, such as the use of the general band to make landlords accountable for their adherents, and existing border-specific laws, such as the ban on cross-border marriage. More innovative attempts to make these measures effective, however, were not carried out, although the concept behind them reappeared in subsequent legislation.

What the act did achieve was to establish the Borders as an area of extra concern in a way that stuck. This sustained perception affected all future policies on the Borders, even at times when government actions appeared to conflict with its expressed intentions. When James travelled to Denmark for his marriage in 1589, he appointed a committee to oversee border affairs under John Lord Hamilton with the wardens, including Cessford, as his advisers. In June 1590 this was taken further with the setting up of a weekly court, first suggested in the 1587 act, to deal with all cases from the Borders.[120] Though this council included two borderers, Carmichael and Home of Cowdenknowes, since the others such as Maitland, the justice clerk and the clerk register formed the nucleus of the main council, this had the effect of setting aside a day a week for the council to consider border affairs – a display of their new prioritisation. Significantly, the register that recorded its deliberations was named *Liber actarum penes Hyberniae, Insularum, et Marciarum regni ordinem*, a clear indication of the council's mental linkage of the regions. Though the meetings of this council petered out after about six months, the separate register continued long after, suggesting the government's enduring concern.[121]

In September 1593 parliament repeated the act of 1587, specifically charging landlords and bailies to find surety for the good behaviour of their adherents and for 'masterless men and vagabonds' to find surety or be declared fugitive. At the same time a muster was ordered to meet at Peebles in November.[122] Another act of June 1594, which referred to the 'vickit thevis and lymaris of the clanis and surnames' in the highlands and isles, also called for a listing of the troublesome surnames of the Borders 'that thair may be ... a perfite distinctioun be[tuix] names and surnames ... that ar and desirit to be estemit honest and trew' and those that were not.[123] Official policy hardened further under the act of 1599, which stipulated that thefts on the border were no longer to be resolved by redress, but rather by punishment 'unto the death'. In an act of 1600 wardens were again ordered not to make redress but to burn offenders' houses and to expel their wives and bairns: it was noted that this should 'be extendit alsweill to heland as bordour'.[124]

---

[120] *RPC* iv. 426; Rae, *Administration*, 127–9, 210–12.
[121] *RPC* iv. 781–814; v. 733–48; vi. 823–9.
[122] *RPS*, A1593/9/2, accessed 7 Oct. 2009; *RPC* v. 94–5.
[123] *RPS*, 1594/4/48, accessed 7 Oct. 2009.
[124] *RPS*, 1599/7/2, 1600/11/48, accessed 7 Oct. 2009.

The incorporation in this legislation of mostly traditional methods of imposing justice was replicated in the continued use of the judicial raid. In the period from 1586 to 1597 at least seven raids were made into the Middle March. James himself accompanied four of these. However, they were not all motivated by border-specific concerns for those in 1591, 1592 and 1593 were to deal with the madman Bothwell and his adherents following his raids at Stirling, Falkland, Leith and Holyrood. Some of Bothwell's supporters, such as his stepson Buccleuch, came from the Middle March but all of them came into line. Buccleuch, with the Scotts of Harden and Whitslaid, received a remission in 1591 for their involvement with Bothwell.[125] Angus's court at Jedburgh in January 1587 and James's at Peebles in November 1587 and Jedburgh in April 1588 were more specifically to address the usual border complaints.[126]

Whilst such measures may appear to mark the Middle March out as an area of special concern, they were symptomatic of a broader approach by James and Maitland to make the administration of justice more effective throughout Scotland. This included the intervention of the council in the resolution of feuding, measures against weapon-bearing of 1593, 1595 and 1596 and attempts to make officials more efficient.[127] It is important to keep this context in mind for the increased report of border affairs might otherwise give them a significance out of proportion to their place within other government preoccupations. Much of this report came from the English wardens who were in a different situation from their Scottish counterparts. It is likely that it was in the interest of English border officials to exaggerate the amount of crime, since its existence justified their continuation in office to their council. Their woeful reports repeatedly referred to the lack of resources available to them to fulfill their duties. However, in the late sixteenth century, border affairs seemed decreasingly important to English central government as the likelihood of further outright hostility disappeared in the face of the increasingly probable succession of James to the English throne.

The growing perception of the Borders as a markedly different region did not mean, however, that it existed in a separate bubble. The politics of central government continued to impact on the Middle March. The balance of power which swung away from the Maitland-Hamilton faction following Maitland's temporary retirement and the Lennox faction's resurgence in 1592, swung back towards Maitland following his reconciliation with the queen in late 1593. Throughout the wardenry remained in the hands of the Cessford Kers, allied to Maitland through the marriage of his niece Margaret,

---

[125] Fraser, *Buccleuch*, ii, no. 209.
[126] Rae, *Administration*, appendix 6.
[127] *RPC* v. 90–1, 247, 274–5, 321–2.

daughter of Maitland of Lethington, to Robert Ker younger of Cessford.[128] However, the keepership of Liddesdale was affected, changing hands five times in the period 1591 to 1594.[129] In 1590 Lord Hamilton's Borders affairs committee included the earl of Bothwell, and his stepson Buccleuch was appointed keeper in July 1591.[130] However, following Bothwell's rebellion, in November 1591 Buccleuch was replaced as keeper by Robert Ker, younger of Cessford, who was himself replaced by Lennox in 1592, on Maitland's forced retirement. Cessford's rival Ferniehirst was appointed as Lennox's deputy in Liddesdale. However, in October 1593, on Maitland's recovery, Cessford replaced Ferniehirst as deputy, and also took over the wardenry from his ageing father William. This combination of roles eventually was to prove too much.[131] In the meantime, Buccleuch's position had recovered and he was granted the lordship of Liddesdale from Bothwell's forfeiture.[132] As a result, Buccleuch was appointed keeper in October 1594 and continued so on an hereditary basis for the rest of the period. He distanced himself from Bothwell's affinity, and when that October he met the Armstrongs at the Hermitage, he 'told them plainly that if any of them dealt with Bothwell, that he would hang them'.[133]

The importance of Maitland in court politics, particularly in the first part of this period to 1592, should not obscure the increasing importance, from around 1588, of James's own authority. James's growing stature, combined with his attempts to suppress feuding, meant that the factionalism, which previously had so dominated court life, began to have less effect on crown policy. Factionalism had not disappeared, but James's own views increasingly directed what the government did. Domestically, he was to continue to intensify government in every region, in the Borders as elsewhere. But his policies did not remain static, necessarily evolving in the face of changing circumstances. Externally, Anglo-Scottish relations were markedly less

---

[128] In 1588 William Ker of Cessford had the grant of the abbacy of Kelso, previously held by his father Walter, for his services in the Middle March: NRAS1100/987, 1196.
[129] See ch. 3 above.
[130] *CSP Scot.* x, no. 592; *RPC* iv. 649, 668; *CBP* i, no. 714.
[131] *CSP Scot.* x, nos 606, 616, 623, 640, 652, 765, 779; xi, no. 157.
[132] Fraser, *Buccleuch*, i. 174–5, 178; ii, nos 209, 211. Buccleuch had been forced into exile in the meantime, but he had used his time profitably, accompanying William Fowler, the queen's secretary to the University of Padua. Alessandra Petrina of that university has discovered recently some love poems written in execrable Italian by Buccleuch amongst Fowler's papers in the Hawthornden papers at the NLS, revealing a more cultured side of him not apparent before. Fowler was an affiliate of Bothwell, who was his literary patron and Buccleuch's stepfather. In 1588, as parson of Hawick, he had granted Buccleuch the tack of his teinds for five years; in 1608, with Buccleuch's consent, he granted these teinds to Buccleuch's ally, Sir Gideon Murray of Elibank. See Alessandra Petrina, *Machiavelli in the British Isles: two early modern translations of the Prince*, Farnham 2009, chs iii, iv, and 'Walter Scott of Buccleuch, Italian poet?', *Renaissance Studies* (forthcoming). NAS, GD224/887/1; GD 224/918/27, fos 4–5.
[133] *RPC* v. 178, 191–2; *CBP* i, no. 986; *CSP Scot.* xi, no. 390.

hostile, even occasionally amicable. However, this did not stop James from continuing to use the Borders as leverage in diplomatic negotiations, rather as he showed himself sympathetic to the earl of Tyrone's rebellion in Ireland until 1597.[134]

Such posturing, however, could not obviate his acute financial dependence upon the English pension, his appreciation of the alliance and his desire for the confirmation of his succession to the English throne. As a result his actions in the Middle March sent out a rather mixed message to the English. In 1588 Lord Hunsdon voiced his confusion. Noting 'the nyghtly spoyles in the Mydell Marches' and his 'smale hope of justis', he questioned the point of James's raid that November to Peebles 'where it was thought hee woulde have taken seveare order with them of Liddesdale and Weste Tyvidale, to be aunserable to England for suche attemptates as they had committed'. Hunsdon thought that James had had little effect wondering 'what leklyhode ther ys of the recovery of thys kynge'.[135] Particularly confusing, the English felt, was James's attitude to specific borderers, most notably Buccleuch and Cessford. Such complaints revealed much about James's intentions in the Borders and his personal style of government. In 1587 the English questioned James's lack of action over their misdemeanours, with Hunsdon later complaining about Buccleuch's raid into the English West March; he thought that such 'great oughtrages durst not be attempted by such men as hath done them, without the Kinges privitie'.[136] The following month both Cessford and Buccleuch were accused of leading a raid by two thousand men into England. Buccleuch was apparently warded in Edinburgh castle for it, but was soon released on surety.[137] Amongst all these complaints Cessford's father continued as warden and, in 1593, Robert was captain of the king's guard. In 1594 the grant to Buccleuch of the keepership of Liddesdale confounded the English.[138]

Both Cessford and Buccleuch attended council meetings in 1594 and 1596, Cessford appearing five times in 1596. That year, the earl of Northumberland complained of the lack of redress from the Middle March warden, whom he felt was protecting Scots who 'have good bands' from Buccleuch and Cessford. Lord Eure, in the English Middle March, complained that he could get no redress from Buccleuch for Liddesdale since its inhabitants were all joined to him 'by oathe and scripte'.[139] Scrope noted that Buccleuch, as keeper of Liddesdale, showed 'a backwardness to justice, except [that] which was solely for the profit of his own friends'. Enumerating Buccleuch's offences, Scrope complained that he 'has ever been the chief enemy (and

[134] Rae, *Administration*, 207, 218.
[135] *CBP* i, no. 563.
[136] *CBP* i, nos 560, 575, 638.
[137] *CBP* i, nos 570, 574.
[138] *RPC* v. 178.
[139] *CBP* ii, nos 231, 232.

still is) to the quiet of the border … yet this man is thought fit by the King and Council to be still officer!'[140] Scrope's outpourings about Buccleuch were mainly inspired by the personal antagonism between the two and should be viewed with some caution. However, such reports were typical of the general attitude of the English. Robert Carey was similarly contemptuous of the 'unworthye officer' Cessford, describing his 'delatarye and doublye' dealings. He thought that Cessford's poverty and his small remuneration as warden lay at the root of the problem and that without the grant of a bigger pension to Cessford there was not much hope of justice.[141] Cessford and Buccleuch were clearly involved in cross-border raiding: that James continued to employ and reward them indicated that, for the moment, he tacitly at least condoned their activities. Even if he did not, the English thought that he did.

One particular incident exemplified James's approach to the Middle March and its officers and the changing effect of Anglo-Scottish relations on his policies there. This was the rescue by Buccleuch of his adherent Willie Armstrong of Kinmont in April 1596 and James's reaction to it. Kinmont Willie had been apprehended on the Scottish side of the border by Scrope's deputy during a day of truce. Buccleuch, protesting against the violation of the customary immunity on such days, demanded Kinmont's return. Scrope refused, so Buccleuch took matters into his own hands. Elizabeth and Scrope were outraged and a diplomatic furore broke out.[142] Six weeks later Robert Bowes addressed the Scottish Convention of Estates, demanding Buccleuch's delivery to English justice; the matter, however, was referred to a meeting of the border commissioners, as Buccleuch had requested.[143] In July the council replied to the increasingly angry correspondence from Elizabeth that, though the king remained 'inviolable observing' of the amity, he upheld Buccleuch's demand for an 'ordinair forme of tryale' by the commissioners. Scrope reported Buccleuch 'openly says the King has freely remitted his deed at this castle as good service to him and his "comune wealth"'.[144] Buccleuch was warded on another charge by James in August but was released in October, despite English protestations.[145] The delayed meeting of the commissioners finally took place the following January; it settled a large number of cross-border bills, but failed to achieve the delivery of Buccleuch. Scrope complained that James and his council 'intend to extenuate and bear out Buccleuch's "proude acte"'.[146] The continuation of James's support for Buccleuch had resulted in an impasse between the Scottish and English governments on the matter,

---

[140] *CBP* ii, nos 237, 253, 336.
[141] *CBP* ii, nos 295, 343.
[142] *CBP* ii, nos 237, 252; *CSP Scot.* xii, no. 196.
[143] *RPC* v. 290; J. Spottiswoode, *History of the Church of Scotland*, ed. M. Napier and M. Russell (Bannatyne Club, 1850), ii. 415.
[144] *CBP* ii, nos 283, 302; *RPC* v. 298–9.
[145] *CSP Scot.* xii, nos 256, 264, 284; *RPC* v. 323n.; *CBP* ii, nos 413, 416.
[146] *CBP* ii, nos 473, 475, 476.

with a question mark over James's commitment to amicable Anglo-Scottish relations.

This remained the case until some change in James's priorities could tip the balance against Buccleuch. There were signs however that James's policies were about to change. In November 1596 the council registered the letter from Elizabeth of 1586 in which she had vaguely acknowledged James's rights to succeed her on the English throne.[147] This indicated that the lack of formal confirmation from Elizabeth was beginning to unnerve James. In the same way that external political considerations had intruded on the Middle March before, so they were to again.

---

[147] RPC v. 324–5.

7

Pacification, 1597–1625

Crown policy in the Middle March had always been affected by external considerations, in particular relations with England. Whilst successive Scottish governments had used disturbances in the Borders as a form of leverage in diplomatic negotiations with England, so had some governments, such as that of Morton, attempted to use the imposition of order to encourage amicable relations. In 1597 James's border policy was affected by a number of concerns, in particular his succession to the English throne, which had led to his involvement in secret negotiations with the earl of Essex. James was keen that these should not be prejudiced by any cross-border incident.[1]

His relations with England were also influenced by his need for the English pension. This meant that he was vulnerable to any delay in its payment, as could be occasioned by a cross-border dispute such as the Kinmont Willie affair. In June 1596 Eure had written to Cecil that James 'is displeased as yt is thought, that the Quene threatneth to withhold her pentione from him in regarde of Baclugh his layte acte to my Lord Scrope'.[2] Payment was finally made in September 1596 but no payment was forthcoming throughout 1597. James's need for the money battled with his indignation at Elizabeth's attitude towards him. He expressed his fury at the queen's 'threatening to stop the payment of his annuity, and treating him as her pensioner'. He thought 'it a greater break of the League than his not giving up Buccleuch'.[3] But the combination of James's concerns over the pension and the succession were to create a watershed, in 1597, in his attitude to the Borders: external concerns were to begin to outweigh his inclination to support his officials there.[4]

Against this more conciliatory background, the English were also in need of amicable relations with Scotland. Throughout the 1590s English worries about a second Spanish Armada finding a landing in Scotland had been exacerbated by James's continuing indulgence of the Catholic earl of Huntly. At the same time, English attempts in Ulster to suppress the earl of Tyrone's rebellion needed James's co-operation in stopping any support for it

---

[1] S. Doran, 'Loving and affectionate cousins? The relationship between Elizabeth I and James VI of Scotland, 1586–1603', in S. Doran and G. Richardson (eds), *Tudor England and its neighbours*, Houndmills–New York 2005, 203–33 at pp. 216, 218–21, 227.
[2] *CBP* ii, no. 284.
[3] *CSP Scot.* xii, nos 195, 212, 215; *RPC* v. 300.
[4] Goodare, 'James VI's English subsidy', 110, 116. For a list of amounts paid to James see *CSP Scot.* xiii/1, no. 153.

from Scotland.[5] Thus, in 1597, the external concerns of both governments resulted in increasingly amicable cross-border relations, despite continued English complaints against Buccleuch and Cessford who remained in office.

In January and February 1597 a meeting of the border commissioners was largely successful, with commissioners meeting daily and a series of compromises being effected.[6] Success was partly due to the well-established mechanisms for resolving complaints but was principally the result of a new determination on the part of both governments that it should succeed. Tensions over the Kinmont Willie incident had demonstrated the necessity for a clarification of border redress and neither government wanted any escalation of the dispute.[7] The commission then went on to collate the existing march laws into a new border treaty, which they finally signed on 5 May. Significantly, a clause on the forcible renouncing of feuds received its first mention in such treaties and reflected both governments' growing perception of the need to deal with it. Tough described the new treaty as 'a great improvement on its predecessors', but this did not stop English wardens subsequently complaining of its 'knottes' which 'nobody goe about to untye'.[8]

For James, concern over the succession underlined the need for the maintenance of the amity evident in the treaty of May with England. No disturbance in the Borders was to be allowed to upset Anglo-Scottish relations, and from 1597 a new consistency was evident in James's implementation of justice in the region. In July 1599 a proclamation against incursions into England underlined James's determination to suppress further raiding 'quhilk may importe the brek of violatioun of the peace' and amity between the two realms.[9] The measures taken anticipated those undertaken in the pacification from 1605 onwards. The beginnings of the pacification can thus be traced to 1597, in preparation for the regal union, rather than to the Union itself. This chapter charts the two phases of the pacification, its origins from 1597, and the official pacification between 1605 and 1625.

I

In 1597 increasingly amicable Anglo-Scottish relations were jeopardised by English complaints over the behaviour of Buccleuch and Cessford and the failure to resolve the Kinmont Willie incident. The English often bracketed Cessford and Buccleuch together in their complaints. However, Cessford

---

[5] CSP Scot. xii, nos 118, 119; xiii/1, no. 98; R. B. Wernham, *The return of the Armadas: the last years of the Elizabethan war against Spain, 1595–1603*, London 1994, 31, 143, 149, 202–3.
[6] CBP ii, nos 481, 520, 594.
[7] Rae, Administration, 218–19; CBP ii, no. 569.
[8] Tough, *The last years*, 135; CBP ii, nos 621, 622, 623.
[9] RPC vi. 13.

and Buccleuch were not working together in the mid-1590s; in fact they were at feud, perpetuating the Scott-Ker feud that had continued for much of the sixteenth century. This was despite the marriage of Cessford's sister to Buccleuch in 1586. Cessford probably felt threatened by the older and more experienced Buccleuch whose increasing power in the march, following his acquisition of Liddesdale, had been formalised by his appointment as keeper. In 1596 the dispute flared again and Cessford challenged Buccleuch to a combat.[10] Though there was much report of this challenge, there was no report of the combat having taken place. It is likely that Cessford was pressured by James to back down, but the bad feeling lingered until at least late 1598, when it was finally reported that 'the King dealt for agreement of Cessford and Buccleuch and made them friends in his cabinet on Tuesday morning ... [Y]et some doubt it will not last nor is heartily between them but [is done] only for obeying the King'.[11] Cessford, a consummate politician, appears to have been the favourite with James, whilst Buccleuch, though a more attractive figure, lacked the finesse needed of a courtier. Furthermore, the Ker card was strong at court, Cessford having the support of his kinsman Mark Ker, commendator of Newbattle, a senior privy councillor.

Whilst Buccleuch and Cessford retained James's favour they were secure, but their political position was vulnerable to any changes in Anglo-Scottish relations. English calls for Buccleuch's surrender had been provoked further by raids by Cessford and Buccleuch in late 1596.[12] But in March 1597 the bishop of Durham, writing about a proposed exchange of pledges, thought that 'the king neither can nor will perform it against the opposition of Cesford and Buccleuch'.[13] In April Cessford felt able to boast that James would never deliver him to the commissioners, whilst Bowes complained that Cessford, Buccleuch and Johnstone had got 'great reputation with the inland lords and gentlemen, for their valorous defence of their charges'.[14] Scrope was even more suspicious: he thought that the only way 'to bridle these wicked clandes' was if the 'king can be persuaded to break their [Buccleuch's and Cessford's] combination'. Since 'these officers hold his full authority', he considered that James's lack of action showed that 'their actions are done by him or for him'. Furthermore, Scrope felt that there was 'little [hope] of peaceable fruit of their commission' when 'the greatest murderers are made the chiefest governors of the frontiers'.[15]

However, the registering of Elizabeth's letter suggested that James's nerve had begun to weaken. He delayed doing anything about Buccleuch and Cessford for the first half of 1597, whilst the commission's negotiations

---

[10] *CSP Scot* xii, nos 197, 224; NAS, GD224/1059/17.
[11] *CSP Scot* xiii/1, no. 279.
[12] *CBP* ii, nos 356, 405, 473, 475.
[13] *CBP* ii, no. 564.
[14] *CBP* ii, no. 595.
[15] *CBP* ii, no. 603; *CSP Scot.* xiii/1, no 3.

went well. In June, however, Buccleuch and Cessford failed to comply with one of the treaty's clauses, which called for the exchange of pledges with the opposite side, both refusing to surrender any one of their own adherents.[16] The following month a change in James's attitude to the Borders was detectable in the order for the return of all English prisoners and goods taken in a recent Scottish raid. A judicial raid was proposed to prevent further raiding which threatened 'a publict weare'.[17] In early October Bowes reported James's 'full assurance that Buccleuch and Cessford would present and enter on the next day to him all the pledges'. Despite a fracas on the day of truce at Norham on 8 October, Buccleuch delivered himself into English custody.[18] James remained concerned at the non-payment of his pension, but Elizabeth made it clear that she connected the payment of the pension with the surrender of Cessford. She looked 'every hour to hear ... some good satisfaction in the Border causes'. Cessford held out until the following year but in January it was reported from the court at Edinburgh that 'we look daily to hear that the gratuity should be paid which will stop the mouths of many'.[19] Cessford was forced to surrender to Carey's custody at Berwick on 14 February 1598. Temporarily his position at court had collapsed. Bowes thought that Cessford's friends 'could no longer bear out his evasion; whilst the king, straitened by her Majesty's last letters' finally realised that Cessford 'was not worth balancing against the Queen's merit'. In addition, the duke of Lennox, working on Buccleuch's behalf to arrange his release, supported Bowes's requests to James.[20] In May £3,000 sterling was received from the English.

The change in James's attitude to the Borders seemed to mark a watershed in the borderers' understanding of what was expected of them. The surrender of Cessford and Buccleuch proved crucial in their re-education. In March 1598 Buccleuch was released in exchange for his young son, regaining him on the surrender of pledges from his adherents. Cessford was freed shortly after.[21] Cessford, in particular, used the opportunity to build an amicable relationship with his warder Robert Carey and with William Bowes. Bowes advised Elizabeth to 'tie fast a knotte upon his faith' since Cessford was 'so well befriended by a stronge faction' and 'better furnished to do hurt on these Borders than any other of his nation' if alienated.[22] Subsequently both Cessford and Buccleuch were drawn into central government. Cessford attended privy council meetings between twelve and nineteen times annually to 1603 when he accompanied James south. In 1600 James, remem-

[16] *CBP* ii, no. 666; *CSP Scot.* xiii/1, nos 6, 32, 40.
[17] *RPC* v. 404–5.
[18] *CSP Scot.* xiii/1, nos 77, 78, 79, 82, 84; *CBP* ii, nos 783, 784.
[19] *CSP Scot.* xiii/1, nos 116, 117, 120.
[20] *CBP* ii, nos 906, 908, 909.
[21] *CSP Scot.* xiii/1, no. 124.
[22] *CBP* ii, no. 909.

bering Cessford's 'gude honorabill and thankfull service', granted him an annual pension of 650 merks from the abbacy of Kelso previously held by Robert's father William. Later that year Cessford was made Lord Roxburgh.[23] Buccleuch's advancement took longer and he was not regularly present on the privy council until 1607. In 1599 he received a new confirmation of the barony of Branxholme, with the consolidation of his lands of Branxholme, the lordship of Ettrick forest and the barony of Minto into one barony. He then spent a few years serving in the Low Countries, returning to help with the pacification in the Middle March. In March 1606 he was ennobled as Lord Scott of Buccleuch.[24]

The only potentially serious diplomatic incident in the Middle March after 1597 was that of August 1598 following Sir Robert Carey's over-enthusiastic pursuit of an unauthorised Scottish hunt into England, but both governments seemed intent on resolving the affair amicably.[25] James's preoccupation with the succession, and with maintaining good relations with England, was not confined to the Borders. In July 1600 a proclamation was made banning the recruitment in the west Highlands of men to assist the Irish rebels 'in thair rebellious and treasonabell courseis against his Majesteis darrest suster' Elizabeth in direct contrast to James's threats of assistance to the earl of Tyrone in 1596.[26] In 1601 James ordered Roxburgh to try a Scottish minister for the murder of an Englishman. He was to put his head 'upoun a publict place of the merche ... to be a testimony to baith the nationis of our eirnest cair that freindschip, love and amitie may be interteneit'.[27] In May 1601 Elizabeth recognised James's efforts, raising the pension to £5,000 and, in 1602, it was reported that Elizabeth 'does much commend the great care which the King does show to preserve the mutual peace'.[28]

James's new vigour and consistency in the Middle March should be seen in the context of these concerns. In Feburary 1598, in anticipation of a planned justice court at Peebles in March, all commissions of justiciary in the Merse, Teviotdale and Tweeddale were discharged to prevent judges showing partiality to their adherents.[29] To maintain this new consistency, William, tenth earl of Angus, was appointed lieutenant over all the marches in June 1598, a post which he retained until at least 1600. He was to be given the necessary support and all border pledges were to be at his disposal. In July 1599 a proclamation against raiding into England reiterated James's determination to suppress any disturbance and Angus's commission was renewed. Another

---

[23] NRAS1100/728.
[24] NAS, GD224/479/1; GD224/890/14; GD224/917/34; RPC vii. 340; Fraser, *Buccleuch*, i. 235.
[25] CSP Scot. xiii/1, no. 186.
[26] RPC vi. 127, 252–3, 304–5, 324.
[27] HMC, *The manuscripts of the duke of Roxburgh*, ed. W. Fraser, London 1894, no. 74.
[28] CSP Scot. xiii/2, nos 659, 828.
[29] RPC v. 444.

act ordered that border thefts were to be punished 'conforme to the first lawis and custome of the saidis Bordouris'. Unusually, wardens were ordered not to accept redress for theft but to 'execute unto the death', a departure from traditional sentencing.[30] Then James addressed the need for a consistently efficient administration of justice in the region, in December 1599 charging the sheriffs of the shires of Roxburgh, Selkirk, Peebles and Berwick with neglect of duty in failing to present fugitives to justice.[31] In July 1600 a large number of border lairds and nobles were summoned to a council meeting to discuss the quieting of the Borders and in November the wardens were ordered to burn offenders' houses.[32]

These measures suggested that significant levels of crime still persisted. There were seven judicial raids recorded in the Borders in the period 1597 to 1603. Only one of these, however, in October 1602, was to the Middle March, and little more from the Middle March troubled the council register in this period. Instead, it seems that the particular region of concern was the West March, which experienced continuing disturbance from the Maxwell-Johnstone feud. It is therefore likely that the measures addressed to the Borders as a whole were in fact more targeted at the West March.[33] And since the council thought that 'the cheiff and onlie caus of the grite misreule and unquietnes of the West Bordour ... hes bene the deidlie feidis' there each branch of each West March surname was required, in December 1598, to surrender two pledges to Angus. In September 1599 Maxwell, Johnstone and Drumlanrig, the leading figures from the West March, were held in ward whilst an ordinance called for the West March surname leaders to submit their feuds to the council for resolution.[34] Some however were slow to learn and the murder by some Armstrongs, in June 1600, of the West March warden, Sir John Carmichael (James's most trusted border official), triggered sustained retribution. In July, the new warden, Lord Herries, was ordered to arrange the trial and execution of an Armstrong pledge held in the 'pledge chamber' at Dumfries. The man was known as 'ane commoun and notorious theiff' but if the court could not prove anything against him, he was to be executed for the involvement of his surname in Carmichael's murder.[35]

All measures taken in the Borders, however, whether or not prompted by concern over the English succession, should be viewed within the context of the implementation of similar policies throughout Scotland. The most compelling example of this was that provided by the act against feuding

---

[30] *RPC* v. 464, 466; *RPS*, A1598/6/1, 1599/7/2, 4, accessed 7 Oct. 2009.
[31] *RPC* vi. 56–8, 68.
[32] *RPC* vi. 136–8; *RPS*, 1600/11/48, accessed 7 Oct. 2009..
[33] Rae, *Administration*, appendix 6; *CSP Scot.* xiii/2, no. 863. An extensive raid to Dumfries had taken place in November 1597 which was not replicated by one to the Middle March. In November it was recorded that James would return every Michaelmas to deal with the miscreants of the West March: *RPC* v. 421–7.
[34] *RPC* v. 503, 537; vi. 31, 46.
[35] *RPC* vi. 117–18, 127–8.

of 1598 in which a problem, often portrayed contemporarily as a peculiarly border characteristic, was addressed on a nationwide basis.[36] Similarly, the charges against the sheriffs of the Middle March in 1599 were swiftly followed by measures in 1600 and 1601 to improve the efficacy of sheriffs in general.[37] All these were symptomatic of James's overriding concern for the better administration of justice throughout his kingdom.

II

Negotiations and preparations in the Borders finally bore fruit in March 1603, on the death of Elizabeth, with James's undisputed succession to the throne of England. It was fitting that Sir Robert Carey, the son of the redoubtable warden Hunsdon, and with extensive Borders experience himself, was the person to bring the news to James. As he passed through Berwick on his slow journey south, James declared that 'the pairt of baith the countreyes quhilk of lait wes callit the Mariches and Bordouris' is now 'be the happie union, … the verie hart of the cuntrey'.[38] The region, he had prophesied previously, 'will be the middest of the Ile, and so as easily ruled as any part thereof'. In James's mind, the Anglo-Scottish frontier had vanished on his succession; the territorial congruity of the two kingdoms 'separated [internally] neither by Sea, nor great River', meant that the borderers could not 'distinguish, nor know, or discerne their owne limits'.[39] This perception was to guide all his future policies within the region, in which he was to strive to eradicate any difference of law or practice between the Scottish and English Borders. It was the new world of 'Great Britain'.

James was ignoring, however, as many subsequent historians have done, the significance of continuing differences between the two regions and what Jane Dawson has termed 'the long-standing enmity' between the two kingdoms: how was he to 'transform their deep-rooted hatred into an enduring amity'?[40] As an English officer in Berwick in 1604 warned, 'the inveterate passions of the two nations who convening here daily engender new occasions of dislike'.[41] The term 'Great Britain', so enthusiastically embraced by James, was premature; as Brian Levack wryly observes, 'the use of a new name to describe one's nationality usually reflects, rather than inspires, a new national identity'. Sir Francis Bacon certainly did not like the term, complaining to the English parliament, in April 1604, that 'we find no precedent, at home or abroad, of uniting or contracting of the names of two

[36] RPS, 1598/6/2, accessed 7 Oct 2009.
[37] RPC vi. 68–9, 233–4, 329.
[38] RPC vi. 560–1.
[39] James VI and I, Political writings, ed. J. P. Somerville, Cambridge 1994, 25, 135.
[40] Dawson, 'Anglo-Scottish Protestant culture', 91.
[41] HMC, Salisbury, xvi. 4.

several kingdoms ... into one name, where the union has grown by marriage or blood' except 'in the case of conquest'. This was dynastic union, a Union of the Crowns and not a conquest. And Scotland, as Levack further notes, 'was qualitatively different' from all other regions that had been subsumed into England.[42] Levack's criticisms are equally applicable to the differences between the Scottish and English Borders, and also to the new name James had for them, the 'Middle Shires'. As events in the Middle March would exemplify, the separate nature of the two kingdoms was to fundamentally undermine attempts to bring them together in the early 1600s. And although James, in 1604, declared his determination 'to extinguishe as well the name, as substance of the bordouris, I meane the difference betwene thaime and other pairts of the kingdome', government continued to use the term the 'former borders'. More significantly, the measures that James was to adopt to 'extinguish' the difference between the Borders and elsewhere, were in themselves to continue to differentiate the Scottish Borders both from the rest of Great Britain, and, indeed, from the English Borders as well.[43]

A memorial of 1604, in James's own hand, spelled out how the Middle Shires were to be united: for the

> doing quhairof it is necessarie that querrellis amoungst thaim be reconcyled and all straingenes betwene the nations quyte removed; that all theeves, murderers, oppressouris and vagabondis be quyte rooted out, ... that severe and indifferent justice be ministered upon all offenders and that no factions be fostered among thaime by the partialitie of thaire judges.[44]

The overriding theme was that the Borders should be the same as anywhere else in the new Great Britain, and as easily governed (somewhat hopeful in itself for government in the new multiple kingdom). The methods that James proposed replicated those undertaken in the 1590s to achieve a more efficient administration of justice in Scotland. All disputes between those of either side of the border were to be resolved, the impartiality of judges ensured and sureties taken to ensure everyone's future good behaviour. In 1604 an Anglo-Scottish commission sat down to draw up articles on the Borders for inclusion in the proposed treaty of union.[45] Whilst they did not take issue with much of James's plans for the Borders, his insistence on the standardisation of laws, to remove any dissimilarity between the two countries, proved more problematic. As Sir Edward Coke, the English attorney-general, observed in 1606, 'it will not appear which will be the middle shires, for a jury of England and Scotland cannot yet join. And for many

---

[42] Levack, *Formation of the British state*, 24, 189; J. Spedding (ed.), *Letters and life of Lord Bacon*, London 1872, iii. 197–9.
[43] HMC, *Salisbury*, xvi. 405.
[44] Ibid. xvi. 405.
[45] Galloway, *The Union of England and Scotland*, 65–6, 84–6.

respects I think that such a proviso would be very offensive'.[46] These differences within the Middle Shires had significant implications for the wider kingdoms: contemporary opinion was that for political union to happen, 'a union of laws appeared to be a necessity'. But it was easier said than done.[47] James's desire to create a union of the laws ignored the 'substantial differences' between the legal systems in each country and the lawyers' self-interested defence of the integrity of their own systems.[48] In the Borders, this protectionism resulted in the continuation of separate administrations in what was supposed to have become one region. Subsequently, it also led to heated resistance to James's demands for the remanding of offenders across the border, on the grounds that this would interfere with each country's jurisdiction. The Union commissioners were faced with three tasks: the abolition of all national statutes in which those of the opposite country were seen as hostile; the abolition of all laws, customs and ordinances which distinguished the Borders from elsewhere; and the setting up of a new system in the region which would administer the laws that existed in the rest of the new composite kingdom.[49] For James, the Middle Shires were to be an exemplar of the benefits of regal union, and an encouragement to further 'perfect Union'. However, though the commission readily agreed on the abolition of hostile laws, the methods for the future administration of justice proved more problematic.[50] Sir Francis Bacon's suggestion for an Anglo-Scottish court to try cases from either side of the border under a practical mix of both countries' laws made no headway.[51] No new legislation was made on the Borders and the treaty of union presented to the English parliament in 1604 made similarly little progress.

By 1605, therefore, despite James's proclamations on the new 'Middle Shires', little had changed in the Borders. His declaration on the abolition of 'hostile' laws at Newcastle in April 1603 was not formally ratified by either English or Scottish parliament until 1607.[52] In administrative terms, though the office of wardenship had lapsed on Union, Lord Home was appointed lieutenant with jurisdiction over the Scottish marches only, with Sir William Cranstoun as his deputy. His commission, like many such before, was to reduce the inhabitants to a 'godlie, peciable, and quyet forme of leving'. What was new, was the grant to Home of a substantial annuity of 1,000

---

[46] HMC, *Salisbury*, xviii. 186–7.
[47] Levack, *Formation of the British state*, 69.
[48] Ibid. 91. See also A. I. Macinnes, 'Regal union for Britain, 1603–38', in Burgess, *New British history*, 33–65 at pp. 35–6.
[49] Galloway, *The Union of Scotland and England*, 67–8.
[50] It was proposed that 'the laws or usage of the late Marches or Borders, instituted or tolerated while they stood separate thereof, are utterly frustrated and expired': *RPC* vii. 706–7
[51] Levack, *Formation of the British state*, 75.
[52] *RPC* vi. 560–1; *RPS*, 1607/3/12, accessed 7 Oct. 2009.

English merks (£8,000 Scots) and a paid force of fifty horsemen.[53] This, at least, demonstrated James's commitment to suppressing crime. As before, however, there were difficulties in getting payment. Home, suffering from contradictory orders and council interference in January 1604, resigned that July. In December 1604 there was an order for those in the Scottish Borders to assist Cranstoun in his duties but problems of communication between London and officials in the Borders abounded.[54] As a result, in December 1604, the captain of the Berwick garrison complained that 'the Borders are much infested with stealing, and now and then some disordered persons of the Scottish side stir up the ancient and barbarous custom of deadly feuds'.[55] Continued instability in the Borders formed an unhappy background to the Union negotiations and the English parliament of 1604. James now realised that something more had to be done if the example of the Middle Shires was to convince both countries of the benefits of Union; a severe pacification of the region was to be undertaken. Ironically, the bi-polar judicial framework created to enforce this pacification was to institutionalise an enduring mutual distrust and to underline the separate administrations of the two regions within the 'Middle Shires'.

III

In March 1605 the Middle Shires were to be an example of 'civilitie and obedience to the haill remanent boundis of his kingdome of Grit Britane' and a new commission of justiciary was appointed to undertake the pacification of all crime in the region.[56] Emphasis was, firstly, on the suppression of crime in each region, but government was keen also to encourage cross-border co-operation, without which pacification could not be successfully sustained. All occasions for further dispute were to be removed, either through the suppression of feuding or the redress of past complaints. The punishment of offences should act as an example to prevent further crime and an effective armed force should be formed to prosecute the pacification. Crucially, this new regional body of commissioners was necessary to oversee the co-ordination of official responses to crime, both internally within each of the 'former Borders' and within the new Middle Shires. The commission anticipated that there would be cross-border co-operation between the two judicial administrations and harmony between the people of both sides.

---

[53] RPC vi. 833–4.
[54] RPC vi. 601, 604; vii. 19. The earl of Cumberland was appointed lieutenant over the English counties of Northumberland, Cumberland and Westmorland but was sacked in December 1604 having suffered, like Home, confusing orders from the English council: Watts, *From Border to Middle Shire*, 133–4, 137.
[55] HMC, *Salisbury*, xvi. 376.
[56] RPC vii. 701–4.

Judicial processes should be standardised. And finally, for the pacification to be deemed a success, it had to work not only in the short term but had to be maintained in the long term. This, it was thought, necessitated a change in mentality on the part of the borderers; offenders were to be expelled since 'the change of air will mak in thame ane exchange of thair maneris', whilst the reformation of the 'godless, lawless, and disordered' of the Scottish Borders was to stimulate the reinvigoration of the work of the kirk there. It 'were fit' Lord Sheffield intoned that the Borders 'should be lightened by the preaching of the Word, being the only way to bring them to civility who are now so barbarous'.[57] Their whole way of life was to be transformed, by force if necessary. Most of the methods used bore remarkable similarity to what had gone before, but what was novel was the sustained commitment of government in both London and Edinburgh to the pacification.[58]

The formation of the commission for the Middle Shires in March 1605 was an attempt to encompass all these aspirations. However, its very form embodied the continuation of mutually exclusive spheres of administration, with five commissioners from each realm having jurisdiction only in their own country. All were men with kinship links in their own region, or experience of it. In Scotland, the obligations of kinship, though under pressure from the suppression of feuding, remained part of the foundation of a government effected through personal relationships.[59] The Scottish commissioners were Sir William Home of Whitelaw and Patrick Chirnside of East Nisbet, both part of extensive surnames in the East March; Robert Charteris of Amisfield, part of the Maxwell network in the West March; and Sir Gideon Murray of Elibank, who was resident in the Middle March and linked to both the Murray and Scott surnames there. He would subsequently become the most important Scottish commissioner. The only outsider was Sir William Seton of Kylesmure who was a younger brother of the new chancellor, the earl of Dunfermline, and embodied the close communication that was to exist between the commission and the council in Edinburgh. Unlike border commissioners of the past, whose commissions had lasted the length of a specific meeting, these commissioners were appointed indefinitely and received an annual payment, initially of 400 merks. Most of them served many years: Elibank acted as a commissioner until 1617 when his duties as deputy treasurer forced him to resign his place in favour of his nephew Sir John Murray of Philiphaugh.[60]

Details of the work of the pacification, its severity and the appointments that James made within it, are sufficiently covered elsewhere.[61] But from

[57] RPC vii. 706–7; HMC, *Salisbury*, xvii. 125; see chapter 1 above.
[58] RPC vii. 701–4; Spence, 'Pacification', 107.
[59] RPC vii. 701–4; HMC, *Muncaster*, 229.
[60] RPC xi. 11; Sizer, 'Middle Shires', 95–7.
[61] The Scottish pacification is covered in greater depth in Groundwater, 'Middle March', ch. vi, whilst an excellent summary of it is Maurice Lee's *Government by pen*, 44–7, 72–4,

the start the efforts of the commissioners, such as Elibank, the captain of the border guard, Cranstoun, and subsequently Ker of Ancrum and then of Oxnam, and the mighty lieutenant, the earl of Dunbar, were to be hampered by the judicial divisions that remained between the two kingdoms, and the separate jurisdictions of the Scottish and English commissioners. The order to the Scottish commissioners to remove 'all occasioun of strangeness and mark of divisioun' between the two regions was undermined by the constitution of the commission itself.[62] Differences surfaced early, in August 1605, when official English observers at a court at Hawick where they were judicially powerless, complained that the Scottish commissioners 'made no bones to kill such fugitives or felons as made resistance'.[63] Here, additionally, judicial differences were being exacerbated by the continuation of centuries of mutual distrust. And it was this distrust that was, disastrously, to hamper the clause that asked for the 'delyverie to be maid of all personis fugitive' from one country to the other when called upon by the opposite officer. This 'remanding' of offenders to the country of their offence, or to repatriate them from any hiding-place, was intended to 'quench all the spark of ony hope of escape from punishment'.[64] The bishop of Carlisle, like James, thought that of the measures taken that 'none was found so powerful as remanding. It brought terror to the thieves of both kingdoms that theft was in a manner banished, and every malefactor feared that he should find justice without favour with those of the opposite nation'.[65] James did not envisage, however, the huge row that this clause would cause, and the ramifications that it had for his Union project.

Of all the contentious articles for Union put before the English parliament, remanding was one of the most bitterly disputed.[66] For James, it was a priority, the lack of remanding at odds with his desire for the standardisation of the laws in the new Britain. However, in this he had run up against the self-defensive protection of jurisdictions by English and Scottish commissioners and parliaments alike; for some it was very personal, Northumbrian officials resisting remanding feared for their own immunity.[67] To James's outraged disbelief the English parliament of 1607 refused to pass an act for the institution of remanding. The only thing that this English parliament agreed was the abolition of the hostile border laws. It was not until 1610 that James succeeded in getting the legislation on remanding, though its ratification was dependent on the Scottish parliament passing a reciprocal act. This

---

116. For the English pacification see Watts, *From Border to Middle Shire*, and Spence, 'Pacification'. For a treatment of the entire cross-border region see Sizer, 'Middle Shires'. For appointments to the commission and to the border guard see chapter 3 above.
[62] *RPC* vii. 706–7.
[63] HMC, *Muncaster*, 236.
[64] *RPC* vii. 706–7.
[65] HMC, *Salisbury*, xix. 300.
[66] Galloway, *Union of England and Scotland*, 122–3, 142–3.
[67] Watts, *From Border to Middle Shire*, 142, 148, 151, 155.

finally happened in 1612, but problems associated with remanding continued.[68] In 1617 it was still a subject of discussion, and in 1623 Buccleuch experienced difficulty in extraditing a fugitive from Northumberland.[69] The dispute had demonstrated the divisive flaw in James's vision of unity in his 'Middle Shires'.

Problems were exacerbated by worsening relations between Scottish and English commissioners. Things had started well: in April 1605 the English commissioner, Sir Wilfred Lawson, wrote that 'I cannot but commend the Scottish Commissioners for their care for his Majesty's service' following their execution of an Armstrong for Carmichael's murder.[70] Initial co-operation, however, was not to last. By July 1605 Seton, whilst protesting friendship, was writing snidely to Lawson that 'though you have wealth, we have liberality. Knightships with you are common merchandise, with us they are rewards of virtue'.[71] In December the Scots complained to the English commissioners that they should search the farms on their side more carefully 'for we are informed that the fugitives have their maintenance there, dreading our side more than their own'.[72] Cranstoun's stinging reproach to the English commissioners in March 1606 exemplified the difficulties: 'If you will needs be commanders, I desire that your discretion may appear as well as your authority. Think not that my body can be everywhere to do all your services.'[73]

The pacification did not, however, rest merely on the efforts of these commissioners in suppressing cross-border and internal crime. More general measures were taken to change a way of life and centuries-old traditions in the Borders. Most illustrative of governmental intrusion was the prohibition of 'the ordinary custome' of hunting in the Cheviots by those of Selkirkshire, Roxburghshire and Liddesdale which might be the cause of further trouble. These were not just threats: in June 1605, for example, the Scotts of Goldielands and Thirlestane and Douglas of Cavers were forced to find caution of up to 1,000 merks not to hunt there.[74] And in May 1608 a horse race at Peebles was banned by the privy council for fear of 'quarrellis leading to trouble', as was another race at Annandale in 1611.[75]

Government intervention was not limited to the secular life of the Borders but targeted its religious life too. Great significance was attached to the lack of competent ministers and regular worship which, it was argued, created a godless society, prone to crime. As James was to reiterate, 'the

---

[68] RPS, 1612/10/9, accessed 7 Oct. 2009.
[69] RPC xi. 290; CSP Dom., 1623–1625, 38, 82.
[70] HMC, Muncaster, 243.
[71] Ibid. 244.
[72] Ibid. 242.
[73] Ibid. 250–1.
[74] RPC vii. 41–2, 601, 623, 709.
[75] RPC viii. 81; ix. 152–3.

bypast barbarite and incivilitie in that parte of the Middle Shyris' was due, he thought, to 'the inhabitantis in most pairt thairof being voyd of all trew feir of God and religioun'.[76] In July 1608, therefore, the General Assembly made a priority of addressing the state of the Kirk in the Borders, approving a visitation there by the scary Archbishop Spottiswoode.[77] The linkage between spiritual and temporal measures was evident in the friendly co-operation of Spottiswoode and James's chief secular henchman, the earl of Dunbar: Dunbar, Spottiswoode wrote, was 'a man of deep wit, few words, and in his Majesty's service no less faithfull then fortunate. The most difficult affaires he compassed without any noise, and never returned when he was employed, without the work performed that he was sent to doe'.[78] They were to prove a formidable joint force in the Borders, Spottiswoode staying with Dunbar at Newcastle in August 1608, perhaps planning the visitation of the Middle March. At council level too their alliance provided a counter-balance to the power of Dunbar's rival, the chancellor, Dunfermline.[79] In November 1610, in official recognition of Spottiswoode's involvement in the pacification, his powers were extended into its secular realm on his appointment to the commission of the peace for Roxburghshire, Selkirkshire and Peeblesshire.[80]

Whilst it is impossible to quantify any decrease in the levels of crime, contemporary report increasingly spoke of the Middle Shires as 'settled in perfyte obedience' and border business troubled the privy council less. By 1609 even Dunfermline was moved to superlatives in a letter to James, claiming that Dunbar,

> had rendered all these ways and passages betwixt ... Scotland and England as free and peaceable as is recorded Phoebus in old times made free to his own oracle in Delphos ... These parts are now, as lawful, as peaceable and quiet as any part in any civil kingdom.[81]

Such hyperbole, however, is an inexact basis for an assessment either of the levels of crime in the region or Dunbar's effectiveness in suppressing it. Central government was prone to generalisations about endemic disorder, and border officials were in the habit of exaggerating it, in order to justify their offices.[82] In 1607 Dunbar's self-congratulatory letters to Salisbury had spoken of his suppression of crime without which there would have been 'a most troublesome winter'.[83] The last old-style raid into England was in

---

[76] *RPC* viii. 266–7, 564–5.
[77] *BUK* iii. 1061–2. See chapter 1 above.
[78] A. S. W. Pearce, 'John Spottiswoode, Jacobean archbishop and statesman', unpubl. PhD diss. Stirling 1998, 116; Spottiswoode, *History*, iii. 516.
[79] Lee, *Government by pen*, 47; Pearce, 'John Spottiswoode', 65, 78.
[80] *RPC* ix. 75–6.
[81] NLS, Denmilne, Adv. MS 33.1.1, vol. 3, fo. 23.
[82] Lee, *Government by pen*, 46; Watts, *From Border to Middle Shire*, 152.
[83] HMC, *Salisbury*, xix. 254, 427.

1611, by the Armstrongs and Elliots. The council expressed disbelief that 'suche ane accident and outrage sould haif fallin out', ordering 'examplar puneshment'.[84] Immediately courts were held at Jedburgh, during which eighteen offenders were executed, whilst a large number from the Middle March were forced to find caution – but it is the last such lengthy record of a court until those held in 1622.[85] Michael Braddick's assessment that James might fairly claim, after 1607, a successful pacification in Northumberland, may have been true of the situation in the English Borders, but subsequent measures in Scotland, and the concern shown by James, particularly in around the period 1617 to 1618, make Calder's assertion, that 'the Border problem melted like snow on the Cheviots in spring', seem somewhat premature.[86]

What had diminished beyond doubt however was cross-border crime. But there was continuing evidence of internal crime in the Scottish Borders, the assurances listed in the registers of acts of caution showing that feuding still persisted there. Such time-honoured practices would take longer to pacify. Of 1,965 acts of caution calendared between 1604 and 1610 the total figure for the Borders was around 330, of which 120 were from the Middle March and 160 from the West.[87] These records suggested that crime in the Borders was about 17 per cent of that recorded in Scotland as a whole, and slightly above the national average. However, such crime needs to be placed within its national context: feuding and violent crime were nationwide phenomena and the problems of a border-specific nature, which continued to define the marches as a region of special concern, should not obscure the similarity of the Borders' experience to that of the rest of Scotland. For instance, James's linking of lawlessness with godlessness motivated much of his plans for discipline in all the parishes of Scotland.[88] Similarly, the grant of commissions of the peace to prominent figures in the Middle March, in November 1610, was part of a programme of government efforts to improve the judicial system throughout Scotland.[89] The government was imposing its will on the region in an unprecedented way, but it was doing much the same elsewhere. Moreover, this was not a government alienated from borderers, for borderers continued to be part of central government, as the frequent attendance at council of such as Roxburgh, Buccleuch, Cranstoun and Elibank attested.

These men were familiar figures to government both in the Borders and in Edinburgh, and, although the pacification represented an unprecedented intensification of government in the Borders, many of its methods were not

---

[84] *RPC* ix. 614–15.
[85] *RPC* ix. 705–14.
[86] A. Calder, *Revolutionary empire: the rise of the English-speaking empires from the fifteenth century to the 1780s*, London 1981, 108, quoted in Braddick, *State formation*, 376, 378.
[87] *RPC* vii. 545–697; viii. 629–733.
[88] MacDonald, *Jacobean Kirk*, 38.
[89] *RPC* ix. 75–6; Goodare, *Government of Scotland*, 203.

new. Kinship continued to provide the framework for the network of support relied upon by local officials, whilst the accountability of surname leaders and landlords for their kinsmen and tenants, under the general band, had been in use since at least the 1560s. Similarly, in 1607, the warding of various Scotts, Elliots and Rutherfords in Fife, Perth and Aberdeen as surety for future good behaviour, replicated the pledge system of the sixteenth century.[90] The Middle Shires commissioners were all connected to old powerful families and the new JPs in the Middle March were all prominent figures already. As Spence notes, 'the roots of reform are to be found in an earlier phase' though this study would not agree with his verdict that the pacification needed 'new men to execute' it.[91] What was new was the maintenance over several years of the consistency and severity of the implementation of justice.

IV

The premature death of Dunbar in February 1611 triggered central government fears about a resumption of crime in the Borders and the Armstrong-Elliot raid seemed to give them further grounds for concern.[92] As a result, for the following few years, the maintenance of the pacification continued to be a priority for the council. Proclamations were issued renewing measures in order to show that there would be no softening of government determination to punish offenders. This prompted a proclamation in December 1616 against the 'auld custome' of hunting in the Cheviots. James was worried that 'the hoip of oversicht and presumptioun of impunitie hes bene the cause of this publict contempt and violatioun'.[93] The severity of justice meted out was meant to be exemplary but occasionally it was perceived to have gone too far. In November 1614 the magistrates of Selkirk, including the provost Robert Scott of Haining, were fined 150 merks for torturing two wool merchants from Leith to force confession of some minor thefts.[94] Another incident, in 1624, gave an indication of the methods used: John Maxwell of Bromeholme, acting as bailie depute to the commissioner, the earl of Nithsdale, was accused of dragging a mother and son 'violentlie further [from their house] under nyght binding thame with coirdis, and carieing thame as captives ... to the Water of Ewes' where they cruelly drowned them.[95]

---

[90] *RPC* viii. 7–8.
[91] Spence, 'Pacification', 97.
[92] Sizer observes that 'All traces of unity between the two sets of Border Commissioners gradually vanished with the death of Dunbar' until the conjunct commission of 1618, his death leaving something of a power vacuum: 'Middle Shires', 112, 114.
[93] *RPC* x. 198–9.
[94] *RPC* x. 793.
[95] Sizer, 'Middle Shires', 169 (quotation from justiciary record books of adjournal, 1637–50, NLS, JC2/8).

The government particularly persisted, in the Middle March, in the suppression of feuding in this period in order to contain any further outbreak of trouble. James continued to intervene, especially when his officials were involved. In May 1612 the continuing dispute between the earl of Angus and his bailie Ferniehirst resulted in a 'great convocation of the lieges in arms for holding courts at Lintellie in the Lordship of Jedburgh Forest, [where] ... both parties were resolved to hold the same'. Angus was accompanied by up to four hundred men. Ferniehirst and one of his sons were warded. James then intervened, ordering their release and the council to arbitrate in the dispute.[96] Cranstoun was Angus's spokesman, whilst Elibank, as was to be expected, supported Ferniehirst. The case was brought before the council for resolution in June; Angus's right to hold courts in Jedforest was upheld but with no more than sixty people in his company. However, the affair continued, prompting James's order in September 1613 to the council to resolve it.[97]

James similarly intervened in December 1616 in an internal Scott dispute between Simon Scott of Bonnington and Sir Walter Scott of Harden, but which involved the border guard. Buccleuch and the Scotts of Goldielands, Haining and Burnfoot were ordered to produce before justice the Bonnington Scotts for the slaughter of Walter Scott of Essinsyde, Harden's second son.[98] In April 1617 a counter-complaint was made by Mary Scott, Lady Bonnington, against a man 'mantenit' by Harden. With two gentlemen of the guard, Harden and other Scotts had violently put the Bonningtons out of their home, the escheat of which Harden had been granted as the kinsman of the slaughtered man. There was an unhappy confusion here between the official and private nature of Harden's actions where he was probably also acting as Oxnam's deputy on the border guard. However, Harden's alliance with Elibank was to his advantage, the council finding in favour of Harden, and in August 1617 William Scott of Harden, Elibank's son-in-law, was appointed lieutenant of the border guard.[99] In September 1617 Elibank wrote to James reminding him that James had agreed to Elibank's disposal of the escheat to Harden and asking him not to undo the grant.[100] The dispute must have continued, however, for James was forced to intervene again in 1619, though the council again found in Harden's favour.[101]

But such intrusion of government into the Borders, as elsewhere, was not confined to the suppression of violent crime; it continued to intensify in all aspects of life. In March 1619, for instance, the earl of Roxburgh

---

[96] *RPC* ix. 372–4; NAS, GD40/13/41.
[97] *RPC* ix. 372–4, 394, 398, 400, 403; x. 152.
[98] *RPC* x. 667; xi. 20.
[99] *RPC* xi. 98–101, 217; papers relating to the Bonnington-Harden feud, NAS, GD157/1246, 1249.
[100] NLS, Denmilne, Adv. MS 33.1.1, vol. 8, fo. 33.
[101] NAS, GD124/15/29, fo. 14; *RPC* xii. 123; GD157/190, 194.

was forced to apologise before the council for setting a bad example by not taking communion in accordance with James's directive to all his councillors.[102] Council concerns also began to include trade. Reacting to the sale of English-processed Scottish skins at a market in Kelso, the council appointed English tanners to teach the tanning and barking of leather to the Scots.[103] It was not a popular measure, and in July 1622 a number of Selkirkshire tanners were denounced as rebels for refusing to comply with the new tanning ordinances, while in 1623 a complaint by Scottish tanners against these laws was subscribed by nineteen men of Selkirk.[104]

The council's attention to such matters suggests that cross-border crime was no longer seen as overridingly prevalent. Trade was becoming more important. Following the reimposition of duties payable on Anglo-Scottish trade, a statute of 1612 named Kelso and Jedburgh as the places for the payment of customs on livestock passing between England and Scotland in the Middle March. This indicated that there had been an increase in cross-border trade, which in turn suggested that a decrease in crime had occurred.[105] Figures for overland trade with England are, as Jennifer Watson observes, 'necessarily incomplete', traders following old droving routes and avoiding the customs posts. Even so, in the period between 1610 to 1619, there was a huge expansion of cross-border trade, particularly in livestock, cloth and grain, which Watson attributes to the suppression of crime in the region.[106] For James this will have underlined the benefits of Union, and the example that the Borders could provide of such benefits.

From time to time James's interest in the region intensified. In November 1616, following some quieter years, James wrote to express his surprise at complaints 'being made unto us of some wronges done on the Bordouris ... [that] are not free of that mischeife of thefte'.[107] In response, in January 1617, the Middle Shires commissioners were ordered to hold a justice court as soon as possible and to report back to the council on the 'caus of the disorderis and thiftis'.[108] It is difficult to analyse the accuracy of these reports of renewed crime. As Jared Sizer observes, 'local authorities tended to interpret incidents of violence as a sign of impending disaster rather than an isolated incident in the long term process of pacification'. James's concerns were almost certainly triggered by his planned arrival in Scotland later that year. His passage through Berwick and Dumfries inescapably brought the Borders to his attention again.[109]

---

[102] *RPC* xi. 635–6.
[103] *RPC* xii. 161, 294.
[104] *RPC* xiii. 9, 247, 635–46.
[105] *RPC* ix. 394–5.
[106] Watson, 'Scottish foreign trade', 171, 192.
[107] *RPC* x. 847.
[108] *RPC* xi. 14.
[109] Sizer, 'Middle Shires', 88–91.

Whilst James was in Scotland, in August 1617, he reiterated his personal commitment to the consolidation of the pacification by summoning a number of senior borderers before the council to sign another band for the good behaviour of their kinsmen and tenants. These included such worthies as Buccleuch, Cranstoun, Oxnam, Sir John Ker of Jedburgh and Douglas of Cavers. In his absence the earl of Angus was represented by his kinsmen and bailies of Jedburgh forest, the Douglases of Cavers and Bonjedburgh. They were ordered to apprehend offenders and 'punishe thame, yf thay have jurisdictioun, or then present thame to the judge ordinair to abyde thair tryall', and replicating the traditional use of financial liability for their errant dependants, lairds were to make restitution for any theft or harm 'conforme to the General Band'. A band made previously in 1602 by the men of the Middle March was reinserted in the register.[110] Stung, these border lairds asked that a letter be sent to James requesting that a similar course of action be taken with the landlords on the other side of the border. The council also agreed to a petition by these lairds that they should have power 'to apprehend thair awne malefactouris and to exhibite thame' to the commissioners if they catch them with the 'red hand' and, with individual commission, try them.[111] All the landlords of the marches were then called to appear before the council in September to 'underly the lyke ordour', prompting the mass subscription of the band by a large number from the Middle and West Marches, including the new earl of Roxburgh, over the next couple of months.[112] Clearly, the prominent local figures being held potentially painfully responsible by the crown, were careful to extract further judicial powers in return for their co-operation – and it is significant that one of their targets of complaint should be their opposites in the English Borders. It was taking time to establish the harmonious cross-border co-operation expected by James. At the same time, the problem of prisoners escaping before a justice court day was remedied by the commissioners being given full power individually 'to fense and hald courtis' and to put criminals to execution.[113] This had been happening anyway before 1610, but suggests that problems within the Scottish pacification continued to exist.

James's return to London did not stem his interest: early in January 1618 the Scottish council received from the English council a long list of proposals on the Middle Shires. The overriding principle behind these forceful suggestions was that the law and its administration should be the same in both kingdoms. This was because it was felt that the 'greitest causis of thair offences is houpe of impunitie' in the other country.[114] In April this resulted in the appointment of a 'Conjunct Commission' the aim of

[110] RPC xi. 215–16, 218.
[111] RPC xi. 216–17, 228–9.
[112] RPC xi. 216, 225–8, 253, 257, 276, 283, 407.
[113] RPC xi. 216–17.
[114] RPC xi. 288–91.

which was to limit such impunity more effectively, with thirty members from each side of the border on the one body. They were to act jointly in apprehending offenders and charged to remand them back to the country where the offence had taken place, which suggested that the distrustful resistance to remanding had not disappeared. The Scotsmen appointed included all the original commissioners of 1605 and added to them the other principal figures in the Borders, most of whom also already held commissions of the peace.[115] An attempt was being made here to achieve a genuinely crossborder institution. Disastrously, however, commissioners from one country never had jurisdiction in the other, a problem that James was never able to resolve, and because of its size the commission ultimately was to prove too unwieldy to be effective.[116] Cross-border co-operation remained elusive.

The Scottish council was keen, however, to maintain the pacification in all its ramifications, in June calling for the appearance before the council of the Commission for the Plantation of the Kirks, and instituting measures to avoid disturbances, such as the suppression of hostelries. In August James ordered that the new regulations be printed and fixed to the mercat crosses in the Borders and to the houses of every freeholder, so that none could claim that they were unaware of them.[117] The most extreme suggestion was 'to send the most notorious leiveris of thame unto Virginia, or to sum remote pairtes, to serve in the wearris or in colloneis'.[118] This replicated the earlier transportation of some unfortunate Grahams and Armstrongs to serve in the Low Countries, and then, with only qualified success, to farm in Ireland. The council was taken aback by these new proposals, skillfully evading outright refusal by drawing attention to some 'points of doubt or delicacy on the Scottish side': since landlords were responsible for notorious thieves under the general band there was no necessity for such a course. Furthermore, the proposals, they said, could only be implemented 'so far as the lawis of this countrie will permit'. This would have been an irritating reminder to James of the un-unified legal systems of his new multiple kingdoms. James became insistent on the transportation proposals and in May the council was forced to concede.[119] The following February the 'Commission for the Transportation of Criminals' was ordered to report to the council 'the evill disposed, vagarant, and idle persones in these schyres' and to transport them. There is no record, however, of this happening within this period, telling evidence of

---

[115] James took a personal interest in the membership, altering those nominated before the final appointments were made: *RPC* xi. 291, 344–8, 360, 386–7.
[116] Watts calls this commission the 'least useful' one, noting the hostility that its duties of remanding engendered amongst the Northumbrian gentlemen: *From Border to Middle Shire*, 194–5.
[117] *RPC* xi. 354–5, 425–6.
[118] *RPC* xi. 289.
[119] *RPC* xi. 313–14, 353–4.

the Scottish council's ability to exercise its own discretion in the day-to-day implementation of policies formed in London.[120]

V

Thereafter, the English council appeared to lose interest in the Borders.[121] In 1621 it decided that since the Borders were 'now brought to a peaceable estate' the commission should be abolished and 'a more ready and less chargeful mode of governing' the English Borders should be devised.[122] The Scottish privy council continued to deal with a few cases from the Middle March each month but no significant action was taken in relation to the region until November 1621. Demonstrating the reduced prioritisation of the Borders, a warrant from the king that month noted that since 'oure kingdome is reduceit to suche quietnes ... thair is no necessitie [for] ane ordinarie Gaird within the same, and that the moneyis bestowit that way may be reserved for more necessarie useis'. The guard was discharged with immediate effect, its fortunate captain, Ker of Oxnam, receiving a royal exoneration for any harm that he had caused, whilst his annual pay was confirmed in perpetuity. (On the same day his father Ferniehirst was created Lord Jedburgh. The Kers had clearly survived the fall of their less lucky kinsman Somerset.)[123] The decision to disband the guard, however, should also be considered within the context of the fiscal crisis of 1620–1, when the government froze pensions, financial expediency perhaps overriding any concerns over continuing internal crime.[124]

It did not take long for complaints to surface. These related primarily to the dales of the West March. In February 1622 the commissioners of the Middle Shires complained to the council of increasing crime in Annandale, Nithsdale, Eskdale and Ewesdale since the discharge of the guard. In response, prominent borderers were summoned to give their advice: this was principally to emphasise the benefits of a standing guard which 'was not onlie ane countenance and grandour to the courtis, bot a grite terrour to malefactouris'.[125] Several men of 'power and friendship' within the region should be appointed to oversee such a resident force. This resulted in a new

---

[120] RPC xi. 506; M. Perceval-Maxwell, *Scottish migration to Ulster in the reign of James I*, Belfast 1999, 25–6, 280–8, 312.
[121] Only seven references to the whole of the Borders appeared for the seven years covered by *CSP Dom.*, *1619–1623* and *CSP Dom.*, *1623–1625*, in contrast to the twenty-eight entries for the eight years in *CSP Dom.*, *1611–1618*, and more than seventy in the eight years in *CSP Dom.*, *1603–1610*. There were no border-related entries in the English *Acts of the privy council* from January 1618 to March 1625.
[122] *CSP Dom.*, *1619–1623*, 331.
[123] RPC xii. 582–4. 657–9, 663.
[124] Goodare, *State and society*, 132, 150.
[125] RPC xii. 650, 670–2, 775–9.

commission of three men, the triumvirate of the earls of Buccleuch, Nithsdale and Annandale, as overseers of the pacification with superior judicial powers and the paid support of ten armed men each. This effectively resurrected the border garrison. The original border commission of 1613 was to continue in existence but in a subordinate role.[126] This meant that Oxnam, Kylesmure and Cranstoun continued as commissioners as did Murray of Philiphaugh, Elibank's replacement, whilst the conjunct commission seems by 1622 to have faded away.

All the triumvirs fulfilled the requirement of being men of 'power and friendship', all holding lands in Annandale, Nithsdale, Eskdale or Ewesdale, but how effective Annandale was, given his duties at court for most of his tenure, is questionable. Relations between the triumvirate seem to have been strained. In August 1623, following a triumvirate court at Dumfries from which Douglas of Drumlanrig had got two men repledged to his regality court, Oxnam wrote to Annandale beseeching his intercession with James: the earl of Nithsdale had apparently taken offence to Oxnam seeking his advice on the repledging and was about to complain to James. The residual antipathies of the Maxwells, not only to the Johnstones, but also to Douglas of Drumlanrig will not have helped relations between commissioners. In a subsequent letter to Annandale, the Maxwell earl of Nithsdale exclaimed that Drumlanrig had said that if 'anie man wald bring his regalatie in question then he intendit to cut his throt' and complained that repledging undermined the effectiveness of the triumvirate.[127] In June 1624, following the departure abroad of a financially-embarrassed Nithsdale, and Annandale's preoccupations in London, two similarly prominent Middle March men, Lord Yester and Stewart of Traquair, were appointed in their place.[128] At courts in Jedburgh in August and October 1622 and February and April 1623, at least forty-one men were executed, nine 'brunt on the cheik with the commone birning irne' of Jedburgh, eighteen had their cases referred to the council and a number banished under pain of death.[129] Exemplary severity was still the hallmark of sentencing policy in the region, surely in response to the continuing reports of internal crime. It was apparently still felt necessary to commission a new 'triumvirate' in November 1625, to include Buccleuch, Yester, Nithsdale (now returned from abroad) and Annandale and a new figure from an old family used to service in the Borders, the earl of Angus.[130]

In many ways the structures of power in the Borders had not much changed, the triumvirs using the traditional methods of effecting justice, their kindreds and alliances providing their manpower, and utilising the

---

[126] *RPC* xii. 672–9.
[127] NLS, Denmilne, Adv. MS 33.1.1, vol. 10, fos 112, 135.
[128] *RPC* xiii. 542–3, 545–6, 621.
[129] *RPC* xiv. 677–714. Sizer calls the triumvirate 'a study in failure': 'Middle Shires', 120–9.
[130] *RPC* 2nd ser. i. 193.

obligations associated with lordship to make the surname leader accountable for the actions of his dependants. The difference here was that Buccleuch was being called to police, in an official capacity, his own lands and men. Traditional authority-holders, like Buccleuch, who embraced the opportunities provided by James's 'new world' of Great Britain, had become a formal part of government, rather than acting as the crown's unofficial agents. An indication of Buccleuch's severity was the description by two English travellers in 1629 of a river, between Langham and Selkirk, where 'my lord Buckpleugh did wapp the outlaws into the dubb'.[131] Unsurprisingly, there is some evidence of local reaction against these changed circumstances: Buccleuch, for instance, was the target of a murderous and disgruntled former associate and tenant, Robin Elliot of Redheugh.

Disaffected dependants were not the only problem facing the commissioners, tensions in the wider cross-border region continuing as pronounced as ever. The formation of the various commissions underlined the continuation of separate administrative and judicial systems, the divisions between which were exacerbated by strained relations amongst commissioners and xenophobic hostility. In 1617 the council felt it necessary to issue the threat of the death penalty for anyone harming any Englishman in the king's company on his forthcoming journey to Scotland. In 1621 a letter from a Scottish commissioner criticised the failure of his English counterparts whilst praising Scottish efforts, which were 'so active and vigilant that the thieves fly to England'.[132] The last years of James's reign continued to be beset with disputes between the two sides. A fitting example of this was that between Home of Wedderburn and Lord Walden over fishing rights on the Tweed which had deteriorated into violence: 'unlawfull assemblies, ryotts, routts, and other misdemeanouris and tumults have bene raised and one of our subjectis killed'. In 1622 James ordered a meeting of Cranstoun, the Master of Jedburgh, the sheriff of Teviotdale and Home of Manderston with the English commissioners to settle the dispute. However, such mutual suspicion remained that Wedderburn asked that 'in evrie thing the commissione be conseved in equall termes for both nationes, and that what ever preveledges the English hath, we may not be depryved of the lyk'. The matter was still not resolved in 1625 and a new arbitration was ordered. Despite his efforts, the dispute outlasted James. The residual hostility of two individual kingdoms continued to bedevil administration.[133]

---

[131] C. Lowther and others, 'Our journal into Scotland AD 1629, 5th of November, from Lowther', in HMC, *The manuscripts of the earl of Lonsdale*, ed. J. J. Cartwright, London 1893, thirteenth report, appendix 7, London 1893, 76.
[132] RPC xi. 108–9; CSP Dom., 1611–1618, 152.
[133] RPC xii. 746; xiii. 178–9, 565–6, 573–4, 675–6, 703–5, 722; 2nd ser. i. 415–16; HMC, *The manuscripts of Colonel David Milne Home*, ed. H. Paton, London 1902, 90.

VI

If the success of the pacification of the Middle Shires, from its hesitant beginnings in 1597, is to be measured by the decreasing amount of privy council record devoted to it, then, by 1625, the pacification can be deemed to have worked. Certainly, if the situation in the Middle March in 1597 is compared with that in 1625, there had been significant changes. The removal of the international nature of the border had irrevocably ended any governmental toleration of crime in the Borders and instigated an unprecedented commitment to the its pacification; cross-border raiding appeared to have ceased, whilst cross-border trade was increasing; the council recorded far fewer crimes from the region and complained much less about it; the kirks had more ministers; a system of JPs had been set up and the hereditary sheriffdom of Selkirk replaced by a yearly appointment; and the office of March warden had lapsed, his jurisdiction absorbed by a supposedly co-operative cross-border body of commissioners.

It is in the cross-border commissions, however, that the flaws in the pacification were most evident. Despite undeniable improvements in the co-operation between the officials on either side of the border, at no time in the whole pacification were the two bodies of commissioners joined within a cross-border jurisdiction. The only person (apart from James) to hold authority on both sides of the border was the earl of Dunbar, from 1606 to 1611, and no attempt was made to replace him after his death. The legal systems of each country remained separate and the mutual suspicion of the Wedderburn-Walden dispute demonstrated an enduring hostility between the inhabitants of either side of the border. If the 'Middle Shires' were to be judged as an exemplar of Union, whereby they would be the same as anywhere else in Great Britain, then, by 1625, this could not be said to have happened. The very existence of border-specific institutions continued to mark the region as an area of concern. Catherine Ferguson notes that the pacification was not complete until the full Union of 1707. Although the scope of this work ends in 1625, the evidence makes it clear that the full ramifications of the pacification had not worked themselves out in the reign of James VI and I.[134]

---

[134] Ferguson, 'Law and order', pp. xi, 205, 459.

Conclusion

'Those confining places which were the Borders of the two Kingdomes, where heretofore much blood was shed, and many of your ancestours lost their lives; yea, that lay waste and desolate, and were habitations but for runnagates, are now become the Navell or Umbilick of both Kingdomes ... where there was nothing before ... but bloodshed, oppressions, complaints and outcries, they now live every man peaceably under his owne figgetree ...The Marches beyond and on this side Twede, are as fruitfull and as peaceable as most parts of England.'[1]

James's portrayal of the Borders to the English parliament in 1607 owed more to wishful thinking than to reality. Similarly hopeful had been his pronouncement in 1604 that the geographical unity of Scotland and England was 'by nature so indivisible, as almost those that were borderers themselves on the late Borders, cannot distinguish, nor know, or discerne their owne limits'.[2] With such protestations James intended to convince a sceptical, somewhat hostile, English audience of the benefits of the 'union of the crowns': if the English recognised these, they might agree to extend the dynastic union into a full political or 'perfect union'. The transformation of the Borders was intended to have epitomised the unification of England and Scotland: the 'Middles Shires' were to have become a microcosm of the unified kingdoms; standardised judicial procedures in the English and Scottish Borders were supposed to have exemplified the uniformity that James VI and I desired within throughout his kingdoms; and the pacification was to have demonstrated a new co-operation between previously hostile administrations.

James's descriptions, however, were a little premature. Enduring hostility, mutual suspicion and separate administrative and legal systems continued to demonstrate the divisions between Scotland and England within a region still demarcated by a frontier. Alan Macinnes's assessment of James's 'civilising projects' is surely right to qualify their success in the Borders, that they were only 'partially pacified'.[3] James did not fully achieve his plan 'to extinguishe as well the name, as the substance of the bordours [and] the difference betwene thaime and other pairts of the kingdome'.[4] Indeed, the existence of institutions such as the border commissioners or the triumvirate continued to mark out the Borders region as different or separate to any other part of Scotland, if only in administrative terms. Any attempt to explain this failure

---

[1] James VI and I to Houses of Parliament, Whitehall, 31 Mar., *Political writings*, 169.
[2] James to Upper House, 19 Mar., ibid. 135.
[3] Maciness, 'Regal union for Britain', 38–9.
[4] HMC, *Salisbury*, xvi. 405.

is bound up with James's aspirations for a fuller union than the dynastic union that he embodied on his succession in 1603. Analysis of events in the Middle March has to consider, therefore, the external influences on the region as well as internal pressures arising from personal relationships and kinship. One of the central themes of this study has been to evaluate and place the experience of the Middle March within a wider political context and within the evolution of government throughout Scotland, and subsequently within the expanded context of government in the infant Great Britain: from the close linkage between crown action in the Middle March and court factionalism of the 1570s and 1580s, to the impact in the Borders of James's hopes for the English succession in the 1590s, to the effects of his desires for union and uniformity after regnal union in 1603.

Conversely, the experience of the Middle March can inform wider debate on the development of government throughout the period and the effect of the succession on Scotland. These broader processes were ongoing, throughout Scotland, and continued after James had left for London. One of the principal themes emphasised here has been the effect on the Borders of what Mike Braddick usefully terms 'the intensification of government'.[5] This included moves by the crown towards its monopolisation of judicial measures, as exemplified by the suppression of feuding, and the drawing in of the resolution of dispute into central courts in Edinburgh. But the crown was also extending its tentacles into all aspects of life, both secular and spiritual, and within all its domains: the introduction of JPs, the plantation of ministers and the work of the presbyteries and kirk sessions, intensified the presence of government throughout Scotland at the same time as linking it firmly to the council and courts in Edinburgh. And it was no less so in the Borders. Indeed it might be said that there was a greater determination, and thus a more vital process of increasing government in the Borders. The privy council was extremely alert to what was happening in the Borders, keeping lines of communication constantly open, and a chain of authority in place from Edinburgh to Jedburgh. For all this to work, however, James VI and I needed the assistance of the existing structures of power in all his regions, and the co-operation of the men who headed them. This he achieved by carefully including the prominent nobles and lairds in each region within his government, both locally and in Edinburgh, and carefully rewarding their service. This brought him their co-operation in his increasingly powerful government, and the manpower that they could provide. In the Middle March these processes were exemplified by the well-remunerated careers of Buccleuch and Cessford, acting as agents of the intrusion of central government, and utilising their networks of kinship, alliance and economic dependants. These former combatants would seem, also, to bear out Keith Brown's emphasis on the co-operation of most of the Scottish landed elite

---

[5] Braddick, *State formation*, 337; Goodare, *State and society*, 100–1.

in the government's suppression of feud, and similarities, too, can be found here with the co-operative Grants and Mackintoshes of Alison Cathcart's work on the eastern Highlands. For those who wanted to, it was very much possible to participate in the intensification of government, from Selkirk to the central lowlands, to the wildest uplands of the north.

There was, as a result of James's initiatives, a significant evolution of the framework of government throughout Scotland between 1573 and 1625. But, as Julian Goodare has so deftly shown, it was not all novel: the new administrative or judicial institutions, such as the body of JPs, worked alongside and used many of the same personnel as the traditional institutions.[6] This co-existence of the old and new indicated the way in which the state machinery was able to evolve without engendering too much resistance from those upon whom the crown had historically relied to govern in all its regions. In the Middle March, Sir John Murray of Philiphaugh's surrender of his hereditary sheriffship of Selkirkshire, rewarded by his occasional re-appointment as sheriff, and as JP and Middle Shires commissioner, demonstrated how successfully James could pacify the old, and emplace the new, within the one man. Goodare's work has been invaluable here, and it is hoped that these findings will provide a small example of Goodare's wider themes within a regional context. Where this study is different from Goodare's is in its analysis of the impact of a change in policy in the Borders, rooted in James's concern over the succession, which was evident in James's treatment of Buccleuch and Cessford in 1597. Subsequently, James's determination to suppress anything that threatened the succession or Union was demonstrated by the prioritisation of the pacification in the Middle March. The way in which the pacification was carried out, the institutions created and the personnel involved, was to illustrate the continuation of traditional mechanisms, utilising traditional obligations of kinship and alliance, which underlay and helped to implement the changes that preceded and followed Union.

The Middle March also needs to be seen within the context of what was happening in the Scottish marches to either side of it. Many of the policies pursued by government in the Middle March were part of those implemented in all the marches: a judicial raid to Peebles displayed similar intentions and methods to those in a raid to Dumfries in the West March, as did the subscribing of the general band by Middle March lairds to that by their eastern neighbours. There were, however, differences. Maureen Meikle has shown the lairds of the Eastern Borders to have been, in the main, of less concern to the government than those further to the west. However, as Meikle also acknowledges 'there may also be Western Borderers who have been incorrectly included as violent men in standard Border histo-

---

[6] Goodare, *Government of Scotland*, 203–7.

ries'.[7] Moreover, this study would suggest that any violence needs to be seen within the context of crown policy in each of the marches: the activities of the Middle March lairds such as Buccleuch and Cessford were useful to the crown in a different way to those of Lord Home in the East. The experience of the West March seems to have been rather different as well. The inclusion of Maxwells and Johnstones in central government took rather longer than the Scotts, the Murrays and the Kers. Feud in the West March was still remarked upon in the 1620s as a continuing cause of disturbance when report of it in the Middle was much decreased. Perhaps the traditional explanations of such disturbance, of an alienation or remoteness from central government, are more applicable to the West than to the more centrally integrated men of the Middle March.

And, finally, the experience of the Middle March seems particularly relevant to any discussion of the influences of one region on another that informs attempts at a 'British history'. Certainly this study of a Scottish region on the frontier with England has tried to counter any anglo-centric appraisal of the Middle March's history. At the same time, however, it is hoped that an account of what governments did in the Middle March before and after the regnal union will provide some Scottish evidence and Scottish perspective to the wider 'British' debate. In particular, this work seeks to ferret out the strains within the new composite kingdoms, evident in the uncomfortable term the 'Middle Shires', to acknowledge the dissimilarities between the two kingdoms as much as any commonalities, and to appreciate the divergent forces between England and Scotland that James's efforts for fuller Union were attempting to constrain. This is to put the Anglo-Scottish frontier back as a line within British history.

I

So what were the particular circumstances in the Middle March in 1573 and had these changed by 1625? Government hyperbole would suggest that the situation was very different: a proclamation for a muster at Peebles, in 1573, noted that the 'thevis and disorderit people' had inflicted on the Borderers 'birningis, slaucheteris, heirschippis of thair guidis, ransoming of thair personis ... quhairby divers gude and proffeittabill landis ar utterlie herreit and laid waist, to the greit hurt of the commoun weill'. Contrast this with the discharge, in 1622, of the guard as a result of the 'quieting and reduceing to his Majesteis obedience of the lait Borderis ... as thair is no necessitie ane ordinarie Gaird'.[8]

[7] Meikle, *A British frontier?*, 279–80.
[8] RPC ii. 242–3; xii. 583–4, 657.

CONCLUSION

If James's claims of 1607 were not wholly justified, how much progress in pacifying the former Middle March could he have claimed by 1625? Of course, success could have been measured in several ways: if it meant solely a reduction in the privy council's preoccupation with cross-border crime there from 1573 to 1625, then James's triumphalism had some basis. Similarly, the council's record of internal crime in the shires of Roxburgh, Selkirk and Peebles no longer spoke of widespread offences; where crime was reported by 1625 it was almost always within arbitrations of specific disputes. Absolute levels of crime are harder to quantify. The hugely increased records of the privy council mean that a quantative comparison of the frequency of recorded crime in 1573 and 1625 would be misrepresentative of the frequency of crime itself. In addition, the increasing monopolisation of the judicial process by courts in Edinburgh meant that there was more record of disputes which previously would have been privately or locally resolved. It is easier to make a qualitative comparison: the concern of 1573 over the wicked men of Teviotdale and Roxburghshire in the Middle March had disappeared from the privy council's records by 1625. Any enduring concern in the 1620s seemed to be reserved for the inhabitants of the dales of the Annan, Esk, Ewe and Nith in the former West March.

How had this change been brought about? Such a dramatic difference in government reporting might suggest that significant changes had been made in the way in which government had implemented justice in the region. Certainly, the volume of government reporting of incidents in the Borders and the measures to deal with them had increased hugely during this period, though it was lessening by 1625. One of the most remarkable characteristics of government spanning Union in the Borders, however, is the lack of change and the continuity apparent both in the mechanisms and personnel that government used to impose its policies. In 1573, during a judicial raid by Morton to Jedburgh, the principal figures of the Middle March subscribed the 'Band of Roxburgh' promising to assist in the suppression of disorder 'conforme to the General Band'; in 1617, following James's visit to Scotland, a general band of 1602 was re-subscribed before the privy council by all the prominent men of the Middle March, including Buccleuch, Cranstoun, Oxnam and Douglas of Cavers. All of these men were from families subscribing similar bonds in the 1570s.[9] They were used to being involved in government, and to being held accountable by it for the behaviour of their dependants.

Underlying the mechanisms for imposing justice, the responsibility of the laird for his men and their co-operation with their superiors, were the obligations of kinship and alliance. The ties of kinship may have been beginning to decline in the lowlands by the end of the sixteenth century at a faster rate than in the more impoverished uplands of the Borders and the High-

---

[9] RPC ii. 549; vi. 825–9; xi. 215–19, 225–8.

lands, where the economic gap between governors and governed remained less visible, but kinship remained of significance throughout Scotland into the seventeenth century. Another of the central themes has been to emphasise the importance of such obligations in the frameworks of power that government used throughout the period to implement its authority in the Borders. The kinship element was implicit within the 'haill men' referred to in the band of 1617 to sustain the pacification, and, similarly, government used the responsibility for kinship in its suppression of feud. In 1607, in order to resolve a feud between Geddes of Rauchan and Jardine of Applegarth, Buccleuch 'takand ye burding upone him for all his kin freindis assistaris pairtie and partakeris and in speciall for Charles Geddes of Rauchane and haill surname of Geddes thair kin'.[10] The continuing significance of the expectations of, and links provided by, kinship and alliance saw the kinsmen and allies of government's greater officials staffing its administrative and judicial institutions. The indemnity that Ker of Oxnam received in 1622 for his actions as captain of the guard was extended to those who had assisted him and all of them were Kers.[11] Men of 'power and friendship' with a 'strang hand' in the Borders were those upon whom government relied to do its work: Buccleuch, the Kers of Roxburgh, Ferniehirst and Ancrum, and the Murrays of Blackbarony, Elibank and Philiphaugh continued to exert authority on behalf of the crown within their followings, and to utilise their followings to govern others. In the 1620s the kindreds and alliances of the Kers, Scotts and Murrays, alongside the Stewarts of Traquair and the Hays of Yester, continued to provide useful power structures within the former Middle March, much as they had in 1573.

Something must have changed, however, to explain the slow disappearance of the Middle March from privy council records by 1625. Most useful in explaining this is an appreciation of the external influences on the march, and the context provided by more general developments throughout Scotland: James's increasing direction of government, central government intrusion into all Scottish regions, mounting concern over the succession and the Union of 1603. Measures taken in the Middle March were often part of a wider programme such as the suppression of feud or, after 1603, James's initiatives to secure a fuller Union, and it is sometimes difficult to tell these apart. What is evident, however, is that the crown was able to impose its will in the Middle March. It may not have been able to do so as quickly or as thoroughly as it may have wanted but when, for instance, James embarked on a more consistent approach to the Borders in 1597, it was relatively easy to bring Buccleuch and Cessford into line. There were mechanisms in place in 1573 which could be used to impose government authority in the region if the government chose fully to implement them. Before 1597, with

[10] NAS, GD224/906/60, fo. 3.
[11] RPC xii. 659.

perhaps the sole exception of Morton's regency, successive governments had equivocated over a full crackdown in the region. After 1597, however, the government's priorities were changed irrevocably by the dynamics of the English succession.

In 1603 the Middle March's position at the geographical centre of the Scottish marches put it also at the centre of the Middle Shires, the exemplary heart of the unified kingdoms. Though James's description of every man living 'peaceably under his owne figgetree' exaggerated the order imposed in the region, it is clear that, contemporarily, the pacification was perceived to have succeeded in the suppression of crime. However, if the pacification was meant to be more than this and to include the co-operative implementation of newly standardised laws within a supra-national region, then little progress could have been discerned by 1625. English parliaments of 1604 and 1607 refused to agree to a fuller Union and upheld the separate legal systems, negotiations undermined by distrust and prejudice, 'the aversion and natural alienation of [the Scots] from the Inglish'.[12] And perhaps James should not have been so surprised by the resistance that he encountered: perhaps, he, like many subsequent historians was too keen to over-emphasise the commonalities, in his words, 'rex, lex and grex', between England and Scotland, at the expense of the consideration due to the differences. The continuation of border-specific institutions with delineated Scottish and English jurisdictions indicated that divisions remained at what was meant to be the heart of a unified Britain. Buccleuch's difficulties in extracting an offender from England in 1623 testifies to the effect of such division. If negotiations over Union and the standardisation of the legal system failed at the highest levels, how much less likely was Anglo-Scottish co-operation over a border defined by hundreds of years of hostility?

II

The Borders had a profound and long-term effect on the development of the British state: enduring tensions and administrative and judicial difficulties, manifesting in the former marches, served to inhibit full union for more than a century after 1603. In any British history, or that of union, it is important to acknowledge the resistance of the component parts of Britain to each other, as much as the forces that brought them together. As Nicholas Canny warns, the 'new' approach to British history has risked masking 'fundamental diversities' by emphasising 'similarity at the expense

---

[12] Galloway, *Union of England and Scotland*, 10, 12, quoting R. Parsons, *A conference touching succession to the crowne*, Antwerp 1594, 118.

of difference'.[13] Cultural, religious, linguistic and social similarities, and the kingship of all residing within one man, may have made union more likely, but they should not obscure the more divergent forces at work in 1603: the logistical difficulties of governing three kingdoms with no email or centralised police force, residual hostility, mutual distrust, a lack of a common identity.[14] We 'find ourselves', concludes Glenn Burgess, 'in a very complex world in which political contingencies and underlying structures do not mesh at all well. This is a world in which Britishness is forged, created, imposed – an act of deliberation and will'. James's efforts to impose 'Britishness' in name, legal and ecclesiastical uniformity, and political union were a conscious attempt by him to constrain the divergent tendencies that were becoming so evident in both the Middle Shires, and in the wider multiple kingdom.[15]

Recognition is needed, too, of the significance of the continuation of different or separate structures within the composite kingdoms, in particular of a separate Scottish government within Scotland. A Scottish privy council had a more immediate effect on the Scottish Middle March than that in Whitehall. For the time being, government of the Middle March continued within a Scottish framework using largely traditional methods which originated in Scotland before 1603. The process at work in Scotland after 1603 was not Anglicisation, finds Mike Braddick, because it had already been in progress before the Union: 'a process of state formation was under way in Scotland independent of that in England'.[16] For Brian Levack, Scotland in 1603 'was qualitatively different from all the other political units that had been incorporated into, or otherwise united to, England'; Scotland was a 'free, independent kingdom, a sovereign state in its own right' with its own institutions and laws.[17] Similarly, Steve Ellis, observing the differing circumstances at Union between Scotland and the conquered Ireland or Wales, finds that Scotland as 'an independent sovereign kingdom' was less susceptible to English policies of 'centralisation and administrative uniformity' towards its peripheries. The English inability to recognise these differences resulted in the English government at dynastic union in 1603 treating Scotland 'as another conquest lordship to be incorporated into England, rather than as an equal partner': this, Ellis concludes, led to tensions that undermined union in 1603 and 1707.[18]

---

[13] N. Canny, 'Irish, Scottish and Welsh responses to centralization, c.1530–c.1640', in A. Grant and K. Stringer (eds), *Uniting the kingdom? The making of British history*, London 1995, 147–69 at p. 148.

[14] Dawson, 'Anglo-Scottish Protestant culture', 91. See also R. A. Mason, *Scots and Britons: Scottish political thought and the Union of 1603*, Cambridge 1994, and J. Wormald, 'O Brave new world? The Union of England and Scotland in 1603', *Proceedings of the British Academy* cxxvii (2005), 13–36.

[15] Burgess, 'Introduction: the new British history', 15–18, quotation at p. 17.

[16] Braddick, *State formation*, 356, 368.

[17] Levack, *Formation of the British state*, 23–4.

[18] Ellis sees the continuation of these tensions to this day: *Tudor frontiers and noble power*,

And caution is necessary in any application of the wider context that syntheses of British history could provide to the histories of either the Middle March or Scotland and *vice versa*. Whilst theorising can lend perspective to a specific region, such theorising needs to be rooted in primary research. As Allan Macinnes warns, 'a post-modern rationalising of theory divorced from archival endeavour' would 'jeopardise seventeenth-century studies as the crucible' for any 'integrated' British history.[19] Similarly, for English history, Steve Ellis points to the limitations of 'traditional surveys of nation and state in England' which were 'generally based, not on primary sources, but on syntheses written by English historians': these were further limited by a failure to address 'regionalism, marcher society and the problems of cultural assimilation'.[20] Care is needed, too, in using syntheses of Scottish history to explain what was happening in the Scottish Borders, and using generalised history of this region to place it within the growth of the Scottish and British states.[21] At the same time, what is suggested by the primary research into a particular region, such as the tensions found in the Middle Shires, could provide one of the foundation blocks for any 'integrated' British history, providing that it has been assessed within in its proper context.

If 'British history' is to achieve Macinnes's worthy objective, an 'integrated history' using a 'wider contextualisation', events in the peripheries should be assessed within their national historiographies as well as in terms of the external influences that affected them.[22] And, obviously, it should counter any anglocentric tendency to explain the development of Britain, in particular by imposing inappropriate English models, or criteria, on Scottish or Irish circumstances. Any methodology which applies English terms of reference is more useful in explaining English rather than British state formation.[23] Thus, when trying to assess a 'British' government's efforts in its borderlands, it is not sufficient to look, for instance, at the pacification in Northumberland or Cumberland. To do so would be to limit the analysis of the British state to the actions of an English government within England. The work of Ellis on Tudor policy in the English north and Watts and Spence is invaluable in understanding the difficulties that an English government faced in prosecuting the pacification in the English north, which in turn

---

271, and 'From dual monarchy to multiple kingdoms', in Macinnes and Ohlmeyer, *The Stuart kingdoms*, 37–48 at p. 41.

[19] Macinnes thinks that no such 'integrated' British history has yet been achieved: Macinnes and Ohlmeyer, *The Stuart kingdoms*, 15.

[20] Ellis notes the importance of Mervyn James's study of Durham for a more balanced evaluation of English government: *Tudor frontiers and noble power*, 9, 254.

[21] Despite the best of intentions, this is an easy hole to fall into: Braddick's careful use of syntheses of the relevant Scottish work, for instance, has led perhaps to an overestimation of the success of the pacification: *State formation*, 373–8.

[22] For a recent assessment of such attempts at an 'integrated' history see J. Ohlmeyer, 'The old British histories?', *HJ* 1 (2007), 499–512.

[23] Macinnes, 'Introduction: awkward neighbours', 15, 23, 25, 35.

can inform a study of Scottish government within the Scottish Borders, but should not be taken at more than that.

Steve Ellis's comparisons of Tudor policy on its northern frontier with that in its Irish pale were made with the context of 'British history' in mind. His valuable conclusions on the English north, however, should not be applied to a very different Scottish situation. The resistance that Ellis describes of men like Lord Dacre to the centralising impulses of Tudor government in the sixteenth century was not replicated in the Scottish Middle March, where the Scottish crown used the acquiescence of prominent figures, such as Buccleuch and Roxburgh. Furthermore, the conclusions that Ellis draws for the difficulties of a Stuart English government in Scotland after 1603 are based on his conclusions on Tudor policy within the English north before Union, and do not take into consideration the continuing significance after Union of a Scottish council exercising its own discretion in the daily implementation of any policy.[24] An acknowledgement is needed here of the separate and particular conditions in Scotland as a whole, in the Scottish Borders, and the specific circumstances of the Scottish Middle March. The scepticism expressed by Keith Brown in 1993 over the dangers of 'British history' becoming merely another vehicle for an anglo-centric account of the British Isles would seem to be prescient.[25]

This study began with a desire to look behind the legends of the reivers of the Middle March. What it has found is a far greater connection between the crown and the inhabitants of the Middle March than that implied by the image of 'King' Johnnie Armstrong's proudly acclaimed independence in 1529. The Middle March may have been geographically on the periphery of the kingdom of Scotland but its inhabitants were anything but remote from the centre: they were involved in government at its highest level and, conversely, central government could and increasingly did use those from the Middle March as agents of crown policy within it. This is to challenge the orthodoxy of accounts which ascribe an 'endemic' violence to an area outwith crown control. In doing so it is hoped to have countered the anglo-centric models traditionally used to assess the Borders and to put the Middle March into its proper Scottish context.

---

[24] Ellis, 'Tudor state formation', 62–3.
[25] K. M. Brown, 'British history: a sceptical comment', in R. G. Asch, *Three nations: a common history? England, Scotland, Ireland and British history, c. 1600–1920*, Bochum 1993, 117–27. Brown has more recently tempered his criticism: 'Seducing the Scottish Clio: has Scottish history anything to fear from the new British history?', in Burgess, *New British history*, 238–65.

Bibliography

Unpublished primary sources

Edinburgh, National Archives of Scotland
Commissary court papers, CC6, CC8
Court of session papers, CS7
Privy council papers, 1578–1609, PC10/3–8A
Register of deeds, first series, RD1
Sheriff court book, Roxburghshire, SC62/2/3–7

Family papers
Buccleuch muniments, GD224
Cuninghame of Caprington papers, GD149
A. O. Curle and J. Curle papers, GD111
Dalrymple (earls of Stair) papers, GD135
Elibank papers, GD32
Erskines of Dun, Angus, papers, GD123
Sir William Fraser charters, GD86
Lothian papers, GD40
Mar and Kellie papers, GD124
Morton papers, GD150
Napier papers, GD430
Scott of Harden (Lords Polwarth) papers, GD157

Presbytery records
Jedburgh, CH2/198/1
Peebles, CH2/295/1
Selkirk, CH2/327/1

Edinburgh, National Library of Scotland
Armstrong papers, Acc. 6110–20
Denmilne MS, Advocates' MS 33.1.1, vols 1–11; 33.3.12; 33.1.3; 33.1.7
Douglas of Cavers papers, Acc. 6803, 6991
Murray of Falahill papers, Acc. 11403
Pont maps, Pont 35(2)
Rutherford papers, Acc. 7676A

Edinburgh, National Register of Archives, Scotland
Pringle of Torwoodlee papers, NRAS482
Roxburgh papers, NRAS1100

Hawick, Borders Archives
Selkirk burgh papers, SC/S/12/33
Walter Mason papers, WM3–12

Published primary sources

Abstracts of the treasurer's accounts (Bannatyne Club, 1867)
Ancient criminal trials in Scotland, ed. R. Pitcairn (Bannatyne Club, 1839–45)
Bell, R., *Book of Marches* (1604), in J. Nicolson and R. Burn, *History of Westmorland and Cumberland*, London 1777
Birrel, R., *Diary*, in Dalyell, *Fragments*, 1–64
Blaeu, J., *Atlas of Scotland*, Amsterdam 1654
Booke of the universall Kirk of Scotland, ed. A. Peterkin, Edinburgh 1839
The Border papers: calendar of letters and papers relating to the affairs of the Borders of England and Scotland, ed. J. Bain, Edinburgh 1894–6
The burghs of Scotland: a critical list, ed. G. S. Pryde, London 1965
Calderwood, D., *The history of the Kirk of Scotland*, ed. T. Thomson and D. Laing (Wodrow Society, 1842–9)
Calendar of state papers, domestic series, 1603–1704, ed. M. A. E. Green and others, London 1856–1947
Calendar of state papers relating to Scotland, ed. J. Bain, G. G. Simpson and J. D. Galbraith, Edinburgh 1881–8
Calendar of state papers ... Venice, 1603–75, ed. R. Brown, G. Cavendish Bentinck, H. F. Brown and A. B. Hinds, London 1864–1947
Calendar of writs preserved at Yester House, 1166–1625, ed. C. Harvey and J. Macleod (SRS, 1930)
Charters and documents relating to the burgh of Peebles, 1165–1710, ed. W. Chambers, (Scottish Burgh Records Society, 1872)
Child, F. J., *English and Scottish popular ballads*, Boston 1898
The complaynt of Scotland, c. 1550 by Robert Wedderburn, ed. A. M. Stewart (STS, 1979)
Correspondence of Sir Robert Kerr, first earl of Ancram and his son William, third earl of Lothian, ed. D. Laing (Bannatyne Club, 1875)
Dalton, M., *The countrey justice* (1618), repr. London 1742
Dalyell, J. G. (ed.), *Fragments of Scottish history*, Edinburgh 1798
The exchequer rolls of Scotland, ed. J. Stuart and others, Edinburgh 1878–1908
Fasti Ecclesiae Scoticana: the succession of ministers in the Church of Scotland from the Reformation, ed. H. Scott, J. Lamb and D. MacDonald, Edinburgh 1915–81
Fraser, W., *The Scotts of Buccleuch*, Edinburgh 1878
—— *The Douglas book*, Edinburgh 1885
The Hamilton papers, ed. J. Bain, Edinburgh 1890–2
The historie of Scotland by John Leslie, bishop of Ross, ed. E. G. Cody and W. Murison, trans. J. Dalrymple (1596) (STS, 1888–95)
HMC, *The manuscripts of Colonel David Milne Home*, ed. H. Paton, London 1902
HMC, *The manuscripts of the duke of Buccleuch*, ed. R. E. G. Kirk, London 1899–1926
HMC, *The manuscripts of the duke of Roxburgh*, ed. W. Fraser, London 1894

HMC, *The manuscripts of the earl of Lonsdale*, ed. J. J. Cartwright, London 1893
HMC, *The manuscripts of the earl of Mar and Kellie*, ed. H. Paton, London 1904–30
HMC, *The manuscripts of Lord Muncaster*, ed. H. M. Maxwell Lyte, London 1885
HMC, *The manuscripts of the marquess of Salisbury*, ed. M. S. Guiseppie and O. G. Dyfnallt, London 1930–70
James I and VI, *Political writings*, ed. J. P. Somerville, Cambridge 1994
Lesley, J., *History of Scotland* (Bannatyne Club, 1830)
The letters of James VI and I, ed. G. P. V. Akrigg, Berkeley 1984
The letters of John Chamberlain (American Philosophical Society, 1939)
The Lochmaben court and council book, 1612–1721, ed. J. B. Wilson (SRS, 2001)
The Maitland folio manuscript, ed. W. A. Craigie (STS, 1919)
Memoirs of Robert Carey, ed. J. H. Mares, Oxford 1972
Memoirs of Sir James Melville of Halhill, 1535–1617, ed. A. F. Steuart, London 1929
Moysie, D., *Memoirs of the affairs of Scotland, 1577–1603* (Maitland Club, 1830)
Nicholson, W., *Leges Marchiarum*, London 1747
Practicks of Sir James Balfour, ed. P. G. B. Neill (Stair Society, 1962–3)
Raine, J., *The history and antiquities of North Durham*, London 1852
Records of the convention of royal burghs of Scotland, ed. J. D. Marwick, Edinburgh 1870
The records of the parliaments of Scotland to 1707, ed. K. M. Brown, G. H. MacIntosh, A. J. Mann, P. E. Ritchie and R. J. Tanner, St Andrews 2007–9; www.rps.ac.uk
The records of the regality of Melrose, 1605–61, ed. C. S. Romanes (SHS, 1914–17)
The records of the synod of Lothian and Tweeddale, 1589–96, 1640–49, ed. J. Kirk (Stair Society, 1977)
The register of the great seal of Scotland, ed. J. M. Thomson, P. J. Balfour, J. H. Stevenson and W. K. Dickson, Edinburgh 1882–1914
The register of the privy council of Scotland, 1545–1625, ed. J. Buron and D. Masson, Edinburgh 1877–98
The register of the privy seal of Scotland, ed. M. Livingstone, Edinburgh 1908
The Scots peerage, ed. P. J. Balfour, Edinburgh 1904–14
Scott, Sir W., *Minstrelsy of the Scottish Border*, ed. T. F. Henderson, Edinburgh 1902
'The sheriff court book of Dumfries, 1573–83', ed. P. Hamilton-Grierson, *Transactions of Dumfriesshire and Galloway Natural History and Antiquarian Society* xii (1926), 126–224
Spottiswoode, J., *History of the Church of Scotland*, ed. M. Napier and M. Russell (Bannatyne Club, 1850)
The works of Sir David Lindsay of the Mount, 1490–1555, ed. D. Hamer (STS, 1931–6)

Secondary sources

Armstrong, B., *The history of Liddesdale, Eskdale, Ewesdale, Wauchopdale and the debateable land*, Edinburgh 1883
Barrow, G., 'Frontier and settlement: which influence which? England and Scotland, 1100–1300', in Bartlett and MacKay, *Medieval frontier societies*, 3–21

Bartlett, R. and A. MacKay (eds), *Medieval frontier societies*, Oxford 1992
Boardman, S., *The early Stewart kings: Robert II and Robert III, 1371–1406*, East Linton 1996
Braddick, M. J., *State formation in early modern England, c. 1550–1700*, Cambridge 2000
—— 'Administrative performance: the representation of authority in early modern England', in Braddick and Walter, *Negotiating power*, 166–87
—— 'Introduction: the politics of gesture', *Past and Present* cciii, suppl. 4 (2009), 9–35
—— and J. Walter (eds), *Negotiating power in early modern society: order, hierarchy and subordination in Britain and Ireland*, Cambridge 2001
Bradley, P., 'Social banditry on the Anglo-Scottish Border during the late Middle Ages', *Scotia* xii (1988), 27–43
Bradshaw, B. and J. Morrill (eds), *The British problem, 1534–1707*, Basingstoke 1996
Brown, J. (Wormald), 'The exercise of power', in J. Brown (ed.), *Scottish society in the fifteenth century*, London 1977, 33–65
Brown, K. M., *Bloodfeud in Scotland, 1573–1625: violence, justice and politics in an early modern society*, Edinburgh 1986
—— 'Burghs, lords and feuds in Jacobean Scotland', in Lynch, *The early modern town*, 102–24
—— 'British history: a sceptical comment', in R. G. Asch (ed.), *Three nations: a common history? England, Scotland, Ireland and British history, c. 1600–1920*, Bochum 1993, 117–27
—— 'The Scottish aristocracy, anglicisation and the court, 1603–38', *HJ* xxxvi (1993), 543–76
—— 'Seducing the Scottish Clio: has Scottish history anything to fear from the new British history?', in Burgess, *New British history*, 238–65
—— *Noble society in Scotland: wealth, family and culture, from Reformation to Revolution*, Edinburgh 2004
Brown, M. H., 'Scotland tamed? Kings and magnates in late medieval Scotland: a review of recent work', *Innes Review* xlv (1994), 120–46
—— *The Black Douglases: war and lordship in the late medieval Scotland, 1300–1455*, East Linton 1998
Burgess, G., 'Introduction: the new British history', in Burgess, *New British history*, 1–29
—— (ed.), *The new British history: founding a modern state, 1603–1707*, London 1999
Canny, N., 'Irish, Scottish and Welsh responses to centralization, c.1530–c.1640', in Grant and Stringer, *Uniting the kingdom?*, 147–69
Cathcart, A., *Kinship and clientage: highland clanship, 1451–1609*, Leiden 2006
Colley, L., 'The significance of the frontier in British history', in W. R. Louis (ed.), *More adventures with Britannia: personalities, politics and culture in Britain*, London 1998, 13–29
Cowan, E. J., 'Introduction', in Cowan, *The ballad in Scottish history*, 1–18
—— 'Sex and violence in the Scottish ballads', in Cowan, *The ballad in Scottish history*, 95–115
—— (ed.), *The ballad in Scottish history*, East Linton 2000
Craig-Brown, T., *The history of Selkirkshire*, Edinburgh 1886

BIBLIOGRAPHY

Croft, P., 'Can a bureaucrat be a favourite? Robert Cecil and the strategies of power', in Elliott and Brockliss, *The world of the favourite*, 81–95

Cuddy, N., 'The revival of the entourage: the Bedchamber of James I, 1603–1625', in D. Starkey and others (eds), *The English court: from the Wars of the Roses to the Civil Wars*, London 1987, 173–225

—— 'Anglo-Scottish Union and the court of James I, 1603–1625', *Transactions of the Royal Historical Society* 5th ser. xxxix (1989), 107–24

Cunningham, I. C. (ed.), *The nation survey'd: Timothy Pont's maps of Scotland*, Edinburgh 2001

Dawson, J., 'Anglo-Scottish Protestant culture and integration in sixteenth-century Britain', in Ellis and Barber, *Conquest and union*, 87–114

Devine, T. and S. G. E. Lythe, 'The economy of Scotland under James VI: a revision article', *SHR* l (1971), 91–106

Dickinson, W. C., 'The death of Lord Russell, 1585', *SHR* xx (1923), 181–6

Doran, S., 'Loving and affectionate cousins? The relationship between Elizabeth I and James VI of Scotland, 1586–1603', in S. Doran and G. Richardson (eds), *Tudor England and its neighbours*, Houndmills–New York 2005, 203–33

Elliott, J. H., 'A Europe of composite monarchies', *Past and Present* cxxxvii (1992), 48–71

—— and L. Brockliss (eds), *The world of the favourite*, New Haven–London 1999

Ellis, S. G. 'Introduction: the concept of British history', in Ellis and Barber, *Conquest and union*, 1–7

—— *Tudor frontiers and noble power: the making of the British state*, Oxford 1995

—— 'Tudor state formation and the shaping of the British Isles', in Ellis and Barber, *Conquest and union*, 40–63

—— 'From dual monarchy to multiple kingdoms', in Macinnes and Ohlmeyer, *The Stuart kingdoms*, 37–48

—— and S. Barber (eds), *Conquest and union: fashioning a British state, 1485–1726*, London–New York 1995

Galloway, B., *The Union of Scotland and England, 1603 to 1608*, Cambridge 1986

Gilbert, J. M., *Hunting and hunting reserves in medieval Scotland*, Edinburgh 1979

Goodare, J., 'Scotland', in B. Scribner, R. Porter and M. Teich (eds), *The Reformation in national context*, Cambridge 1994, 95–110

—— 'James VI's English subsidy', in Goodare and Lynch, *Reign of James VI*, 110–25

—— *State and society in early modern Scotland*, Oxford 1999

—— 'The admission of lairds to the Scottish parliament', *EHR* cxvii (2001), 1103–33

—— 'Witch-hunting and the Scottish state', in J. Goodare (ed.), *The Scottish witch-hunt in context*, Manchester 2002, 122–45

—— *The government of Scotland*, Oxford 2004

—— and M. Lynch (eds), *Reign of James VI*, East Linton 1999

—— and M. Lynch 'The Scottish state and its Borderlands, 1567–1625', in Goodare and Lynch, *Reign of James VI*, 186–207

—— L. Martin, J. Miller and L. Yeoman, 'The survey of Scottish witchcraft', University of Edinburgh, http://www.arts.ed.ac.uk/witches/ (archived Jan. 2003)

Goodman, A., 'The Anglo-Scottish Marches in the fifteenth century: a frontier society?', in Mason, *Scotland and England*, 18–33

—— 'Introduction', to Goodman and Tuck, *War and border societies*, 1–29
—— 'Religion and warfare in the Anglo-Scottish Marches', in Bartlett and MacKay, *Medieval frontier societies*, 245–66
—— 'The impact of warfare on the Scottish Marches, c. 1481–c. 1513', in L. Clark (ed.), *The fifteenth century: conflicts, consequences and the crown in the late Middle Ages*, Woodbridge 2007, 195–211
—— and A. Tuck (eds), *War and border societies in the Middle Ages*, London 1992
Grant, A., 'Crown and nobility in late medieval Britain', in Mason, *Scotland and England*, 34–59
—— 'The Otterburn War from the Scottish point of view', in Goodman and Tuck, *War and border societies*, 30–64
—— and K. Stringer (eds), *Uniting the kingdom? The making of British history*, London 1995
Grant, R., 'Politicking Jacobean women: Lady Ferniehirst, the countess of Arran and the countess of Huntly, c.1580–1603', in E. Ewan and M. M. Meikle (eds), *Women in Scotland, c. 1100–1750*, East Linton 1999, 95–104
Greengrass, M., 'Introduction: conquest and coalescence', in Greengrass, *Conquest and coalescence*, 1–24
—— (ed.), *Conquest and coalescence: the shaping of the state in early modern Europe*, London 1991
Griffiths, P., A. Fox and S. Hindle (eds), *The experience of authority in early modern England*, Basingstoke 1996
Guy, I., 'The Scottish export trade, 1460–1599', in T. C. Smout (ed.), *Scotland and Europe, 1200–1850*, Edinburgh 1986, 62–81
Hewitt, G. R., *Scotland under Morton, 1572–1580*, Edinburgh 1982
Hindle, S., 'The keeping of the public peace', in Griffiths, Fox and Hindle, *Experience of authority*, 213–44
James, M. E., *Society, politics and culture: studies in early modern England*, Cambridge 1986
Kirk, J., *Patterns of reform: continuity and change in the Reformation Kirk*, Edinburgh 1989
Lee, M., *John Maitland of Thirlestane and the foundation of the Stewart despotism in Scotland*, Princeton 1959
—— *Government by pen: Scotland under James VI and I*, Urbana 1980
—— *Great Britain's Solomon: James VI and I in his three kingdoms*, Urbana 1990
—— *The heiresses of Buccleuch: marriage, money and politics in seventeenth century Britain*, East Linton 1996
Levack, B. P., *The formation of the British state: England, Scotland, and the Union, 1603–1707*, Oxford 1987
Lynch, M., 'The crown and the burghs', in Lynch, *Early modern town*, 55–80
—— 'Introduction', in Lynch, *Early modern town*, 1–35
—— 'Preaching to the converted: perspectives on the Scottish Reformation', in MacDonald, Lynch and Cowan, *Renaissance in Scotland*, 301–43
—— (ed.), *The early modern town in Scotland*, London 1987
—— (ed.), *The Oxford companion to Scottish history*, Oxford 2001
McAlpine, K., 'Proude Armstrongs and border rogues: history in "Kinmont Willie", "Jock o the Side" and "Archie of Cawfield"', in Cowan, *The ballad in Scottish history*, 73–94

MacDonald, A., *Border bloodshed: Scotland and England at war, 1369–1403*, East Linton 2000
MacDonald, A. A., M. Lynch and I. Cowan (eds), *The Renaissance in Scotland: studies in literature, religion, history and culture offered to John Durkan*, Leiden 1994
MacDonald, A. R., *The Jacobean Kirk, 1567–1625: sovereignty, polity and liturgy*, Aldershot 1998
MacDonald Fraser, G., *The steel bonnets: the story of the Anglo-Scottish border reivers*, London 1971
Macinnes, A. I., 'Regnal union for Britain, 1603–38', in Burgess, *New British history*, 33–65
—— and J. Ohlmeyer (eds), *The Stuart kingdoms in the seventeenth century: awkward neighbours*, Dublin 2002
Madden, C., 'The feuing of Ettrick forest', *Innes Review* xxvii (1976), 70–84
Malcolm, C. A., 'The sheriff court: sixteenth century and later', in *An introduction to Scottish legal history* (Stair Society, 1958), 356–62
Mason, R. A., *Scots and Britons: Scottish political thought and the Union of 1603*, Cambridge 1994
—— (ed.), *Scotland and England, 1286–1815*, Edinburgh 1987
Meikle, M. M., 'A godly rogue: the career of Sir John Forster, an Elizabethan border warden', *NH* xxviii (1992), 126–63
—— 'The invisible divide: the greater lairds and the nobility of Jacobean Scotland', *SHR* lxxi (1992), 70–87
—— *A British frontier? Lairds and gentlemen in the eastern Borders, 1540–1603*, East Linton 2004
Morrill, J., 'The British problem, c.1534–1707', in B. Bradshaw and J. Morrill (eds), *The British problem, 1534–1707*, Basingstoke 1996, 1–38
Murray, A. C., *Memorial of Sir Gideon Murray of Elibank and his times, 1560–1621*, Edinburgh 1932
Neilson, G., 'The March laws', in T. I. Rae (ed.), *Miscellany* (Stair Society, 1971) i. 11–77
Neville, C. J., *Violence, custom and law: the Anglo-Scottish Border lands in the later Middle Ages*, Edinburgh 1998
Newton, D., *North-east England, 1569–1625: governance, culture and identity*, Woodbridge 2006
Ohlmeyer, J., 'The old British histories?', *HJ* l (2007), 499–512
Opalinski, E., 'The path towards the commonwealth of the two nations', in MacInnes and Ohlmeyer, *The Stuart kingdoms*, 49–61
Peck, L. L., 'Monopolising favour: structures of power in the early seventeenth-century English court', in Elliott and Brockliss, *World of the favourite*, 54–70
Perceval-Maxwell, M., *Scottish migration to Ulster in the reign of James I*, Belfast 1999
Petrina, A., *Machiavelli in the British Isles: two early modern translations of the Prince*, Farnham 2009
—— 'Walter Scott of Buccleuch, an Italian poet?', *Renaissance Studies* (forthcoming)
Rae, T. I., *The administration of the Scottish frontier, 1513–1603*, Edinburgh 1966
Read, C., *Mr Secretary Walsingham and the policy of Queen Elizabeth*, Oxford 1925

Ridpath, G., *The Border history of England and Scotland*, London 1776, repr. Edinburgh 1979
Sanderson, M., *Scottish rural society in the sixteenth century*, Edinburgh 1982
—— *A kindly place? Living in sixteenth-century Scotland*, East Linton 2002
Scott, J. C., *Domination and the arts of resistance: hidden transcripts*, New Haven–London 1990
Sizer, J., 'The good of this service consists in absolute secrecy: the earl of Dunbar, Scotland and the Border (1603–1611)', *Canadian Journal of History* xxxvi (2001), 229–57
Spedding, J. (ed.), *Letters and life of Lord Bacon*, London 1872
Spence, R. T., 'The pacification of the Cumberland Borders, 1593–1628', *NH* xiii (1977), 59–160
Todd, M., *Culture of Protestantism in early modern Scotland*, New Haven–London 2002
Tough, D. L. W., *The last years of a frontier: a history of the Borders during the reign of Elizabeth I*, London 1928
Walter, J., 'Public transcripts, popular agency and the politics of subsistence in early modern England', in Braddick and Walter, *Negotiating power*, 123–48
—— 'Gesturing at authority: deciphering the gestural code of early modern England', *Past and Present* cciii, suppl. 4 (2009), 96–127 at pp. 113–15, 126–7
Watts, S. J. and S. J. Watt, *From Border to Middle Shire: Northumberland, 1586–1625*, Leicester 1975
Wernham, R. B., *Before the Armada: the growth of English foreign policy, 1485–1588*, London 1966
—— *The return of the Armadas: the last years of the Elizabethan war against Spain, 1595–1603*, London 1994
Whyte, I. D., *Agriculture and society in seventeenth-century Scotland*, Edinburgh 1979
—— *Scotland before the Industrial Revolution: an economic and social history, c. 1050–c. 1750*, London–New York 1995
—— *Scotland's society and economy in transition, c. 1500–c. 1760*, Basingstoke 1997
Williamson, A. H., 'Scots, Indians and empire: the Scottish politics of civilization, 1519–1609', *Past and Present* cl (1996), 46–83
Wormald, J., 'Bloodfeud, kindred and government in early modern Scotland', *Past and Present* lxxxvii (1980), 54–97
—— *Court, kirk and community: Scotland, 1470–1625*, Edinburgh 1981
—— *Lords and men in Scotland: bonds of manrent, 1442–1603*, Edinburgh 1985
—— 'Taming the magnates', in K. J. Stringer (ed.), *Essays on the nobility of medieval Scotland*, Edinburgh 1985, 270–80
—— 'O Brave new world? The Union of England and Scotland in 1603', *Proceedings of the British Academy* cxxvii (2005), 13–36
Wrightson, K., 'The politics of the parish in early modern England', in Griffiths, Fox and Hindle, *Experience of authority*, 10–46

Unpublished theses

Adams, S., 'A regional road to revolution: religion, politics and society in south-west Scotland, 1600 to 1650', PhD, Edinburgh 2002

Dixon, P. W., 'Fortified houses on the Anglo-Scottish Border: a study of the domestic architecture of the upland area in its social and economic context', DPhil., Oxford 1976

Ferguson, C., 'Law and order on the Anglo-Scottish Border, 1603–1707', PhD, St Andrews 1981

Groundwater, A., 'The Middle March of the Scottish Borders, 1573 to 1625', PhD, Edinburgh 2007

Juhala, A., 'The household and court of James VI of Scotland, 1567–1603', PhD, Edinburgh 2000

Macpherson, R. G., 'Francis Stewart, fifth earl Bothwell, c.1562–1612', PhD, Edinburgh 1998

Pearce, A. S. W., 'John Spottiswoode, Jacobean archbishop and statesman', PhD, Stirling 1998

Sizer, J., 'Law and disorder in the "Middle Shires" of Great Britain, 1603–1625', PhD, Cambridge 2001

Symms, P. S. M., 'Social control in a sixteenth-century burgh: a study of the burgh court of Selkirk, 1503–1545', PhD, Edinburgh 1987

Wasser, M., 'Violence and the central criminal courts in Scotland, 1603–1638', PhD, Columbia 1995

Watson, J. C., 'Scottish foreign trade, 1597–1640', PhD, Edinburgh 2003

Zulager, R. R., 'A study of the middle-rank administrators in the government of King James VI of Scotland, 1580–1603', PhD, Aberdeen 1991

Index

abbeys: Dryburgh, 106; Jedburgh, 97–8, 106; Kelso, 97, 106; Melrose, 35, 97–9, 106
Abirnethie, Mr John, minister of Jedburgh, 42, 44–5, 100
access, *see* communication
acts of caution, *see* bonds
acts of parliament, *see* legislation
agriculture, 40; crops, 31–2; effects of warfare, 33; enclosure, 33–4; pastoral, 31–3. *See also* trade
Alensone, John, 76
alienation, 2, 15, 27, 120, 126–7, 195, 208
allegiance, 63, 76–7, 80–2, 83, 86, 126, 150; alliance, 3, 62–72, 140, 142–5, 162, 178, 209–10; faction, factionalism, 69–70, 85–6, 146–7, 149, 155, 162–8, 184; interdependence, mutually beneficial relationships, 39–40, 56–8, 62, 74, 87, 106, 126; use of by government, 1–2, 3, 128–9, 158, 159–60; use of in office, 1–2, 76, 80–6, 89, 93, 101–2, 114, 120–1, 155, 156–7, 162. *See also* co-operation, feud, kinship, lordship, marriage, obligation
Anglo-Scottish relations, 2, 109, 110–11, 112, 119, 151, 154–5, 181–2; amity, 133, 135–6, 148, 151, 154–5, 155–6, 160, 164, 169, 170, 173, 177–8, 179, 182, 185; Anglo-Scottish alliance (1586), 171–3, 174; death of Lord Francis Russell (1585), 170–1; hostility, 130–2, 154, 160, 187, 203–4, 211; Kinmont Willie incident, 57, 179–80, 181–2; Raid of Redeswyre, 156, 157, 160, 162; Rough Wooing, 33, 83, 141; tensions, 164, 165–7, 168–9, 170–1, 172–3, 178–80, 182–4, 203–4, 208; treaty, treaty negotiations, 82, 131, 150, 170, 171, 182. *See also* cross-border relations, Elizabeth I, England, James VI and I, Union
Annandale, 54, 93, 104, 108, 201–2

Annandale, John Murray, 1st earl of, *see* Murray of Lochmaben, John
Argyll, Colin Campbell, 6th earl of, *see* Campbell, Colin
Armstrong, family, 27, 28–9, 54, 86, 87, 144, 149, 150–1, 159, 177, 193, 194–5, 200
Armstrong, 'King' Johnnie, 28, 214
Armstrong of Kinmont ('Kinmont Willie'), 57, 86, 93, 112, 113, 131–2, 179–80, 181–2
Armstrong of Mangerton, Sym, 68–9, 150
Armstrong of Whithaugh, family, 93
Armstrong of Whithaugh, Lance, 68–9, 150
Arran, Capt James Stewart, earl of, *see* Stewart, James
assurance, bonds of, *see* bonds
Atholl, John Stewart, 3rd earl of, *see* Stewart, John
authority, *see* power

Bacon, Sir Francis, 187–8
ballads, 10–11, 28; 'Battle of Otterburn', 10, 28; 'Johnnie Armstrong', 28; 'Raid of Redeswyre', 160
bailies, 74–5, 80, 95, 96–101, 102, 175, 197, 199. *See also* baronies
baronies, 96–7. *See also* jurisdiction
Batey, Bateson, 49, 159; of Eskdale, 67
Berwick, 7, 26, 33, 78 n. 21, 91, 142, 173, 184, 186, 187, 190, 198
Berwickshire, 92, 102, 127, 164
Blaeu, 30–1
bloodfeud, *see* feud
bonds, bands: acts of caution, 61–2, 63, 69, 71, 129, 136, 143–6, 158, 172, 173–4, 195; band of Roxburgh, 60, 209; band of Teviotdale, 53, 158; binding over, 61; bonds of assurance, 52, 68–9, 86, 143–6, 150, 152–3, 158, 178, 210; general band, 59–60, 68–9, 71, 93, 149, 158, 196, 199, 200, 207, 209, 210; letters of assythment, slains, 69, 145; manrent, 49–50, 55, 56, 63,

225

67, 70, 129, 165; pledges, 60–1, 63, 82, 156, 158–9, 173, 183, 184, 185, 186, 196. *See also* cross-border relations, feud, obligation
border: frontier, 24, 25, 26, 87, 154, 205, 208; frontier mentality, society, zone, 3, 19, 23–5, 26–8. *See also* cross-border relations
border guard, 81, 87–90, 118, 161, 168, 173, 189–90, 192, 201–2, 208. *See also* Middle Shires
border-specific offices, 80–94, 102, 106. *See also* lieutenant, marches, Middle Shires, wardens
borderers: in central government, 2, 3, 11–12, 104–6, 106–11, 112–20, 120–7, 195, 206, 208, 209, 214; contemporary descriptions, 9, 10, 11, 20–1, 23, 30, 132–3; diet, 32; English, 126–7; identity, 26–9. *See also* alienation, perception of borderers
Borders: equated with Highlands, 9, 17–18, 53, 132, 174–5; historiography, 8–9, 12–13, 22, 23–4, 26–7, 51, 207–8; population, 32–3, 36, 40; topography, 5, 23, 30–2. *See also* crown policy, perception of borderers
Bothwell, earls of, 54, 106, 149
Bothwell, Francis Stewart, 5th earl of, *see* Stewart, Francis
Bowes, family, 147, 152
Bowes, Sir Robert, 21, 160, 162, 163, 169, 179
Bowes, Sir William, 57, 84, 150, 184
Branxholme, 7, 155
Branxholme, Sir Walter of, *see* Scott of Branxholme, Sir Walter
British history, 19–20, 208, 211–14
Buccleuch, Anna, duchess of, *see* [Scott of Buccleuch], Anna
Buccleuch, Walter Scott, 1st Lord, *see* [Scott of Buccleuch], Walter (*d.* 1611)
Buccleuch, Walter Scott, 1st earl of, *see* [Scott of Buccleuch], Walter (*d.* 1633)
burghs, 94–6, 145–7

Calderwood, Mr David, 45, 162–3
Campbell, Colin, 6th earl of Argyll: alliance with Ker of Cessford family, 70, 147, 162, 163
Carey, Henry, 1st Lord Hunsdon, 152, 178, 187
Carey, John, 147

Carey, Sir Robert, 1, 53, 173, 179, 184, 187
Carmichael, family, 81
Carmichael, Sir John of that ilk: *m.* Margaret, sister of James Douglas, 4th earl of Morton, 85; keeper of Liddesdale, 85, 149, 156–7, 160, 163–5, 167; privy councillor, 112, 114, 119, 175; West March warden, 112, 186, 193
Cecil, Sir Robert, 1st earl of Salisbury, 92, 123, 138, 152
Cecil, Sir William, 1st Lord Burghley, 157
Charlton of Hesleyside, family, 147
Charteris, Robert, of Amisfield, 191
Cheviots: ban on hunting in, 69, 128, 193, 196
Chirnside, Patrick, of East Nisbet, 191
Chisholme, Walter of that ilk, 98
Church, *see* Kirk
clans, *see* kindred, kinship
communication, 126–7, 190, 191, 200, 206; access, 106, 108, 118, 120–2, 124–5; advice, information, 108–9, 121, 124–5, 126, 201; contact, 111–12, 126; correspondence, 92, 117–18, 121, 123–6; geographical channels of, 5, 104; personal lines of, 123–6; of policy, 90, 104, 106, 110–11, 121–2, 124, 191
co-operation, 82, 154; cross-border (or lack of), 161–2, 170, 190, 192–3, 200, 204, 205, 211; elite with crown, 13–16, 47, 51, 73, 79, 91, 94, 104–5, 113, 116–17, 121–2, 129, 140–1, 199, 206–7; subordinate with superior, 15–16, 62, 87, 118, 124, 129
court, 105–6, 116, 119, 120–6, 163; at Edinburgh, 120–1; at Whitehall, 116, 121–6
Cranstoun, family, 88
Cranstoun, Helena, Lady Newton, 43
Cranstoun, John (son of Sir William Cranstoun): *m.* Elizabeth daughter of Walter, 1st Lord Buccleuch, 88
Cranstoun, Sir William, Lord Cranstoun, 80, 197, 199, 209; *m.* Sara daughter of John Cranstoun of that ilk, 88; captain of the border guard, 44, 87–9, 118, 189–90, 192, 193; commissioner, 88, 90, 92–4, 109, 118, 202, 203; JP, 88; lieutenant, 88; privy councillor, 88, 116, 118, 119, 195

INDEX

Cranstoun of that ilk, Sir John, 44, 88, 90, 107
Cranstoun of Morriston, Alexander (brother of Sir William Cranstoun), 88
crime: border-specific, 128, 130, 133–4, 136–7, 138, 195; report of, 2, 132–3, 134–5, 169, 173, 176, 194–5, 204, 208–9; reset, 128, 136, 158–9, 161–2; suppression of, 2, 3–4, 73, 87, 110, 122, 128–30, 152–3, 155, 156–60, 197, 204, 208; theft, spulzie, 133–4, 135, 149, 150–1, 161; violent crime, 13, 110, 130, 134, 136–7, 140, 151, 152–3, 167. *See also* cross-border relations, feud, judicial policy, pacification
cross-border raiding, 33, 128, 134–7, 147, 148–51, 151–2, 167, 169–70, 174, 178, 182–4, 194–5
cross-border relations: assimilation, fraternisation, 27, 29; marriage, 27, 175; pledges, 183, 184; tensions, 29, 106, 160–2, 165–7, 169–71, 172–3, 182–5, 192–3, 203–4, 205–6. *See also* co-operation, jurisdiction, Middle Shires, trade, Union
crown policy: Borders, 2, 11, 17, 112, 115, 128, 154–5, 156, 170, 173–6, 181, 204, 206, 207–9, 210–11; crime, 3, 73, 110, 128–30; ecclesiastical, 41–3, 46, 193–4, 206; feuding, 3, 110, 140–1, 148, 186–7; Highlands, 17, 53, 132, 174–5; judicial, 73, 102, 110, 128–30, 151, 154, 156, 173, 176, 185–7; transmission of policy, 122

Dacre, Lords, 19, 214
diaries: Birrel, John, 10; Melville, Sir James of Halhill, 157. *See also* Carey, Sir Robert
Douglas, Archibald, 8th earl of Angus (d. 1588), 67, 112, 119, 163, 171; as lieutenant, 70, 77, 81–2, 156–7, 162, 164–5, 173–4, 176
Douglas, Archibald, parson in Peebles, 77
Douglas, earls of, 51
Douglas, earls of Angus, 51, 54, 73, 97, 106, 112–13, 130–1
Douglas, family, 54, 142, 144, 155
Douglas, James, 4th earl of Morton, regent, 7, 67, 69–70, 82, 83, 85, 147–8, 149, 155–67, 210–11; anglophilia, 82, 154, 155–6, 157, 160,
 164; judicial raids, 111, 156–8; pledge system, 60, 158–9
Douglas, Margaret (sister of James Douglas, 4th earl of Morton, *see* Carmichael, Sir John of that ilk), *m.* (1) Sir Walter Scott of Branxholme (d. 1574); (2) Francis Stewart, 5th earl of Bothwell, 148, 150. *See also see* Scott of Branxholme, Walter (d. 1574)
Douglas, William, 8th earl of Douglas, 131
Douglas, William, 9th earl of Angus, (d. 1591), 119
Douglas, William, 10th earl of Angus, (d. 1611), 97, 113; as lieutenant, 81–2, 185–6
Douglas, William, 11th earl of Angus, (d. 1660), 97, 113, 197, 199, 202
Douglas of Bonjedburgh, family, 81
Douglas of Bonjedburgh, George, 44, 70, 82–3, 108, 144, 174
Douglas of Bonjedburgh, William, 93, 109, 156–7, 159, 199
Douglas of Cavers, family, sheriffs of Roxburghshire, 51, 55, 75, 81, 94, 107, 144
Douglas of Cavers, James, 75, 77; *m.* Margaret Cranstoun, 88
Douglas in Cavers, James, 76
Douglas of Cavers, William, 75, 77, 85, 110, 158, 168, 174
Douglas of Cavers, William, feuar of, 75–6, 78, 93, 109, 118, 193, 199, 209
Douglas of Drumlanrig, family, 51, 81
Douglas of Drumlanrig, William, 9th baron, 96–7, 122, 202
Douglas-Scott alliance, 69–70, 81–2, 85, 112, 142, 144, 155–6, 160
Dryfe Sands, battle of, 70
Dunbar, George Home, 1st earl of, *see* Home of Spott, George
Dunfermline, Alexander Seton, 1st earl of, *see* Seton, Alexander
Dumfries, 114, 118, 161, 202, 207

economy: trade, 32, 198. *See also* agriculture, cross-border relations
Elizabeth I, 155–6, 166, 167, 171–2, 187; and James VI, 169, 172, 179–80, 184–5; meddling in Scottish affairs, 165–6, 170, 171; and Scott of Buccleuch, 179, 181

227

Elliot, family, 27, 37, 54, 60, 62, 68, 86, 93, 144, 149, 150, 159, 194–5
Elliot, Gilbert, 68
Elliot of the Banks, Sym, 150
Elliot of Braidley, [?], 68
Elliot of Gorrumberrie, Will, 68
Elliot of Lauriston, Robert, 69, 150
Elliot of Redheugh, family, 110
Elliot of Redheugh, Robert, 68, 69, 203
Elliot of the Stobs, Gavin, 69
England, English: incursions, 7, 33, 41; northern England, 14, 213–14; subsidy to James, 161, 172, 174, 178, 181, 184. *See also* Anglo-Scottish relations, Middle Shires, Union
Eskdale, 54, 88, 93, 104, 108, 109, 201–2
Ettrick forest, 74, 169, 185; bailie, chamberlain of, 100–1; feuing of, 35–6
Ewesdale, 54, 93, 108, 201–2

farming, *see* agriculture
fees, 78, 81, 84, 88, 89, 90, 92, 101, 113, 117, 118, 161, 168, 179, 185, 189–90, 191
feu-ferme, *see* Ettrick forest, landholding
feud, 62, 69, 77, 137–48, 149, 152–3, 195; in the Borders, 53, 61, 84–5, 138–9, 152–3, 159, 168, 182, 186, 190, 208; cross-border, 147, 172, 182; day of combat, 142, 172; geographical distribution, 13, 134, 138–9; kinship structures of, 48–9; origins of, 128, 134, 139–48; political factionalism, 69–70, 83–4, 85–6, 147–8, 149, 154–5, 155, 156–7, 158, 162–8, 171, 176–7; suppression of, 3, 110, 128–30, 137–9, 140–2, 145, 148, 186–7, 206–7. *See also* allegiance, crime, James VI and I, legislation, ordinances
feuing, 35–6. *See also* Ettrick forest
fishing, 31, 203
Forster, Sir John (warden of English Middle March), 148, 152, 160, 166, 168, 170–1, 172, 173; at feud, 138; complaints against, 161–2
Foster, family, 27
friendship, 94, 124, 126, 146, 156–7, 162, 167, 170, 183, 184, 185; as basis of power, 74, 93, 201–12, 210; in bonds, 56, 67, 68, 69, 210. *See also* allegiance, Anglo-Scottish relations
frontier, *see* border

Galashiels, 63. *See also* Pringle of Galashiels, family
Geddes, Charles of Rauchane, 69, 210
General Assembly, 42–3, 44
general bands, *see* bonds, bands
gesture, 17
goodwill, 78–9
government: central, 104–27; intensification, 17, 73, 101–2, 104, 130, 177, 186–7, 193–4, 195–6, 197–8, 206–7, 210; linkage between central and regional, 88, 90, 94, 104–6, 107–8, 111, 112–20, 126–7, 206, 214; regional, 17, 73–103; of Scotland after 1603, 105–6, 108, 111, 115, 200–1. *See also* crown policy, office-holders, parliament, privy council
Graham, family, 27, 200

Hamilton, John, Lord, 175, 176, 177
Hamilton, Thomas, Lord Binning, 1st earl of Melrose, 99
Hawick, 5, 7, 40, 91, 95, 192
Hay, family, 54
Hay, James, 7th Lord Yester (d. 1609), 76, 77, 114
Hay, John, 8th Lord Yester, 1st earl of Tweeddale, 76, 93, 94, 202. *See also* Yester, Lords
Hay, Lords Yester, 51, 55, 63, 75–7, 95, 106, 144–5, 147, 210
Hay, William, 5th Lord Yester (d. 1586), 73, 76
Hay, William, 6th Lord Yester (d. 1591), 76, 77
Hay of Smithfield, John, 77
Hepburn, earls of Bothwell, *see* Bothwell
Heron, 147, 160
Highlands, 9, 17–18, 53, 60, 132, 174–5
histories, *see* Calderwood, Leslie, Spottiswoode
Home, Alison, 45
Home, family, 52, 83, 92, 100, 102
Home, Lords, 52, 73, 90, 102, 112
Home of Cowdenknowes, Sir James, 119, 155, 160, 162, 163, 168, 175
Home of Cowdenknowes, Sir John, 43
Home of Lessudden, William, 69
Home of Manderston, George, 203
Home of Spott, George, 1st earl of Dunbar, 88, 91–2, 112, 116–17, 120, 122–3, 194, 196, 204
Home of Wedderburn, David, 203–4

INDEX

Home of Whitelaw, Sir William, 191
Home-Ker alliance, 70, 147, 163-4
honour, 57, 86-7, 160; martial prowess, 57. *See also* reputation
Horsburgh, family, 77, 95, 147
Howard, Thomas, 1st Lord Howard de Walden, 203-4
Hunsdon, Henry Carey, 1st Lord, *see* Carey, Henry

identity, 26-9, 187, 212. *See also* borderer, kinship
interdependence, *see* allegiance
Ireland, 178, 181-2, 185, 212, 214; transportation to, 200

James VI and I, 175, 177-8; Borders policy (to 1603), 18, 87, 113, 135, 151-2, 163, 167, 168-9, 170, 172-3, 176, 178-80, 181-2, 183-6, 203, 207, 210; Borders policy (after 1603), 18, 119, 122-3, 187-90, 198-201, 205-6, 211; and Elizabeth I, 164, 167, 169, 172, 179-80, 184-5; favour, 117, 123, 124, 142; against feuding, 61, 142, 177, 197; and Ker of Cessford, 113, 114-15, 152, 183-5; pension, 172, 174, 178, 181, 184, 185; and Scott of Buccleuch, 113, 152, 181, 183-5; succession, 1, 18, 87, 112, 137-9, 154, 172, 175, 180, 181, 183, 185, 187, 206, 207, 210; visit to Scotland (1617), 93, 198-9; writings on the Borders, 89, 91, 187, 188, 205; writings on Union, 187, 211. *See also* crown policy, government, privy council
Jardine, Sir Alexander, of Applegarth, 69, 210
Jedburgh, 5, 33, 40, 89, 94, 96, 104, 106-7, 161; courts at, 111, 157-8, 173, 176, 195, 209; feud in, 77, 96, 146-7
Jedforest: regality of, 51, 67, 81, 113, 197. *See also* Douglas, earls of Angus
Johnstone, family, 52, 83, 208
Johnstone, Sir John, 70; *m.* Margaret Scott of Branxholme, 70
Johnstone of that ilk, Sir James, 94
Johnstone of Westraw, Sir James, 94
Johnstone-Maxwell feud, *see* Maxwells
Johnstone-Scott alliance, 70
judicial policy: crown judicial control, 1, 110, 128-30, 151, 153, 176, 206; private justice, 110, 128-30, 153;

public justice, 110, 128-30, 153, 207, 209; sentencing, 122, 133-4, 135-6, 151, 157-8, 175, 192, 196. *See also* crown policy, James VI and I
judicial raids, 82, 151, 152, 156, 157-8, 176, 186, 207; courts in the Borders, 77, 78, 91, 92, 111, 114, 151, 157-8, 173, 185, 195, 202; musters, 132, 151, 170, 172, 174, 175, 208
judicial system: birlaw court, 36; commissions of justiciary, 80; court of High Justiciary, 153, 130, 206, 209; court of Session, 128-30, 153, 128-30, 206, 209. *See also* baronies, Middle Shires, sheriffs
jurisdiction, 81, 83, 90, 91, 149, 151, 199; dispute over, 76, 97, 130-1, 197, 202; exemptions from, 85, 94; national sovereignty, 106, 188-9, 190, 191-3, 200, 203-4, 205, 211, 212; overlapping, 76, 79-80, 80-1, 82, 130-1; private, 96-8, 100-1; re-pledging, 97, 101, 130, 202. *See also* legislation, lieutenants, remanding, sheriffs, wardens
Justices of the Peace, 88, 200, 207; function, 79; introduction, 8, 75, 79, 195, 206; jurisdiction, 8, 79-80

Kelso, 5, 40, 84, 152, 171, 172
Ker, family, 51, 54, 62, 114, 121, 140-2, 144, 147-8, 172, 208, 210
Ker, Robert, 1st Lord Roxburgh-Buccleuch feud, *see* Scott of Buccleuch
Ker of Ancrum, family, 37, 85, 96, 100, 210
Ker of Ancrum, Robert, 1st earl of Ancram, 44, 45, 116; *m.* Elizabeth daughter of John Murray of Blackbarony, 66; captain of border guard, 66, 89, 192; gentleman of Prince Charles's bedchamber, 67, 118, 122-6
Ker [of Ancrum], William, 3rd earl of Lothian (son of Robert, 1st earl of Ancram), 85, 109, 114, 172; *m.* Anna, countess of Lothian, 64
Ker of Ancrum-Roxburgh feud, 114, 125
Ker of Cavers, Thomas, 85, 143
Ker of Caverton, family, 142
Ker of Caverton, William, 158
Ker of Cessford, Andrew (*d.* 1526), 55, 141

229

Ker of Cessford, family (wardens of the Scottish Middle March), 36, 37, 39, 51, 72, 83–5, 96, 99, 100, 102, 147
Ker of Cessford, Margaret, sister of Robert Ker of Cessford, m. Sir Walter Scott of Buccleuch, see Scott of Buccleuch, Sir Walter
Ker of Cessford, Robert, 1st Lord and 1st earl of Roxburgh (d. 1650), 1, 57, 108, 197–8, 199, 206–7, 210; m. (1) Margaret, niece of John Maitland of Thirlestane, 64, 176–7; m. (2) Jane Drummond, sister of James, 1st earl of Perth, 64; children's marriages, 65; complaints against, 165, 167, 182; at court, 120–1, 122, 125, 183; descriptions of, 163, 179, 183–5; in feud, 142–3; involvement in cross-border raiding, 178, 183; and James VI and I, 113, 114–15, 142, 178, 183–5, 207; JP, 79, 116; keepership of Liddesdale, 85–6, 176–7; and the Kirk, 44, 99, 100; Middle Shires commissioner, 93, 109, 116; privy councillor, 107, 113–14, 115–16, 119, 178, 195; warded in England, 183–4; warden, 84–6, 114, 151–2, 179
Ker of Cessford, Walter (d. 1581), 52, 83, 141, 159; m. Isabel Ker of Ferniehirst, 64
Ker of Cessford, William (d. 1600), 7, 64, 114, 120, 146, 165, 170, 171; warden, 70, 82, 84, 149, 155–7, 161–2, 163, 164, 166, 171, 172, 173, 175
Ker of Cessford-Argyll alliance, see Campbell, Colin, 6th earl of Argyll
Ker of Cessford-Home alliance, 70, 147, 163–4
Ker of Cessford-Ker of Ferniehirst feud, 85, 96, 142–3, 146, 148, 156, 162, 165
Ker of Cessford-Lennox alliance, 70, 147, 163–5, 167–8
Ker of Cessford-Scott feud, 140–4, 160, 163, 182–3
Ker of Crailing, Thomas (brother to Sir Andrew Ker of Ferniehirst), 96, 146–7
Ker of Faldonside, family, 63, 141, 155, 159–60, 164, 168
Ker of Ferniehirst, Sir Andrew (d. 1545), 64
Ker of Ferniehirst, Sir Andrew, Lord Jedburgh (d. 1631), 44, 45, 65, 84, 85, 96, 97, 109, 110, 119, 121, 123–4, 142–3, 146–7, 197, 201
Ker of Ferniehirst, family, 37, 39, 51, 55, 64, 89, 94, 96, 97, 98, 99, 100, 113, 130–1, 172, 210
Ker of Ferniehirst, Janet, m. Walter Scott of Branxholme (d. 1552), 141
Ker of Ferniehirst, Sir John (d. 1562): m. Catherine Ker of Cessford, 64
Ker [of Ferniehirst], Robert, Lord Rochester, earl of Somerset, (half-brother of Sir Andrew Ker of Ferniehirst, Lord Jedburgh), 66, 89, 118, 121, 122–4, 125, 201; alliance with Murray of Elibank, 66, 124
Ker of Ferniehirst, Sir Thomas (d. 1585), m. (2) Janet, daughter of David Scott of Kirkurd, 66, 142, 167, 169; 7, 45, 83–4, 85, 96, 141, 146, 158–9, 161–3, 165, 166, 169; warden, 157, 161, 167–9, 170–1
Ker of Ferniehirst, Thomas, the 'first', 55, 64
Ker of [Ferniehirst] Oxnam, Andrew (d. 1628, son of Sir Andrew Ker of Ferniehirst, Lord Jedburgh), 66, 96, 99, 108, 123–6, 143, 199, 203, 209; m. Margaret, daughter of Mark Ker, 1st earl of Lothian, 64, 114; captain of border guard, 66, 88–9, 96, 118, 123–4, 192, 201, 210; commissioner, 90, 92–4, 109, 118, 123; privy councillor, 90, 96, 116, 118–19, 123
Ker of Ferniehirst-Murray alliance, 66, 89, 197
Ker of Ferniehirst-Scott alliance, see Scott of Buccleuch-Ker of Ferniehirst alliance
Ker of Gateshaw, family, 63
Ker of Grange, William, 89
Ker of Greenhead, Andrew, 84, 109, 143
Ker of Greenhead, family 100
Ker of Greenhead, James, 84;
Ker of Heiton, Andrew, 84
Ker of Hirsel, Andrew, 142
Ker of Jedburgh, Sir John, 93, 199
Ker of Lintalee, James, 109–10
Ker of Linton, family, 63, 100
Ker of Linton, George, 142
Ker of Littledean, family, 63, 142–3, 155
Ker of Mersington, family, 63
[Ker of Newbattle], Anna, countess of Lothian, 64

INDEX

Ker of Newbattle, family (later earls of Lothian, 55, 63–4
Ker of Newbattle, Mark, commendator of Newbattle (*d.* 1584), 55, 114, 155
Ker of Newbattle, Mark of Prestongrange, 1st earl of Lothian (*d.* 1609), 55, 108, 114, 119, 120
[Ker of Newbattle], Robert, 2nd earl of Lothian (*d.* 1624), 119
Ker of Primsideloch, family, 63, 142
Ker of Woodhead, William, 77
Ker of Yair, Andrew, 79, 146
kindred, 2, 47–8, 49–62, 71–2, 98, 102, 140–8; clans, 47, 53. *See also* kinship, surnames
kinship, 1, 3, 7, 47–8, 49, 102, 120, 126, 128–9, 140, 154, 209–10; expectations of, 49, 210; fictive kinship, 49–50, 63–67, 126; governmental use of networks of, 3, 48, 51–2, 71–2, 81–3, 88–90, 93–4, 101–2, 116, 120, 126; identity, 7, 48, 49; loyalty, 55–6; networks, 81–2, 83–4, 114, 123–4, 155–7, 161, 164, 172, 191, 196, 210; obligations, 48, 156, 158, 191, 209–10; relations within kinship, 16–17, 39. *See also* lordship, marriage, obligation, surnames
Kirk, Church, 41–6, 92; communion, 198; godlessness, 133, 149, 174, 191, 193–4, 195; 'godly' society, 43, 46, 133; kirk sessions, 41, 206; landholdings, 97–9; plantation of ministers, 42–3, 200, 206; visitations, 194. *See also* General Assembly, ministers, parsonages, presbyteries, recusancy, Reformation, synod, teinds
Knox, Mr John, minister of Melrose, 100

lairds, 75, 105, 128–9, 207–8; bonnet, 37–8; greater, 37–8, 73–4; 'the invisible divide', 37–8; lesser, 37–8, 73–4. *See also* lordship, wealth
landholding, 40; in the Borders, 48 (map 3), 62–3; enclosure, 33–4; kindly (customary) tenancy, 34–5, 49; tacks, 34, 35–6; tenancy, 68. *See also* feuing
landlords, 108; accountability, 68–9, 93, 109, 159, 174–5, 196, 200, 209; landlord-tenant relations, 33–5, 36–7, 38, 39–40, 68–9, 159, 203; obligations, 68–9. *See also* jurisdiction
Langholme, 88

language: of opprobrium, 9, 20; rhetoric, 102, 126, 132–3. *See also* perception of borderers
Lauder, 106, 161
Lauderdale, 88, 115
Lauderdale, John Maitland, 1st earl, *see* Maitland, John
Lawson, Sir Wilfrid, 193
legislation: border or march law, 130–2, 182, 188–9; border-specific, 174–5, 185–6, 192–3, 199; domestic, 130, 132, 174–5; on feuding, 128, 138, 186–7; on fire-arms, 128; on Highlands and Borders (1587), 9, 53, 54, 60, 68, 112, 132, 174–5. *See also* ordinances
Lennox, Esme Stewart, 1st duke of, *see* Stewart, Esme
Lennox, Ludovic Stewart, 2nd duke of, *see* Stewart, Ludovic
Lennox-Ker of Cessford alliance, *see* Ker of Cessford-Lennox alliance
Leslie, John, bishop of Ross (1566–9), 10
Liddesdale, 54, 60, 109, 135, 148–51, 169, 193; bonds for, 68–9, 159; inhabitants of, 29, 167, 178; keeper of, 85–6, 112, 113, 142, 148, 149–50, 156–7, 163–5, 167, 174, 177, 178–9, 183; lordship of, 63, 85–6, 177
lieutenant, 153, 158; Borders, 80–2, 151, 162
Littill (Liddle), family, 149, 159
lordship, 129, 154; accountability to crown, 59–61, 68–9, 71, 150; good lordship, 14, 47, 50–2, 56–9, 71; maintenance, 57–8, 67; protection, 56–7, 150. *See also* obligation, power

Maitland, John, 1st earl of Lauderdale, 119
Maitland of Lethington, Sir Richard, *see* poetry
Maitland of Thirlestane, Sir John, chancellor, 64, 107, 114–15, 119, 148, 169, 173, 175, 176–7
manrent, bonds of, *see* bonds
marches, English, 5, 86, 102, 138, 150, 161–2, 169, 172, 199, 213–14
marches, Scottish, 5; East, 5, 52, 70–2, 83, 102, 104–5, 112, 129, 137, 148, 207–8; West, 5, 52, 70–2, 83, 102, 109, 112, 129–30, 135, 137, 138–9, 150, 159, 186, 195, 207–8
Marian wars, 7, 45, 142–3, 155, 161–2

marriage, 64–7, 88, 114, 116, 141–4, 148, 176–7, 183; contracts, 63, 160; cross-border, 27, 175; elite, 27. *See also* allegiance
Mary, Queen of Scots, 45, 155, 166, 169, 172–3
Mary de Guise, 83, 141
Maxwell, family, 52, 83, 159, 191, 208
Maxwell, John, 9th Lord Maxwell, 72, 88, 110, 118, 123–4
Maxwell, Robert, 10th Lord Maxwell, 1st earl of Nithsdale, 93–4, 112, 196, 201–2
Maxwell of Bromeholme, John, 196
Maxwell-Johnstone feud, 70, 72, 94, 129–30, 186
Melrose, 5, 141. *See also* abbeys
Melrose, Thomas Hamilton, Lord Binning, 1st earl, *see* Hamilton, Thomas
Middle Shires, 80–1, 87, 187–204, 205, 208, 211; commissioners, 75, 78, 80–1, 87, 90–2, 108, 190–3, 201–2, 205, 207; commissions to survey idle persons, fugitives, 109, 134, 200; conjunct Commission, 93–4, 108, 199–200; creation of, 2, 7–8, 155, 187–9; English commissioners, 87–8; example of union, 188–90, 193, 198, 204, 205, 211; lieutenant, 87, 88, 90, 189–90; tensions in, 19, 87–8, 106, 187, 192–3, 203–4, 205, 211, 213; triumvirate, 58, 73, 93–4, 201–3. *See also* border guard, jurisdiction, remanding, Union
ministers, 41–3. *See also* Abirthnethie, John; Douglas, Archibald; Knox, John; Shaw, Patrick
Mitchelhill, family, 107
Moscrope, family, 172
Murray, family, 51, 100, 208, 210
Murray of Blackbarony, Andrew (*d.* 1572): *m.* Grisel Beaton, 65
Murray of Blackbarony, family, 36, 44, 51, 54, 55, 61, 66, 76, 91, 107, 210
Murray of Blackbarony, John (*a.* 1603), 65, 66–7, 124; also known as Eddleston, 61, 145
Murray of Elibank, Sir Gideon, 44, 57, 61, 78, 107, 210; JP, 91; lieutenant, 117; Middle Shires commissioner, 66, 91–4, 117, 191–2, 202; privy councillor, 66, 116–19, 195; treasurer depute, 66, 91, 117, 197

Murray of Elibank-Ker of Ferniehirst alliance, *see* Ker of Ferniehurst-Murray alliance
Murray of Elibank-Scott of Buccleuch alliance, 65–6, 91, 98–9
Murray of Elibank-Scott of Harden alliance, 66, 144, 197
Murray of Elibank-earl of Somerset alliance, *see* Ker, Robert, earl of Somerset
Murray of Falahill, family (subsequently Philiphaugh), 51, 54, 55, 61, 65, 78–9, 91, 100, 210
Murray of Falahill (subsequently Philiphaugh), Sir John (*d.* 1640), 65, 77, 78, 91, 92, 107, 191, 200, 207
Murray of Falahill, Patrick (*d.* 1580), 65, 77
Murray of Falahill, Patrick (*d.* 1601), 65, 77, 78; *m.* Agnes daughter of Andrew Murray of Blackbarony, 65
Murray of Kilbaberton, James, 118
Murray of Langshaw, Patrick (son of Gideon Murray of Elibank), 1st Lord Elibank, 117
Murray of Lochmaben, John, 1st earl of Annandale, 93–4, 118, 122, 124–6, 201–2
Murray of Romanno, John, 76
Murray-Scott alliance, *see* Scott-Murray alliance
musters, *see* judicial raids

negotiation, *see* power
Newark castle: captaincy of, 74, 100–1
Nithsdale, 104, 201–2
Nithsdale, 1st earl of, *see* Maxwell, Robert
Nixon, Nickson, family, 149, 150

obligation, 16–17, 39, 47–8; accountability, 59–61, 68–9, 71, 93, 109, 150, 158, 199, 209; of alliance, 67–9, 101, 207, 209–10; in feuding, 58–9; used by government, 59–62, 68–9, 71, 101, 121, 150, 159, 191, 196, 202–3, 206–7, 209–10; of kinship, 49, 55–6, 58, 62, 71, 74, 101, 191, 207, 209–10; of lordship, 56–8, 67, 71, 74, 150, 159, 202–3. *See also* bands, honour, kinship, lordship, power
office-holders: border-specific, 80–94; central, 2, 3, 117–27; crown (private), 74; expansion in local, 17, 73, 79,

INDEX

101–2, 129; local, 3, 173–203. *See also* bailies, government, Justices of the Peace, lieutenants, Middle Shires, patronage, power, privy council, sheriffs, wardens

ordinances, 198; Borders-related, 54, 59–60, 109–11, 132, 172, 184, 185–6, 193, 196, 200, 208; feuding, 137–8, 153, 176, 186; fire-arms, 128, 153, 176; hunting in the Cheviots, 128, 193, 196; justice, 187. *See also* legislation

pacification, 81, 87–94, 108, 115–20, 122–6, 154–5, 182, 190–204, 209–11, 213–14; objectives of, 3–4, 18, 87, 90, 92–3, 188, 190–1, 193–4, 199–200, 207; success of, 194–5, 198, 201, 204, 205, 208–9

parliament, 106; admission of lairds to, 105, 107; burgh representatives, 95, 106; shire representatives, 105. *See also* legislation

parsonages, 43; Hawick, 99; St Mary of the Lowes, 42, 58, 99

patriotism, 28. *See also* ballads, identity

patronage, 1, 11–12, 74, 87, 89, 106, 114, 115, 118, 120–7. *See also* court

Peebles, 5, 40, 92, 94–5, 104, 106, 161; courts, musters in, 114, 132, 157, 172, 174, 176, 178, 185, 207, 208; feud in, 29, 56, 134, 147

perception of borderers, 9, 11, 12–13, 20–1, 53, 132–3, 149, 174–6, 214; barbaric borderer, 9, 12–13, 22, 30–1, 174, 191, 193–4; caricature, 4, 10. *See also* diaries

pledges, *see* bonds, cross-border relations

poetry: Maitland, Sir Richard, 10, 137, 149, 152; Lindsay, Sir David, 10. *See also* ballads

power, 108, 113, 122, 183, 201–2, 210; authority, 47–8, 57, 73–4, 83, 86, 87, 88–9, 90, 93, 98, 108, 120, 155, 162, 167, 183, 206, 210; consensus, 15–16, 39–40; discourse of, 16–17, 50, 55–6; exercise of, 73–4; frameworks, networks of, 47–8, 73–4, 86, 91, 93, 96, 101–2, 116, 155, 196; governmental, 128–30, 151, 153; governmental use of networks of, 48, 71, 81–2, 83–4, 87, 114, 115, 120, 121–2, 123, 124, 126–7, 128–9, 201–3, 206–7, 210; influence, 117–18, 121–6;

interdependence, 39–40, 47, 50–1, 74, 126; legitimation, 16–17, 47, 50, 74, 116; relations between governor and subordinate, 15–17, 33–5, 36–7, 39–40, 210; 'strang hand', 73, 87, 93, 210. *See also* allegiance, co-operation, friendship, kinship, landholding, lordship, reputation, surnames

presbyteries, 41–2, 43–59, 99–100, 206; Jedburgh, 41, 43, 45–7, 100; Peebles, 42; Selkirk (Teviotdale), 41, 44, 100

Pringle, family, 51, 54, 63, 100, 144–5, 159

Pringle of Buckholm, James apparent of, 145

Pringle of Buckholm, John, 145

Pringle of Galashiels, family, 39, 55, 97

Pringle of Galashiels, Sir James, 78, 79, 107

Pringle of Tinnis, John, 145

Pringle of Torwoodlee, family, 39, 55

Pringle of Torwoodlee, George, 78, 107, 145

privy council, 87–94, 104–5, 108–11, 111–20, 159–60, 174, 178–80, 199–201, 212; council for Borders affairs, 175, 177; Prince Charles's council, 116

provost, 74–5; of Annan, 88; of Jedburgh, 76, 94, 96, 143, 146; of Peebles, 76, 94–5; of Selkirk, 76, 94–5

Radcliffe, Thomas, 3rd earl of Sussex, 7, 141, 154

raiding, *see* crime, cross-border raiding

recusancy, 45–6

Redesdale, 86, 147

Redeswyre, *see* Anglo-Scottish relations

Reformation, 41, 46

remanding, 19, 189, 192–3, 211

reputation, 57, 86, 183. *See also* honour, power, status

reward, 87, 89, 113, 116, 118, 119, 120, 121, 123–6, 184–5, 206. *See also* fees, patronage

rhetoric, *see* language

rivers: as corridors of communication, 5; Ettrick, 5; Gala Water, 5; Leader, 5; Teviot, 5; Tweed, 5, 31, 145; Yarrow, 5

Roxburgh, Robert Ker, 1st earl of, *see* Ker of Cessford, Robert

Roxburghshire, 70, 88, 193, 209. *See also* sheriffs

Russell, Lord Francis, 170–1
Rutherford, family, 51, 54, 62, 94, 107, 144, 146, 158, 159, 163–4, 165, 168, 172
Rutherford, John, provost and burgess of Jedburgh, 76, 95, 107
Rutherford of Edgerston, Richard, 85, 110
Rutherford of Hundalee, Andrew (a. 1581), 165
Rutherford of Hundalee, family, 55, 85, 94
Rutherford of Hundalee (a. 1616), Nicol, 44
Rutherford of Hunthill, family, 55, 94, 96
Rutherford of Hunthill, John (d. 1577), 108, 159
Rutherford of Hunthill, John (d. c. 1610), 76, 85, 99, 109–10, 165
Rutherford of the Tofts, John, 134
Ruthven raid, 166–7, 171

Salisbury, Robert Cecil, 1st earl of, *see* Cecil, Sir Robert
Scott, Andrew 'a commoun rydar', 57, 91
Scott, family, 51, 54, 58, 62, 63, 95, 121, 143–4, 159, 163–4, 165, 208, 210
Scott, Mr James, vicar of St Mary of the Lowes, **99**
Scott, Janet, 160
Scott, Robert, captain of Hermitage, 86
Scott, Walter, in Bowhill, 56
Scott, William, in the Glack, 56
Scott of Allanhaugh, family, 63
Scott of Allanhaugh, Robert, 37, 56
Scott of Birkenside, Sir Walter, 159
Scott of Bonnington, Mary, Lady Bonnington, 197
Scott of Bonnington, Simon, 56, 66, 144, 197
Scott of Borthwick, John, 57
Scott of Branxholme, family, 35, 51, 55, 72, 97–9, 100–1, 162; landholdings, 97–9, 100
Scott of Branxholme, Sir Walter (d.1504): m. Elizabeth Ker of Cessford, 141
Scott of Branxholme, Sir Walter (d.1552), 52, 59, 65, 83, 141–2
Scott of Branxholme, Sir Walter (d. 1574), 37, 39, 70, 159; m. Margaret Douglas, 69, 81–2, 144, 156
[Scott of Buccleuch], Anna, duchess of Buccleuch (d. 1732), 39
Scott of Buccleuch (or Branxholme), Sir Walter, 1st Lord Buccleuch (d. 1611), 54, 57, 95, 97, 108, 155, 168, 171, 206–7; m. Margaret Ker of Cessford, 64, 183; cross-border crime, 135, 147, 151–2, 165, 178–9, 183; crown action against, 69, 173–4, 176, 178, 179, 183–4, 210; descriptions of, 86, 178–9, 183; in feud, 147; and James VI and I, 61, 142, 178, 179–80, 181, 183–5, 207; JP, 79–80; keepership, lordship of Liddesdale, 85–6, 113, 149–50, 177, 178–9; and Kinmont Willie, 57, 58, 131–2, 179–80, 181–2; and the Kirk, 43, 45, 58; landholdings, 63, 72, 86, 97, 177; as landlord, 37, 63, 68–9, 86, 150, 203; leadership of kindred, 55–7, 60–1; Middle Shires commissioner, pacification, 80, 93, 109, 115, 185, 193; other offices, 73, 98–9, 101; poet, 177 n. 132; power, 74, 86; privy councillor, 107, 113–14, 115–16, 119, 178, 195; oversman, 57
[Scott of Buccleuch], Walter, 2nd Lord and 1st earl of Buccleuch (d. 1633), 66, 101, 115–16, 119, 199, 201–3
Scott of Buccleuch-Douglas alliance, 81–2
Scott of Buccleuch-Ker of Ferniehirst alliance, 85
Scott of Buccleuch-Murray of Elibank alliance, *see* Gideon Murray of Elibank
Scott of Buccleuch-Roxburgh feud, 64, 142–3, 148, 182–3. *See also* Ker of Cessford-Scott feud
Scott of Burnfoot, family, 110
Scott of Burnfoot, William, 197
Scott of Deephope, Adam, 159
Scott of Dryhope, John, 64
Scott of Dryhope, Walter, 159
Scott of Essinsyde, Walter, 66, 197
Scott of Gamescleuch, Sym, 159
Scott of Goldielands, family, 110
Scott of Goldielands, Walter, 52, 55, 58, 70, 86, 142, 193, 197
Scott of Haining, Robert, 55, 69, 79, 86, 94–5, 110, 143, 146, 150, 173–4, 197
Scott of Haining, Thomas, 98
Scott of Harden, family, 55, 58, 110, 148
Scott of Harden, Walter, 58, 61, 78, 176; m. Mary Scott of Dryhope, 64
Scott of Harden, William, m. Agnes Murray of Elibank, 66, 89, 144, 197
Scott of Harden-Murray of Elibank alliance, *see* Murray of Elibank-Scott of Harden alliance

234

INDEX

Scott of Harden-Scott of Bonnington feud, 66, 144, 197
Scott of Hartwoodmyres, Walter, 159
Scott of Haychesters, Walter, m. Mary, countess of Buccleuch, 64
Scott of Howpasley, family, 55, 63
Scott of Hundleshope, John, 56
Scott of Kirkurd, William, 65
Scott of Newark, James, 101
Scott of Synton, Walter, 57, 63
Scott of Thirlestane, family, 63
Scott of Thirlestane, Robert, 56, 66, 78, 107, 134, 144, 159, 193; m. Margaret Scott of Branxholme, 64
Scott of Tushielaw, family, 144
Scott of Tushielaw, John, 66
Scott of Tushielaw, Walter, 150–1
Scott of Tushielaw, William, 159
Scott of Whitslaid, Walter, 144, 148, 176
Scott-Douglas alliance, see Douglas-Scott alliance
Scott-Johnstone alliance, see Johnstone-Scott alliance
Scott-Ker of Cessford feud, see Ker of Cessford-Scott feud
Scott-Ker of Ferniehirst alliance, 66–7, 85, 89, 142–3
Scott-Murray alliance, 65, 67, 191. See also Murray of Elibank-Scott of Buccleuch alliance
Scrope, Thomas, 10th Lord Scrope of Bolton (warden of the English West March), 86, 135, 150, 167, 169, 172–3, 178–9, 183
Selkirk, 5, 40, 76, 95, 106–7, 157–8, 161, 196, 198; dispute over common lands, mills, 79, 95–6, 143, 146. See also provost
Selkirkshire, 70, 193. See also Teviotdale
Seton, Alexander, 1st earl of Dunfermline, chancellor, 122, 126
Seton, Sir William of Kylesmure, 191, 193, 202
Shaw, Mr Patrick, minister of Selkirk, 146
sheriffdoms, shires: Peeblesshire (Tweeddale), 5, 60, 77, 107; Roxburghshire, 5, 60, 107; Selkirkshire, 5, 60, 77, 107
sheriffs, 75–9, 80, 153, 187; of Peeblesshire, 75–7, 186; of Roxburghshire, 75–8, 80, 186; of Selkirkshire (Teviotdale), 76,

77–9, 186, 203, 207; surrender of sheriffdoms, 78, 207
Spottiswoode, John, archbishop of Glasgow (1603–15), of St Andrews (1615–39), 194
status, 74, 91, 94, 116. See also reputation
Stewart, Esme, 1st duke of Lennox, 70, 147, 163–8
Stewart, family, 63, 145
Stewart, Francis, 5th earl of Bothwell, 73, 112, 148, 176, 177; forfeiture, 72, 148, 152
Stewart, Capt. James, earl of Arran, 7, 82, 83–4, 85, 162, 167–8, 170
Stewart, John, 3rd earl of Atholl, 162
Stewart, Ludovic, 2nd duke of Lennox, 86, 176–7, 184
Stewart of Shillinglaw, Sir Robert, 93, 145
Stewart of Tinnis, James, 145
Stewart of Traquair, family, 36, 51, 55, 107, 144–5, 147, 210
Stewart of Traquair, Sir John, 94, 202
Stewart of Traquair, Sir William, 61, 114, 165
Storey, family, 147
surnames, 47, 52–4, 71–2, 143–4, 175, 210; leaders, 54–62, 71–2; loyalty, 55–6, 58; responsibility of leaders for, 59–62, 68–9, 71, 150, 196, 202–3. See also kindreds, kinship
Sussex, Thomas Radcliffe, 3rd earl of, see Radcliffe, Thomas
synods, 41–2, 99–100; Lothian and Tweeddale, 41–2, 44, 45–6; Merse and Teviotdale, 41–2, 43, 45

teinds, 42, 99, 118–19, 143, 177 n. 132
tenancy, see landholding
Teviotdale, 93, 109, 135, 141, 163–4, 174, 186, 209. See also Selkirkshire, sheriffdoms, presbyteries
trade, 32, 46, 198, 204
transportation, 105 n. 5, 200–1
Turnbull, family, 76, 77, 81, 89, 146–7, 163–4, 165
Turnbull, Thomas, 146
Turnbull of Barnhills, William, 67
Turnbull of Bedrule, Sir Thomas, 43–4, 55, 67, 77, 110, 165, 173
Turnbull of Hallrule, family, 55, 67
Turnbull of Minto, John, 67, 159
Turnbull of Minto, Thomas, 146

Turnbull of Stanyledge, Hector, 146
Tweeddale, 109, 186
Tweedie, family, 63, 95, 145, 147
Tweedie, Gilbert, 95
Tweedie, Walter, reader at Broughton, 95
Tweedie, William, 17
Tweedie of Dreva, Alex, 95, 110, 147
Tweedie of Drumelzier, family, 147
Tweedie of Drumelzier, James, 77, 108, 110, 145
Tynedale, 86, 147, 161

Union, 187–90, 207, 210; Britishness, 187, 212; composite kingdom, multiple monarchy, Three Kingdoms, 46, 105–6, 200, 208, 211–12, 213–14; Great Britain, 187–8, 190; negotiations, 90, 188–90, 211; parliaments, 190, 191, 192–3, 205, 211; 'perfect union', 189, 205; sovereignty, 8–20, 29, 106, 187–9, 200, 205–6, 211, 212; Union of Crowns, 188, 205. *See also* Anglo-Scottish relations, British history, jurisdiction

Veitch, Andrew, portioner of Stewarttoun, 145
Veitch, family, 63, 95, 145, 147

Veitch, James, 95
Veitch of Dawick, William, 108, 147
violence, *see* crime

Walden, Thomas Howard, 1st Lord Howard de Walden, *see* Howard, Thomas
Walsingham, Sir Francis, 156, 160, 166 n. 62, 168–9
wardens, 80–1, 82–3, 87, 90, 138, 158, 161–2, 189
wardens, English, 84–5 n. 55, 134–5, 138, 151–2, 158, 160, 161–2, 176
wardens, Scottish: East March, 83; Middle March, 82, 83–5, 141–2, 155–7, 158, 155–7, 168, 174; West March, 83, 156–7, 174. *See also* Cessford, family; Forster, Sir John; Ker of Cessford, Robert; Scrope, Thomas 10th Lord
Wauchopedale, 88
Widdrington, 138
wealth, 37–9, 84, 161, 179
witchcraft, 44, 128
Yester, Lords, *see* Hay, Lords Yester

Lightning Source UK Ltd.
Milton Keynes UK
UKOW06f0522220316

270637UK00008B/128/P